MEMOIRS FROM THE EDGE

Memoirs From the Edge: Exploring the Line Between Life and Death is published under Catharsis, a sectionalized division under Di Angelo Publications, Inc.

Catharsis is an imprint of Di Angelo Publications.
Copyright 2022.
All rights reserved.
Printed in the United States of America.

Di Angelo Publications
4265 San Felipe #1100
Houston, Texas 77027

Library of Congress
Memoirs from the Edge: Exploring the Line Between Life and Death
Second Printing
ISBN: 978-1-955690-23-2
Hardback

Words, Cover image: Jeb Corliss
Cover design: Savina Deianova
Interior design: Kimberly James
Editors: Cody Wootton, Ashley Crantas, Willy Rowberry

Downloadable via Kindle, NOOK, iBooks, and Google Play.

For educational, business, and bulk orders, contact sales@diangelopublications.com.

1. Biography & Autobiography --- Personal Memoirs
2. Biography & Autobiography --- Sports
3. Sports & Recreation --- Extreme Sports

MEMOIRS FROM THE EDGE

EXPLORING THE LINE BETWEEN LIFE AND DEATH

JEB CORLISS

CONTENTS

PROLOGUE: Fragmented Memories of a Child 9

1. Nepal and India 15

2. Searching for Home 23

3. Don't Get Caught 39

4. Adjusting to a New Life 53

5. The Work Begins 67

6. A Leprechaun's Hat 73

7. The Road to BASE 89

8. My First BASE Jump 101

9. The 260-Foot Antenna 111

10. Kjerag Norway 121

11. Arco, Italy, and the French Connection 131

12. The Poorly Planned Expedition 139

13. Meeting McConkey 153

14. Iiro the Magician 159

15. South Africa 177

16. Connecting with Reality 199

17. The Israeli Doctor and the Cave of Swallows 207

18. Circus Circus 213

19. The Eiffel Tower 221

20. Tim the Stuntman 229

21. The Psilocybin Solution 239

22. Journey to the Center 257

23. Stunt Junkies 273

24. Grinding the Crack 281

25. Heaven's Gate Single Dragon 293

26. Table Mountain—The Impact 317

27. Recovery from Hell 337

28. The Flying Dagger 345

29. Point Break 361

30. The End is Near 377

EPILOGUE: Final Thoughts 385

FRAGMENTED MEMORIES OF A CHILD

Here I am, standing on a razor's edge between life and death. I'm looking out into the abyss, trying to understand how I got here. Who am I? Why do I keep doing this? Does any of this have a purpose? I look down, memories bubbling over, and remember that I almost died here seven years ago. Why have I come back?

Wait, I'm getting ahead of myself. This won't make any sense yet. Let me start at the beginning...

My journey to the edge began inside my mother's belly when she was just twenty-three years old and seven months pregnant with me. Along with my father, she was attempting to hike the 105 miles from Jiri, Nepal, to Everest's base camp on the Khumbu Glacier, which was over 18,000 feet above sea level. This was the kind of thing she thought would be fun, and for some reason, she didn't seem to think having an almost fully formed baby in her stomach should hold her back.

After almost twenty days of hiking, my parents had ascended from 7,500 feet to just over 16,000. My mother began to feel light-headed, and extreme fatigue settled in. My parents had a feeling that altitude sickness was the likely culprit, so they retreated to lower altitudes to give themselves more time to acclimate before resuming their trek. As they dropped altitude, they stumbled across a temporary tuberculosis clinic that had been set up along the trekking trail. With me kicking my mother in the ribs, they stopped to see if there was a doctor who could possibly check on her. The clinic had been set up by Sir Edmund Hillary, the first man to ever climb Mount Everest. As luck would have it, he happened to be visiting on that particular day.

As my parents entered the structure, Sir Hillary saw my mother and quickly whisked her and my father away to a private area, where he sat my mother on a table covered with paper. He gave her drinking water, checked her vitals, and performed a physical. When he was finished, he told her she had a slight case of altitude sickness, but it wasn't serious.

With a stern tone, he looked at her and said, "I have to ask, what are you thinking hiking at these altitudes in your condition?"

My mother told him, "It has been a dream of mine to hike to Everest base camp—" but he cut her off mid-sentence.

"You will have plenty of opportunities to turn that dream into a reality in the future, but for now, you need to head back down the mountain and get to a sanitary environment." She tried to protest, but he shook his head and continued. "We are in the middle of a TB outbreak in this area. This has become a dangerous place for an expecting mother who is almost eight months pregnant."

Mom was resistant, but once she understood that tuberculosis was running rampant—and the risks that posed to her and her baby—she took his advice to heart and, with my father in tow, headed back down the mountain towards the nearby town of Phaphlu. The altitude sickness faded with each step, and they made it safely back.

From Phaphlu, they made their way to Kathmandu to make one last stop before heading home. My father had heard of honey collectors who climbed high in the Himalaya to find massive colonies of bees that gleaned nectar from poppies. This poppy nectar gave the honey an almost psychedelic effect, which intrigued my father.

Having been a true product of the sixties and the hippy movement, my father was obsessed with all things drug related. He felt that drugs expanded his mind and helped him see things in a way that his parents would never be able to understand. The truth was that my father suffered from some undiagnosed form of mental illness and turned to drugs to alleviate his condition. As a child, I never truly understood why my father was the way he was: emotionally unstable and extremely aggressive. It wasn't until I was in my mid-thirties that I realized my father most likely suffered from bipolar disorder (I'm no psychologist, but that's my best guess after observing his behaviors my entire life). His parents came from a time when men just sucked it up and put on a tough façade; I'm not certain my grandparents even believed mental illness was a real thing. I think Dad just felt more right in the head when he sedated himself. The honey was just one treatment in a long line of self-medication.

As part of his quest for psychedelics, my father hired a group of honey collectors from the area to carry as much as they could manage. It was late in the season and winter was coming, which would prove to be an issue since the bees needed their honey to survive hibernation. That meant when the honey collectors brought the sweet treasure back to my parents' camp, the bees followed them.

During the night, they arrived in swarms, their buzzing echoing through the hills like low murmured hums. The workers heard the bees before they saw them, but when the bees descended from above, they were in full attack mode and stung anyone they could reach. My mother tells the story like a scene straight out of a horror film, and according to her, she was the only one who didn't get stung. Even though everyone else around her was stung multiple times, not one bee touched her. My mom has a bit of a mystical side to her, and she believes they spared her because of me; the bees didn't want to harm little me in her stomach. Being the skeptical person that I am, that doesn't seem super rational, but it does make for a great story.

I only have fragmented memories of partial stories about how my mother and father met and what they did for money. I know my father loved traveling. He went to remote, off-the-beaten-path locations to buy art, bring it home, and sell it for a profit. When he met my mother, she owned a small health food store in Santa Fe, New Mexico, which was a business ahead of its time. There are Whole Foods on every corner now, but in 1975, health food was still a niche industry. They fell in love, got married, and within a year, Mom was pregnant with me.

My parents got me my first passport when I was eight months old, and within that same year, they took me on my first international trip. For some reason, they decided Afghanistan would be a lovely place to take a toddler while my father sought out unique artwork to help expand his business. Why they felt it would be a great idea to take me along still boggles my forty-five-year-old brain. It just doesn't seem like a reasonable place to take a baby, but my parents were risk-takers, so off we went. While traveling in remote regions of the country looking for deals on art, they heard rumors that the Russians were going to invade Afghanistan. This scared my mother for rather obvious reasons, so my parents decided to cut the trip short and head home. As it turns out, the Russians did invade about two years later in 1979, sparking the Soviet-Afghan war. All I can say is: I'm glad we weren't there when the tanks rolled in.

Over the years, I have had a recurring memory that only comes to me in flashes of images and feelings. I experience it more like a photograph in my mind with emotions attached. Even now, I can see it so vividly. I am standing on my mother's lap, hands pressed against a glass window in the back of a broken-down bus. I look out at a vast desert and see two large camels pulling a huge wooden wagon. This image has flashed in my mind for as long as I can remember. When I was in my early twenties, I asked my mother where, in all our travels during my childhood, did we see camels?

"The only place we saw camels in that kind of setting was Afghanistan, but you were only about eight months old. You were too young to remember any of that." Regardless, based on her response, I believe this may be my earliest memory.

But I have another early memory that likely occurred around that same time. My mother believes it happened on our return from Afghanistan to see her family in Santa Fe. I remember being in a car at night, riding along with my family to a location unknown to me at the time. I remember seeing a large structure with blinking red lights reaching far into the sky. I now know this was a large AM/FM antenna tower, which would come to have a much greater meaning and purpose later in my life. In my memory, we passed the tower and pulled into a driveway, where I met my grandparents on my mother's side for the first time.

My father called their home "The Hill," so that's how we always referred to it. My grandmother set me down in their den, where she gave me a little box of orange gummy candies dipped in large sugar granules. I savored every bite, loving the feel of the rough granules against my tongue. This experience was the beginning of my love affair with sugar; to this day, I still crave those gummy candies.

At some point during this unconventional childhood of mine, my mother realized I was someone who enjoyed pushing boundaries. She hadn't learned how to swim until she was in her early twenties, and because of that, she was terrified of the water. She considered it to be a paralyzing condition and didn't want me to suffer from the same affliction, so she started taking me to "Mommy and Me" swimming classes when I was eight months old. I learned to swim before I learned to walk.

At around eighteen months old, I became obsessed with the high dive. Every time we went to swimming lessons, I would get upset and throw a tantrum because they wouldn't let me go to the top of the tower. I couldn't talk yet, but I had a few words and hand gestures that I used to make it very clear what I wanted to do. One day, the swim coach had enough and told my mom he was taking me up there.

After my mother's protests about the height and my safety, he said, "You're right. It's way too high. He'll get scared and won't jump. I'll take him up and settle this once and for all. We'll be right back."

The coach carried me to the top of a tall ladder and walked me to the edge of the diving platform. But the instant his hands let go of my little shoulders, I stepped off the edge before he had time to react.

My mother said I screamed, "WHEEEEE!" all the way to impact, and as I hit the water, my swimming diaper blew off my body. I then swam to the edge of the pool—my little tallywhacker swinging on display for everyone to see—and looked up gleefully at my mother's horrified face. With a smile from ear to ear, I used one of the few words I had in my vocabulary.

"Again!" I demanded at the top of my little lungs. This was the moment my mother knew she had a serious problem on her hands.

CHAPTER ONE

NEPAL AND INDIA

My first recollection of strong memories—more than just bits and pieces with missing context—started when I was around five years old. This was a formative age in developing the person I have become, and my memories from this stage in life are still quite vivid.

In a bold move, my mother decided to sell her health food store to fund a massive one-year trip through Nepal and India. She and my father wanted to buy artifacts and import them back to Santa Fe, New Mexico, where my father intended to open a new store called Yazzie Muhammad and Muldoon. If you consider the level of risk they took with this venture, the background for how I became who I am today is strikingly obvious.

My mother and father decided to sell the store—the only thing they owned at the time—for only $50,000. As a kid, I couldn't really fathom what was happening, but as an adult, I cannot imagine how they just packed it all up and went. It's odd how you tend to just do things in life and then one day, years later, you wake up and think, *Wait, what the fuck did I do?*

Anyway, my parents headed out on a journey that would rattle most adults, wealthy or otherwise, and they did it with their three children in tow: my older sister Sonia, age eight, myself, age five, and my little sister Scarlett, age one. This all happened before the age of credit cards, so they had to carry all their money in cash and traveler's checks. Had we been robbed on day one, we would have been screwed.

Prior to setting off on our adventure, we were living close to my father's parents in Palm Springs, California, and I was attending kindergarten. I remember being pulled out of school early one day and my mom informing me that we were about to go on a little trip. I obviously had no idea what that meant, but as any child would, I just kind of went along with whatever my parents did.

Using a borrowed car, we then began a massive road trip that spanned from California to New York, where I sat for hours in the backseat with my sisters. In an effort to ease boredom, I played a little game where I would bob my head between telephone poles, back and forth, for hours on end to keep myself busy. This game would later manifest itself in a very odd nervous tic, and to this day, I bob my head without realizing it's happening. But it helps me relax and it soothes me, so I don't let the strange looks people give bother me. I only really sit still around people who make me uncomfortable. The rest of the time, I'm bobbing.

When we reached New York, we stayed there for a few days with my father's friends. Mom took the opportunity to take my sisters and me to an amazing toy store that seemed to come from every child's dream—F.A.O. Schwarz in Manhattan. I had never seen so many toys. My sisters and I were allowed to pick out one toy each, which was extremely difficult for kids our age to do. There were too many choices. We ran around the store looking at everything and playing with whatever we could get our grimy little hands on while Mom carried Scarlett, who was too little to keep up with us. After passing up a lot of toys that didn't feel quite right, I ended up finding a wind-up bird with flapping wings that, if you threw it in the air, could glide for hundreds of feet. I was instantly obsessed with that little piece of plastic, and it became my favorite toy of the trip. When we finally made it to Nepal, I recall running through fields, throwing that little bird up in the sky and chasing after it.

The children in Nepal were super friendly, so I made friends to play with wherever I went; that little wind-up bird seemed to make me very popular. My days were filled playing with other children as we chased that bird for hours on end. Eventually, they also showed me a local game where they would take hoops made of wood, plastic, or metal about knee-high and push them along the ground with sticks and chase them through the streets..

But in life, there is always contrast. Even though the children played and smiled, this was my first time seeing real poverty. As a child, I truly couldn't comprehend why everyone was so incredibly poor. The helplessness of their condition, like an endless sea of suffering, was disturbing to my young mind. I constantly asked my parents for money to give to desperately poor people who I could tell really needed it. On one particular day, my mother had given me a little candy wrapped in wax paper, and as we walked along, we passed an old homeless man who was obviously starving, so I handed him my candy. I watched as he put it in his mouth, wrapper and all, and swallowed. I remember wondering why he did that, and the feeling of so much overwhelming poverty wrenched at my heart and left it raw. I couldn't process that level of pain; I only knew I felt sad and wished I could do something more to help. But I was only five, so there wasn't much I could do. As we walked away from the homeless man, I cried.

We had flown as a family from New York's JFK Airport to Kathmandu and stayed in a hotel a few miles from the famous Swayambhunath Stupa, also known as the Monkey Temple. I visited this temple with my parents the first day we arrived and was fascinated by the chanting of the Buddhist monks. The deep, dark rumbling of their voices all vibrating in unison mesmerized me.

The following day, I snuck away from my parents and walked for miles by myself to the base of a hill leading to the temple. I looked up to see hundreds of stairs rising from the jungle, with monkeys chattering all around. Reaching the top of the staircase, I was greeted by two gigantic eyes painted on the walls of a square building with a massive golden dome on top.

My mother said the first time I disappeared, she panicked and started frantically searching for me. One of the hotel maids had seen me head in the direction of the Monkey Temple, so my mother started running that way. She passed people, asking if they had seen a small, five-year-old blond boy, and they would nod and point in the direction of the temple. She finally found me sitting in the middle of a group of monks as they sang from the Tibetan Book of the Dead. She kept an eye on me until they were finished, then scolded me and tried to convince me not to sneak off ever again. Even at that age, I never really paid much attention to people telling me what to do, and my mother was no exception. I was not easily controlled, so during our stay in Kathmandu, I snuck away every chance I got to spend time with the monks.

My mother was very strict when it came to what I was allowed to eat. As a child, I was forced to be vegetarian, and I was only allowed to eat sugar on special occasions (like the candy from our walk). Our hotel offered these delicious little chocolate cakes, and every time we could, my older sister and I would sneak them when my mother wasn't watching. One day, my sister and I were playing behind the hotel and saw a table sitting outside the kitchen, loaded with our favorite freshly baked little cakes. We ran over to steal a few when no one was looking, but as we inched closer, we discovered they were crawling with thousands of flies. The visual was unnerving, and it suddenly clicked that this was how they let the cakes cool before handing them out. We had been eating the exact same fly-covered cakes for days! The image and sickening realization of that moment has been burned into my mind ever since. To this day, I can't stand chocolate cake.

On a walking trip to buy a few artifacts, my parents, with me in tow, found our path blocked by a gaping hole in the ground. Locals had arranged long wooden planks across the hole to act as a makeshift bridge. In this immensely deep hole—by a five-year old's standards—were the biggest pigs I had ever seen in my life. They looked like their backs were higher off the ground than I was tall, and for some reason, they absolutely terrified me. They squealed and grunted, all the while acting super pissed off. I suppose being stuck in a big hole all day would have upset me, too.

My parents crossed the bridge first and waited for me on the other side. The planks, narrow and unstable, creaked and bent as I put my weight on them. How could my mother and father have made it? I thought about falling in the hole with those frightening beasts, and I started to cry. I didn't want to walk across those flimsy wooden planks anymore.

"Listen to me, Jeb," said my father. "This is the only way to get where we're going." I just sobbed in reply, so he continued, "You need to deal with your fear. No one can do this for you. You have to do it on your own."

It was the first time I remember being super afraid and forced to face it. After some further prompting, I managed to swallow my fear and hustle across the bridge to the outstretched arms of my parents, but I didn't want to take another glance at those pigs.

As the New Delhi leg of our trip began, new memories imprinted in my mind. I remember eating poached eggs sprinkled with Spike (a healthy salt substitute my mom put on everything) in a large garden behind the hotel we were staying at. There were massive trees covered in strange blue-and-yellow leaves. When I was done eating my eggs, I decided to walk closer to the trees to get a better look at the colors, which is when I realized the colors were not actually leaves, but thousands upon thousands of parakeets. My movement spooked the birds, so they exploded into flying flocks, scattering into the sky and leaving the trees bare, empty, and silent. I felt embarrassed at having chased away all the pretty birds, but my mom just smiled and patted the chair for me to sit back down.

Later that same day, our family went on a little trip down the Ganges River, starting in the town of Varanasi. We rode in a small wooden boat with the captain sitting in the back by a tiny out-board motor. My mother casually dipped my baby sister's toes in the water, making her giggle as we went upstream against the current. The captain noticed and politely asked her to stop.

"Why?" asked my mother, somewhat offended.

"Because," replied the captain in a casual tone, "the river has many large crocodiles, so it is best not to drag bait through the water."

Mom hauled the baby away from the edge and moved to the center of the boat, where she sat with Scarlett firmly secured on her lap, and she proceeded to glare at each passing ripple.

As we continued motoring upstream, we witnessed a handful of religious ceremonies taking place along the shore. The Ganges is one of the most sacred rivers in the Hindu religion, so much so that people actually worship the river. It originates in the western Himalayas and empties into the sea at the Bay of Bengal. Spanning over 1,500 miles, it is the third largest river in the world based on highest average discharge of water. The Hindus believe bathing in the water purifies their souls, and many want to have their bodies burned by the riverside after their death. I would say the smell was the thing that had the greatest impression on my young mind. It's what I noticed first about the area, and it was one of the strongest, most horrible odors I have ever experienced. It was so powerful that it brought tears to my eyes. I have yet to smell anything like it anywhere else.

I saw fires on the shore and pointed them out. My mother had trouble making out what they were burning at first, but as we got closer, it became clear they were human bodies. Colorful frames surrounded the bodies, made to look like canopies over elaborate beds and covered with flowers and all kinds of exotic fabrics, all ablaze. My young mind couldn't really process what I was seeing, but the sense of loss and moving on definitely left an impact.

Shortly after the Ganges, my parents took us to see snake charmers. On our way, we saw a new level of poverty that made what we had seen in Nepal seem mild. There were people sitting on blankets who had severed their own limbs to make begging for money easier. The truly horrifying part was that they set those severed limbs out on blankets for display. The level of helplessness in their eyes pierced straight through me. So many desperate hands grasping at nothing. I remember an overwhelming sense of sorrow that completely consumed me as I walked past them, giving what little I had here and there. As a five-year-old, I didn't possess much, so I repeatedly asked my parents for money to hand out. It didn't take long for the well to run dry, and the tide of poor kept rising beyond my comprehension. Honestly, it's still beyond my ability to understand.

After walking through what seemed like the Seventh Ring of Hell, we finally arrived in an open field where a man sat by himself, surrounded by large baskets. We all sat down in front of him, and as we settled, he took out a tiny flute and began to play. He swayed from side to side with the tune as a second man approached from behind. He walked by us and took the lid off the largest basket, situated directly between the snake charmer and us. From within the basket, a massive king cobra slowly rose up with its hood spread wide open.

A strange feeling welled up inside me at seeing the snake. I was scared and I didn't understand why. It was my first experience with snakes, and for some reason, the fear seemed built into my DNA; it was instinctual. I had no true reason to be afraid, didn't even know what the word "venomous" meant at that point, but the fear I experienced was real. I didn't know why this creature made me feel this way, but my response to the feeling was not an urge to escape. Instead, it drew me in. Despite the warnings in my head, I wanted to get closer, to see the glittering scales and watch the tongue flick in and out. I wanted to understand why this animal made me feel this way.

Throughout the next few hours, the two men brought out more and more snakes, each one more exotic than the last. Finally, they pulled out an odd brown snake that my sister and I were allowed to hold. My mother explained that the snake's head would migrate down its body and change sides each year. This fascinated me at the time, but as an adult, I realize she was just making things up to engage our imaginations. She was the kind of mom who loved fantastic stories of leprechauns and fairies, and I think she really enjoyed seeing the wonder in our eyes. But, by pretending this snake had imaginary abilities, along with the powerful fear I felt, she fueled an obsession with these creatures that would dominate my childhood. From that point forward, all I wanted to do was catch and play with snakes.

As we neared the end of our ten-month journey, I noticed an odd tunnel next to the stairs that led to my room. It kind of looked like a drain for water run-off. After some searching, I found that all the rooms around us had them, too. I asked my mom what they were for.

"Mongooses live in them," she explained. She might have said "mongeese," but it's "mongooses," if you didn't know.

"What's a mongoose?" I asked.

"They're little animals that kill and eat snakes."

"What do they look like?"

"Sort of like a ferret, or a long rat. There are lots of cobras around, and the mongooses hunt them to keep everyone safe."

That evening, I was outside, watching those odd tunnels to see if I could catch a glimpse of a mongoose, when I was startled by a strange growl and a menacing hiss. As I looked over, I saw an animal that looked a little like a ferret, but larger. It moved low to the ground, ready to kill. The hissing came from a medium-sized cobra, maybe four feet long, that was reared up with its hood open. The fight was over in an instant as the mongoose struck with force and took the cobra right at the back of the neck, just behind its hood, and shook it violently from side to side. I watched as the mongoose dragged the snake into one of the holes, and they were gone. I couldn't believe what I'd seen, or how fast it had happened.

I spent the next few days searching for both mongooses and snakes. As I looked in holes and walked through the gardens, just hoping to get another look at either of them, I was struck with a sudden, sharp pain in my stomach. I had to go to the bathroom in the worst way, so I sprinted for my room. I frantically jerked down my pants as I stumbled into the bathroom, barely making it to the toilet as diarrhea sprayed everywhere. During this bout of explosions, I realized I needed to throw up as well, so the only thing I could do was lean over and barf into the tub beside the toilet—and I was a bad aim.

This sickening vacillation between toilet and tub went on for what felt like an eternity. My parents walked in on my ordeal, and when I no longer had anything left to expel, they took me to a local doctor for an examination. When he finished, he told my parents he had bad news, explaining I had something called "Delhi Belly" and that a child my age was unlikely to survive.

Delhi Belly is a very strong form of amoebic dysentery, and fulminant amoebic dysentery is reported to have a 55–88% mortality rate in adults. The numbers are even worse for children. Between 40,000 and 100,000 people die each year from it, placing this infection second only to malaria in mortality.

When the doctor informed my parents that I would likely die, they took me straight to another doctor for a second opinion, thinking that a more "westernized" professional would be more thorough or give a better diagnosis. However, this specialist informed them it was bad—*really* bad—but he would do what he could. He gave my mother all kinds of medications for me and told her to let me eat and drink anything I wanted. He explained it was important for me to get as many calories into my body as possible, and my usual diet just wouldn't give me the nutrients I needed to fight this illness. That was a tough pill to swallow for my mother, who was a strict vegetarian and thought meat and sugar were the devil. But she listened to the doctor, and it took almost four weeks of being very sick before I finally started to recover. Over that time, I lost about a third of my body weight and suffered from powerful hallucinations. I only remember small glimpses of reality during those weeks, but those glimpses serve as the beginning of a deeper understanding of my own mortality, and it would shift the way I approached my life. At five years old, I had begun to grasp the concept of death.

CHAPTER TWO

SEARCHING FOR HOME

After almost a year of traveling, it was finally time for us to head back home—or rather, find a place to turn *into* a home. My parents decided to move our family to Santa Fe, New Mexico. Dad felt it would be the easiest place to set up his art dealership since Santa Fe was a tourist hub. Mom liked the area because we would be close to her family in case we needed a little support.

My family rented a small apartment and my father set up what would be the family business for most of my early childhood. Just as he had planned, he called his shop Yazzie Muhammad and Muldoon, situated right in the middle of the main plaza of central Santa Fe. His business created a kind of feast-or-famine lifestyle for our family. He had all kinds of art for sale, but there was no money until he sold something. Sometimes he would sell a large piece and we would have money for a little while, but most of the time we struggled to get by. We endured long periods where we couldn't afford food, and in some cases, we weren't even able to pay our gas bill to heat our apartment; at an altitude of over 7,000 feet, Santa Fe gets quite cold in the winter.

My sisters and I used to go to the market with my mother to buy groceries, and we'd go down the aisles picking out what we wanted to eat. Mom always found it difficult to say no to us, even when she knew we didn't have the money to pay for everything, which taught me about humiliation. Each time this happened, we would get to the register, smiling and laughing as the cashier rang up each item. The total amount would appear, and Mom would reach into her purse, pretend to search for more cash, and confess she didn't have enough to pay. While the other shoppers looked on, my sisters and I had to take our chosen items back to their respective shelves, one by one. The shame I felt is something I have never forgotten.

Regardless of our situation, Mom did her best to shelter us from the idea that we were poor. She constantly talked about how valuable all the art in the shop was and told stories about how certain items once belonged to royalty from the four corners of the world. I had a very active imagination, so I found it easy to buy into her stories and feel like we were rich. I was never concerned about money because I knew Dad would sell something valuable soon and everything would be okay. But looking back on it now, I realize how precarious our situation really was.

Our constant lack of resources meant we had to move around a lot. We moved three times within six years, and each move involved transferring schools. My parents made the mistake of enrolling me in a Catholic school for first grade, setting the tone for the next six years of my life. I had just spent a year traveling around Nepal and India and learning from Hindus and Buddhists, so when the Catholic priests started talking about Jesus and Christian doctrine, I had a lot of questions. One thing I learned very quickly was that Catholic priests do not like being questioned by seven-year-olds about their religious beliefs. I was confrontational and stood my ground, which resulted in me being punished constantly. After my first year, the school informed my parents that it would be in everyone's best interests if I did not return. That started the trend of me changing schools regularly, which meant I was almost always the new kid. The schools I attended were made up of a primarily Hispanic and Native American demographics, which usually meant that I was the odd one out. I was blond, tall for my age, and white, so I stuck out like a sore thumb. That, combined with always being new, meant I was the one who got picked on. But I was never in a fight with just one other person; it was always me against four or five other kids at once. School quickly became a war zone for me. I wasn't going somewhere to learn; I was going somewhere to fight.

Contrary to how I felt, I wasn't completely alone during my grade school years. I made friends here and there, but the friendships didn't seem to last long. The constant moving, new homes, and school transfers made it almost impossible for me to maintain relationships for any length of time.

The few friends I did make and the limited amounts of time we got to spend together were fun for me. However, the games we played usually revolved around violence, like throwing rocks or sticks at each other. We ran down alleys and through yards, slinging whatever we could grab, laughing and screaming the entire time. The games only ended when someone was left bleeding from their head or needing stitches on some part of their body. Blood was a good sign that it was time to go home.

Sometimes the games evolved. My grandfather was a plumber and had enormous piles of tin disks in all shapes and sizes behind his workshop. We would fashion some of the larger disks into shields and use the smaller ones as razor-sharp frisbees to throw at each other. They made it easy to draw blood. The right side of my head is covered in scars from this particular activity, and I can actually remember pulling one of those disks from my skull; it had hit me so hard it was embedded in the bone. The sound it made coming out was disturbing. Why we thought this game was entertaining is beyond me.

The only people my age who were around for my entire childhood were my cousins, Tommy and Richie. They lived at The Hill with my Aunt Linda, Uncle Richard, and our grandparents on my mother's side. Sometimes I spent weekends with my cousins, who were probably my best friends growing up. Uncle Richard, however, was strict and had a horrible temper. He would spank my cousins all the time, and I can say now that what he did was child abuse. It wasn't spanking; it was beating. He was cruel and vindictive—but he was afraid of my father, so he never laid a finger on me—thus, his children became the proverbial whipping boys for every mistake or problem he could find. He punished my cousins whenever he wanted to punish me, which was just as psychologically effective at inducing fear; I knew that if I fucked up, Tommy and Richie had to take the heat for it. I tried to avoid going to The Hill whenever possible, but my uncle didn't like my cousins to visit me where I lived because he thought I was a bad influence. So, if I wanted to see them, I was forced to go to The Hill so he could keep an eye on our interactions.

Still, I didn't get to see my cousins or my other friends very often. Their parents quickly came to dislike me because someone always seemed to get hurt when I was around. You know how most parents say things like, "If your friends jumped off a bridge, would you?" Well, my mom never said anything like that to me. Instead, she said, "Jeb, you need to stop taking your friends off bridges. They're getting hurt and their parents keep calling me."

Most of my time between first and sixth grade was spent by myself. I played in creeks and the desert around where I lived. After my experiences in India with the cobras, snakes were my obsession. They frightened me, but I wanted to understand why. So, when I wasn't getting into fights at school or hitting my friends with metal disks, I went looking for snakes. If I came across lizards, scorpions, frogs, or spiders, I would catch them, too, but snakes were always what I was searching for.

In the beginning, I was terrified of snakes. But even as a six-year-old child I had a process I used to help confront the things that frightened me. I started with a harmless snake, like the garter snake. The fear would well up inside me just at the thought of touching one, but I knew it couldn't hurt me, so I'd force myself to touch it. Over time, it got easier to deal with that fear. I was small, but I was able to rationalize how I had nothing to worry about when dealing with a garter snake, simply because it had small fangs and no poison. After desensitizing myself to the irrational fear of the safe snakes, I could then step it up to a slightly more difficult and scarier situation. Bull snakes were larger and more aggressive, and even with bigger fangs, they still lacked poison. If they bit you, it would cause more pain than a garter snake, but wouldn't cause any lasting damage. Facing the bull snake, I felt the fear just as powerfully as when I faced the garter snake the first time, but slowly, the fear became manageable.

Once this happened, I felt ready to take the next step towards bigger and more dangerous creatures. Rattlesnakes were my final goal. These snakes were the biggest and nastiest in my area, moved much faster than the others, and were way more aggressive. They were also venomous, meaning I would finally face something that could kill me outright. This was the first snake that had real consequences for making mistakes. But I had been training my fear response in safer conditions with safer snakes, so by the time I caught my first rattlesnake, I had my fear response in check and was able to control it. The process took me about a year, and I was seven when my fingers wrapped around my first rattlesnake neck. The day I brought it home, my mother was not pleased. She said, "You can play with that outside, but do not bring it into this house." She had already come to realize there was no way to stop me from doing things like this. She knew that if she forbid me to touch rattlesnakes, I'd just do it anyway and not tell her. She would rather me handle them in our yard where she could keep an eye on me than out in the woods by myself.

One day, I was in my father's shop—just playing in the back—when a box showed up. It had holes poked in it and said "Live Tarantula Inside" in big letters. It was from one of my father's friends and it had my name on it. Apparently, the friend had heard how much I loved snakes and thought I might like to have a large spider as a pet. My father thought it was a joke and that the box was going to have a fake, spring-loaded snake inside. He pointed the box away from himself with his eyes squinted, ready for the spring to shoot out, but that's not what happened. As he opened the box, a massive black and orange spider jumped out with tremendous force. My dad threw the box in the air, and the spider went running across the floor at top speed. It's amazing how fast they can move when they want to get away. Dad scrambled around, tossing things aside, searching for something to capture the spider with. He found a large jar and somehow managed to trap the spider inside it. My dad handed me the jar and asked, "Are you interested in a pet spider?" Honestly, I was terrified of the thing. It was the biggest spider I had ever seen, and I wasn't sure I wanted anything to do with it. One thing was for sure, though: I was never going to let that creepy thing get out of that jar, whether I kept it or not.

My parents were friends with a married couple named Willy and Judy Mackey. They had traveled through parts of Nepal with us, but my father had been friends with them for many years before that. I had gotten to know them, and I liked them. My mother was protective when it came to her children, so she never let anyone babysit us. She would either take us with her wherever she went or she just wouldn't go. But something came up at the last minute one day and bringing us just wasn't an option, so against her better judgment, she asked if Judy could watch us for a few hours. Judy was thin with long, straight blonde hair, and she wore odd round glasses and a wool beanie that gave her a distinct hippy look. She told my mother not to worry, that she wouldn't let anything bad happen. And with that, my mom rushed out the door.

As Judy walked into our living room, she saw my new pet spider sitting in its jar on the table. She was fascinated by how huge it was and asked me what I fed it.

"Grasshoppers and crickets," I told her with a grin.

"Do you ever hold it?" she asked, wide-eyed.

"No way. It has huge fangs." As if on cue, the tarantula reared up and spread its fangs for us to see. Judy shuddered.

"But you love snakes," she said, "and they have fangs." She tapped a fingernail on the jar, but the spider didn't budge. "You should take it out and hold it."

"You're insane," I said. Judy reached into her purse and pulled out a wad of crumpled dollar bills.

"If you hold it and it bites you, you can have all this money." She held the money right in front of my nose, baiting me. I glanced down and saw that there was maybe twenty bucks, but to an eight-year-old, that was a fortune that would keep me in candy for weeks. I hesitated because I hadn't used my snake technique on spiders yet. The tarantula was an unknown, and that meant danger.

Judy noticed my hesitation, set the money on the table, and said, "Well, tarantulas aren't poisonous, so it would just hurt a little. Nothing bad would happen anyway."

I looked at the wad of cash sitting there and thought, *How bad could the bite really be?* So, I grabbed the jar and unscrewed the lid. I put the jar on the table and set the lid next to it. The spider placed its front two legs at the mouth of the jar and started pulling itself up the inner glass walls. As it came over the lip of the jar, I put my hand out and let it crawl onto my fingers, across my wrist, and all the way to my elbow. I was mesmerized at how slowly the spider moved, every movement controlled and cautious. Eventually, it made its way to my shoulder, crawled across my face, and settled on top of my head. The spider was actually quite gentle and never bit me, so I didn't get the money after all. I did, however, end up conquering a new fear that day.

I started trying to use my fear process with the bullies at school. The problems with the bullies I faced were: they were always much bigger than me, and I was always outnumbered. I initially tried to avoid them, but when avoidance wasn't possible, I tried to ignore them. That rarely worked, so I would then be forced to fight. Being outnumbered by bigger people is typically a recipe for disaster. It took me time to learn the subtle mind manipulation to win in these situations. Every now and then I won a fight, but it never seemed to slow them down. They just kept coming.

By fifth grade, I had had enough. One day, a group of bullies decided to gang up on me where no adults were around. There were just too many of them and the fight was unfair. They came in fast and got me before I had a chance to even respond. They beat me up worse than usual, and this flicked a switch inside me. A rage built that I no longer had control over. All the years of being picked on and beaten up came to a head, and I snapped. After they had their fill and walked away, I stood up and brushed the dirt off myself. I walked past all the lines of kids waiting to be let back into the school and headed for my classroom. Once I got there, I looked for the most dangerous weapon I could find: a heavy pencil sharpener with a blunt edge that perfectly fit in my hand.

I turned and walked back out to the playground, where I saw the leader of the little gang that had just attacked me standing next to a teacher. He had this smug little grin on his face, thinking I couldn't retaliate with him standing right next to her. I walked straight to up to him, grabbed him by the throat, and cracked his skull open with the sharpener. I dropped him right where he stood as everyone watched in stunned disbelief. I then turned around and walked slowly back into the school. I went straight to the principal's office and sat down in a chair across from her desk.

"What are you doing here?" she asked in confusion. "Did a teacher send you here?"

I told her, "I just cracked a kid's head open with a pencil sharpener, and if anyone else touches me, I'm going to kill them." She looked at me with sheer terror in her eyes, and that was the day everything changed at school.

They took away all my books, pencils, scissors...pretty much anything I could use as a weapon. They set up a partition in the classroom to separate me from the other children. They called in my parents and had meeting after meeting about what they should do. They brought in three different psychologists to evaluate me. Through all this chaos, my mother and the principal decided that being around other children in that school system was not a healthy environment for me. They reasoned that if things were getting this violent in fifth grade, it would only get worse as I entered junior high and high school. They felt there was a real possibility of true violence emerging, so they determined that I should be homeschooled from that point forward.

Honestly, looking back, I believe this was one of the single most important decisions my mother made to save my life. School had become nothing but pain and suffering for me. I was psychologically damaged from years of bullying and fighting. If I had stayed in school, there was a strong possibility I would have killed someone. I had *The Anarchist Cookbook* and I knew how to make bombs. I had so much rage and anger from how I was treated throughout my childhood that I was on the edge of exploding. You can only kick a dog for so long before it turns on you. Luckily for me, my mother was aware and paying attention.

The day I started homeschooling, the rage seemed to evaporate. I no longer felt a constant knot in my stomach. The anxiety that I had felt every day of my life just went away. A new life opened up for me, and the violence was no longer necessary. After that year in fifth grade, I have never been in another physical fight.

My mother told me something at this stage of my life that would forever change the way I conducted myself. She told me she didn't have a set of rules for me to follow, that I could do whatever I wanted. She explained she knew I was a good person and she trusted me to make the right decisions. There was only one thing she insisted on: I couldn't lie to her about the choices I made. If I felt like I needed to lie to her about something, then maybe that was something I shouldn't be doing. This simple concept made me think deeply about every choice I made from that point forward. Anytime I was about to do something, I asked myself, *Would I be willing to tell everyone about this?* If I felt I had to keep something secret, then I knew there must be something wrong with whatever it was. I'm not sure if this technique would be effective for anyone else, but it really worked for me. To this day, I don't drink, smoke, or use drugs of any kind. Not that those things have anything to do with honesty, but it's just the way I am. I try to be honest with others and with myself. If I do something, I own it, and I feel totally fine telling the world what I have done.

There's a reason I don't drink. When I was eight, my mother needed a babysitter, and seeing as we had all liked Judy, she asked her to watch us again. As we played boardgames, Judy was drinking this odd-smelling, clear liquid called Ouzo. It's a Greek alcohol with a strong black licorice odor. At the time, I loved black licorice and asked if I could have some. She smiled and gave me a sideways glance. She said, "I don't think that would be a good idea," but I could tell she wanted to give me some. She went to the kitchen and got the biggest glass she could find, then filled it all the way to the top with Ouzo. She handed it to me and said, "Okay, Jeb. I will let you drink this, but you have to drink the entire glass."

I smiled and said, "No problem." I only weighed about seventy-five pounds, which she clearly didn't take into consideration. Maybe wanting to impress or surprise Judy, I drank the entire glass in less than ten minutes. This obviously made me very drunk, but it also made me super sick. I began to throw up and didn't stop for what felt like hours. By the time my mother got home, I wasn't doing any better; it was clear I had alcohol poisoning. That was the second and last time my mother ever allowed anyone to watch us.

I'm unsure whether Judy was trying to teach me a lesson, but this experience changed me forever. After that, the smell of either alcohol or licorice always made me gag. If the smell didn't go away quickly, I would throw up. This lasted well into my mid-twenties, and the effect was so strong that I couldn't even be around a woman wearing perfume, which reminded me too much of alcohol. In a college psychology class, I learned that this was called "classic conditioning." This experience, combined with growing up watching my father smoke weed nonstop, gave me an extreme dislike for drugs and alcohol. Even when we had no money for groceries or heat, somehow my father always had money to buy pot. This always bothered me, because even though I was young, I knew his actions didn't make any sense.

Similarly, I also spent my childhood watching my mom smoke cigarettes. For most of my life, I can remember watching her try to quit, but no matter how hard she tried, she always started again. It seemed strange to me seeing someone that I knew was strong be controlled by a substance. For most nonsmokers, smoking smells horrible, and it made me feel sick just being around her when she did it. She explained it was an acquired taste, and it was unpleasant at first, but after you did it for a while, it became soothing. But she then went on to say, "Never start smoking, because it is horrible for you." So, I decided early in my life to never start.

I've noticed the combination of not drinking, smoking, or using drugs has been, without question, the thing people find most strange about me and the number one point of friction I experience with others. The questions they ask are like they're talking to an alien. I have now traveled the world more times than I can count, but

I have met only a handful of people like myself. You meet quite a few who had drug or drinking problems who have given them up, but it's rare to find someone who just never started in the first place. Seems odd to me that our preferred default recreational state as human beings tends to be intoxication or sedation.

As children, my sisters and I spent many summers with my paternal grandparents, who lived in Palm Springs. They loved putting us to work and would pay us in quarters to wash cars or work in the garden. At the time, I felt like it was slave labor, and I was resentful for being forced to be at their beck and call. But after all these years, I see the true lesson they were teaching me: the importance of work ethic. It's funny that as you grow older, you start to see how the world really works, and you find the wisdom in your grandparents' actions. I wish I could go back and thank them now, but such is life.

But my grandparents also had some old-world views that weren't as positive. They noticed I would bob my head back and forth—that relic from the game I played during my family's cross-country trip to NY. They felt it was strange and thought they needed to break me of the habit, or else people would never take me seriously. Every time I did it, they made fun of me, thinking this would somehow get me to stop. But I wasn't even aware I was doing it anymore. It had become completely subconscious, so no matter how much they ridiculed me, I wasn't capable of stopping.

They also felt I had a serious hearing problem. When I was playing or watching TV, I would ignore them when they spoke to me. They didn't realize I heard everything they were saying, and I just refused to acknowledge them. I didn't like being interrupted when I was doing things, and they loved interrupting. These perceived issues prompted them to take me to the UCLA Medical Group in Los Angeles to receive testing for mental and/or hearing disorders. I was put through a battery of tests checking anything and everything from my I.Q. to my vision, hearing, memory, reflexes, and so on.

My grandparents were surprised when the tests came back, because not only was my hearing perfect, but I had a nearly audiographic memory. It also turned out my I.Q. was 136, which was unique for a ten-year-old. They explained my head bobbing was a manifestation of attention-deficit/hyperactivity disorder, or ADHD. They said that aside from the ADHD, I was in perfect health both physically and mentally. I'm not sure I would have agreed with the "mentally" part, but that was their determination. They told my grandparents I should take Ritalin to calm me down and help me focus. They sent all the test data to my mother and informed her of the medication they wanted me to take. My mother expressed, in no uncertain terms, that there was no way in hell she was going to let me take drugs that alter brain chemistry while my mind was still developing. My grandparents became incredibly angry and had a big argument with my mother. They ended up compromising on me taking a super small dose to see what effect, if any, it would have on me. I took a quarter of a tiny pill, once a day, for a week. It made me exhausted and zoned out all the time.

At the end of that week, my mom said, "I've seen everything I need to see. This little experiment is over. Children are supposed to have energy and be hyper. There is nothing wrong with that." So, I never took Ritalin again and am still a super hyper person to this day. I am far from perfect and have dealt with many mental issues my entire life, but I do not feel ADHD is the root of those issues. If anything, I feel it has helped me. That energy was invaluable when I started channeling it into my future endeavors.

Back home in Santa Fe, during my tenth trip around the sun, other things happened that shook my world in big ways. At the time, our home was about two miles from my father's store in the center of town. I would ride my bike from our house to my father's shop on most weekends to hang out and just be around him while he worked. I loved riding down this one huge hill on the way there. I had a ten-speed mountain bike and was riding it in hard gear as fast as I could down the steep grade. A large van passed me on my left doing about 50 mph, and then suddenly turned right in front of me.

I had just enough time to squeeze both my brakes as hard as I could as I impacted the van on its passenger-side sliding door. I crashed at high speed and was just able to duck my head into my shoulder and take the hit on my left side. These were the days when people thought helmets were for the weak, and they cost money that I didn't have. My impact completely caved in the van's sliding door and bent the frame of my bike. It was the first time I understood the term "seeing stars." I hit so hard that my eyes sealed shut. I couldn't open them and there were strange blotches of light flashing out in the perceived space in front of me. The driver got out of his van and started asking me questions, but I couldn't understand what he was saying. I remember trying to stand up, but somehow my legs had become intertwined with the frame of my bike. The driver helped separate my legs from the metal wrapped around them and then lifted me up off the ground. I stood up and found that my eyes had become sensitive to the light. My head felt like it was bleeding from the inside, building pressure. The pounding was overwhelming.

The guy with the van continued asking me questions, but I—for no known reason—grabbed my bike and started walking away from him, dragging it behind me. He yelled after me, demanding that I stop, but I just kept walking. Unable to fully open my eyes, I squinted through the two little slits I could muster and walked the mile-and-a-half distance to my father's shop in a daze.

As I walked in, I told my father I had just been hit by a car. He laughed at me in blatant disbelief. I showed him my destroyed bike and he finally noticed the blood running down the side of my head. He quickly realized I wasn't kidding and, as he looked closer, he could see I was really hurt. We didn't have health insurance or the money to go to a doctor, so the only thing he could do was tell me to "walk it off." Lucky for me, I didn't have any broken bones, and if my brain did bleed, it didn't bleed enough to kill me. But that may help explain a few of my mental disorders.

A few days later, I headed to Palm Springs to spend time with my grandparents. The day I got there, they took me and my older sister swimming in a neighbor's pool. During a round of Marco Polo, a bad pain started in the lower right side of my belly. The pain grew worse and worse until I couldn't even stand up on my own. My grandfather decided to take me to the emergency room right away. For over three hours, I sat in a hospital waiting room before a doctor could see me. They conducted a bunch of tests but couldn't find anything wrong.

"It's most likely food poisoning," the doctor told my grandfather. "Take him home, and he should get better in a few days."

A few days went by, but the pain didn't go away; it actually got much worse. I kept telling my grandparents that I was getting worse, but they just repeated that the doctor said it was food poisoning and I would be fine. In their minds, it was a false alarm and they had already wasted enough money taking me to the emergency room for nothing. That night, while my grandparents were asleep, I snuck into the kitchen and called my mom.

"Jeb?" she asked through her grogginess. "What is it, honey? What's the matter?"

"Mom, I am one hundred percent sure I'm dying."

"You're dy—so it's not just food poisoning, is it?"

"Something is really wrong. Grandpa and Grandma don't believe how bad it is. I need you to come here immediately or I'm not going to make it."

My mother got on the first flight she could find the next morning. The moment she walked into my grandparents' house, everyone started yelling. Mom was screaming at them about not taking care of her child, and they were shouting right back that the whole thing was ridiculous. My grandfather had survived WWII and acted like a drill sergeant most of the time. He told my mother I was just being a mama's boy and I needed to toughen up. He said they did every test they could, so I was going to be fine.

But the reality was I had been unable to stand up for days and was barely able to get to the bathroom to relieve myself. I had to walk in a hunched-over, almost fetal position. When my mother saw me, she said, "We are going to get another opinion now."

"You're overreacting, Gigi," my grandfather told my mom. "The kid's already been to the doctor, and money doesn't grow on trees."

Without another word, my mom picked me up, put me in the car, and drove me to another doctor. This doctor performed another series of tests that also came back negative. He said my condition was strange because I was showing all the signs of appendicitis, but their instruments couldn't detect it. He explained that my other organs were covering up my appendix, making it hard to see. My mother asked, "What should we do?"

He responded, "We should go in and take it out. He doesn't need an appendix. The worst thing removing it will do is eliminate one of the possible issues affecting him. Judging by his vitals, he is extremely sick. We're just finding it difficult to figure out why."

Seeing no other option, my mother said, "Take his appendix out right now."

My grandparents, who had followed us to the new doctor, decided to chime in at this point.

"Who's paying for this little operation, huh?" asked my grandfather. "Seems like you're trying to prescribe an unnecessary procedure so you can charge an arm and a leg for it."

"Sir," said the doctor, "that's not the case here at all. This boy needs his appendix out today."

"Well, I'm not paying for it," Grandpa continued, knowing full well that my mother couldn't afford it.

"I don't care how much it costs," Mom told everyone. "I'll find a way to pay for it. Just help my boy."

"Look," said the doctor, "I'll do the procedure for free, and if it makes you feel any better, I'll try to get the rest of my team to give whatever deductions they can."

Within hours, they had opened me up and removed my appendix. The doctor saved it to show my mother and grandparents. He explained it had been perforated for over a week and had disintegrated in his hands upon removal. He said the only reason I didn't die was because the muscle in my abdomen had contracted around it, holding everything together. That was why I was in the fetal position for so long: it was my body trying to save itself.

"If you had stood up straight at any point," he continued, "the organ would have

ruptured, killing you almost instantly." The silence that followed his remarks was deafening.

Because my appendix was so severely damaged, its contents had spilled into the surgical opening the moment the doctor touched it. Due to this contamination, they had to leave a gaping hole in my abdomen for an entire week to drain the wound. I was on an IV for over ten days in the hospital before being discharged. The doctor told my mother that most people with comparable levels of appendix damage die within twenty-four hours, but somehow, I survived for seven days. He told her I had a powerful will to survive.

This story makes my grandparents sound like bad people, but they were not. They just came from a different era in time, and it was a stressful situation. They took me to the doctor the instant I got sick, but they just trusted what the first doctor said without questioning him. To their minds, any diagnosis was final. They trusted his expertise over what a ten-year-old child had to say. I don't blame them for this. I understand why they acted the way they did. They were kind and generous throughout my life, but none of us are perfect. We all do things we later regret, and I know they regret what happened to me.

My grandparents helped foster my love for the ocean by taking me and my sisters on summer trips to Hawaii. My grandfather was not a strong swimmer, but that didn't stop him from taking me in the water almost every day. He bought me my first snorkeling gear and spent hours doggy-paddling next to me while I looked at all the beautiful tropical fish. He also bought me boogie boards and took me into the beach break when I was only four years old. He would push me into waves as I giggled all the way to shore. He made me strong, and only when I grew older did I begin to understand the powerful impact he had on me.

When my mother and I returned to Santa Fe after my appendix surgery, she started working more and more. My father's art business wasn't doing well, meaning things were becoming more famine than feast. My mother had been going to the Kototama Institute for acupuncture for many years, and she began using what she had learned to earn money by treating people. She was fascinated by the Japanese culture and wanted to practice their style of medicine. She trained under a Japanese man called "Sensei M" for almost a decade before she started her own practice. Once she focused her energy on her practice, it grew quickly. She began getting clients from all over the country. But for some reason, a small community in Palm Springs, California, called Smoke Tree became the epicenter of her client base. Mom started traveling between Santa Fe and Palm Springs to work on clients every week. It became clear that the family needed to make another move.

We made a permanent move to Palm Springs when I turned thirteen years old. For the next three years of my life, I became increasingly isolated. I didn't interact with other people besides my parents and sisters. I withdrew into myself, and as the years passed, the aggression I suppressed after leaving the toxic environment of school began to manifest itself in odd ways. I became dark and depressed. I was lonely and lost, had no friends, no real hopes or dreams. There was nothing I wanted, nothing I cared about. I became a walking dead person, growing darker and darker until the idea of suicide invaded my thoughts and took over my mind. Even waking up was a painful process. I just wanted the sweet release of death.

It's hard for me to understand exactly what my issues were, and even in adulthood, I am not exactly sure what made me so unhappy. My mother was doing everything she could to make sure I had everything I needed. My father wasn't any help and kind of oblivious to everything but his own needs, but he wasn't the problem, either. I think I was just broken somehow. I know this experience wasn't unique to me. It seems like lots of children go through similar experiences when they hit puberty. Maybe it's a chemical imbalance that strikes as you're making that transition from child to adult? I think in my case, it may have been a combination of many factors—a chemical imbalance coupled with crushing loneliness, plus feeling like a complete outcast by having zero contact with people my own age. All I know is that by sixteen, I felt like a bomb just waiting to go off.

After years of putting up with him, my mother finally divorced my father, who had become nothing more than a negative, useless human being. Instead of working on his business or finding a new gig, he did nothing but smoke weed and lie on the floor, reading books and watching TV. My mom probably could have handled his extreme laziness, but it was just the sheer meanness of his personality that made him an impossible person to be around. My mother tried to tell him to leave many times, but he just refused to go. I watched this process happen over and over again until one night, I just snapped. They had a fight and, after she left for work, Dad just lay down on the floor, started watching TV, and rolled himself a joint like nothing had happened.

I walked up to him, looked at him, and said, "You need to go. We don't want you here anymore."

At this point in life, I was filled with rage and extremely unstable. I was ready to do combat with pretty much anyone willing to give me a reason. I believe I was angry enough to kill, and in that moment, my father would have been as good a target to destroy as anyone else. He threw down his joint, stood up, and got in my face in his usual aggressive fashion.

"Don't you talk to me like that, you little shit!" he shouted.

I looked him right in the eye and said, "You will leave here on your own two feet or in a body bag. Your choice. I know where you sleep."

One aspect of my personality that has not changed over the years is that when I say I'll do something, you know I'll do it. I do not make threats. I just say exactly what's about to happen, so people tend to take me very seriously. I could see my father was upset and calculating what he should do. He puffed up like he was going to hit me, but I didn't move. I thought about facing the rattlesnake and just looked him in the eye with the gleaming stare of a psychopath, calm but poised to strike. Something in him shifted. He realized I was ready to go all the way. He left that night, and that was basically the end of our relationship. Since he left, I can count the number of times we have spoken on one hand.

A few months later, my mother decided to send me back to Santa Fe for private tutoring. My maternal grandparents had a friend who agreed to help get my education to a higher level. Mom was working a lot and just didn't have time to homeschool me, and he was a friend of the family she could afford to pay. She could see I was lonely and suffering in silence, and I think she felt that socializing with my cousins might bring me out of the dark funk that seemed to be overtaking me.

Being around my cousins actually served as a release valve at the time, and it calmed me down a bit. That, along with having a more structured curriculum and learning about interesting new things, helped activate my mind. It got me out of my own head and gave me a feeling of temporary purpose. I was educated by the tutor in subjects like Russian history, math, science, English, and philosophy. He was an important mentor at a pivotal point in my life, and I was so absorbed with myself and trapped so deeply in my own mind that I can't even remember his name. This makes me feel bad, realizing how completely broken I was for so many years.

My tutor was trying to prepare me for the GED, and when I informed him I didn't care about passing it, he was very clear that my prospective job opportunities would be greatly limited if I didn't take it seriously. He explained that without a high school diploma or GED equivalent, pumping gas was probably my only option for work in the future. At that point, I wasn't sure I really cared, because I didn't see myself living long enough for any of that to matter. I thought about suicide almost every waking hour of the day, but I didn't feel the need to share that information with him or anyone else. I am pretty sure no one was aware of just how unhappy I truly was. For some reason, I tried to keep my feelings—or the lack thereof—to myself.

CHAPTER THREE

DON'T GET CAUGHT

Right around my sixteenth birthday, something strange happened. My mother disappeared for over a month. I had no idea what happened to her, couldn't get in touch with her, and was left completely in the dark. Every time I called, her phone would just ring and ring with no answer. My birthday came and went without so much as a birthday card. I was getting really upset, but then my grandmother handed me the phone and said, "Jeb, your mom is on the line and needs to speak with you." I grabbed the phone with excitement and asked where she had been.

She responded, "Jeb, I don't have a lot of time to talk right now. I need to ask you an important question."

I said, "Okay, what?"

She said, "I have a client named Barry...you met him just before leaving for New Mexico. He has two children: a little boy named Chris who is six and a little girl named Nicole who is four. I need you to fly to Los Angeles and pick them up in Santa Monica, grab fifty thousand in cash, and bring them and the money to Cancún, Mexico, tomorrow."

I was like, "Are you kidding?"

My mom said, "No, and I need to know right away if you are comfortable doing this."

I responded with, "Sure, why not." She went on to inform me there was a plane ticket waiting for me at the airport and to get moving.

I hung up the phone and my grandparents said, "Get packed. We need to get you to the airport right now." The next ten hours were a blur. Packing, driving to the airport, getting on a plane, flying to LA, and bang, I'm suddenly at baggage claim where some odd woman named Jeannine was waiting to pick me up. She was Barry's ex-wife, which was weird. She informed me I would be staying at Barry's house that night with her and her two children. I would then be leaving early in the morning with Chris and Nicole for Cancún. As we got to the house in Santa Monica, she proceeded to hand me $50,000 in cash. I had never seen that amount of money. I was shocked at how much space $50,000 took up. I asked, "How am I supposed to carry all of this without someone seeing it?"

She said, "I have no idea, but you need to figure it out. And whatever you do, don't tell anyone you have it." I asked why and she explained, "Because they will take it from you if you do." To call the situation strange would be an understatement.

A little later, Chris and Nicole showed up from daycare and I met them for the first time. They were cute kids and very friendly. I had never really been around little kids (aside from my younger sister), so I didn't know what to say or how to act around them. They seemed a bit wild. I wasn't sure how I was going to control them during our journey to Mexico. I was also concerned that it would seem odd for a sixteen-year-old to be traveling with a six- and four-year-old with different last names. I think it's important to note that I had extreme antisocial tendencies at the time and was horrible with people in social situations. Plus, having that much cash on me was frightening because I really didn't want to get robbed. It all felt pretty illegal, but I wasn't sure why. All I knew was that my one thought was, *Don't get caught.*

I eventually excused myself and went to the room Geniene had told me I could use. I took all my bags and the money with me. When I got there, I closed the door and tried to find places to hide the giant bricks of cash. I placed the money evenly between my three different bags. Some were going to be checked bags and some were carry-on. Grandpa had even given me a money belt and I hid some in there. I just tried to spread it around as much as I could so if one bag got stolen, I wouldn't lose all of it.

The next morning, Jeannine left me at LAX with two small children and absolutely no idea what was coming. I was nervous, but traveling to Cancún was actually easy. The kids listened to everything I said, which was a huge surprise and made everything go smoothly. They were much better behaved than I first thought. I also didn't get bothered at customs; they just kind of waved me through without asking any questions whatsoever. Waiting for us outside the baggage claim in sweltering, steamy Cancún heat were my mother and her client, Barry. I was so happy to see her after so long. I also recognized Barry immediately.

I had met Barry right before leaving for New Mexico for tutoring. My mother had just taken him on as a client a few days before I left. The first time I met him, I remember coming home and seeing a Porsche Turbo parked in our driveway and thinking it was the single coolest car I had ever seen. I wondered why it was there. As I walked through the front door, my mom quickly introduced me to Barry, and I was instantly struck by his appearance. Barry had long blond hair and a massive mustache that made him look a little like a light-haired Tom Selleck from *Magnum P.I.* At that moment, I didn't really know what to think, but he seemed like a friendly person. Mom's clients tended to be nice people in general, so that wasn't out of the ordinary. Her acupuncture practice had about fifty clients at that point—most of them older women—but she treated many people of all ages.

Seeing Barry in Cancún with Mom confused me. The last time I had seen them together, my mom was a caregiver and he was her patient. Now, I was delivering him his kids and $50,000 in cash. I wasn't sure what the situation was but knew Mom would fill me in later. We all got in a rental car and Barry drove everyone to a massive resort on the beach.

After checking into our rooms, Mom came over to mine, and I asked her where she had been for the last few months and why I hadn't heard from her. She told me a crazy story that started with how she had been treating Barry regularly since I left. He had come to her with an illness that was difficult to pinpoint, but he had been getting better. My mother would often get cases that had no cures. Most of the time it would be people who had been to regular doctors who told them there was nothing modern medicine could do to help, and they might want to look into alternative treatment methods. This usually meant the doctors had given them only a few months to live or that they just didn't know what to do with them. Barry was no exception. He was building a new home in Malibu, and the contractor on the job was one of my mother's clients. He referred Barry to her, explaining she was good at helping people no one else could. Barry would make the drive from Santa Monica to Palm Springs to be treated every week while I was gone. Over time, he decided it would be easier to just move to Palm Springs until his treatments were complete.

After about six months, he started getting stir-crazy and decided he wanted to go on a trip to La Paz in Baja, Mexico. He asked my mom if she would be willing to do a road trip with him for ten days so he wouldn't have to miss his treatments. Mom tried to explain she couldn't because she had other clients and couldn't be away from her practice that long. Barry told her he would pay her three times the amount she would normally make in the ten days they would be gone. Being financially responsible for three children, she decided it was a good opportunity to make some extra money. So, she told her clients she was going on a short trip to treat a patient, and that was when she disappeared. Barry picked her up in a car, and they just started driving. Seven days into the trip, Mom started to get anxious. They had been driving south in one direction the entire time. She told Barry they should probably turn around now so they could make it back in time for her other clients.

Barry then said, "I think you are going to get mad at me."

She asked, "What do you mean by that?"

He explained they were no longer in Baja, Mexico. They had actually crossed over into mainland Mexico and were driving towards Cancún.

Mom got furious and said, "What are you doing? You know I have work! What about my children? I can't just leave them for unknown periods of time. What is wrong with you?"

But he said, "No problem, just have the kids meet us in Cancún. We'll spend a few more weeks traveling around and sightseeing together. This will give me a chance to get to know your kids better."

Mom explained to me that that was why she couldn't get in touch. This was before cell phones were common, and landline phones were few and far between during their drive through Mexico. But once they agreed to bring all the kids down, they found a phone and began setting everything up. I came with Barry's kids in the first wave. My sisters, Sonia and Scarlett, would come in the second wave a few weeks later.

I looked at Mom and asked, "What now?"

She said, "We travel around Mexico and have fun while I continue to treat him. His condition has improved significantly during this trip." This all felt really weird, but I decided a trip through Mexico sounded like fun, so why not?

From the moment I met Barry, I liked him. He was an oddball for sure and had an explosive temper from time to time, but in general, he was nice to me. I saw him as the father I never really had. My real dad was never mentally there, even when he was physically there. Dad was always checked out, totally consumed with his own thoughts. He had no space left for anyone or anything else. But Barry seemed like he wanted to be a part of my and my mother's lives. He tried hard to connect and went out of his way to communicate with me, which, at that point in my life, was a difficult thing to do. My mind felt fragmented, and I was detached from everything, not to mention depressed and angry. He worked hard to find ways to get me interested in things.

One of the first things he did on the trip was ask me if I wanted to learn scuba diving. He had done a little diving a few years earlier and felt it would be a good way for us to bond. I had always loved the ocean and the animals that lived in it, so I jumped at the opportunity. I said, "Yes, I would love to learn to dive."

He decided I should take a resort course first, just to see if I liked it before committing to a full scuba certification. A resort course is a simple class where they teach you the basics of diving while in a pool. Once they show you simple diving skills in confined water, you head out in the open ocean with an instructor who takes you for a shallow dive and guides you around for thirty minutes. It's a great way to see if you would like to learn more.

My resort course took about twenty minutes, and the only things I learned were how to recover a regulator if it was knocked out of my mouth and how to clear a flooded mask. That was it. The next thing I knew, I was in line with a bunch of other people getting on a boat to go diving. Barry bought me a mask and fins for the class, but the rest of the gear was included in the course. Unfortunately, he said he had a bit of a cold and couldn't come with me. As I was loading onto the boat, he told me if I liked the experience, he would get me certified so we could go do some real dives together over the next couple of weeks.

They sat me on the bow, where I quickly noticed the boat was overcrowded. There were lots of people and gear everywhere—so much gear that every square inch was taken up by something. As we set off, the weather seemed perfect: almost no wind and a sunny sky without a cloud in sight. The ocean was as flat as a pancake, with waves so small you couldn't even feel them as the rusty old engine pushed the boat through the water. We were headed to a reef about two miles offshore between Cancún and Isla Mujeres.

Once we got over the reef, they dropped anchor and told everyone to get their weight belts on. They had given me a weight belt with twelve pounds of weight on it. I didn't know at the time, but this was way too much for my size. I was sixteen years old and had about 5 percent body fat. I only needed four pounds at most. As I put the weight belt on, I didn't understand what a problem this was about to become. As I sat quietly, watching people gearing up for the dive, I noticed something off in the distance. A massive darkness was approaching us. I pointed to it, trying to get the captain's attention, and asked, "What is that?"

The ocean started to move under us in an ominous way. Waves suddenly rose up, seemingly coming from nowhere.

The captain screamed, "Squall!" as the darkness reached us and hit full force. Rain flew sideways, carried by a powerful wind that made the raindrops feel like they were piercing my naked skin. A giant wave made the bow go fifteen feet into the air. I was holding on with everything I had, just trying not to get ejected off the boat into the ocean. All I was wearing were board shorts and a twelve-pound weight belt. As this wave pushed the bow into the sky, the stern slipped under the surface and water poured into the back of the boat. The bow came slamming back down with teeth-shattering force. People just started bailing off both sides as we were hit by another gigantic wave. This time, the boat went completely vertical—nose up, tail down. I was clinging to the nose, looking at a twenty-five-foot drop into dark, angry water, when I heard someone scream, "JUMP NOW!" I instantly let go of the boat and went into a freefall, then hit the water hard as the boat completely flipped over. Its wood frame slammed right next to my head, missing me by only a few inches. I was now struggling to keep my head above water, treading in place and swallowing water with every gasping breath. I was drowning. All I could think about was getting that weight belt off, but I couldn't find the release. It was old and one of the weights was covering the buckle. I could feel the weight pulling me down and I began to lose consciousness.

I'm not completely sure what happened next. I don't trust my memory because my brain shut down. Everything is disjointed and cloudy, but I am pretty sure I drowned. One minute I was choking and suffocating, then nothing. There was no time between going down and coming back. It's as if that period was clipped out and no longer existed. As I came back into consciousness, the sky had cleared, the rain had stopped, and the ocean had calmed, and I had forgotten where I was and what I was doing.

People held onto me as they clung to the side of an over-turned boat. I was confused at what had happened and how I'd ended up in the water. I remember one of the people holding me saying, "You were dead, bro, and you had to be revived." I didn't understand what was happening and couldn't process what he had said. As we held on, drifting for what seemed like hours, my head began to clear and I started to grasp what was happening. Our boat had just sunk, and we were drifting in the open ocean. Luckily, though, it was heavily trafficked water, so a boat spotted us before too long. They rescued us, and we headed back to shore.

Mom, Barry, and the manager of the dive operation were all at the harbor waiting for us when we got there. Mom was visibly upset, but Barry was so furious that he got aggressive with the manager. The manager held up his hands, apologizing, and told Barry he would do everything in his power to make this up to us. The manager asked how I was feeling, and I said, "I feel fine. I guess I'm a little cold, but I am okay." He then suggested I could go on a dive the next day, free of charge, if I still wanted to try scuba. As I stood there, I noticed it was a bit difficult to breathe. I think quite a bit of water had gotten into my lungs and my head felt groggy, but since I wanted to go diving, I kept those details to myself.

Barry asked me if I still wanted to do this, and I said, "Yes, but they need to use a bigger boat with less people tomorrow."

The next day the conditions were perfect, and this time they stayed that way. I'm not sure why, but my near-death experience from the day before didn't deter me in the slightest. I completed my first open-ocean dive using scuba gear, and it turned out to be a relaxing experience. The water was a bit murky, but I still got to see two sea turtles mating. I also saw beautiful coral and so many tropical fish it made me feel like I was swimming in an aquarium. I had dreams as a child of breathing underwater, and there I was, doing it. I was hooked, and the instant I got back to shore, I told Barry I wanted to get certified and dive as much as we could. My first diving lesson gave me the experience of what it was like to drown, but on my second experience, I saw what it was like to live a dream. I felt death was a reasonable thing to risk for the chance to do something so extraordinary.

Barry was right: we did end up bonding through scuba diving. Shortly after I got my certification, we went on a trip to Belize. We used Cancún as a home base and spread out from there to different countries around the area. The trip to Mexico was supposed to be two weeks long but ended up extending for over eight months and spanned across Belize, Guatemala, Honduras, Cuba, and Costa Rica. During the Belize portion of the trip, Barry, Mom, Nicole, Chris, and my little sister Scarlett— who had just flown in from California—all went on a small snorkeling adventure off an atoll called Ambergris Caye. We were all swimming together, soaking up the beautiful reef and colorful fish, when we saw our first shark. It was just a six-foot nurse shark—completely harmless, but a shark was a shark and it sent shivers down my spine. I mean, come on; I was in the open ocean with a shark.

Barry and I became obsessed with the idea of diving with sharks after that. We started planning everything around seeing them. Whenever we would do a dive trip, we asked the dive masters where the largest congregations of sharks would be. They'd give suggestions and we would go wherever they pointed us. This was the main reason the trip didn't seem to have an end. Every time we would do a dive with sharks, we'd find out about another location where we could see another species. Barry ended up buying an underwater camera so we could take pictures of the different types of sharks and collect them like baseball cards. It became all about diving with the biggest, most dangerous sharks we could find. Our goal was to get pictures of the top three: Bulls, Tigers, and Great Whites. But those were difficult to find, so we mostly filmed different types of reef sharks.

When we weren't looking for sharks, we visited ancient Aztec ruins. My mother wasn't a strong swimmer and feared the ocean, so Barry had to come up with fun things for her to do instead. Mom still had a passion for the artifacts she used to find with Dad, so Barry would take Mom around to the shops to buy as many as they could. Barry felt they might be a good investment and Mom had the knowledge about what was real and what was fake, so I think they managed to land a lot of quality pieces. The trip became about buying old artifacts for Mom and diving with sharks for me. Looking back, I can see Barry was working hard to become part of the family.

About five months into the trip, Barry and I broke off from the rest of the family. We were in Costa Rica when we heard of a recently discovered place called Devil's Island. It was supposed to have enormous sharks, but few people had explored its waters. We were going to be one of the first non-local groups to dive it. Most of the stories surrounding its shark infestation were told by fisherman who talked about losing loved ones who fell overboard. They said the sharks were like piranhas, grabbing you and pulling you under the instant you hit the water. This was music to Barry's and my ears. We knew the stories were bullshit but hoped they were based on fishermen spotting large numbers of sharks. Barry and I decided to go for a week-long trip to Devil's Island to see what we could find.

We traveled to a remote area of Costa Rica that is considered the largest mangrove swamp in Central America. It was hot, humid, and had little bugs called no-see-ums. These little buggers are so small they can fit through window screens and mosquito nets. The only defense against them is a fan. The pests were so small they couldn't fly against the airflow, but the power in our huts came from generators that shut off after 6:00 p.m. to save fuel, so our nights were spent being eaten alive by invisible insects.

This area was also known for having large saltwater crocodiles. I was excited at the possibility of seeing one while diving, but the dive guide expressed great concern at this idea. He said if we saw them, we had to get out of the water instantly. He felt they were extremely dangerous and diving with them would prompt an attack for sure. Something inside told me he was wrong. I had started to realize that most people had the wrong idea about predators; they were not mindless monsters, and they would only attack if they were threatened or if they felt they could eat you without too much of a struggle. As long as you don't threaten them or act like their food, you should be fine. Humans fear what we don't understand, and I could tell this man just didn't understand. At some point, with or without his help, I was going to meet a croc.

We didn't stay on Devil's Island itself. It was a sixty-minute boat ride from the mainland, and we had to time our plans around the tides to make it out to the dive locations each morning and back again each evening. We stayed in a cottage by a river that emptied into the ocean. At low tide, the water became dangerously shallow and created huge waves. The locals wouldn't even attempt to travel during this time. They said many boats had capsized because of the rough conditions, and swarms of sharks hunted around the river mouth. We needed a high tide when the waves were calm to make the journey safely, but that only happened twice each day. They also told us not to swim in the river next to our cottage, explaining that the sharks fed on anything that entered the water.

When we finally made it to Devil's Island, the diving was truly amazing—by far the best we experienced on our trip. Eels, rays, and huge schools of fish swam everywhere. We saw dolphins and, of course, sharks. Lots and lots of sharks. It was a super exciting trip, and Barry and I really got along, aside from a few arguments here and there.

About five days into our trip, we left a little out of sync with the tides and ended up hitting massive surf. It was so big we almost had to turn back. The captain of our small metal dingy was visibly shaken, but we made it through and pressed on for the one-hour ride to the small island. When we got there, the currents were stronger than we had experienced on previous days. The sky was darker and something just felt off. We did three dives that day, and as we were on our final dive, Barry accidentally cut himself on some jagged lava rock. He got my attention and showed me he was bleeding pretty badly, and we gave each other a look of understanding. We both knew blood and sharks didn't play well together, but we hoped it wouldn't become an issue. We hadn't seen more sharks than usual on the dive, and they were all behaving normally, so we felt like everything would be fine. As the dive came to an end, we headed to fifteen feet to do a safety stop and let off nitrogen for three minutes. During our safety stop, we just drifted with the current. Suddenly, the water became murky and visibility dropped below three feet. We all gathered close and held on to each other so we wouldn't get separated.

The current carried us into the river mouth pouring from the island—not an ideal location when one of your team is bleeding. As we surfaced, I made eye contact with Barry right as he saw something terrifying. His eyes opened so wide I could see all the white around his blue irises, and he yelled, "SHARKS!"

I turned around and put my face underwater to try and see them, but I couldn't see anything. As I lifted my head, Barry asked, "What did they look like?"

I told him I hadn't seen anything.

He said, "Jeb, they couldn't have been more than one foot in front of your face; they almost touched you."

Our dive master was waving at the boat and yelling, "Get over here, now!" As the captain headed our way, the boat suddenly stopped for a few moments, which sent a panic through our small group. We all moved back-to-back, then took off our tanks and put them in front of us to defend ourselves. As the boat came close, I dropped my tank and was on board in less than five seconds. I grabbed the dive master's hand and pulled him in as Barry was helping push him up from the bottom. Once he was up, we grabbed Barry by the hands and pulled him up, just as the captain shouted that one of the sharks was going under the boat. When Barry was safely onboard, I looked over the edge to see, but the sharks were gone.

Barry, the dive master, and the captain all started talking at once about what they had seen. The dive master asked the captain why he had stopped. The captain said, "I stopped because the sharks were coming at the boat, and I was trying to get a better look at them." He had seen three large dorsal fins with stripes on them and estimated the sharks' size at around 600 to 800 pounds each. The captain and dive master were trying to figure out what kind of sharks they might have been, but couldn't be sure. We looked them up later in a book about shark species and determined that they were tiger sharks. I was upset that tiger sharks had shown up and I hadn't seen a single one.

The dive master tried to tell me I had indeed seen them, I just didn't know it. He explained, "Jeb, when you put your head underwater, you were looking right at one of them, but it was so close and so big you couldn't tell. You didn't realize you were looking at the side of a massive tiger shark. To you, it must have just looked like murky water."

Barry and I didn't have wetsuits on this trip. He thought the water was too warm for them and seemed to be treating it like some test of manhood to go without them. When I mentioned being cold, he told me I was being a pussy. On our ride back to the cottage, he learned to regret his decision. It started raining—or I should say: the sky opened up and dropped a second ocean on us. It's remarkable how much water can fall from the sky in such a short time frame. The sky went black as death and lightning spiderwebbed across it, illuminating a raging sea. Our only protection was the board shorts we were wearing, which weren't adequate. We sat on an iron anchor in our metal boat as rain pelted us sideways. We could see lightning striking the water all around us, and the peals of thunder drowned out the noise of our small engine struggling against the strong current. In horror, we imagined one of those forks of lightning striking the surrounding metal, electrocuting us and ending our existence prematurely. I couldn't understand how the captain could navigate in such harsh conditions. We were blinded by the chaos of the elements. Our small boat was not designed to survive in such circumstances.

As we shivered, I turned to Barry and said, "We really should have gotten wetsuits."

When our little boat finally got to the river mouth—our last obstacle to get back to shore—we found our way blocked by huge waves. We had mistimed the tide.

"Prepare to capsize!" the captain shouted over the storm. The waves were too large, and our chances of making it past the surf break intact were slim. We braced for the worst, but somehow the captain caught one of the waves like a surfer and rode it all the way to the river mouth. At long last, we made it back to the cottages and heaved a sigh of relief.

Towards the end of the eight-month odyssey that was our trip through Mexico and Central America, Mom and Barry fell in love. They decided to get married and join the two separate families into one. I liked Barry; he had become the father figure I desperately needed at the time, but I noticed he was a bit volatile with two distinct sides. He was friendly and giving but also had some odd views about reality and the world in general. He was kind most of the time, but without any apparent reason, he would suddenly get aggressive and say cruel things, especially toward my mother. This dual personality bothered me, but at the time, I just figured no one was perfect, especially not myself. Plus, it wasn't any of my business anyway. If Mom said she loved Barry, then she was well within her rights to marry him. It all had very little to do with me; this was her life, after all, and she had a right to live it.

By this time, the rest of the family had headed home to go back to school and get back to normal life. Mom, Barry, and I were the last ones still traveling. Mom and Barry decided to get married in Oaxaca, Mexico, in front of a justice of the peace two weeks before making the trek back home. The morning of the wedding, we were all eating breakfast in the courtyard of our hotel when something dropped from the ceiling and landed on my mother's arm; it was a scorpion. She watched as its tail flipped up and over, burying its stinger deep in her flesh. She slapped it away as a burning sensation started radiating outward from the wound. We moved as quickly as we could to the lobby, where we asked the receptionist to call a doctor immediately. We took her up to my mom's room, but by the time a doctor got to us, all the muscles in her body had begun contracting.

"What color was the scorpion?" the doctor demanded.

"Uh, yellow...I think," my mom said through clenched teeth. The doctor's face darkened with concern, and he drew a small glass vial from his bag. The label was marked "anti-venom."

He said, "The yellow ones are the most venomous in this region, and if you are allergic to them, they can kill."

The doctor unwrapped a fresh syringe with a large needle and stuck it into the vial, pulling back the plunger and sucking all the liquid up. He then injected my mother with the anti-venom. Mom said she could feel the stuff working its way through her veins, but it didn't look pleasant. Her muscle spasms subsided within a few minutes, and within a few hours, it was as if nothing had ever happened.

Barry asked if she felt well enough to still go to the courthouse that day, or if she would like to postpone. She replied, "Today is the day. Let's get married."

The courthouse was just around the corner, so Barry, Mom, and I walked there together. I bore witness as a judge married them. They got their marriage certificate, and that was that. Mom got a husband, and I got a stepdad.

As the trip finally came to an end, I was sent home ahead of my mom and new stepdad. For the past eight months, they had collected artifacts and various art pieces, and they wanted to send a lot of strange things home with me. That feeling of not wanting to get caught came back; I wasn't sure how legal any of it was. They had Cuban cigars, Aztec and Mayan artifacts made from jade, and all kinds of other weird shit.

As they loaded up my bags, I asked, "Am I going to get in trouble for this?"

With a smile, Barry said, "You're sixteen—no one is even going to check you."

"Dude," I questioned, "what if they do?"

"Just tell them it's all fake. Just a bunch of tourist trinkets."

"This jade skull right here doesn't look like a tourist trinket, bro."

He smiled and said, "No one at the border patrol knows what they're looking at. And besides, they're looking for drugs, not artifacts. You'll be fine."

I wasn't convinced, but what was I going to say to my brand-new stepdad? I was a kid and I had to do what I was told, period. So, my parents packed up five oversized duffle bags, filled with art and who knows what else, that I was expected to transport back to Barry's house in Santa Monica.

The trip back to the US was an unusual kind of experience for a sixteen-year-old. I was being forced to transport a load of items that constituted a legal gray area. My parents dropped me off at the airport with a friend and client of my mother, who had come down to visit for the final part of the trip. Her name was Jennifer. She had somehow let Barry rope her into becoming a mule alongside me. Neither of us were excited about this venture, but together we headed into the airport with way too much baggage for two people. We checked in separately and didn't sit next to each other, which only added to the feeling of criminal activity. All we did was walk into the airport together and fly on the same plane; aside from that, we traveled separately. But somehow, we both managed to get flagged as we went through customs. As I was being pulled out of line, I looked over and saw her getting taken, too. My first thought was, *Yup, saw this coming a thousand miles away.*

They took me to a special area with armed police and security dogs. I was like, *Great, isn't this just exactly what I knew was going to happen?* A bearded guard took my passport and looked through it while another guard started going through my bags one by one. The man holding my passport asked, "Why is a sixteen-year-old traveling through Central America for eight months by himself?"

I told him the abbreviated story of the trip and how I was traveling around filming sharks with my mom and new stepdad. He asked me about school, so I told him I had been homeschooled most of my life and was taking a little break. As this was going on, the man opening my bags kept pulling out strange, old-looking things. He would pull one out, look at it, and put it right back in to reach for another. I quickly realized he didn't give two shits about the art. Barry was right: they really were just looking for drugs. I instantly relaxed, and a grin spread across my face as I understood I wasn't in any trouble and everything was going to be just fine. The guard with my passport asked me a few more questions, then said, "Have a nice day," and pointed me towards the exit.

I met with Jennifer outside customs, and she told me a similar story about her experience, but she was a bit more shaken, even on the edge of tears. But for me, I thought the whole thing was kind of funny. I had been crapping my pants for no reason. As Dan Zadra put it, "Worry is a misuse of the imagination." I couldn't agree more.

CHAPTER FOUR

ADJUSTING TO A NEW LIFE

A few days later, Mom and Barry returned to the Santa Monica house. My older sister, my younger sister, Barry's two kids, and myself all moved in together. This living arrangement didn't last long, though. Barry had been building an enormous 11,000-square-foot mansion on a private beach in Malibu, CA. The framing of the house was finally complete, but only one room was ready for use: a maid's quarters with a service entrance. Barry had been informed that, for insurance reasons, he needed to post a full-time security guard on the premises. Barry decided he had a brand-new sixteen-year-old stepson who didn't have anything better to do, so he moved me into the Malibu property to act as the onsite twenty-four-hour-security detail. So, within just a few weeks of my return from the south, I found myself in Malibu to live in a construction site, by myself. The house was remote, and I didn't have a driver's license, so it was hard to get around. There were no grocery stores within walking distance, so each week, Mom and Barry came to Malibu so I could get groceries. We would buy enough food to last me seven days, until my parents could come again.

There wasn't much for me to do except go to the beach. Barry had an old, nine-foot-long surfboard and he suggested I teach myself how to surf. The house he was building just so happened to sit at the top of a trail leading to one of the best surfing beaches in Malibu. It was the only beach in all of California that was 100 percent private, with massive gates covered in razor wire like some kind of prison. The community was always in court battles over the gates because, technically, you can't have a private beach in the US, but they argued that the gates weren't to keep people off the beach, only to keep beachgoers away from the houses. Somehow the gates remained, but regardless, they kept most people away. While other famous Malibu surf breaks had over a hundred surfers in the lineup, this beach usually had about ten.

Even though the Californian waters were cold, Barry still didn't feel I needed a wetsuit. He said it was summer and, as far as he was concerned, the water was warm. He also made it clear that the board didn't belong to me—I was just allowed to use it, and any damages would come out of my pocket. I felt it was a fair enough deal; I should be held responsible for using his things. But I also had no way of making money at the time, so I tried to be careful with the board.

For months, I was all alone. Every morning, after eating breakfast by myself, I would walk to the beach with the board in tow, where I spent hours on end trying to teach myself how to surf. I was surprised how hard it was to learn. I got hurt every single day. The beach had shallow water over jagged rocks, and large, black sea urchins covered in spikes lurked under every step. Tripping or falling meant getting cut or punctured in some way. I fell a lot in those first few months.

It was a lonely time for me. When I wasn't surfing, I would go for walks on the beach by myself. Aside from our long vacation, I had been living a life of isolation from twelve years old to sixteen. I had no friends and never talked to people my own age. The only people I regularly communicated with were my parents. I was awkward to the extreme, and to call me weird would be a true understatement. The short time I had spent in New Mexico with my cousins didn't really help in the long term. I still felt broken inside, and being around strangers made me feel uncomfortable. Looking back, I'm not exactly sure what my problem was, but I think it may have been a combination of things I had carried since my early childhood. First, I had serious unresolved issues with my real father. Second, my isolation created a crushing loneliness that was overwhelming. And third, I was going through puberty, which probably helped create a hormonal imbalance and made my mind unstable. All these things combined to create a state of suffering that led to severe suicidal depression, which I tried to keep locked up inside myself. This negative energy was bottled up inside me for years and just didn't have anywhere to go. The longer I held it in, the more it festered.

Up to this point in life, I was just going along for the ride, kind of like excess baggage on a trip. Wherever my parents went, I went. I was just drifting with the wind, going wherever it blew me. I think this movement helped distract me from the turmoil within, but now, being trapped in this construction project, completely alone all the time, having nothing but my own crushing thoughts to keep me company, everything started to become overwhelming. The oppressive darkness trapped inside me started bubbling over like black tar, seeping through my pores. As a defense mechanism, I found myself detaching from all emotion. I stopped caring about anything and pushed everything away. My mind began to implode. Every day, I would wake in a massive, empty house all alone, wondering *why?* I felt trapped in my own body and couldn't figure out what the point of existing was. Why did I need to keep breathing? I no longer had dreams or felt the need to persist. I saw no future—no reason to be. The loneliness became all I could think about, and I came to the realization that I was done.

I had no reason to live, and I was going to kill myself.

I told no one, said nothing. I just went deep inside myself, and all I wanted was death. One night, after being in the ocean alone for eight hours straight, I came back to the house and tried to warm my frozen body while clicking through countless boring channels on the TV. Suddenly, I came across an image that made me stop dead in my tracks. A feeling of electricity began coursing through my body as I watched a man standing on the edge of a massive cliff in France. He looked at the camera, stuck out his tongue, and stepped off the cliff, opening his arms as gravity began pulling him towards earth.

BANG!!!

Instantaneously, a memory flashed in my mind. I was sitting in the backseat of my aunt's car in Santa Fe, New Mexico. I was maybe five years old. I had my hands pressed against the window as I was looking out. I was watching birds perching on telephone wires attached to poles. I watched them step off, open their wings, and fly. I remembered telling my aunt that when I got older, I was going to do that. I was going to fly. She glanced out the window to see what I was talking about, then looked back at me and said, "Jeb, you are very young, but when you get older, you're going to realize that's not physically possible."

I looked her right in the eye and said, "Maybe you can't, but I'm going to fly."

I don't think she was purposely trying to quash a child's dream, but adults do have a tendency to think it's their place to teach children to be practical. However, in many cases, adults are not as intelligent as they think they are. How does the saying go? "You don't know what you don't know." A child's imagination doesn't possess the same arbitrary boundaries adults have built up over time. Children see possibilities without limitations. As they get older, that magic seems to be erased with time and older people telling them what can and can't be done.

I had my dreams stomped out of me so many times as a child that, by the time I reached sixteen, I didn't really have dreams anymore. All that seemed to exist in my head were demons ripping vast holes straight through my psyche, leaving empty voids in their wake. When I saw this man standing on the edge of that cliff, a dormant desire came back to life. It was like a spark of light appeared and started glowing in a dark place. It dawned on me that I had been lied to my entire life—people could fly; this man was living proof. That little glowing light quickly became a fire in my mind, filling the dark voids that had been growing for years with a warm illumination. I decided I would stop at nothing to repeat what I had just witnessed. I would do anything it took, sacrifice everything I had, to make this a reality—or I would die trying.

With the way my mind had been collapsing for years, this seemed like the perfect activity for me. If I did it and survived, then I would have accomplished something I had been told was impossible my entire childhood. If I died while doing it, then I would be released from my suffering on this planet. It was a win/win situation; either way, I'd get what I wanted.

As twisted as this way of thinking was, I feel like it saved me. That fixation helped me hold on during the darkest periods of my teenage years. I know I'm not the only adolescent person to have had these feelings, but I am happy I found something to channel my negative energy into. Whenever the darkness began snuffing out my light and the suicidal thoughts started rushing in, I would focus on this thought: *NO! I am not going to waste my death. Anyone can kill themselves. If I'm going to die anyway, I want it to be special. I'm going to use my death to do something others are unwilling to do.*

In an odd way, BASE jumping saved my life. The thought of it dragged me, kicking and screaming, through time. It would be many years before I became a BASE jumper, but during that journey, I would grow to love my life. By the time I did my first jump, my depression was gone and I no longer wanted to die. Somehow, in my search for death, I found my life. It's somewhat paradoxical that such a dangerous activity is what ended up saving me. I am convinced that had I not found BASE jumping when I did, I would have killed myself before my life—the one with meaning—had even begun.

Once the image of that person flying had entered my mind, I couldn't think of anything else. I started researching what I needed to do in order to make this happen. I called the closest skydiving center to see if they knew where I could get BASE jumping training. The person who answered the phone listened to me explain how I wanted nothing more than to learn how to BASE jump, but suddenly cut me off.

"Hold on. How old are you?"

"Uh, I'm sixteen," I said as nicely as possible.

"You're not even old enough to start skydiving yet, kid. You have to be eighteen to do the training. That's *before* you learn how to BASE jump."

"There's got to be another way," I insisted.

"Nope. Even after you get your skydiving license, you still have to do hundreds of skydives before any BASE jumper will even *think* about mentoring you."

BASE jumping didn't have any standardized instruction, and the only way to learn was to find someone that was already doing it and convince them to teach me.

"No, screw that," I told him. "I'm not even interested in skydiving. I only want to BASE jump."

"Sorry, kid. Skydiving comes first. If you don't do it that way, you're dead for sure."

That was when I realized BASE jumping would have to be a long-term goal, something that was going to take me years to accomplish. I didn't know it at the time, but this turned out to be a good thing. A goal of that magnitude was exactly what I needed. It gave me something I wanted to live for; it gave me direction and added purpose to my life.

This was also around the time I started wearing nothing but black. I had read somewhere that Einstein would only wear one outfit because he didn't want to waste energy of thought on how he dressed, preferring to focus his mental energy on more important things. I liked this idea and agreed: thinking about what I was going to wear and separating laundry did waste a lot of time. So, I decided I was only going to wear one color. Black happened to be my favorite color, so it became the default. Everything I bought from that point forward was black. It started out as a practical thing, but it would eventually become something deeper.

After a few years of wearing nothing but black, I felt strange whenever I wore color. Even to this day, seeing myself in colored clothing makes me feel uncomfortable. I don't fully understand the psychology behind why this is, but that preference has now extended to everything I own. If I have a color choice for anything, it's always going to be black.

When black clothing first became compulsory for me, I think it was a reflection of how I felt inside. Also, I didn't want to stand out; I just wanted to blend into the shadows and be left alone. I was misanthropic and didn't want people to be around me, and I felt bright colors would draw too much attention. But as the years went by and I became happier, the black began to symbolize something else: an internal rebellion against exterior forces. Older people told me it was a phase that I would grow out of. I would just smile and think to myself, *No, it isn't, I am going to wear nothing but black till the day I die.* I also hate dress codes for the same reason. I can't stand being told how I should dress, and I refuse to go places or do things where people dictate what I wear. The only exception is work. If it's for a stunt job where I am being paid to double an actor, then I will do it, but I must be paid well.

When I finally told Mom and Barry I wanted to become a BASE jumper, they didn't seem surprised. They said, "Yup, seems like something you would want to do, but you do realize you can't make a living that way, right?" Barry expressed concern and felt he needed to explain life to me.

"You're going to eventually need to get something called a 'job' and make something called 'money.' We are not going to support you for the rest of your life."

I responded with, "Yes, I know I won't be able to earn a living this way, but it's just something I want to do. I feel like it will give my life purpose and bring me happiness."

Barry said, "That is wonderful, Jeb, but how do you plan on making money in the future to pay for this new, expensive hobby?"

I didn't have an answer for him. I wasn't planning on living long, so earning money wasn't something I was worried about at the time.

Barry decided right there on the spot that it was time for me to get a high school diploma so I could go to college and get an education. He felt the best way for me to figure out what I wanted to do for a living would be college. I was concerned because I remembered how horrible my experience in school had been. I hadn't gotten along with children my own age, and I was worried the violence that had planted seeds in my grade school years might sprout. But I was also suffering from mind-crushing loneliness. I thought maybe being around people my own age might help me work through some of my darkness and antisocial mindset. It could've gone either way; I just didn't know which to expect.

I had been living in the Malibu construction site by myself for over a year before the rest of the family was able to move in. Once they did, Barry's first act of business was to enroll me in a private high school called Colin McEwen. He drove me down to the heart of Malibu, right across from the famous John's Garden, where we walked up the stairs of what looked like a small office building. We opened a door with the name of the school on it and were greeted by a man named Mr. Wilson; he was the principal of the school. Barry began discussing our options on what it would take for me to get a high school diploma. After hearing about my homeschooling since sixth grade, Mr. Wilson informed us I would have to take and pass the GED. If I did that, he would be able to add it as credit, and if I was able to pass another series of standardized tests, he could enroll me as a senior. I would then have to earn a certain number of credits through the school to get a full high school diploma. We asked how long it would take, and he said if I was able to pass all the tests, it could be as few as six months, which meant I could possibly graduate with the senior class that year. Barry signed me up, and school started bright and early the next day.

I was nervous as Barry drove me to Colin McEwen for my first day. The memories of grade school haunted me: the constant fighting, the evil children ganging up on me, the cracked skulls and shattered faces. The rage that had grown inside me as a child had lain dormant for years, but I could still feel it just below the surface, like molten lava under high pressure. I had developed a true, deep-seated hatred towards people my own age, and that concerned me. But as I walked into class for my first time, I was pleasantly surprised. The school was small: only fifty students evenly distributed from ninth through twelfth grade. Everyone I encountered seemed pleasant. Most just smiled at me as I walked by or greeted me in friendly ways. It was disarming and disorienting. I had walked in ready for battle, but there was no one to fight. Just happy people and teachers ready to teach.

During my first break, I was sitting in the common room, just minding my own business, when a young kid named Loki sat down next to me. He seemed way too young to be there. Colin McEwen was a high school that went from ninth to twelfth grade, and this kid looked maybe twelve at the oldest. I asked him how old he was, and he said fifteen. I thought, *Damn, this is the youngest-looking fifteen-year-old I have ever seen.* I didn't find out until much later this guy was a chronic liar and he was eleven years old at the time. There was a chess board on a table between us and I asked him if he would like to play. He said, "I have never played chess before, but I would love to learn."

I responded, "Not a problem; I can teach you to play." So, for the next couple of weeks between classes, we sat together and I would teach him the strategy of the game. This is how my friendship with Loki began.

Loki and I played so much chess that the other students got interested in what we were doing. I started noticing one guy in particular named Shawn who would walk by multiple times a day as we played. After a few days of circling us like a shark, he finally walked up and said, "I play the winner." Turned out Shawn had played a little chess and wanted to learn more about it from us. Shawn was an outgoing character with an odd sense of humor. He would purposely say inappropriate things at inappropriate times to see how people would respond. He was also the master of all procrastinators. He did no schoolwork—like zero—until a week before the semester ended. He would then do all-nighters for a week and finish everything all at once. Seemed like a stressful strategy to me, but somehow it worked for him.

I didn't have a car or a driver's license at the time, so I had to take the public metro each morning to get to school. About a month into my high school experience, I was sitting at the bus stop when a black Mercedes pulled up and rolled down its passenger-side window. A blond head poked out and I recognized it as Shawn, the boy I had played chess with a few days earlier. He asked what I was doing.

I looked at him and said, "What does it look like? I am waiting for the bus."

"Wanna ride?" he asked, revving the engine. "I drive this way every day. If you want, I can pick you up here each morning and drop you off after school, so you don't have to wait for the bus. Buses suck."

I smiled and said, "Thank you, I would love that." I ended up carpooling with Shawn the rest of the year. He became my first real friend, and to this day, over twenty-eight years later, we are still good friends.

As Shawn was driving me home from school that same day, I asked him if he had ever tried surfing. He looked at me with an odd expression and said, "No, Jeb, and I never will."

I shook my head and asked, "Why?"

He said, "When I was young, maybe five years old, I was playing in knee-deep surf with one of those foam boogie boards at Zuma Beach with my parents. I got caught in a riptide and pulled out to sea. My parents called the lifeguard, but by the time he got there, I was too far from shore for him to get me. They had to call in a boat and it turned into a full-on rescue operation. It traumatized me, and I haven't put one toe in the water since."

I said, "Bro, I can help you fix that problem if you want."

"I'm not sure that's possible, but if you could, that would be amazing. This is something that has bothered me my whole life, and the fear is crippling. I don't know how you'd do it, but if you could show me how to work through it, I'd be forever grateful."

That evening, I went over to Shawn's house to hang out and talk. I told him about my travels around the world from childhood and the crazy shark diving trip I had been on with my parents through Central America. I explained my dream of becoming a BASE jumper and that on my eighteenth birthday, I was going to begin my skydiving training. In return, he told me about his love for acting and making music. He could listen to any song and recreate it on almost any instrument, which I found incredibly impressive. Personally, I am tone deaf and can't play a note. He also loved writing and was thinking about becoming an author. Towards the end of the conversation that went on for hours, we started planning on how I would teach him to surf. I could see the idea scared him but could also see his excitement.

I am not sure why, but even early on I had a gift with fear—not only my fear, but other peoples' fears as well. My extreme fascination with fear and my understanding of it seemed to put people at ease about their own fears. The things I had done were obviously dangerous, many of them bringing me face to face with death. I think this made them feel more comfortable facing their own fears because usually, their consequences were nowhere near as dire. Being around someone that does truly scary shit makes a person feel more comfortable because their own fears seem smaller and easier to manage by comparison. If my dream was to jump off buildings with parachutes, then it almost seemed silly to fear swimming in the ocean.

When Shawn brought up sharks—people's number one fear about the ocean—my response was simple: "Shawn, you would be the luckiest human being in the world to be eaten by a shark. You are more likely to be struck by lightning twice or killed by a falling coconut. Plus, what better way is there to die? Getting eaten by an animal is a man's death, and we would all be so lucky to go out that way."

As odd as it sounded, my words made him feel better. He just laughed and said, "Okay, what do I need to do?"

A few days later, we were in Becker's Surf Shop looking for a longboard for him to buy. He picked out a single-fin, nine-foot-long flat tail. It was a beautiful board and perfect to learn on. I lived on Little Dume with some of the most perfectly-shaped waves in all of Malibu. It was the ideal place to bring Shawn for his first lessons.

There are four distinct breaks at Little Dume. As you come out of the wildlife guard gate, you see the first break. It's called Gully and it's the best one for beginners. It breaks in the deepest water and has a sand bottom. This makes it much nicer on the student when they fall, and less likely for them to get hurt. The next break, to Gully's right, is called Middles. This break usually has a rock bottom with shallow water. Falling here means falling on rocks covered in sea urchins. This break is for an intermediate surfer and not the best place for a beginner. A little farther to the right is the best break on Little Dume (when it comes to the waves' shape and size) called Point. On good days, you can catch a wave at Point and ride it to Middles, then transition through Middles and keep going. On a great day, you can then transition from Middles to Gully and ride that wave all the way to shore. The last break only goes on huge days (by Southern California standards). The waves must be overhead, meaning seven feet high or more. When they get that big, they break on a reef called Outers. On perfect days, when the waves are just the right size, Outers can shape a wave that connects from Point to Middles to Gully, then takes you all the way to the beach. These days are far and few between, but when you get one, it's magical.

We were going to start Shawn's training at Gully on a relatively small day. I started him on the sand, lying on his board doing pop-up drills. He would lie on his belly and I would yell, "Pop up now!" He would jump up into a squatting position, standing on his board. I would then yell, "Down!" and he would drop back down to his belly. I made him repeat this over and over until his arms got so tired they felt like noodles. When I could see he was tired, I allowed him to rest but made him count the waves as he did. I told him that waves come in sets, and he would need to know how many average waves there'd be per set. The best way to do this is to count them and watch for at least four to five sets. Each day you go surfing, you need to do this before going out, because the numbers change each time. This can give you an understanding of which waves you should catch and how much time you have between sets. Usually, the biggest and the best waves come towards the end of the set. This was important information when it came time to paddle out. You wanted to start the paddle at the end of a set, and you wanted to know how much time you had before the next set was coming. On big days, this was crucial information that could help keep you safe. Also, you never wanted to catch the first wave in a set. If you were to catch the first wave and wiped out in the impact zone, it would mean you would have to take all the rest of the waves on the head before you could paddle away. On giant days, this could be life-threatening, especially if you're not a strong swimmer. Shawn was not a strong swimmer, so he listened very carefully to everything I said.

I think Shawn appreciated my almost-drill-sergeant approach to teaching. I have always felt it's important to take things seriously when they can potentially hurt you. I had been hurt a lot while surfing, so I wanted to help Shawn avoid some of that if possible. The more drills I put Shawn through, the more confident I saw him become. By the time we started heading to the water, I could see he was more excited than scared. I think he felt ready, and the fact that his board was more like a boat seemed to bring him comfort, too.

Shawn had a friend named KC who lived just down the street from me, and KC showed up at this point. He was actually a pretty good surfer and was surprised to see someone had been able to convince Shawn to give it a try. He had been trying for years and heard nothing but, "No way in hell. Not going to happen," from Shawn.

Before we all paddled out together, I explained one final important thing to Shawn. I told him that on longboards, a big part of catching a wave is finding the board's center of gravity. If you are too far back on the board, you can't catch the wave. If you are too far forward on the board, you will push the nose underwater as you go down the face of the wave. This is called "pearling" and will result in you being ejected over the front of your board. The wave will then keep pushing the nose of the board deeper into the water until, at some point, it builds enough pressure that the board will shoot up in the air with force. I told him if this happens, stay underwater as long as you can. As you come to the surface, make sure you have your hands and arms above your head to protect you from the board. Remember, the board has a sharp blade on the bottom called a "skag." If you get hit in the head with this part of the board, it can open you up in a serious way.

As we paddled out to the line-up, I set him right next to something called a water boil. The water boil is the place where the waves first begin to break. This is the spot where the water starts getting shallow enough to slow down the energy that has been traveling over the surface for thousands of miles. It creates a disturbance that looks like water boiling—hence the name. As that energy going over the surface starts to slow down, it forces the water to jack up and form the wave. If you are close enough to the water boil in just the right spot, you can paddle into the wave the water boil creates and follows that energy all the way to shore.

As I was explaining all this and putting Shawn in the perfect position, I saw a set coming. Shawn started paddling for the first wave of the set. Usually, I would have made him wait for the third or fourth wave, but since it was a small day, I wasn't worried about him getting caught on the inside of the impact zone. He paddled for his life, and to my surprise, he caught the wave and slid down its face as he got to his feet. He stood up and rode the wave all the way to the beach. It's rare for a person to catch a wave and manage to stand up on their first try. Shawn was a natural athlete and had no trouble surfing. I was impressed. For someone scared of the ocean, he learned ten times faster than I did. That was a great demonstration of how important having a coach can be. Trying to learn things from scratch without any guidance makes everything harder.

We surfed for about an hour before the accident happened. A nice set was coming and Shawn went for the second wave. He caught it and, for an instant, I thought he made it. Suddenly, I saw the nose of his board go underwater, and he pearled big time. He went over the front of the board, and I saw the board go vertical and dip super deep into the water. This created huge power, and the board rebounded out of the wave, flying high into the sky above where Shawn was getting pounded by the wave. The board actually traveled so high, I could see that Shawn's leash (the long strap that holds the board to your leg so you don't lose it) was fully extended. On a nine-foot board, you usually have a ten-foot leash, so it was way up there. Before the board came down, I saw Shawn's head appear above water and his hands were by his side. I watched as the board smashed down onto his head with full force. Both KC and I paddled to Shawn as fast as we could. We knew he was hurt; we just didn't know how bad. As we approached him, the water around him was bright red with blood. He had naturally blond hair, but at that moment, he looked like a redhead. The skag on the bottom of his board had hit him and sliced his head open. Head wounds bleed a lot and usually make things look worse than they are, but we weren't going to take any chances and went straight back to my house. We put Shawn in his car and KC drove it to the nearest emergency room.

Shawn was calm and didn't seem worried about what was going on, but blood was pooling all around him. Every time he removed the paper towels we had given him to take a look, blood would just squirt everywhere. Malibu is remote, so it took us over thirty minutes to get Shawn to the emergency room. As we got there, we saw a large line of people waiting to be seen.

I walked in front of everyone and told them, "We have an emergency over here." The person admitting people handed me a clipboard with paperwork and told me to have him fill it out.

"Are you fucking serious?" I said. "He just got his head crushed by a surfboard and he's bleeding everywhere." They informed me that all the doctors were busy at the moment dealing with a child in critical condition who had just been run over by a car. They said Shawn would be looked at as soon as they could get to him. Shawn quietly filled out the paperwork, and we ended up sitting there for about two hours before they called his name. The wound turned out to be mostly superficial. He didn't have a concussion, and all they needed to do was give him ten stitches. He was worried about them shaving his head, but they were able to just shave the small area where the wound was. You could barely see it when they were finished.

As Shawn drove us back to Malibu, he thanked me for helping him get over his fear. Even with the accident, he said, "That was a freeing experience. Releasing that fear of the ocean after so many years was amazing." After that day, Shawn was no longer scared of the ocean.

A few days later, as Shawn was driving me to school, he started making fun of my odd curly hair and asked, "Why don't you just shave your head? Your hair makes you look like a total dork." My real father had been forced into military school when he was young, so he had a hatred for crew cuts and shaved heads. But seeing how I didn't speak to him anymore, I thought, *That was Dad's hang-up, not mine.* In fact, shaving my head could actually make everything I did much easier. I hated how my hair got caught in my dive mask, making it flood with water. I didn't like how long it stayed wet after getting out of the surf. It just seemed to be in the way, serving no real purpose other than annoying me. I asked Shawn if he had shears and would shave it for me. He said, "I sure do; I have horse shears in my barn, and we can use those."

Shawn's family lived on a ranch and raised quarter horses for racing. We went in his family's stables, and he opened a drawer with the crustiest looking shears you can imagine. They had horsehair trapped in the blades, and I wasn't sure if they had ever been cleaned. It was disgusting, but as teenagers who didn't really give a shit about hygiene, we used them. Shawn told me to get on my knees in the dirt right in the middle of the stable, and he shaved my head with those nasty shears. After he was done, the feeling of having no hair was strange. I could feel the air touching the skin on my head. I went home and took a shower. The feeling of the water hitting the skin on my skull was something different, and I liked it. As I stepped out of the shower and rubbed a towel over my head, I reached up to feel my scalp and it was already dry. I knew at that moment I was going to shave my head for the rest of my life. Hair was completely pointless, and I had no use for it.

I ended up going to Colin McEwen for six months. I got my credits, passed all their tests—including the GED, which was a shockingly easy test, by the way—and got my high school diploma. This seemed to make Barry and my grandparents happy, but it did little in helping me figure out what I was going to do with my life. I was still pretty lost, but my eighteenth birthday was coming. After two years of dreaming, I would finally be able to start my training and do my first skydives. For my birthday, my grandparents bought me my first two skydives. There was a small drop zone in Bermuda Dunes called Parachutes over Palm Springs. About twenty minutes from my grandparents' house, Parachutes over Palm Springs was located on a small local airport, and the drop zone used Cessna 182 aircraft as jump planes. We showed up early in the morning on March 26, 1994, the day after my birthday. My grandparents signed me up for two tandem jumps back-to-back. A tandem is where they attach you to an instructor's belly and they pretty much do all the work. I went through a short thirty-minute class that basically told me to arch and have fun. Then we went up in a tiny aircraft that only had space for a pilot, two tandem instructors, and two students.

This is when I got my first glance at the fear threshold. I think fear is kind of like pain: you only feel it to a certain point and then it just cuts off and you go numb. I was surprised, because not only did I not feel scared, I kind of felt nothing at all. I got on the plane and went to altitude, then the instructor hooked me up to his harness and opened the door, and we jumped out. I felt nothing. When I landed, I found myself disappointed with the experience. I had an instant dislike for skydiving, which went against everything I'd been told about doing it. So many people claimed skydiving was a life-altering experience. This jump made me feel otherwise.

We had a thirty-minute break before we got back in the plane to do it all again. This time was different, though. I started to feel something the moment I got in the aircraft: an uneasy feeling in my stomach. As the airplane gained altitude, the feeling became more and more uncomfortable. As the tandem instructor hooked me in, the feeling became almost unbearable. He then opened the door at 14,000 feet and started leaning out of the aircraft to see where we should jump. As he was spotting the aircraft, I noticed I wasn't leaning out with him. I was actively fighting him to stay in the plane. I could sense that feeling in my stomach was fear creeping up on me. I think for the first jump, I was so overwhelmed by what was happening that I passed the fear threshold and just shut off. I have friends that call it "data dumping." The brain becomes overwhelmed and just purges everything in response. All thought was gone. This time, because I had the first experience earlier, my body was not as scared, so I wasn't passing the fear threshold. The ironic thing is the first time I didn't think I was scared, but as it turns out, I was petrified and just couldn't tell. This time I was far less afraid, but I felt it more powerfully.

I didn't truly come to terms with this concept until much later in life. You must experience a wide range of horror to truly grasp this concept. As the instructor tried to lean out of the aircraft, I remember reaching up and grabbing the frame around the door with my hand. As I did, I noticed the frame was bent from people grabbing it with so much force that they had physically bent the metal. My hand was right in this indentation, holding on for dear life. When the instructor went to jump, I wouldn't let go and he had to grab my hand and forcibly pry my fingers from the doorframe. This time, the jump was scary as shit, and when we landed, I realized I truly hated skydiving. It wasn't something I wanted to do. I didn't like the way it made me feel—not on the first jump where I felt nothing, and definitely not on the second jump where I felt like I was going to crap my pants.

All I wanted was to BASE jump, but skydiving was a barrier to that dream. It also occurred to me that if a tandem skydive scared me that badly, how the hell could I ever BASE jump? It sent pangs of doubt through my core. I had just been scared on a level I had never come close to experiencing before, and it was the easiest level of what I was planning to do. Fear and self-doubt began spreading their roots through my skull.

My grandparents took me to lunch afterward and asked me what I thought about the experience. I didn't know how to respond, so I just said, "It was interesting." They thought I was just trying to downplay the experience, but I honestly didn't know how to process what I had gone through. It had shaken me in a way I couldn't express. I'd never been so scared that it made me short circuit before. I had never felt fear so powerful that it made me go numb. My concept of fear was so limited at this point; I just couldn't comprehend how much stronger it could get. I still had a child's mentality that was too sensitive to stimulation. It takes time and constant hammering to desensitize your soft molten brain into hardened steel. Gut-wrenching horror is the fire that can help forge a strong mind. This type of fear was looming on the horizon for me, though. I had just received a small glimpse of what was to come.

CHAPTER FIVE

THE WORK BEGINS

While on a trip to the Florida Keys with my parents, I became a scuba diving instructor. Barry was concerned about my future and wanted me to have a skill I could use to earn a living. He felt it was important to make that skill something I could be passionate about, so he made me an offer I couldn't refuse: he said he would cover the expenses for me to become a scuba instructor if I would let him teach me the insurance business. I would then have to work for his company for six months after my training to pay him back. I didn't have any interest in insurance, but the idea of being a scuba instructor intrigued me, so I agreed. I stayed in Florida for half a year and went from open-water diver to scuba instructor.

When I returned home, I had a sense of accomplishment. I had learned something I could always use to earn a living. That idea brought me comfort. Teaching scuba diving was a great plan B. I didn't exactly have a plan A yet, but that was a work in progress.

Barry greeted me with a schedule as I walked through the door of his insurance brokerage building. Our days were planned out, and my training in his company began. Secretly, I think he wanted me to take over the business one day. We would go on long walks on the beach and hikes in the Malibu hills where he explained the inner complexities of the insurance industry. I hate to say this, because Barry was trying to help me, but every word was the most mind-numbingly boring shit on planet Earth. I could tell from day one this was not going to be a job I would enjoy. But we had made a deal, and I would do my best to honor it.

After about four weeks of Barry training me for the position, I showed up at his office in Thousand Oaks, California, to begin what was supposed to be a six-month contract. He gave me a list of companies with names of people to cold call. My first job was to call the people on this list and ask them specific information about their corporate structure. The goal was to talk to a CEO or COO to ask who was in charge of human resources. If I could get this information from one of the heads of the company, Barry could then call whoever that person was and claim that their boss told him to contact them. This was one of Barry's tricks to get people to talk to him about their insurance. If people just get a cold call, they usually try to get off the phone as quickly as possible, but if they hear the name of their boss or their boss's boss, they listen carefully to anything you have to say. It's an effective technique, if a bit sneaky. So, it was important that I did this well because having the names of the CEO or COO mattered to Barry. But I was horrible at this job. I spent a few hours just having people hang up on me. I couldn't even get through to 99 percent of the secretaries. The task required a skill you just can't teach someone. People either have it or they don't, and I was in the don't category for sure. Sitting under those fluorescent lights, staring at a phone, calling number after number, and having people just hang up on me over and over again was making me anxious. The office setting was making my heart rate speed up. I felt sick to my stomach. I realized there was a zero percent chance I could last four days, much less six months, doing this. I was not emotionally stable enough to do this kind of work. I was not what you would call a "people person."

Halfway through the day, I walked into Barry's office. He looked up at me and asked, "How is everything going? How many names have you been able to get so far?"

I said, "Zero. Not a single person is willing to speak to me." I had a little breakdown while trying to explain to Barry how this wasn't something I was going to be able to do. I began begging him to let me do anything else. I pleaded with him, "I will do any other job you want; I just can't work in insurance. It's soul-sucking and I'm horrible at it."

He looked at me and said, "Okay, Jeb. I understand. Tomorrow morning you'll start working as a day laborer, on the house. You will be paid fifty bucks a day like all the other day laborers, and you'll work until you pay back the money you owe me." Unless I'm mistaken, I think Barry had some financial frustrations at this point and maybe vented them on me. The house in Malibu was still under construction and would remain that way for another six years. We didn't know it at the time, but the Malibu house was the never-ending construction project from hell.

I instantly said, "No problem, Barry, and thank you from the bottom of my heart." I was honestly so relieved to be released from that damn office environment and that infernal cold calling that I didn't give two shits what I had to do. I would have done anything else. Working outside digging ditches seemed like a welcome alternative. The only thing that kind of sucked was the pay he offered—it would take an exorbitant amount of time to pay him back.

The next day, I woke up bright and early and met with the contractor on the project, who put me to work instantly. This was going to be my first lesson in what it truly meant to work hard. The day laborers I worked with were amazing human beings. I had never seen anything like them before and have never seen anything like them since. The head laborer, a foreman, was a lovely older man from El Salvador who wore a little suit with a hat. He didn't speak a word of English but smiled all the time. He was also the strongest human being I have ever met in my life. The first task he gave me was to dig up a massive boulder and carry it up a huge hill to be removed from the property. I was able to dig the boulder up, but it was way too huge to be moved by one person—or so I thought. I couldn't get the rock to budge, even with all my bodyweight. The foreman just stood there, watching me with a grin on his face. When he could tell there was no way I was going to be able to move it, he just walked over, put a rope over it, turned around, and used leverage to lift it onto his back. He gave me a nod and walked up the hill. It was one of the most impressive acts of sheer power I have ever witnessed. What shocked me most was he was a little guy. He didn't look like he had any muscle at all, and he must have been in his late fifties. I was so impressed, but I don't think I can convey how truly amazing what he did was. It looked like one of those army ants in Brazil carrying a load way too big for their body but handling it effortlessly.

That day, I was given a list of things I needed to do, including digging a huge hole through some rock to create space for a swimming pool. This needed to be done by hand because it was on the side of a hill where they couldn't get earth-moving equipment. Also on the list were helping to dig twenty, five-foot-deep holes around the perimeter of the pool to place beams for a wall support; clearing brush from the entire hillside, which took up about a quarter acre; jackhammering concrete that had been poured in the wrong area; helping cut tiles for the new marble floors to be installed later that week; and the list went on and on. You might say Barry was trying to teach me a lesson, but I didn't care; anything was better than being stuck in that office.

I worked as a day laborer for almost a year to pay Barry back, and I feel it was a thousand times better than working in his office for even half a day. I loved the people from south of the border I got to work with. They came from places like Mexico, El Salvador, Guatemala, and more. They were honest, hard-working people, constantly smiling, constantly telling jokes. I rarely understood the jokes because I didn't speak Spanish, but I had a feeling the jokes were about me most of the time. My short time in Barry's office didn't give me the same feeling of satisfaction. Going to the office was like walking into a funeral home. Everyone seemed gray and cold, as opposed to the day laborers who were vibrant and lively. With such a polar opposite comparison, I felt I had made the right choice.

About two weeks before I finally finished paying Barry back for my instructor rating course, Barry and I had a falling out. My workday had ended, and I was making myself some dinner. I hadn't eaten all day and I was starving. Barry walked into the kitchen and informed me there was a mess outside and wanted me to go clean it up. Now, remember, we were living in a construction site, so there were messes everywhere. There would continue to be messes everywhere until the building was complete. It was 6:00 in the evening and I was tired. I tried to explain, "Barry, I will get to it in the morning when I start work again, but my food is ready and I need to eat."

He exploded, grabbing the food I had just prepared and throwing it in the trash. He then reached for a broom and hit me with it. Now, it's important to remember I was just under nineteen years old and extremely mentally fragile at this point in my life. I was still suffering from severe suicidal tendencies, and this scenario escalated very quickly. It was the spark that set off a chain reaction that was going to end badly. I looked at him with a rage so extreme that he could tell he had crossed a line. He had pushed me over an edge that was taking us somewhere new, and something destructive was about to occur. I looked him right in the eye and said, "I am going to show you pain like you have never felt before," and I walked out of the house.

He must have realized just how serious this was going to be, because he ran after me as fast as he could. He put his arms around me and said, "Jeb, come back inside. We need to talk right now." I had been triggered and was not in any position to talk at that moment. I was about to do something bad and all I could see was red. Thinking quickly, Barry pleaded with me, "Jeb, I want to help you become a BASE jumper."

That was probably the only thing he could have said at that exact moment to bring me back from oblivion. I glared at him and growled, "What do you mean by that?"

He went on, "Come inside and let's talk with your mother about this. We will figure something out." This managed to calm me down and defused the situation. As my red haze lifted, I walked with him upstairs to their bedroom and sat down across from him and my mother. Barry started with, "Jeb, I want you to go to college. I need someone to do graphic art for my company, and I know you love taking pictures. I will make you a deal. If you go to college, carry a full load of credits, and study graphic art, I will buy you a BASE rig after two years. I will also hire you once you've learned enough about graphic art so you can start earning money to train more."

I asked him, "How am I supposed to get to a college without a car or driver's license?"

"You will need to get your driver's license ASAP," he said, "and I will buy myself a truck that you can use to get to school. As long as you carry a full load of classes and get a GPA of three point five or higher, you won't need to work while going to school." That is how Barry saved my life that night. I think Barry could tell I was going to kill myself right then and there, and somehow, he came up with exactly the right words to prevent it.

After that encounter, Barry and Mom could see that I was suffering from something they didn't understand, so they took me to a psychologist to see if talking to someone might help. I remember walking into an office and sitting on a little couch while I waited for the mental health specialist to come in the room. We sat across from each other and talked about my life, thoughts, and feelings for around an hour. Towards the end of our session, she informed me that I most likely had a condition called "counterphobia," along with a series of other issues that would take time to grasp the full scope of. When she told me what counterphobia was, I laughed out loud. It sounded like a completely made-up condition that described everything I had just been telling her for the last sixty minutes—kind of like telling a doctor your elbow hurts and them responding with, "You have elbow-itis." She told me I was pathologically compelled to confront fear and that this condition was rare because most living things that had it wouldn't survive in nature. Fear was built into our DNA through generations of evolution to make us shy away from dangerous things. It was a self-preservation mechanism, but people with counterphobia just didn't respond to fear the same way. This usually meant that counterphobes inadvertently died from things that would otherwise be avoided.

I found this all interesting, but not helpful. She hadn't told me anything I didn't already know, and it seemed she was just mirroring everything I was saying without any real insight. Her input wasn't helpful in dealing with my excessive rage and the underlying deep-seated pain that was burning me alive from within. I realized she wasn't going to be able to help me and that our little meet-and-greet would be the last time I talked to someone about what I was feeling.

CHAPTER SIX

A LEPRECHAUN'S HAT

My first step in getting ready to head to college was getting my driver's license. I had zero training and had only driven once or twice with my grandpa when I was a child, but Barry was convinced that driving was easy and just sent me to take the test. I asked, "Shouldn't I practice a little?"

He shrugged, "No need. If you fail the test, you can just take it again. It's the easiest test on Earth; any dumbass can get a driver's license." I wasn't sure if he was implying I was a dumbass, but he clearly felt getting a license wouldn't be a problem for me. Barry had the general contractor who was building our house give me a ride to the DMV while Barry continued working. When we got there, I went in and took the written exam and passed...barely. I then got behind the wheel of the car, and the driving portion of the exam began. They had me drive around the block, then do a three-point turn, and that was it.

I looked at the examiner and said, "Is that really all there is?"

The guy nodded and said, "Yup, that's all."

"Okay...so did I pass?"

He looked at me sideways. "Yes, but just barely." He told me to practice more and waved his hand as he said, "Have a lovely day." To be perfectly honest, there was zero reason I should have passed that test. The fact that I was given a driver's license without knowing how to drive a car is terrifying and shows just how broken the system is. I was a danger to myself and everyone else on the road.

When I got home, Barry asked if I had passed, and I winced. "Yes, but I really shouldn't have."

He didn't seem to care and said, "Good, I need you to drive to Melrose and pick up some tiles for me."

In shock, I said, "Barry, you don't understand—I just barely passed. I think I should practice driving a bit more before doing something like transporting tiles."

He explained, "This is the perfect way for you to practice; now go get the tiles." He then threw me the keys to his Jaguar.

"Are you insane?" I asked. He just smiled and gave me the address.

I almost crashed three times and probably broke about ten major laws during that drive to get the tiles. GPS didn't exist at the time, and I had to use something called the Thomas Guide, which was a massive book of complicated maps that made navigating by yourself in a car hazardous to the safety of everyone around you. It was an evil book that I hated with a passion. By the time I got home, I felt like I had been to war and was suffering from a mild case of PTSD. Barry asked, "Did you get the tiles?" I handed him a large, heavy box filled with tiles. Barry dumped the box on his desk and then questioned, "Did you damage the car?"

I said, "No, but I almost got in three car accidents on the way."

He smiled and said, "Well, almost getting in an accident isn't the same as getting in one, so good job." Then he walked away.

With my license in hand, my next step was to find a school within driving distance. I didn't need anything more than a junior college with a good graphics art program because I didn't need to get or care about getting an actual degree in anything. If they had a good photography department, that would be a bonus, too.

For the first time in my life, I had a small group of friends that I had built while attending Colin McEwen. Loki, Shawn, and I became good friends during my six-month high school experience. Through my friendship with Shawn, I met KC and a boy named Chris.

Chris became a pivotal person in my life during my college years. He was a hardcore born-again Christian and my first real exposure to that belief system. He had lost his parents when he was a child and was living with his adoptive parents in a house around the block from where I lived on White Sands. Chris's adoptive parents were super religious, and that pretty much meant Chris was, too. His house had emus in the front yard that worked as effective guard dogs. They were huge, mean birds that attacked anyone who came near. Those birds frightened me, so I tried my best to avoid them. Chris was one of those people you meet who can only be described as big. As the saying goes: he wasn't fat, just big-boned. Some people get big from eating too much, but that wasn't the case for Chris. The dude just had massive hands and feet and everything else to match. He was one of the nicest people ever, and super smart. He was the kind of person who could teach himself computer programming by reading C++ textbooks. That is what Chris ended up becoming: a self-taught computer programmer working at places like Net Zero doing things I was never able to understand.

One day, I was talking with Chris, explaining how I needed to enroll in a college ASAP. I would have to carry a full load of credits while focusing on graphic art and photography. He informed me there was an amazing junior college called Moorpark. It had a great graphic arts and photography program, and if I wanted, he would take me to see if I liked it. He was interested in seeing it and maybe taking a few classes, too.

When we got to the campus, we just walked around, looking at the grounds and getting a sense of what the school was like. As we walked from the food court to the graphic arts department, we saw a student walking a giant tiger. I later learned Moorpark was also known for its amazing Exotic Animal Training and Management program, but seeing that tiger made a big impression on me. After spending a day touring the grounds and talking to other students, I decided this would be the perfect place to go to school. It was a long drive from Malibu, but I could put all my classes on two full days so I would only have to drive there twice a week. A few days later, Chris and I signed up. Over the years, we ended up taking many of the same classes and developed a strong friendship.

One day, Chris invited me to something called "youth group." I had never heard of it before, and if someone had asked me what religion I was, my answer would have been "Nothing." I didn't believe or disbelieve in anything. I think my parents felt religion could be a form of brainwashing if introduced to children at too young an age. They wanted me to be a free thinker and question everything, preferring to just expose me to everything and let me learn for myself. Their approach was to tell me, "This is what some people believe," and not, "This is something you have to accept." I think it made all the difference.

After my experiences in Nepal with the monks and going to Catholic school in first grade, I realized there was a lot of contradicting information out there regarding "truth." I viewed most religions as interesting stories, like reading a Dr. Seuss book. I saw them as fictitious tales that sometimes had a moral or catchy tidbit of information. So, when Chris asked me about going to youth group, I was open to it. I didn't feel strongly about it one way or another; it seemed like a place to meet new people my own age, and maybe some girls. This was my chance to try working on being less antisocial. I knew if I was ever going to function on this planet, I would have to be able to interact with other human beings eventually.

So, the next Saturday that came along, Chris took me to a church with a group of about thirty people, all around our age. They were drinking punch and just hanging out. At first, it didn't seem like a religious thing; it was more like a party for children. I think the average age was around sixteen, and at this point, I had just turned nineteen, so I was on the older edge of the group. There was a person they called a pastor, who I gathered was some kind of leader or chaperone, which only increased the kids' party vibe. The conversation was light and mindless until Chris introduced me to a friend of his named Michelle. Michelle was a redhead, and for some reason, I was quite taken by her. She was bubbly and friendly, and this was my first time talking to a girl my own age since grade school. The first question she asked me was, "Do you know my friend, Jesus Christ, and have you accepted him into your heart as your personal Lord and Savior?"

I burst out laughing because I thought she had to be joking, but she was straight-faced and confused about why I was laughing at her. After getting a hold of myself, I responded, "I have heard of Jesus, but don't really know much about him other than he was a mythical person who walked on water, turned that same water to wine, and brought people back from the dead."

She looked at me again, this time with a concerned face and said, "You do realize if you don't accept Jesus, you are going to burn in Hell, right?"

Again, I couldn't help laughing. What she had just said was the equivalent of someone telling me I was going to burn on planet Zeltron. But I was intrigued and fascinated that someone could believe such strange stories and then insist that other people had to believe the same things or they'd be punished forever when they died. I decided I wanted to learn more; plus, despite being condemned by her for my choices, I was attracted to Michelle and wanted to learn more about her.

Being isolated for most of my life without many human interactions had both good and bad aspects to it. The good thing was that I had developed a strong personality in the absence of any kind of peer pressure. At this point, it was close to impossible for people to influence my decisions. In high school, a kid offered me some pills and I said, "No, thank you."

He pushed by saying, "What, are you scared?"

I responded with, "I only need to say no once. Now get the fuck away from me." I didn't give a shit if he liked me or not. Actually, it seemed the more pressure someone applied, the more likely I was to go the opposite way.

The bad thing was that I hadn't learned how to properly socialize with people, which made me socially awkward and combative. I have noticed that when people can't influence your behavior, they tend to avoid you. In other words, my demeanor and obstinance made me a difficult person to be around.

But it seemed like Michelle was interested in being around me even though I was an awkward and super weird non-believer. It was like we were grade school children. She told Chris she liked me, so he told me and asked if I was interested in her. I told him I thought she was cute, so he played matchmaker and set up a date for us. It's funny thinking about how silly the whole exchange was, but I was much younger mentally than my nineteen years would have implied.

Michelle and I avoided the topic of religion and tried to just get to know each other instead. Her friend Gina and my buddy Chris came along because Michelle's parents did not want her going out with a boy by herself—they were strict Promise Keeper Christians, and she was only seventeen, so going out with me was questionable in their eyes at best. We talked about her love for little fuzzy animals and my growing passion for BASE jumping and shark diving. Those were the topics that dominated everything in my life at that point, and they still do to this day. The group date went well, and within a few weeks, I was in my first relationship.

One day, I finally got to meet her parents, and they sat me down to explain a few things. They were not happy with the fact that I wasn't Christian. They felt it was a serious problem and called our relationship "unevenly yoked." I'm still not exactly sure what they meant by that phrase, but I said, "Okay..." They informed me they would only permit me to date their daughter if I would read the Bible and attend youth group so I could learn about their Lord, Jesus Christ. I nodded and said, "No problem," without really understanding what I'd just signed myself up for. I didn't drink, smoke, or use drugs of any kind. I hadn't even kissed a girl, so in many ways, I was more Christian than any of them, at least by my actions if not my beliefs. Christians have often told me how a person couldn't be moral without accepting Christ, but I always found that to be an odd statement. Morality isn't owned by anyone, or exclusive to one belief system. I made the choices I made without fearing punishment after death, and I didn't have to be told by some book what the difference between right and wrong was. My mother had just raised me properly. But at that moment, I didn't care to debate any of my own philosophies with them. I was just interested in Michelle, so much so that I would read the Bible, if that was a requirement.

But it turns out the Bible is not an easy book to read. It's not what I would call a real page-turner. The King James version was dry and boring to me, and many of the stories were incredibly disjointed, to put it mildly. But I trucked along. Every few months, they would ask me if I had finished it. I would say, "You know how complicated this book is. This is going to take some time." Her parents couldn't wait for me to finish so they could sit me down and have a conversation about it. I was able to put off that conversation for about two years.

In the meantime, my relationship with Michelle flourished. She ended up becoming my first kiss and my first love, or at least what I thought was love at the time. Looking back, it's kind of hard for me to use that word because I was too young to know the meaning. Not just by age, but by mental state; I wasn't mature enough to understand how love works. If I am being honest, I wouldn't call her my first love, but she was my first everything else.

Despite trying to avoid the topic of religion with me, Michelle said something one day that shook our relationship to its core. While I drove us to a restaurant for lunch, she suddenly made a passing comment that evolution wasn't real. I felt like I had just heard someone say the Earth was flat and science wasn't real. I couldn't believe my ears. It was the first time I had heard anyone not just question the validity of evolution, but deny it outright. To me, that's as close to fact as facts can get. It didn't seem like there was even the slightest room for debate on the subject. I instantly pulled the car over and said, "What did you just say?"

"I said evolution's not real," she explained, gauging my reaction. "The Bible teaches that the world is only six thousand years old, and evolution is a lie that Satan spreads to confuse people."

I was so shocked by her statement that I couldn't respond. She could tell I was not taking this information well, and we almost broke up right then and there. It was the first time I truly understood how different our minds were, but I didn't want to lose her over a disagreement. I think I was just silent through lunch until we finally started talking about something else, returning to our default mode of avoiding any discussion about religion to keep the peace.

When I finally finished reading the Bible, I knew her parents wouldn't be happy with what I had to say. During this period, I was taking a class at Moorpark called Logic 7. This was a philosophy class that dealt with truth tables, Venn diagrams, and fallacies of relevance. It focused on logical reasoning and how to properly argue. This may have been the single most important class I ever took, because it armed me with the ability to focus conversations and not let people sidetrack. It made me even more difficult to argue with, but it also taught me how to yield when the other side's logic and reason outweighed my own. The class was not about winning arguments; it was about finding truth through logic and proper reasoning.

When our uncomfortable conversation could no longer be avoided, Michelle's parents sat me in their living room with Michelle close by and asked, "So, what have you learned about our Lord, Jesus Christ."

I tried to open with a warning that they didn't want to have this conversation with me. I told them, "I don't think you're going to like what I have to say."

"No, we want to know what you think."

I took a deep breath and said, "Okay, you better brace yourself. I feel the book has some good stories in it, and some of those stories have good lessons. I also find many of the stories troubling and feel all the different books that were compiled into this Bible were trying to manipulate other human beings through the written word. But beyond the Bible, I feel religion in general came into existence for two major reasons. First, it seems to have been one of the first systems of law dating back long before Jesus was written about. It appears most religions grew from trying to control people during a time when they just didn't have the infrastructure to keep most people from doing bad things. In ancient times, they didn't have effective governments, police, or prisons. They tried to convince people that, after they died, they would either be punished if they were bad or rewarded if they were good. This was a good approach because no one could prove or disprove this ideology. It was an effective way of dealing with human psychology thousands of years ago because knowledge was limited, and convincing people of nonsense wasn't hard.

"Second, I feel religion came into existence to try and explain things people didn't understand. When there is a gap in knowledge, people tend to make up stories to help fill in the blanks. Most people would much rather have stories that give answers than have nothing at all. For most, it doesn't seem to matter if those answers are based in reality or fantasy. If they have answers and think they understand how something works, that is usually enough to feel like they have some kind of control. However, I think humanity has developed senses over tens of thousands of generations that allow us to see the reality that exists outside ourselves without having to make up bullshit. These senses have their limitations, though, and we are only capable of previewing a small spectrum of this reality. If you were to take your thumb and index finger and spread them about one centimeter apart, that space between your fingers would represent what our senses can experience from the natural world. Now, if you spread your fingers as wide as possible, that space between them would represent all the technology and science we have developed since the dawn of humanity to expand our senses (like the Hubble telescope or x-ray machines, for instance). Now, with your fingers still spread as wide as possible, if you go an infinite distance in either direction from the outside of that space, that represents what we don't know or can't experience. It exists but is outside our understanding. This is the great majority of everything in what we call the universe. Human beings do not like lacking knowledge or understanding of things. Religion simply throws out guesses at what's in this vast, dark unknown area beyond our ability to perceive. The problem with this is: when you start guessing at the unknown, everything is just as valid or likely as everything else. When you leave science and reason behind and operate on belief and faith, Thor becomes just as likely as Jesus. Buddha becomes just as likely as Muhammad. Leprechauns become just as likely as angels. I can believe all I want that a unicorn took a crap in a leprechauns hat and that created the universe, but that doesn't make it true or give it any validity. To me, belief is meaningless."

As you can imagine, Michelle's parents were not receptive to this line of reasoning and instead said, "That is an interesting view, but we feel what you're saying has little to do with the Word of God contained in the Bible." The conversation then continued for hours back and forth, but I will boil it down to the final points to spare you having to read a book longer than the Bible itself.

At some point, the conversation shifted to the concept of morality, and her parents expressed that to be moral, one must accept Jesus as their Lord and Savior. They had said this to me on many occasions before, but this time I looked at them with a sideways glance and said, "Really? That seems logical to you?" I asked them, "Have you heard of Jeffrey Dahmer?"

They said, "Yes, we know who he is and what he has done. He's a monster."

I said, "You do know that he became a born-again Christian while in prison, right?"

"Yes, we've heard that before."

I then asked, "If Dahmer did accept Jesus as his Lord and Savior, where did he go when he died?"

They said, "If he truly accepted Jesus as his Lord, then he went to Heaven."

I didn't expect them to fall into the trap so easily, but I responded, "That is interesting." I then asked, "Do you know who Gandhi is?"

They responded, "Yes."

I said, "He was Hindu, and therefore did not accept Jesus as his Lord and Savior. Where did he go?"

"He went to hell."

I shook my head and asked, "What kind of morality does that teach? This would mean you can rape and eat little boys every day, and, according to your belief system, if you accept Jesus, you go to heaven. Or you could be like Gandhi, dedicating your entire life to helping others, and still burn in hell for all eternity. You really feel this somehow qualifies as morality? Be honest with yourselves; what morality does that teach?" This was the first crack I saw in their resolve, and I could tell it shook them.

I was using the Socratic method during this conversation, and on my next line of reasoning, I tried to get at the core of their beliefs. I asked them a series of simple questions. First, I asked, "Do you believe God is all-powerful, creating everything in the universe without exception?"

They answered, "Yes."

I asked, "Is God all-knowing, as in he knows everything without exception?"

They answered, "Yes."

I then asked, "Is God evil?"

This question was hard for them to answer. They realized the trap they were in. If God created everything and knew everything, then he had to be just as evil as he was good. But this logic contradicts the teachings of the Bible, which they believed had no contradictions of any kind. This caused a short circuit in their ability to argue any further, and they went to a fallback position of, "You don't have faith, Jeb. If you did, this would all make sense to you."

I then asked, "If I wrote a book and told you it was inspired by God, and you had faith in that, who would your faith be in...God or me, the person who wrote the book? If your faith was based on something inside yourself, I could maybe give you that, but your beliefs come from the Bible, which you know was written by human beings. Your faith is entirely based on that book. That would mean you do not have faith in God; you have faith in what human beings wrote down in a book about God."

Michelle's parents had reached a crisis of faith. I could see widening fissures inside them and their eyes filled with tears. They said, "Jeb, we now understand exactly why you think the way you do, and you have shaken the very foundation of our lives. We don't ever want to talk to you about this subject again."

To be fair, I had warned them.

They didn't ban me from dating her, but that was the end of talking about religion with Michelle's parents. We dated for almost four years. There was something special about her that made me smile, and I respected her regardless of our disagreements about religious beliefs. She loved animals in a way I have never seen in anyone else. If there was a small kitten or puppy—really any cute, fuzzy creature—she would lose her shit, shaking from head to toe as she got down on the ground to start playing with them, no matter what she was wearing or what she was doing. I remember watching in awe every time this happened. I would think, *Wow, how amazing is that? I wish small animals had that kind of effect on me. For me to even get close to what she's experiencing, I'd have to travel halfway around the world, climb some super dangerous mountain, jump off it, almost die, and even then, I wouldn't get as excited as she is right now.* I envied her ability to be excited about ordinary things. For some reason, I couldn't do the same; I was just wired differently.

Michelle and I were opposites. Her favorite color was pink; mine was black. I loved sharks; she loved kittens. I became a militant atheist; she was a born-again Christian. We were always doomed to failure in the long run. I learned later in life that relationships do require similarities in order to last. Opposites attract but seldom work out. I was never going to be content with a person who didn't do the kinds of things I did. I needed someone I could share my passions with. I guess that's what her parents meant by "unevenly yoked."

Before meeting Michelle and spending time with her family and friends, I would never have called myself an atheist; I would have just said I was neutral on the subject, no opinion one way or the other. But after seeing the born-again Christian community Michelle was surrounded by, I changed. I just couldn't believe what they were saying. The way they lived their lives seemed to be in total contradiction to what they claimed to believe. It defied all logic. They seemed like children with an imaginary friend who they believed created the entire universe for their benefit. It seemed like such arrogance to believe that a god created the vastness of space all for them, and if they believed in him, they got to hang out with him for all eternity when they died. To me, it was a laughable concept and still is. Seeing how I didn't have even a basic belief in a god of any kind, the mental stretch it would have taken for me to accept the next step of believing—that this God sent himself to Earth as his own son to die on a cross and absolve the human race from some made-up set of sins—felt insane. It seemed remarkable to me how indistinguishable their religion was from serious mental illness.

After this whole experience, I decided that I didn't believe what these people were saying, period. After reading their book, I saw it as poorly written fiction that had little basis in reality. This is how I became an atheist. Ricky Gervais said something that fits here perfectly. I'm paraphrasing, but the gist is this: "There are roughly 4,200 religions in the world today. Atheism means you do not believe in religion or the gods they represent. Well, people usually only believe in one of those 4,200 religions. That means they are atheists when it comes to disbelieving 4,199 different religions. I just don't believe in one more than they do."

While in college, I took classes that revolved around subjects I was interested in learning. I had to take all the graphic arts classes because of my deal with Barry, but seeing as I also had to carry a full load of courses, I decided to take as many photography, psychology, philosophy, and math classes as I could fit in each semester. I loved philosophy the most. I loved the way it forced me to think, and I could feel my mind growing the more I studied it. I also took creative writing classes, but until the very moment I started this book, writing was never something I could see myself doing. My course schedule revolved around taking the opportunity to learn as much as I could while I had the time.

There was one college professor in particular who had a profound impact on my life. His name was Mr. Grey, and to call him a character would be an understatement. He was head of both the graphic arts and photography departments, and I took every single class he taught. He had a bumper sticker over his desk that read, "Comfort is Your Enemy." He was vocal about being a socialist and convinced me to read Karl Marx and Thomas More. It was illuminating to read about their concepts of utopia and social equality. I'm not sure how practical the ideas are, given the nature of mankind, but that isn't what's important. It's nice to just read thoughts and ideas of other human beings from other times who see things differently. One piece of advice I picked up thanks to Mr. Grey is: understand that you don't have to agree with something to learn from it.

About halfway through my first year of college, Barry decided he wanted to take the family on a trip to Costa Rica. I had lots of schoolwork, but I loved diving in Costa Rica and thought filming some sharks could fill a requirement for a photography class I was taking. With that in mind, I agreed to go. About a week before we were supposed to leave, Barry decided he didn't want to go to Costa Rica anymore and changed the trip to Hawaii. I loved Hawaii, too, but the diving there wasn't as good, and my chances of getting shark images were small. I decided I would rather stay home and work on my assignments, but this made Barry furious. He felt I was being a stuck-up little prick, and if I didn't feel Hawaii was good enough, that meant I had lost touch with reality and needed to get a job right away. You could say I was growing accustomed to Barry's overreactions by this point, or at least wasn't surprised by them anymore. He informed me that if I didn't have a job and wasn't working at least twenty-five hours a week by the time he got back from Hawaii, I would need to find a new place to live. One of Barry's character traits was that he loved changing deals after they had been made. He never put things in writing because he always wanted the option of changing his mind. He would then try to do a Jedi mind trick on people, pretending the deal wasn't what they thought it had been (otherwise known as gaslighting). It was annoying, but in my case, the deal we had made was a fair one and meant to save my life, so I decided there was no fight to be had. I would just go find a job, hopefully one that would let me do homework while I worked.

After the family left for Hawaii, I dropped by the lunch area on campus and saw a sign at the Taco Bell (yep, there was a Taco Bell in our school) that read, "If you can breathe, we will hire you." I thought, *Maybe this will be an easy job I can do between classes.* I walked over and asked them, "What do I need to do to apply for a job?"

They said, "You're hired. See you tomorrow at nine a.m."

I wasn't sure I really wanted the job, but at least it would stop me from getting kicked out of my house. On the way home from my creative writing class, as I was getting off the 101 onto Kanan, I saw a movie theater called the MANN 8 in Agoura Hills and wondered if they were hiring any projectionists. That seemed like it would be a good college job: just watching movies all day. I thought that in between setting up films, I might have time to get schoolwork done, so I pulled over and parked. After taking a moment to get mentally prepared for interaction, I walked in and saw a "Help Wanted" sign on the door, which I took as good news. I asked to talk to the manager and, within a few moments, I was sitting in his office.

"How do I apply to work as a projectionist?" I asked.

He smiled and said, "We already have all the projectionists we need."

"Oh. Well, okay."

"In order to handle projection," he explained, "employees have to work their way up, and we have quite a few waiting in line for the next opening. But we do have floor staff positions open that pay minimum wage."

Minimum wage was $3.75 an hour back in 1995 (yeah, I know, just think about *that* for a minute). I just needed a job, and the theater was a shorter drive than Taco Bell, so I agreed to take it. I filled out a bunch of paperwork and was given a dress shirt, a red vest, and a little black bowtie. The manager told me the cost of the uniform would be taken out of my first paycheck. I didn't like the uniform and thought having to pay for it was bullshit, but I needed a job to stay in my house, so I was going to do what I needed to do.

When Barry got home from Hawaii, he asked me if I had gotten a job, so I explained I was working at a movie theater. For some reason, he seemed really pleased by this. I was still suffering from extreme social anxiety, so getting a job was a big deal for me. It was still difficult for me to talk to strangers, and having a boss telling me what to do was a new level of stress. In the long run, though, I actually have to thank Barry for forcing me to get a job. It helped me grow as a person and it broke down some of the walls I had surrounded myself with. My duties provided the perfect amount of contact and interaction with strangers to help me deal with other humans. My social antenna was awful in the beginning, and I was awkward, but people seemed to realize I had issues and would help me out when I needed it.

I was nineteen-going-on-twenty, which made me one of the older employees working the floor. My job included cleaning theaters, bathrooms, and anything else the managers told me to. This was the entry-level job at the theater, and it seemed to attract a lot of younger high school kids. Because of my age, I was given one of the worst jobs they had to offer: closing the theater with the managers. You had to be at least eighteen to be a closer because you had to stay until after all the movies were finished, and they ran fairly late. One of the things that made this particular job suck donkey nuts was having to clean what they lovingly referred to as "Circle

K." This was the concessions stand, and at its center was the popcorn machine—a greasy, disgusting mess of butter and grossness. After I got done cleaning Circle K, a manager would come around with white gloves—yes, like some ridiculous cartoon—and make sure it was spotless. If it wasn't, I had to clean it again. Some nights I was there until 2:00 a.m. cleaning that evil thing.

I worked my way through all the different positions until I finally got to the box—that's where the tickets were sold. It took me about eight months of working twenty-five hours a week to reach that point, all while still having a full load of classes in college. I didn't mind the job in the box; it was relatively braindead work, and the days seemed to move along quickly. There were no seats allowed, though. For some odd reason I never understood, they wanted people to stand on their feet all day. I was okay with it, however, because I preferred that to sitting all day. I'm telling you all this because something happened here that became a crossroads moment in my life.

It was the end of a long eight-hour shift and I was tired. All the other registers were closed, and the head manager of the theater was counting out a register next to me. I was the only window still open selling tickets, and the line was starting to get long when a rude human being walked up and said, "Give me two tickets."

I said in the politest way I could, "What movie would you like to see, sir?"

Our theater had eight different movies playing at the time. He looked at me like I was the single stupidest human being on the planet for not magically reading his mind and just knowing what movie he wanted to see.

He scoffed and said, "Obviously *Heat.*"

This flicked a switch and I suddenly felt anger building inside me. He then proceeded to drop a bag of pennies, nickels, and dimes in front of me. I looked at the manager because we were not supposed to take anything smaller than a quarter, but the manager shrugged and said, "Just count it, Jeb."

So, I took a deep breath and began counting. As I was halfway through counting this guy's pennies, he said, "Why are you counting so slow?"

Instantly, a dark force welled up inside me and unleashed. The rage was so extreme that even now, over twenty-five years later, I still get angry just thinking about it. I looked up slowly and, with a fire in my eyes that left zero doubt about my intentions, I roared, "IF YOU SAY ONE MORE WORD, I AM GOING TO FUCKING KILL YOU!" He froze, and the smirk on his face disappeared. He looked like he knew for an absolute fact that if anything came out of his mouth at that moment, he was going to die. The manager retreated against the wall, then slowly backed his way to the door and left as quietly as he could.

This was a pivotal moment in my life. I know that if this man had said one more word, I would have taken off my little red vest, placed it on the cash register, then gone outside and beaten this person to death with my bare hands. I would have chased him to the edge of the world and thrown him off it. The only thing that would have stopped me would have been him killing me. One way or another, one of us would have had to die. The level of rage inside me burned with the power of a thousand suns. I was ready to unleash all the rage I had built up from childhood, and it was nearly impossible to contain.

Luckily for both of us, this man took what I said seriously and just picked up his tickets and walked away without saying another word. In the box, fuming as my anger slowly dissipated, I waited to be told I was fired.

My friend Chris, who had also gotten a job at the theater, was working in Circle K when this man walked up and bought some popcorn and candy. Afterward, Chris asked me what I had said to the guy. I honestly didn't know who he meant and asked, "What guy?"

Chris said, "Jeb, a man came in shaking after buying a ticket from you. He looked like he had seen a ghost. As I was selling him popcorn, he looked at me and said, 'That guy over there selling tickets, he really doesn't have a sense of humor.'"

I smiled and said, "I told him I was going to kill him if he said another word. And if he had said another word, he would be dead."

No one fired me that night, but the next day, the manager called me into his office. I walked in absolutely certain I was getting fired. He asked me to sit down and said, "Jeb, I don't think you should deal with customers anymore."

I said, "No kidding."

The manager suddenly smiled and said, "I'm going to promote you to projection so we can keep you away from people. I'm giving you a raise and I want you to report to Paul, the head of projection, immediately to begin your training."

I couldn't believe it and blurted out, "Okay, thank you!"

To this day, I have no idea what they were thinking with that promotion, but I'm grateful I didn't get booted out the door.

Projection turned out to be a dream job for a college student. Most of my day was spent working on school assignments. Every now and then, I would be called to check the temperature or make sure a movie was in focus, but most of the job was automated. You just took film that was laid out on a big plate and threaded that through the projector, then set a timer. Easy.

We had eight theaters that required prep and cleanup. Otherwise, the job provided lots of downtime, and I took full advantage of that time to study. I also liked the solitude of the job. After my outburst at the ticket counter, it was clear that not having to deal with people was a good thing for me at this stage of life. This was the perfect environment for someone with my special brain chemistry, and it helped me work on my antisocial tendencies at a more reasonable pace than my other positions. I had bosses and people I had to interact with, but it was easy and low impact. Everyone seemed to understand my issues and gave me plenty of space, which allowed me to work around people in a comfortable way. Plus, I loved watching movies, and it gave me the opportunity to watch every single movie that came out. I loved that job, and I would probably still be doing it to this day if it had paid better.

CHAPTER SEVEN

THE ROAD TO BASE

Skydiving was an expensive sport, and I wasn't earning enough money to do it properly. My projectionist job only paid $4.75 an hour, so I got a second job, hoping it would help. I began teaching scuba diving on weekends, using what I had learned in Florida for a change. Unfortunately, teaching scuba diving didn't pay any better than the movie theater. My schedule also made it difficult for me to be available for teaching classes; carrying a full load of units at school took up a lot of time. Weeks just didn't have enough hours in them to go to school full-time and make enough money with low-paying jobs to afford skydiving.

This serious lack of money made it difficult for me to advance my training. I tried to not spend money on anything else. I lived in my parents' guest house to save money on rent. I ate French bread pizzas, ramen noodles, and Hot Pockets. The years I worked the movie theater job and taught scuba, I saved every paycheck I could, 100 percent focused on saving everything for jumping. When I had enough money saved, I would go do a skydive, then save up again until I had enough for another jump. This went on for years, one jump at a time, in a painfully slow process.

Around my twentieth birthday, I finally completed enough graphic arts and photography classes to be able to work for Barry's company. In the beginning, he hired other freelance graphic artists to teach me how to create pamphlets and brochures for large corporate insurance packages. College had given me a strong understanding of the programs I needed to use, and the hired artists helped me with the real-world application.

This job finally unlocked the resources I needed to take my jumping to the next level. I also started jumping at a much larger skydiving drop zone called Skydive Perris. At last, I could focus on real training for BASE jumping. When I showed up in Perris, I only had twenty-two skydives, done over a three-year period. Once I got my own skydiving rig and started jumping at Perris, I did that same number of jumps in a weekend.

The graphic arts job Barry gave me didn't just pay me more money; it also gave me lots of free time. That was an amazing combination. Most people who earn a lot of money don't have time off, and those who have time off rarely make enough money. So, to have both was truly fortunate. My work became project-based, meaning I would do a project, get overpaid, and then have time off so I could use that money to train.

During one of my training weekends at Perris, I overheard someone talking about BASE jumping. They mentioned wanting to take a course from a company called Basic Research. I stopped what I was doing, walked up to the person, and asked, "What is Basic Research?" They explained how it was the first company to build commercially available, BASE-specific canopies and containers. The company was owned by Todd Shoebotham and Anne Helliwell. Before I could say anything else, the man pointed over my shoulder and said, "If you have any more questions, just ask Anne. She's standing right over there." I turned around and couldn't believe it. I was so excited that I didn't know what to do with myself. This was something that had been burning a hole in my mind for almost five years. It was all I could think about, and up to this point, I had zero idea how I was going to get someone to mentor me. Now, standing ten feet away, was someone I could just hire to teach me. I wouldn't have to find a BASE jumper and somehow magically convince them I was worthy.

I walked right up to Anne and said, "Hello, my name is Jeb, and I want to take your BASE-jumping course."

She smiled and replied, "No problem. We have a class going next week that still has a few spaces open. But I have to ask you a few questions first."

I beamed with energy. "What do you need to know?"

Her first question was, "How many jumps do you have?"

"Forty-two skydives," I responded, with an ever-expanding smile on my face.

But the grin on her face said, "You're clueless." She informed me in the nicest way possible that it was going to be a while before I would have enough jumps to take the course.

"Our course has a minimum requirement of two hundred skydives to be eligible, but we suggest you do five hundred. The more time you have training in both tracking and canopy control, the better. Your chances of surviving your first hundred BASE jumps will go up dramatically the more skydives you do. BASE jumping is a hazardous activity that kills people when they make mistakes. I suggest you take your time and don't rush."

Now, all I heard was "minimum two hundred jumps," so I said, "I'll have my two hundred jumps done ASAP and then I'll call you. What's your number?" She handed me a business card and smiled again. Looking back now, I understand that her smile meant she understood the kind of person she was dealing with: overzealous and dangerous.

After you've been in BASE long enough, you can see the ones who are just a little too eager; the ones who want everything to happen *right now*. They feel a little bit off and don't seem to care about their own safety in the slightest. You know they're going to jump whether you help them or not, so your only hope is to give them enough knowledge in a short time to keep them alive long enough to calm down naturally. I find myself giving Anne's same smile when I see a new jumper who is obviously insane and impatient, just like I was.

Over the next few months, I jumped as much as I could. On my days off, I would go to the drop zone early in the morning and jump all day. I wasn't there to socialize (big surprise) and tried to avoid people whenever possible. Trying to up my numbers, I would just show up, jump, and leave. I needed two hundred jumps, and I needed them yesterday. I wasn't there to make friends.

Many years later, after I became less socially awkward, I made friends with a free flyer named Eli. He was one of the best to have ever lived and a genuinely nice person. One day, Eli told me his thoughts about this period in my training. He explained how he couldn't understand what I was doing. He would watch me show up at the DZ, talk to no one, and jump by myself repeatedly. He said, "Jeb, we all thought of you as a ghost; you were there and then you would just disappear without ever communicating with anyone." I told him I was completely uninterested in any of the social aspects of the sport at the time. I was on a mission. For me, skydiving was a barrier to my goal, and I just wanted to get through that chore without any distractions.

When I got close to the magic number of two hundred jumps, I called Anne. "Hello, this is Jeb Corliss. We talked a few months ago about your BASE-jumping training course."

"I remember you," she said. "How are things? Have you been practicing your tracking, landing accuracy, and correcting those off-heading openings?"

I explained, "Yes, but I'm running out of money from my last contract. My options are to either spend the remainder on fifty more skydives to get to two hundred or use that money to pay for your course. I've done a hundred and eight jumps in two months, bringing me to one hundred and fifty skydives total. I've been waiting for years, and I can't wait any longer. Please let me join your next course. I don't know when my next contract will come, so I don't know when I will have the money to do your class again."

She paused for a moment, then responded, "I will have to ask my partner, Todd. I understand you've done a lot of jumps in a short time, which is good. It shows you're motivated, current, and have focused over a hundred jumps on training BASE-specific skills, which is helpful. I will call you back after I talk with Todd."

A few hours later, my phone rang and Anne informed me, "Todd said yes, so we will be willing to teach you. You need to be at our shop in Perris on Saturday morning to begin your rigging training and ground course. We will be teaching you about packing, object selection, and BASE ethics." The class, taught by both Anne and Todd, would be private. I think they may have felt I was a bit unstable and needed some special attention, which was pretty understandable.

On that Saturday, I walked into the Basic Research shop early in the morning and met Todd for the first time. Anne introduced us and Todd informed me we had a lot of information to cover and needed to get started. I was bursting at the seams with excitement; I had been dreaming about this for five years—it was my reason for waking up each morning. I wanted it so bad I could taste it. Todd took me to a small room, where he began explaining the different categories of jumps that make up the acronym B.A.S.E., which stands for Building, Antenna, Span, and Earth. These are the four main types of fixed objects jumpers use as platforms for human flight, determined by how the wind interacts with each one. He explained them all in detail and how they fit each classification.

We then spent hours going over technical information about wind, on-heading performance, object selection, landing area selection, alternate landing area selection, pilot chute selection, rigging for both slider-down and slider-up, canopy sizes, and packing techniques. It was a ton of information to absorb in a short time frame. Todd was pouring his twenty-plus years of BASE-jumping experience into my shot glass of a brain, and a lot of it was spilling out. We finally made it to the ethics portion, where he explained the concept of legality in the sport and preserving sites. Well-known BASE-jumping objects existed all over the world, and the goal was to keep them open for jumping. If you broke certain ethical rules, sites tended to get shut down. Laws would get made and security would be tightened. If you jumped a well-known location in an unethical way and it got shut down by the authorities, this was called "burning a site." If you became known for burning sites, you would be ostracized by other jumpers. This was a self-regulating group with punishments ranging from being publicly humiliated to blacklisted, and in extreme cases, tarred and feathered.

To illustrate what being an unethical BASE jumper looks like, I will tell you the story of a man we'll call Bob Doe. Bob's story was told to me secondhand, but I did see footage of Bob being tarred and feathered, so I know it happened. This man was interested in publicity and started jumping for different news programs with the goal of making a name for himself. This in itself wasn't considered unethical at the time, but it was frowned upon. Bob took it a step too far when he found out about a crane on a construction site that a group of local Houston jumpers were frequenting. Bob was not from Houston, so he traveled there from his hometown of New Orleans. But he also decided to bring the media along to film his jump in the middle of the day, which was a huge no-no. The locals had made a deal with the crane operator that, each night, he would lock the crane off so the end hung over a large parking lot the jumpers could use as a landing area. For doing this, the jumpers would leave him a sixpack of beer after each night of jumping. The story goes that Bob jumped the crane in the middle of the day, it went on the news, and the crane operator ended up getting fired. Security increased and the locals could no longer jump the object. This enraged the local Houston jumping crew, and they decided some old-school retribution needed to be handed out. They knew where Bob lived and devised a plan to teach him a lesson.

Sometime later, Bob was relaxing in his living room when he heard a knock on his door. He asked who was there and heard a young woman's voice. Bob wasn't expecting anyone but went to see who it was. He looked out the peephole and saw an attractive woman standing there, waiting for him to open the door. I should point out that Bob sold weed as a side business, so random strangers showing up at his door wasn't out of the ordinary for him. As he opened the door, four large men wearing ski masks rushed past the woman and tackled Bob to the ground. As three of them held him down, the remaining one headed over to Bob's stove and turned it on. He looked through Bob's cupboards for a pot to heat up some black substance they had brought with them. Bob was totally confused at this point and didn't understand what was going on. He kept franticly asking who they were and what he had done to deserve this, but they refused to answer. He started throwing out random things he might have done, trying to figure out why this was happening, but they stayed quiet until he mentioned a woman's name and asked if it was because of something he had done to her. One of the men started laughing and said, "Yup, you shouldn't have fucked with her."

At this point, the black substance turned into bubbling hot tar, and they started putting rolls of plastic down on the floor. Once the plastic was down, they picked

Bob up, took off his shorts and shirt, and laid him out on the plastic. Then they slowly poured hot tar all over Bob's body, causing him to scream in pain. After he was covered in tar, they ripped up a bunch of pillows, dusted him with feathers, and left him writhing in agony. I'm not sure if Bob ever connected his punishment to the crane, but my guess is he was pretty careful about everything after that.

Making sure I understood the ethics in BASE was a big portion of Todd's training; he felt it was that important because the sport draws in big personalities and a rebellious type of person. BASE jumpers are notoriously hard to control, and most will not or cannot follow rules. I'm pretty sure Todd could see I was on the more extreme side of the spectrum. During the class, before I had even done my first jump, I was already talking about jumping the Golden Gate Bridge, and the look on his face was one of deep concern. He decided to reiterate everything he'd taught me to drive the point home, but I had stars in my eyes.

Once we were done with the practical classroom portion of training, we began the packing lessons. Todd took me into the main factory, where they built all the canopies and BASE rigs. It had a massive open floor plan covered with rows of sewing machines, and fabric in all different colors everywhere you looked, set on giant spools that were longer than I was tall. Todd pointed to a large open space on the floor and said, "You will practice packing right there, and Anne will take over from here." Anne walked over and asked me how it was going so far. I told her it was an enormous amount of information and I felt like I was learning a lot. She handed me something called a "stash bag" filled with unpacked BASE gear, then told me to spread it out across the open space in front of us. She explained I was going to learn how to do a flat pro-pack. This was the technique used to pack reserves in skydiving. After I stretched everything out on the ground, she handed me a bag of tools that held four electrical clamps with orange rubber bumpers on the edges, a pull-up cord, small but thick rubber bands, and something called a "tailgate." She explained the tailgate was used to prevent a malfunction known as a line-over.

"What's a line-over?" I asked, trying to process everything.

Anne said, "We'll get into that later. Right now, let's just focus on packing."

She then laid out another BASE rig right next to mine and began showing me how to pack it. She would perform a step on the rig in front of her and then watch me copy it on mine. We did this over and over as we went through the process of packing a canopy. When she watched me finally close my first pack job, she nodded with approval. She then grabbed the pilot chute at the bottom of the rig I had just packed and pulled it open, then stood up and pointed at me.

"Pack it again."

I ended up doing about six pack jobs with her watching my every move and

correcting me when I made mistakes. By the end of the day, I was feeling pretty good about everything I had learned. As I was stowing the pilot chute on the last pack job, Anne walked up with Todd and asked, "How do you feel about that pack job?"

"Pretty good," I said with a nod. "I think I'm getting the hang of this."

Todd said, "Good, because you'll be jumping that pack job tomorrow morning." I'm not sure why, but his statement gave me an uneasy feeling in my chest, like my heart was trying to escape from my body via my throat. It was a feeling I would get accustomed to over time.

The next morning, my alarm went off at 4:30 a.m. The plan was to meet Anne and Todd in an open field next to Perris Valley Skydiving. When I pulled into the parking lot, I saw Anne and Todd helping a man unload a massive basket from a trailer attached to a large truck. As I got out of my car, Todd yelled over, asking me if I could help them move the basket into position behind what looked like a gigantic tube of cloth that stretched for over seventy feet. It was a hot air balloon, and my first jumps using BASE equipment would be done from that very basket. In 1997, there were no easy legal places to train for BASE jumping in Southern California. Hot air balloons were the closest thing Basic Research could get to a legal fixed object in the area. They would tie a 400-foot rope to the balloon so it wouldn't drift away and then use it like an elevator to altitude.

They told me I would start with bungee jumps to get the feel for dead-air exits. Jumping from an airplane feels completely different because the aircraft is traveling at over eighty miles per hour. As you exit, you hit a powerful wind that gives you support right away, making it feel like you're floating on a cushion of air, and you can use this wind resistance to control the way you fall through the sky. But when you step off a fixed object or hot air balloon, you only feel the sensation of falling as you accelerate from 0 to 120 miles per hour in less than twelve seconds. For the first three seconds, you have no wind resistance to use for control. Those seconds are crucial, and everything depends on how you exit the object. If you go a little head-low, you will continue rotating until you end up on your back. If you go a little head-high, you end up rotating into a stand, which can also put you on your back. Both are bad if you're jumping something low and must quickly deploy your parachute. Deploying on your back increases your odds of a malfunction, which can lead to death, so you need to avoid them whenever possible.

Anne and Todd would have me do as many bungee jumps as needed until they felt I had my exits down perfectly. Once it looked like my exits were stable without going either too head-high or too head-low, I would graduate to wearing a BASE rig.

Our goal was to do four jumps with BASE rigs that day after the bungee training was complete. Two slider-down from 400 feet and two slider-up from 1,000 feet. (A slider is a piece of fabric with four holes that slides up and down the lines of a canopy and acts as a braking system. You use them when doing jumps with delays longer than four seconds. When you jump low objects where you need your parachute to open quickly, you remove the slider.) The rig I had packed earlier was sitting on a tarp with six other rigs lined up next to it.

When I showed up that morning, it had been pitch-black around us and I could only see thanks to the illumination from the car's headlights. But as I helped them fill the balloon with hot air from a roaring flame, the sun started slowly coming up over the horizon. Problem was, we couldn't see the horizon as it was cresting—we were in a thick fog bank and could only see about eighty feet in any direction. As the balloon filled with heat, it began to tower over our heads. The top disappeared into a gray fog, making it look even more colossal than it was. They attached a hundred-foot-long bungee cord to a specially designed hook system at the base of the basket. This bungee would stretch to double its length under the load of a human body. They put a strange-looking harness on me that was unlike any I had seen before. All the bungee jumps I had seen on TV were attached to people's feet, but that wasn't how this one worked. You would step into it and then pull it over your shoulders while attaching a buckle at your chest. The bungee attached at a point close to your shoulders on your back. This was supposed to make the training more comfortable and more accurately depict the sensation of opening shock from a BASE deployment. The thing was ingenious.

Once the balloon was filled with enough hot air to begin pulling against gravity, they hooked the bungee cord to the back of my harness and had me get in the basket. This was my first time being near a hot air balloon, and I was feeling overwhelmed by what I was about to do. As I stood there with a heavy bungee cord dangling over the edge, I felt like it was trying to tug me out into open space. I began to feel detached from my body; it was a similar feeling to my first tandem skydive, almost as if I wasn't actually there or like I was watching myself doing this from an outside perspective. There was the sound of fire blasting heat into the balloon, the feeling of the basket rising towards the sky, and the ascent into fog making it impossible to see where I was in three-dimensional space. I am not sure if these white-out conditions were better or worse for the fear welling up inside me. All I knew was when they gave me the signal, I was going to climb over the lip of the basket, stand on a little wooden step, and push off.

I felt a tug against the rope anchoring the balloon to the ground. This meant we were at 400 feet and it was time to go. They asked me if I was ready; I wasn't.

I don't think you can ever truly be ready for these kinds of things. But I said yes anyway. They told me to step over the side of the basket and place my feet on the little wooden step. I did as I was told but I could now feel how fragile everything was. The basket was made of wicker, and if you have ever sat in a wicker chair, you know how weak that material feels. I felt exposed standing on a little piece of wood, just holding on with my fingertips. I was looking out into fog at a blank and desolate view. I couldn't see the ground and I had no idea where I was. It felt like I was in a huge, empty, white room. When the burner isn't firing, hot air balloons are actually silent, which meant there was no sound except for the heart in my chest and the creaking wicker holding my body weight on that step. It was surreal and terrifying.

I heard Todd say, "Jump when you're ready and remember to look out at the horizon."

I responded, "What horizon are you talking about. I can't see shit."

He laughed and said, "It's somewhere out in front of you. Imagine there is an invisible bar six feet up and six feet out. Just jump out and try to grab that invisible bar."

I took a deep breath, imagined an invisible bar out in front of me, and stepped out with my hands reaching for something that didn't exist. The sensation was one of stepping over the edge, crossing an invisible line of some kind. The acceleration was surprising, but before I even realized what was happening, the bungee grabbed at my harness, resisting the gravity that was pulling me towards the ground. As the bungee reached its maximum extension, I came to a complete stop, and for a second, I thought it was over, but it wasn't. I felt the cord start pulling me back up towards the balloon at a high rate of speed. I started feeling the acceleration, but now it was happening in the opposite direction. I then came to a stop again and felt something called "Zero-G" for the first time. This is when your momentum runs out and you float for an instant at the top of your arc in what feels like zero gravity. It only lasts a short time, but in that moment, your stomach feels like it's falling out of your ass and everything in your body tingles as you start rocketing back towards the earth again. This is all repeated about six or seven times before the momentum from the original plummet is completely spent. It's a jarring sensation, and I didn't like it. I wouldn't consider it habit-forming. This all happened in a disorienting fog bank where I could neither see the ground nor the balloon above me. It was impossible to tell which direction was up or down. I then dangled on the end of a string for quite a while as they lowered the balloon back down.

I was forced to repeat this nine more times. By the end of the bungee training, I was nauseous and feeling terrible. I didn't mind the stepping off and falling part, but the Zero-G was awful. I started dreading that moment and developed a true dislike for bungee jumping that day. There didn't seem to be any skill involved—and it was just an unpleasant experience for me—but it did do a great job of preparing me for my first jump in dead air with a BASE rig. During bungee training, Todd was able to see if I was going head-down or head-high on each exit, and he was able to explain the adjustments I needed to make. The bungee jumps were far more forgiving if you exited with bad body position, and you could reset the jumps much faster, so that made training safer and more efficient.

Suppressing my urge to vomit, I followed Todd and Anne over to the tarp with all the BASE rigs lined up. Todd handed me the rig I had packed the day before and said, "Gear up." I put the rig on and realized we still couldn't see anything—the fog had actually gotten worse while I did my bungee jumps. Our visibility was maybe sixty feet at best.

I asked, "Is it safe to try and land a parachute in this?"

"We're in a huge open field with nothing to hit," Todd said. "All you have to do is avoid the tether, which shouldn't be a problem. By the time you open and grab your toggles you'll be able to see well enough to land."

I decided he knew more than I did and got back in the balloon.

This time, as we reached the end of the balloon tether, we broke free from the fog bank and saw an endless blanket of blue sky above us. We had risen past the marine layer into a bright and sunny world above the clouds. We were floating above a fog ocean that was breathing and moving just beneath us. It looked as though I could step off the balloon and gently settle into a bed of puffy, white cotton candy. For some reason, this thought made me feel more comfortable. I think not being able to see the ground helped suppress my fear. A calm came over me and I felt almost peaceful.

My ten bungee jumps had desensitized me to the fear of standing on that wicker step. My first jump with BASE gear was going to be something called a "static line," which is when you are attached to the object you're jumping from with a cord that breaks when its load exceeds one hundred pounds of weight. This means the parachute opens almost instantly as you step off. Todd wanted to make sure I wasn't going to go head-down, which is a common mistake people make on their first balloon jumps. The basket moves as you push off, and this tends to affect people in different ways. Todd had me climb over the rim of the basket and get myself ready. I was standing on the edge, feeling the sun on my face and looking at soft fog pulsating underneath me. I was calm and relaxed. Todd said, "Jump when you're ready." I took a deep breath and stepped off, entering a quiet white room made of fog. A couple seconds later, I was sitting in my harness, unable to see anything but the whiteness around me. The ground slowly started to materialize beneath me, and as I got closer,

I was able to make out where I needed to land. I flared the canopy and set down with a tiptoe landing. This was a much better experience than the bungee jumps. It was gentler and gave me a warm, pleasant feeling in my tummy.

As the balloon landed, the fog lifted and the sun finally made its full appearance. We ended up doing three more jumps that day, going a bit higher with each one. We were able to cover both slider-down and slider-up trainings.

When I finished my day of jumping, we all headed back to the Basic Research shop. The course was now complete, and it was time to order my gear. Todd helped me pick out the proper equipment based on my weight and experience, and he said, "Jeb, this is only the beginning of your training. You'll need to meet and jump with more experienced people. You are now in the most dangerous phase of the sport. Since you're in your first one hundred jumps, you know just enough to get yourself hurt. So please, take it slow and easy. Jump high bridges with nice landing areas until you know your body position on exit is good, then move up to high antennas or even higher cliffs so you can track and get distance. Save buildings and low cliffs for after you get more experience. And remember: be conservative."

Anne was standing next to him and chimed in, "Come with me, Jeb. I want to show you something." She took me into another room with a medium-sized refrigerator and a receptionist named Nick sitting at a desk. All over the refrigerator were pictures of people. Anne pointed at the pictures and told me, "All these people are dead, and they all died BASE jumping. You need to make sure you take this sport seriously so you don't end up with your face on our fridge."

Nick got up from his desk and added, "The average lifespan of a BASE jumper is about five years from their first jump. In that time, one of three things usually happens. One, something horrible occurs and the jumper gets scared, making them quit the sport. Two, the jumper gets seriously injured and is forced to quit. Three, the jumper dies. Now, there are people who last much longer and there are people that don't last as long, but from my experience, it's usually about five years."

When I left Basic Research that day, I felt I had a good grasp on what I was about to face. Of course, I was wrong. I couldn't possibly have understood what was about to come.

CHAPTER EIGHT

MY FIRST BASE JUMP

After two months of waiting, I finally got the call that my BASE gear had come in. I drove for almost two hours through LA traffic to Basic Research's headquarters to pick up my gear, but I also wanted to talk with Todd about possible locations I could use for my first real BASE jumps. To me, this was a magic backpack with wings packed inside. It would give me the ability to fly. The level of excitement trapped inside my body made my skin tingle; it felt like energy was pulsating just below its surface. I was about to pick up my brand-new, Velcro-closed Reactor container with a BASE-specific 260-square-foot FOX canopy. At the time, this was the cutting edge in BASE-jumping technology. BASE containers used Velcro to close because people felt it was less likely to have malfunctions when opening with low airspeed, but that was just before they started experimenting with pins on BASE-specific gear.

I rang the buzzer next to a sign that read, "No Solicitors." That sign always caught my attention for some reason, even after years of visiting BR. I also found it interesting that they had a huge wrought-iron security door and bars on all the windows. Turned out the neighborhood they were in was a bit shady. Apparently, Perris, CA, was good for two things: first, it had one of the biggest drop zones in the United States; and second, it had lots of crack cocaine. Todd answered the door and brought me into the factory. Sitting on a table was my box of gear. He pulled my rig from the box, helped me put it on, then checked it for size. It was a perfect fit—love at first sight.

As Todd inspected the rig, I asked him if he knew of any good objects I could use for my first jump. He seemed a bit hesitant to answer this question. BASE objects were kept secret and highly protected. Everyone constantly worried about losing access to the few objects regularly jumped. He just stood there looking at me for a while, and I could see the wheels turning in his head, debating whether he should say anything or ignore me. I think he saw me as a bit of a loose cannon and felt the chances of me doing something silly were high. But I think he also understood I would probably figure it out on my own if he didn't help, and that could be even worse. In the end, he decided to tell me about one of the safer places to do my first jumps so he could at least teach me the correct way of going about it.

He took a deep breath and said, "Okay, Jeb. There is a place in northern Cali called Auburn Bridge. I'll tell you what to do, but if anyone asks, you didn't hear any of this from me. I will not be held responsible for anything you do."

"No problem," I agreed. "No one will know you told me anything, so...tell me?"

Todd went on, "The bridge is seven hundred feet high and has a nice long trail for you to land on. It's the site most people on the West Coast use for teaching students and training, so treat it with respect and don't get caught. The police in the area know about BASE jumping and actively search for and catch jumpers. Do not, under any circumstance, jump from the deck of that bridge. Also, do not jump that bridge in daylight. Most jumpers will jump in the dead of night between 12:00 a.m. and 5:00 a.m. They usually jump during full moons so they have light for landing, but if you have bad night vision or end up going during a new moon, you can get glowsticks and set three of them about fifty feet apart down the center of the landing zone. As long as you land in the middle of them, they will give you the depth perception you need to flair your canopy for a soft landing."

I asked, "If I can't jump from the deck, how do I jump it?"

Todd went on, "I'm getting to that. The bridge has a catwalk that stretches the entire length of the bridge about thirty feet below the main deck. There are two ways to get on this catwalk. You can either drop down onto it from the side farthest away from Auburn, or you can climb up the steel from where the bridge is secured to the cliff under the roadway. The best method is to climb up the steel from the bottom. You have the least chance of being seen this way. Dropping down from the top is not as good an option because it can expose you to traffic, making you more likely to be seen. Only use this method if you feel climbing the steel is too dangerous for you." He ended with, "Be careful and DO NOT GET CAUGHT."

The next day, I went to my buddy Shawn's house with my new gear to practice packing in his living room. He sat watching me pack while we talked. I asked Shawn if he would like to go on a road trip to Auburn and help me do my first BASE jump. Having a driver would make it easier to do multiple jumps in one night. Plus, if I got hurt for any reason, it would be nice to have someone there. A huge smile spread across his face as he said, "Yes, what are friends for? I would love to come help you do this." He had been listening to me talk about BASE jumping for years and knew exactly how important this was to me.

We decided to drive up that coming Saturday. I would stay the night at his house on Friday and we would start driving early the next morning. The drive would take about eight hours, and we wanted to get there during the day so we could scout the bridge and landing area while we still had light.

Friday came and neither of us seemed to be able to sleep. We were still awake when the sun came up. We had talked all night in a nervous, almost manic state. I had been through BASE training, but this was going to be for real, so I was scared. Shawn was also nervous, because what we were about to do had serious consequences both legally and physically. I could see his concern in his body language.

I told him, "Don't worry. If anything goes wrong and I die, just leave my body where it is for the animals to eat and leave. No reason for you to get in trouble because I made a stupid mistake." For some reason, this didn't seem to comfort him, but I meant every word. To me, it was an acceptable outcome.

By the time we finally got out of bed the next morning to begin the drive, we were not doing well. We hadn't slept one wink. Both of us were so tired we could barely keep our eyes open, and the long drive ahead was daunting. Shawn decided to start driving first. We drove over Kanan through the Malibu hills to get to the 101 South freeway. We took that to the 405 North, which eventually turned into the 5 North. We pulled over for gas as we were passing Magic Mountain, and Shawn asked me if I would please take over driving. He was falling asleep and felt like it had become dangerous for him to continue behind the wheel. I said no problem, but I was also tired. We got back on the 5, and the drive seemed to go on forever. I had the music playing low so Shawn could sleep, but I could feel my eyes getting super heavy. It got to the point where I was fighting to keep them open. I would close one eye to let it rest and then switch eyes so the other could rest.

Next thing I knew, I was in a dream. I don't remember what the dream was, but I do know I was in a deep sleep when a loud sound jarred me awake. The car had drifted off the road onto the rumble strips designed to make sound for this very occurrence. I'm not sure if you've ever woken up behind the wheel of a car doing 75 mph in the fast lane of a freeway before, but I can tell you, it's a fucked-up experience. Coming out of a dream behind the wheel of a car will wake you up faster than 10,000 cups of coffee. The instant I opened my eyes, I realized exactly what was going on as adrenaline rushed through my veins like a speeding locomotive, splashing into my brain and firing every synapse simultaneously. I had almost just killed my best friend and myself. He woke up, too, as I jerked the car back into our lane.

Shawn yelled, "What the fuck?! Did you just fall asleep at the wheel?"

"Yes," I said, trying to keep the car from fishtailing.

Shawn screamed, "Pull over right now!" I had never been more awake in my life, but I pulled the car over and let Shawn drive from there on.

We were both wide awake as we continued driving up the 5 towards Sacramento, when we started smelling something bad. At first Shawn said, "Jeb, did you fart?"

I said, "Nope, not this time," but the odor got worse and worse. We opened the windows to try and get the smell out, but we realized it was coming from outside the car. That is when we saw it: the biggest cattle ranch in California. This ranch produced over 150,000,000 pounds of beef per year. It was a horrible sight to see— an endless sea of cows that went off into the horizon. Nothing was green; there was only the perpetual brown of dirt and fences. We noticed something odd: they were watering the cows like they were fields of grass. I had never seen cows being watered with massive sprinklers before. It was a strange sight to see, and the smell was terrible. I had no idea that many animals could be kept alive in conditions like that. It was disturbing and left a lasting image in my mind.

We finally pulled into the Foothills Hotel in the late afternoon with plenty of light to do the scouting. Todd had told me most jumpers liked staying at this hotel because the rooms were long and great for packing. Plus, it was cheap. Shawn and I checked in and unloaded our bags, then got right back in the car and headed for the bridge. As we drove over it, I could feel butterflies in my stomach, and a sense of euphoria began to take hold. There was a pull-out at the far end of the bridge, exactly where Todd said it would be, and we parked there. Shawn and I walked out to the middle of the bridge and just stood there, looking over the edge. It was much higher than I was expecting. I was in awe and didn't have much to say. Excitement ran through me.

I suddenly became quite emotional; here I was, standing on an object that I was about to BASE jump from. I had spent the last five years of my life obsessing over this moment. Every move I made was about getting to this place. I was a little worried it couldn't possibly live up to my expectations because it had been all I could think about for so long. Dreaming about this had helped me hold on during dark periods in my life. How could it ever be as amazing as I had built it up to be in my mind?

I need to be clear here. I was twenty-one years old at this point. My depression and suicidal tendencies had subsided at around nineteen. I no longer wanted to die, so mentally, I had to figure out a way to reconcile the fact that death would no longer be a winning scenario. I had become a happy person by finding purpose in life through the pursuit of an activity that could prove lethal. This became a paradox that would prove difficult to rationalize, but here I was, standing on top of what I felt my purpose had become. I was finally going to step off a fixed object, but I also now had something to lose.

All this was going through my mind as Shawn asked, "Should we go check out where you're going to land? Those trees look huge." I took a closer look at the trees all around the thin road I was going to land on, and he was right: they did look huge. If we were standing on a 700-foot bridge, those trees must be giant, and hitting them under a canopy would suck. So, we headed back to the car to drive to the bottom for a closer look.

Once we got there, we parked and started walking the trail to the landing area under the bridge. As we got close, I realized the trees were going to be an issue when jumping in complete darkness. There were also other obstacles that could prove tricky. Looking up at the bridge from the landing area, we noticed a steep hill to our right that went 650 feet up to where the bridge spanned over the top of us. That hill was covered in trees that must have been at least sixty feet tall. To the left and below the road was a very steep drop-off, descending about fifty feet to a river surrounded by ankle-breaking boulders. To land, I was going to have to burn my altitude over the river, because that was the only area clear of trees. I knew it would be impossible to see them in the dark, so I had to avoid the slope where they were. I was also going to have to be careful not to overshoot the walkway, which was about ten feet wide and probably a hundred feet long. If I overshot, I would fly into tree branches that had grown over the walkway. It was going to be the smallest area I had landed in and I had to do it in pitch-black conditions. I also noticed the ground had lots of small, jagged rocks embedded in the dirt. If I fell during a landing, it would be like sliding across a cheese grater.

On our way back to the hotel, we stopped to buy glowsticks for the landing area and have dinner. We talked and waited for the sun to drop so the night could cloak what we were about to do. At midnight, I grabbed my stash bag with my BASE rig and we hit the road. In my course, Todd had told me I should invest in some body armor, like kneepads, elbow pads, and a helmet at bare minimum. Of course, I didn't do any of that. I just had my rig and the clothes on my back. My priorities were distorted, and I was going to regret not listening to Todd about the body armor.

Shawn drove me to the bottom of the bridge, where I ran as fast as I could to the landing area. I broke three glowsticks and watched them light up a florescent green. I put one at the beginning, the middle, and the end of the landing zone. For some reason, it made the landing area look much smaller, and without the flashlight on, I couldn't see any of the trees, which was disconcerting. Shawn drove me back up to the top of the bridge and pulled over at the same place we had stopped earlier. I decided it was super late and I could see cars coming from almost a mile in each direction. I didn't see any reason to get on the catwalk and didn't want Shawn to have to climb down there. He wasn't breaking the law by watching me jump, but he would be if he trespassed on the catwalk. We decided to just walk out to the center of the bridge, but if headlights shone in the distance, we could hide behind the concrete barriers until they passed. I told myself that Todd was being overly dramatic about my getting caught. As we got to the center of the bridge, Shawn realized he had forgotten something in the car and ran back to get it. I lay down behind the barrier and watched Shawn run back to the car, ducking each time a set of headlights approached.

As Shawn got to the car, I could see light from a car coming from the opposite direction. The car made an abrupt U-turn and pulled into the turnout right behind our car. Shawn was rummaging through the backseat with the door open as this happened. I watched two men jump out of the back of a flatbed truck and walk over to Shawn. I couldn't hear what was being said but wondered why people were riding in the flatbed of a moving vehicle. I could tell there was a heated exchange between them. After only a few moments, the men backed away from Shawn and jumped back in the truck as it sped off. When Shawn got back to me, I asked, "What was that all about?"

"I have no fucking idea," he replied, out of breath. "This truck pulled over and two high school kids jumped out and told me if I didn't give them everything in my pockets, they were going to kick the shit out of me. I reached in my pocket, pulled out my Spyderco knife, and informed them that the first one who got close enough was getting cut. They got back in their truck and were gone."

With a shocked expression, I said, "Damn! Good thing you had your knife on you."

Shawn explained, "I don't go anywhere without my knife. Are you ready to jump?" I smiled, pulled out my pilot chute, and started preparing for the jump. I felt having the pilot chute in my hand for my first jump would make me feel more comfortable. If it went well, I would do the next one stowed (which is when you have the pilot chute folded and placed in a pouch at the bottom of the rig).

Once the pilot chute was in my hand, I stood up, looked at Shawn with a look that said I may never return, and said, "I am ready." The guardrail was just below chest level and about four inches wide. I checked to make sure no cars were coming, and when I saw the coast was clear, I stepped up on the rail and just balanced there for a moment. As I stood there balancing on the rail, I thought, *Man, this is terrifying. If I were only six inches off the ground balancing like this, there would be no problem at all; I could do it all day.* But being 700 feet off the ground made my legs turn to jelly, and it took everything I had to stay upright. I looked down and couldn't see anything. It was complete darkness. All I could see were three green lights that looked so tiny and far away. I was desperately trying to make out trees or the river or anything, but there was nothing. It was a new moon and the sky was overcast. I started losing my balance and decided it was time to go. I leaned forward and dropped into what felt like a dark void. It was disorienting—I had no reference of up or down—but as my body began picking up speed, the air started rushing up and hitting me in the face. This automatically allowed my brain to discern precisely which direction was down. I threw the pilot chute and it filled with air, creating drag that forced it to rocket behind me, pulling my parachute along with it. The canopy opened with a smack. I was now sitting under lines and fabric supporting my body weight as I drifted in the darkness.

The problem was, I couldn't see anything, which meant I had no idea where I was going. The glowsticks were to my left, but it was hard to judge exactly how high I was. I made a few adjustments and did a 360-degree spiraling turn to lose a little altitude. I was trying to position myself so I could land between the three glowing dots on the ground, but I totally misjudged where I was. As I turned in to make my landing, I could tell I had done so too early and I was going to fly past my markers. I knew from walking the landing area that there were trees beyond the glowsticks— big trees—and if I hit them, I would get hurt. As I passed the last glowstick, I lost all altitude awareness and had no idea how high off the ground I was. I knew I was going to have to flare but couldn't judge when. I made a guess and that guess was wrong; I flared too low and impacted the ground at high speed, sliding across the jagged little stones that acted like a cheese grater, tearing holes in my jeans and stripping all the flesh from my knees, elbows, and palms. I had deep gashes and was bleeding everywhere but didn't have time to worry about that. I grabbed my canopy and stuffed it into my stash bag along with my rig, and I started moving as fast as I could to the pick-up location.

I got there first, but Shawn was close behind. We got in the car and Shawn asked how it went. I turned the interior lights on and we looked at the damage together. My pants were completely shredded, and I didn't have any skin on either of my knees. You could see the flesh had been torn off in chunks. My palms were the same. Everywhere had deep gashes filled with dirt and gravel. I was bleeding a lot. We kind of looked at each other and Shawn asked what I wanted to do. I said, "Lets head back to the hotel so I can pack. I want to do at least one more jump tonight."

"Are you serious?" he shrieked. "That looks like a lot of blood!"

"I'll be fine," I assured him. "Let's get going." Shawn shook his head and started driving, but he kept one eye on my leaking wounds.

At the hotel, I laid my gear out and started packing. It didn't take long before all my lines were red with blood. By the time I finished packing, the room looked like a murder scene. The carpet, most of the towels, and somehow the ceiling all had blood on them. I had not stopped bleeding and was still in a lot of pain when Shawn asked, "Don't you think we should call it a night?"

I said, "No way, dude. We didn't drive all this way to do one jump. Get the keys and let's go."

I tried to wash as much blood off as I could, but it just kept coming. I put on a new pair of black jeans, knowing no one would be able to see the blood soaking through at night. We got in the car and headed back to the bridge. We parked in what was becoming a familiar parking spot and started the process of walking back out to the center of the bridge. About halfway to the launch point, we saw a car coming so we ducked down behind the concrete median. We listened as the car drove by, then watched as the lights slowed down and then pulled in directly behind our car. Suddenly, the area flooded with red-and-blue lights and we knew it was the police.

Shawn whispered, "We are so fucked."

"Just be quiet and get as close to the median as possible."

We lay down flat and placed ourselves against the median like we were part of it. The police car turned around and started driving up the wrong side of the road, shining its search lights back and forth. I was sure they knew jumpers were on the bridge and they were looking for us. I mentally kicked myself when I realized that Todd wasn't being so paranoid after all. Close to where we were hiding, the police stopped their car and got out. With flashlights in hand, the two cops started walking up the bridge while looking over the edge. They shone the light over the median in our direction, less than a hundred feet away. How they didn't see us is beyond me. We were wearing all black, but so were they, and I could see them perfectly. I felt like my heart was trying to get my attention by tapping the inside of my ribcage. But right when I felt they were going to discover us, they turned off their flashlights, got back in their car, turned around, and drove away. Shawn and I just lay there for a moment when he broke the silence with, "Holy shit." We started moving again, but this time at a much faster pace, trying to get to the exit point without being seen. I was going stowed this time, so everything happened much faster. I just jumped up on the handrail, balanced for about three seconds, and jumped off. It was a smooth jump. I still couldn't see shit, but I had a better sense of where I was and lined myself up much better for the landing area. I made my turn-in and was sure I had nailed it, but again, I was wrong and overpassed the glowsticks a second time, totally eating shit just as badly as my first jump. The cheese grater of a landing area destroyed another pair of pants and took even more flesh. I was a little lightheaded on the drive back, but still so happy I'd gotten in two jumps.

The next morning, we packed up all our stuff and tried to clean the blood off the carpet and walls as much as possible. I couldn't reach the blood on the ceiling, and still to this day have no idea how it got up there. The room looked like awful things had happened in the night, but that was someone else's problem now. We packed up our car, checked out of the hotel, and started our drive home. During the drive, thinking about the experience, I felt it had been a productive trip where I had learned a lot. Todd had been correct that jumping from the deck was a bad idea. Also, never leave cars at the top...I kind of remembered Todd saying that, too. Also, body armor was something I needed to invest in. Kneepads, helmet, and some gloves would have been helpful. I still have scars on the palms of my hands from that trip. I guess when you're young, you need to experience things for yourself. Even though Todd had given me all the information I needed to make that trip successful, I still needed to make those mistakes to truly learn the lessons.

Oh, to be young again.

CHAPTER NINE

THE 260-FOOT ANTENNA

I made a friend in my MANN 8 movie theater days named Brian. During our first conversation together, we talked about many things: skydiving, scuba, aviation, and the subject of religion. He explained how he had been brought up Catholic. Because of my situation with my girlfriend at the time, I had developed strong opinions on the matter, and we ended up talking about it for hours. By the end of the conversation, Brian informed me he wanted to go skydiving with me, and, as of that moment, he was now atheist. I was like, "Wait, what? You're an atheist now?"

He explained, "I've always been one, I just didn't realize it until now. My parents are Catholic and I just went along with it to make them happy, but I never actually believed any of it. There's no reason to keep pretending." I was impressed with how switched-on and logical he was. I knew how hard it was to break free from a life of programming and I could tell his mind was something special.

A while later, Brian and I were talking about the experience I had at Auburn Bridge. I told him that as I was driving up, I noticed a couple large antennae and wondered how tall they were. Brian said, "Jeb, you know there is something called an aeronautical chart that pilots use to avoid tall, man-made structures, right? Every tall building, high electrical tower, and antenna are on these charts." I asked him if he would get me a few of them.

He said, "Of course, that's easy. You just need to let me know what area of California you would like to cover." I told him I wanted the charts for the Sacramento area, and as I was saying this, I remembered something. I had been driving by an antenna on the 101 going down the grade towards Camarillo. It was close to where my girlfriend lived, and every time I would drive by it, I wondered how tall it was. I thought it couldn't be more than seventy-five feet high, but thought it was worth checking out. I asked him to get me two charts. One for Sacramento and one for the Camarillo area. He said, "No problem."

A few weeks later, he had the charts for me. As he handed them over, I opened the chart for Camarillo first. I needed to see if that antenna on the 101 freeway was on it. Sure enough, it was there, and it said something I couldn't believe. It showed the antenna was 300 feet tall. There was no way that could be correct. It was on top of a hill, so I thought maybe the chart was measuring it from the bottom of the hill. I had to go investigate.

I wanted to have at least three different measurement devices to make 100 percent certain it was really that high. So, I bought a laser rangefinder that would give me distance, and an altimeter watch that would measure altitude in five-foot increments. With those two devices, combined with the aeronautical chart, I felt I could confirm the true height of the object. A few days later, I drove to the antenna about an hour before sunset. I wanted to scout the location with light first and then, when it got dark and no one could spot me, climb to the top to take my measurements.

You could only drive to the base of the hill the antenna sat atop of. The offramp from the 101 dropped you right at a small turnout where you could park. From there, all you had to do was walk around a small barrier blocking the road to the base of the antenna. I took a quick look around and noticed the hillside was completely covered in cactus—evil, spiky-looking cactus. I saw that the road leading up to the antenna would be the only possible place to land, assuming I could even jump in the first place. If I couldn't set down on that road after jumping off the antenna, it would mean landing in cactus at night. That seemed less than ideal. The walk up wouldn't be hard, but I would have to wait until it got dark. There was too much traffic with too many eyes watching to do it during the day. I decided I would head to dinner to burn a few hours and let it get dark. I had seen as much as I could from the bottom and wouldn't be able to learn more until I walked up that hill.

I returned around 11:00 p.m., ready to go. For some reason, I felt calm. It was a chilly spring night with a full moon, which made it easy to see. My uneventful walk to the top only took ten minutes, but as I got to the base of the antenna, I found it surrounded by a large razor-wire fence about ten feet tall. I threw my jacket over the razor wire, giving me something to climb on without getting cut. I made a note that I was going to need to bring a piece of carpet next time to make this process easier. As I stood under the antenna, looking up, I noticed its ladder was rinky-dink. I couldn't believe this thing was 300 feet high. The antenna only had two lights: one on top and one at the middle. The guywires holding this antenna upright were also super ghetto. I wasn't sure this antenna was even safe to climb, much less jump off. The ladder was on the outside of the antenna with zero safety features of any kind. Even thirty feet up, a fall could equal death. Like I said before, in my mind, this thing was maybe seventy-five feet tops, and the aeronautical chart had to be measuring from the bottom of the hill. All the same, I set my altimeter watch to zero and started to climb with the rangefinder in my backpack. The climb took a bit longer than I expected, and it took a lot of exertion to get to the top. I was sweaty by the time I got there. As I looked down, I could see a bunch of odd-looking dishes sticking out in all directions that made it impossible to jump from the top. I would have to climb underneath this equipment to make a clean exit. This meant I was going to lose quite a bit of the antenna's already low altitude.

I moved down under the dishes to take my measurements and climbed inside the antenna's structure, which was shaped like a triangle. The entire antenna was built using hundreds of thin metal beams fashioned into triangular shapes stacked on top of one another, interconnected by metal rods. As I climbed into the hollow structure, I placed each foot on a separate support strut and placed my butt on a third. I looked down between my legs and could see I was hovering high above the ground. Had one of my feet slipped, I would have fallen down the middle of the hollow structure, hitting metal bars all the way to the ground. I checked my watch and it read 260 feet. I couldn't believe it. I leaned over and looked down the structure, but it still looked too low for that readout. I took out my rangefinder, picked a point directly under me, and pushed the button. To my surprise, it read 260 feet. I was shocked; this didn't seem possible. I looked up past all the dishes and wondered, *Could the top really be forty feet away?* My ability to eyeball distance wasn't trained yet, and my eyes were lying to me, but three different sources all said the same exact thing; I had to trust the technology. According to the numbers, this object could be jumped.

I sat there for a moment, high above the world, looking down at red and white lights inching their way up and down the 101 freeway. I started thinking about all the people sitting in those cars. Where were they going and why were they going there? I then started wondering the same thing about myself. What was I doing and why was I doing it?

A few weeks later, I called Anne from Basic Research. In my class, Todd was clear that I should use a static line if I wanted to jump under 300 feet at my level of experience. A static line, used for jumping ultra-low objects, attaches your bridle to the object you are jumping from and opens your parachute almost immediately when you jump. I didn't have training in the use of static lines yet, so I had a few questions for the experts.

Anne answered the phone, and in a rushed tone, I said, "Hello, Anne. I found a three-hundred-foot antenna but can only jump from the two-hundred-and-sixty-foot mark. How many feet do you think it will take for my parachute to open if I use a forty-eight-inch pilot chute?"

She responded, "Whoa, slow down Jeb. Why don't you tell me a little about the antenna first? Is it free-standing or does it have guywires?"

I said, "It has guywires."

Her voice changed. "Do not jump that antenna. You do not have the experience yet, because if you did, you would already understand that thing is a bad object. You would need to take a short delay, which means two things: one, you will have no time to get separation from the object; and two, if you get even the slightest off-heading opening, your chances of hitting a guywire are incredibly high."

I tried to explain, "That wasn't the question I asked you. I asked how long it would take for my parachute to open if I did a go-and-throw using a forty-eight-inch pilot chute."

A long sigh came out of her as she pleaded, "Jeb, remember the pictures? Do not jump that antenna."

I again stated, "Thank you for the advice, but that isn't what I asked you."

Exasperated, she said, "It could take your parachute a hundred and fifty feet to open. This would give you little time to release toggles and flare."

"Thank you," I said cheerily. "That is exactly what I needed to know," and I hung up the phone.

I then called my friend Shawn and told him what I was planning to do. Now, Shawn and I had talked enough through the years about BASE jumping for him to understand that what I was suggesting was extremely dangerous. He didn't like the idea. He explained, "Jeb, I love you, so I don't feel comfortable coming to watch you kill yourself. I think this sounds like a bad idea. You just started jumping, and I don't think you're ready for something like this."

"I get that, Shawn, but I'm going to jump whether you're there or not, and I could really use your help."

This didn't sway him, and he said, "If you're going to hurt yourself, you can do it without me there."

I was annoyed but realized I couldn't say anything to change his mind, so I said, "Okay." If I wanted to do this, I would be on my own.

A few weeks after my conversation with Shawn, I decided I needed to jump that antenna and I needed to do it right that instant. Something inside me decided I couldn't wait another minute. It was going to be my first seriously dangerous BASE jump, and I needed to know if I was capable of pushing myself through it. By now, I had done five jumps at Auburn Bridge but didn't feel like that was a true test. I was still searching for myself, and I just wasn't sure I had what it took to be a real BASE jumper. Auburn wasn't what I had been looking for, and I was actually a little let down by the overall experience; it just hadn't challenged me the way I had hoped for.

At this point, I was living in a guestroom of my parent's house in Malibu, and as I was loading my car with BASE gear, my mother caught a glimpse of me. She quickly ran out and asked, "What are you doing?" in that frantic tone that only mothers can pull off.

I told her, "I found a two-hundred-and-sixty-foot antenna close by and I am going to BASE jump off it tonight." She had been listening to me talk about BASE jumping for over five years and knew what I just said was ludicrous given my level of experience.

"Jeb, that doesn't sound like a good idea. Don't you think it would be better to train a bit longer and work your way up to something like that?"

I said, "Probably, but I can't wait any longer; I have to do this now."

She got upset. "Jeb, I have never told you not to do anything in your entire life, but I am telling you not to do this. You are not ready. You need more training. Don't be stupid."

"I'm sorry, Mom, but I have to do this. I need to know if I am capable."

This made her even more upset, and she went on to say, "Okay, Jeb. If you feel you need to do this then you need to find a new place to live after you do. I am not going to support this kind of reckless behavior. I can't stand by while you make decisions that will kill you. I love you, and I will do everything in my power to stop you."

With an understanding gaze, I replied, "Well, you do what you need to do, and I am going to do what I need to do."

I then got in my car and watched my mother break down in tears in the rearview mirror as I drove away. It was upsetting, and it shook me, but I had decided nothing was going to stop me from doing this—nothing. It was time to see how far I was willing to go. I wanted to know if I could do something with real consequences. This was going to be my first true test: how much fear could I take before my mind would break?

This time, as I pulled off the 101 and drove down the offramp, I was having a different experience than a few weeks earlier. I was terrified on a level that was and still is impossible to put into words. I knew exactly what I was about to do, and I knew it was a horrible idea. I parked my car in the same place as before, opened my trunk, and pulled out my gear. I put the stash bag on my back, along with my BASE rig, kneepads, helmet, and gloves—I had learned my lesson about body armor from Auburn. I then began walking up the hill towards the antenna. It was 12:00 a.m. and a new moon hung in the sky above, so it was pitch black. This made it difficult to make out where the road ended and the cactus began. The air was perfectly still. It was much warmer this evening and the chill in the air from a few weeks earlier was completely gone.

As I started up the hill, I heard something that startled me: something moved in the weeds between the cactus maybe three feet away. I instinctively moved away right before I heard the rattle from a snake explode with sound. I instantly jumped out of my skin. Judging from the sound, I knew it was big. Then I heard another one behind me, and that one set off a chain reaction. The sound of rattlesnakes was all around me. I couldn't believe it. There had to be at least thirty or forty of them in less than a hundred square feet. I was wondering why I hadn't come across any a few weeks earlier, but quickly understood it was much warmer now so they must have come out of hibernation. The fact that it was pitch black meant this was going to be a serious issue. My childhood spent catching rattlesnakes had taught me this was the worst possible scenario I could find myself in. You never want to startle a rattlesnake, but I had just startled several—that's how you get bit. In utter darkness, I had no way of knowing where they were or if I was going to step on one. I realized this was going to make my landing astronomically more dangerous. If I didn't land on the road, I wouldn't just be landing in cactus anymore; I would also be landing on pissed-off rattlesnakes. Even if I did a perfect landing on the road, I would have no way of telling if I was landing on a snake as I put my feet down. The situation was bad all around, and a feeling of absolute dread filled me.

I felt around on the ground, looking for a stick, and got lucky. I found one about four feet long, thin and wispy, but strong enough to sweep out in front of me and hopefully scare away any snakes before I stepped on them. I noticed the rattling sounds were mostly in the cactus and I didn't hear many on the actual road. But that didn't make me feel much better as I continued walking up the hill.

Every twenty or thirty feet, I would hear another snake burst into sound. I was sweating now, badly. I could feel my heart in my chest, and it felt like it was trying to crawl up my throat and out of my mouth. Absolute terror had gripped me and was squeezing my mind. As I got to the razor-wire fence, I couldn't wait to get over it. I felt like it might be keeping some of the snakes out, which didn't make sense, because it was a chain-link fence, and snakes could easily slip right through. But a false sense of security is better than no security at all. I took a small piece of carpet out of my stash bag and threw it over the razor wire, then climbed over the fence as fast as I could. The fear was coming on in waves, pulsating through me, growing by the minute, and just when I thought it couldn't get any worse, it did.

As I geared up, I began telling myself I wasn't going to do this. Once I finished threading my chest strap, I put my hands on the metal ladder and noticed they were soaking wet. I tried to dry them off on my shirt, but it was soaking wet, too. I then tried rubbing them on my pants, but sure enough, they were even more wet than my shirt. I was sweating so much it was like I had just stepped through pouring rain, and I had no way to dry off my slick hands. I also noticed my breathing was deep and irregular. My heartbeat was unnaturally fast. I could feel it throbbing from my fingertips to my hair follicles. I was on the edge of total panic. But I shook my hands off and sweat went flying. I put my hands on the metal ladder and started pulling myself against gravity. I felt this gravity was trying to chain me to the ground (not just pull me down, but imprison me).

As I put one hand in front of the other, pulling myself up the ladder, I noticed my mind was repeating a mantra. It just kept saying, "I am not going to do this. This is too dangerous. I do not have the proper training yet. I am just going to go to the top, take a look, and come back down. I am not ready for this." I would pull myself up another step, and the mantra would repeat. Pull myself up another step and repeat again. I finally made it to the 260-foot mark, just under all the dishes perched atop the antenna like gargoyles, then slipped inside the frame of the steel structure like I had a few weeks earlier. As I sat there in the dead, calm air, I realized the conditions were perfect. The air was completely still. I saw cars winding up and down the 101 and watched them move off towards Camarillo. I decided I wasn't going to jump. I knew I didn't have the experience to do this safely. I needed to get more training, and I would come back after I did at least fifty more jumps. As I was saying this to myself, I began pulling my pilot chute out of my rig. I told myself that if I jumped, I might not die, but I would probably get seriously hurt and I didn't have anyone to help me this time. I started gathering the pilot chute in my right hand, S folding the bridle in the loose fabric.

I told myself, *You're planning on heading to Norway later this year and you should wait until you get back from that trip.*

With this, I slipped out of the antenna's structure and leaned over, holding on with my left hand and holding my pilot chute in my right. My eyes grew as I looked down at the ground. Every nerve ending in my body screamed, "DO NOT DO THIS!!!" It became like a hurricane raging through my mind, completely consuming my thoughts. My body fought, every muscle clenching desperately to hold on for dear life as the fingers of my left hand let go one by one. I leaned forward, and my legs pushed away from the antenna. Suddenly, time froze. Everything just stopped. I was suspended in mid-air. The fear disappeared, replaced by a heightened sense of things—a new awareness. I could see. My surroundings had gone from the blinding darkness created by the new moon to a beautiful night illuminated by distant stars. I could see the individual guywires stretching down to the ground to hold the antenna upright. I could see the metalwork of the antenna and all its little rungs, one after the other. I noticed that the antenna was moving. Ever so slowly, the metal rungs were moving past me.

I let go of the pilot chute clutched tightly in my right hand and it drifted away like a tissue caught in a slow breeze. Everything seemed to be moving in ultra-slow motion as I watched. In this odd distortion of time, I saw the red light marking the center point of the antenna pass by. I knew I had just traveled more than 150 feet without my parachute opening, and this meant something had gone wrong. I focused on the ground and saw my impact point—directly on the razor-wire fence. As I watched the fence approaching, I raised my hands up to cover my face, bracing for impact. I then heard the sound of Velcro peeling off the back of my container, instantly followed by the sensation of getting hit in the chest with a baseball bat. The chute opening knocked the wind out of me as it sat me upright in my harness. I was dazed and confused but sitting under an open parachute with very little altitude to land. I didn't have time to unstow my toggles, so I just grabbed my left rear riser and pulled, turning my canopy towards the road under the antenna. I impacted the road on my left side in a rear riser turn and bounced off the asphalt. The landing was hard, but I was uninjured.

I lay there trembling and completely overwhelmed. My body had truly believed I was going to die, and it released everything it had to try and save my life. All adrenaline, all endorphins, everything. I was like a live wire just shaking on the ground. I could hear insects crawling in the grass around me. I could see in the dark. I could feel the air touching my skin. I could smell the dirt. All the little hairs on my body were standing at attention. Each of my senses was operating at its most optimum levels. I had never felt more connected to the world in which I lived, ever. In an instant, I knew exactly who I was and what I was capable of. I knew that nothing could ever stand in the way of what I wanted to do again. Not friends abandoning me, not my parents threatening me. Not even I could stop me. From that point forward, I knew that if I decided to do something, I was going to do it. This was probably the single most important moment in my life. I had dreamed of being something for over five years, and this was the moment I had gone from wanting to be something, to actually being that something.

I was free.

CHAPTER TEN

KJERAG NORWAY

Not long before I jumped the antenna, Todd and Anne from Basic Research organized a training trip for advanced BASE jumpers to a three-thousand-foot cliff in Norway called Kjerag. When they asked if I would be interested in attending, I said yes without hesitation. I knew I needed more training and felt that massive (and legal) cliffs like Kjerag would be the next logical step in my progression. I asked Mom and Barry if I could take some time off work to do a few big cliff jumps, and they were supportive. Lucky for me, the job was contract-based and pretty much allowed me as much time off as I wanted.

"I'd never waste my money on it," said Barry, "but it's your life. Do what you want."

"You decide how you want to spend your money," said Mom. "I'm just so proud of you for chasing your dreams with so much passion."

I had never thought about BASE jumping as a passion before, but as soon as my mom said those words, I knew she was absolutely right.

A few months later, in the heart of summer, I found myself heading to a little village nestled deep inside a remote Norwegian fjord called Lysefjorden. Getting there required me to fly into the city of Stavanger, spend the night in a hotel, then catch a ferry early the next morning. The ferry ride would take about three hours to reach Lysebotn, a town with a summer population of around three hundred people.

As I rode the ferry into Lysebotn, I passed under Kjerag and its eight separate exit points. Huge cliffs surrounded us during the entire trip, but the three-thousand-foot vertical walls of Kjerag were overwhelming on a different level. They are so massive and overhanging that it's hard to understand how nature could have created them. How did enormous glaciers carve through granite to create such beautiful platforms for human flight? Knowing that tomorrow I would hike up the back of these monsters and jump off them for the first time was something magical to me. Here I was, finally getting to live my dream.

On the ferry, I met two jumpers who had also signed up for the BR training course. Ed, an older man from northern California with a mustache, and a big guy who called himself "Bubba." Bubba had a loud voice and was wearing a t-shirt that said "Super Pig" across the chest. The way he was dressed and his larger size surprised me. We had been informed this was a trip with rigorous hikes in ever-changing weather; Bubba looked like he would have a hard time walking across the street, not to mention up a three-thousand-foot mountain. But he was a nice guy with strong opinions on all subjects big and small, and he brought a lot to our group. He filled a room when he entered it, and everyone knew he was there, like it or not. Ed, on the other hand, was quiet with a gentle disposition. He owned a small business, had a family, and for some reason, just didn't seem like someone who would be interested in BASE jumping. But after talking to him for a little while, I learned that he had thousands of skydives and had been doing it for over twenty years.

As the ferry arrived at the dock in Lysebotn, we saw Todd and Anne there waiting for us. Being "back in the day" at this point, there were no hotels to stay in and only one camping area, which had a big white house they also rented out as a hostel. Naturally, the house was completely booked, so the locals let our group stay in an abandoned schoolhouse. Many of the families with children had moved away, and the building had been empty for some time. Two other BASE-jumping students were waiting for us at the school when we arrived: a lanky English gentleman named Tony and a blond, long-haired expat who lived in Yemen named Steve. We were all given rooms and instructed to lay out our sleeping bags for a hybrid version of indoor camping, Norwegian style.

That evening, everyone got busy setting up their gear for the next day. Todd and Anne were doing gear inspections to make sure everyone had what they needed to jump safely. Some people needed to borrow pilot chutes, others needed longer bridles, but in most cases, our gear was up to date and BASE specific. The only exception was the Englishman, Tony. He was the only one who had brought a skydiving rig, apparently having asked BR in advance if he could bring it and modify it for jumping high cliffs.

Todd and Anne weren't fond of this idea for many reasons. In BASE jumping, we pull so low that a reserve is useless and just gets in the way. The reserve in skydiving gear is heavy, making the hikes on big mountains more difficult. Skydiving equipment isn't manufactured to deal with the extra stresses of the BASE environment, whereas BASE equipment is over-built to handle the heavier opening shock of slider-down deployments. Even when you are jumping slider-up, you tend to pack for much faster openings, which can be hard on skydiving equipment. In other words, a skydiving rig just makes the system more complicated, and the more complicated the system, the more likely something can go wrong. Simple is best when it comes to BASE jumping. But BR had been experimenting with different ways to make skydiving gear suitable for big walls, so they decided to allow Tony's rig. They helped him set it up with a special deployment bag that had a tail pocket, allowing him to free stow his lines to make a bag lock less likely and hopefully prevent off-heading openings. They gave him a longer bridle and a larger pilot chute that wasn't collapsible, and that was the extent of what they could do to make his gear more BASE friendly. I didn't like the looks of it, but I wasn't in charge.

But there was one other issue with using skydiving gear at this location. One thing that makes Kjerag a relatively safe place to jump is that you land on a beach close to a saltwater fjord. If you have any issues with your canopy, like a tension knot or line-over malfunction, you still have the water as an out. There is a saying in BASE: "You dry faster than you heal." Water is much softer than rocks when you are coming in fast. But skydiving equipment costs about double what BASE gear costs. Just landing in saltwater can add years to a rig, and if you allow it to dry without rinsing it with fresh water first, the saltwater can cause a lot of damage. In some cases, people will try to land dry so they don't damage their equipment, making bad decisions at the last second and getting themselves hurt.

Tony seemed like he was all set, but something felt off. Would he try to land dry if something went wrong? I reminded myself I was only there as a student, and the instructors had given him a green light. Once my own gear was secured, I went to sleep with a lot on my mind.

The next morning, we woke up bright and early to head out for our first big hike and, hopefully, big flight. The sky looked like it might rain, but you can't be sure what the weather will do in Norway. In a three-hour hike, there can be sunny skies, rain, hail, then sunny skies again. The best bet is to just go for it no matter what the weather looks like and hope it clears by the time you get to the exit point. So that's what we did.

The owners of the campsite also ran the van that would drive us up the mountain to the beginning of the hike, and the boat that would pick us up in the landing area. The boat didn't just ferry people back to the camping area; it was also used for safety in case someone landed in the water. Even strong swimmers run the risk of drowning if they land in the water with a lot of gear on.

We all loaded into the van to drive up the mountain. The road is one of the windiest roads on Earth and snakes back and forth for over two thousand vertical feet. There's even a tunnel that does a 180-degree turn through the mountain itself. This tunnel has one lane and a turnout inside so cars can pass each other, but with so little traffic in the area, that doesn't happen often.

I was starting to feel a bit carsick by the time we got to the trailhead. The constant switchback turns and the camp owners' son driving like a psychopath made for a nauseating combination. When the van finally came to a stop, I couldn't get out fast enough. I stepped out of the van and looked at the first slope we would have to climb. Anne called it "Wakeup Hill."

Our larger friend from the Midwest didn't look excited, but he went with Anne to the front of the pack anyway. About twenty minutes later, he had dropped to the back and was turning a slight shade of red with a mix of yellow. Bubba's "wakeup" was that he was in bad shape, and we needed to take regular breaks to ensure his heart didn't explode. It took a while, to say the least, but we enjoyed a slight downhill bit at the top of Wakeup Hill. Then we reached Warmup Hill, which was way steeper and much longer. We were all pretty sure Bubba was going to pass out, so we took turns carrying his gear for him. His big personality and booming voice had taken a backseat to gulping for air and wiping sweat from his eyes. By the time we crested Warmup Hill, Bubba didn't look good at all. Anne informed him that we had another decline ahead with a stream where we could rest, but after that we still had Hell Hill to deal with. Bubba's face twisted into a look of horror and desperation. We all felt for the dude; he really looked like he was being tortured, and our hike was only getting harder by the minute.

When we got to the stream, we all sat down and took turns drinking the fresh water coming off the glacier. It was some of the most amazing, refreshing, and tasty water I had ever experienced, and I needed it badly. I keep mentioning how hard things were for Bubba, but to be honest, I wasn't exactly an Olympic athlete at that point in my life, either. I was suffering too. That was, hands down, the hardest hike I had experienced, especially since I was carrying over thirty pounds of gear on my back. Hell Hill lived up to its name. By the time we made it to the top, I was pretty sure I was going to die; I still have no idea how Bubba was able to do it. He moved on sheer willpower alone. I kept thinking, *If he can't jump, they'll need a helicopter rescue to get him back down.*

Luckily, the rest of the hike was mostly flat. We ended up passing exit point after exit point. Todd and Anne liked to take their students to the highest, most-overhanging part of the wall, and that was Exit Point 7. Of course, that exit was the farthest away and took the most effort to reach, but no one complained. There was an unspoken agreement among us that if we were going to come all this way, we wanted the biggest and best jump. We finally made it after about four and a half hours. Many Norwegians can make that same hike in an hour and a half, which is one reason Americans have a bad reputation for being fat and lazy.

After everyone rested for a bit, we all started gearing up. Todd and Anne were in walkie communication with the boat below and asked if the other exit points were clear. The boat responded with an all-clear, and Todd asked me if I would like to go first.

"Absolutely," I said, and he informed me I should take a fourteen- to eighteen-second delay and track straight for the water.

Exit Point 7 slopes downward and comes to a point that looks kind of like a hawk's beak, and at the tip of that beak is a chip in the rock that's the perfect place for a foot. I stood there with my foot on the edge and looked down at the three-thousand-foot vertical drop. For the first time, I saw how stunningly beautiful the fjord was.

The jade green vegetation hanging on the massive gray granite cliffs looked like an enchanted forest floor from that distance. The water from the ocean running up the fjord was a deep, dark blue. The feeling of exposure, of being a tiny creature standing on the edge of something so immense, was awe inspiring. Not only being immersed in nature, but seeing it from a bird's-eye perspective was beyond anything I could have imagined. I wasn't sure what I would experience when setting out on this journey, but Kjerag was way bigger and much more beautiful than my mind's eye could have envisioned. My senses were overwhelmed.

Something occurred to me then, something I hadn't considered until that very moment. I thought, *This is why I exist. This is why I eat food, drink water, breathe air, and wake up in the morning.*

This is my purpose.

I counted down from five, but as I got to one, I couldn't help hesitating. I took one more deep breath, then stepped off, opened my arms, and started to fly. I put my arms to my sides, straightened my legs, and slid across the air away from the cliff. This movement is called tracking. I tracked over a series of ledges first, watching them approach and then disappear behind me as I moved at ever-increasing speed away from the gigantic wall of rock. I watched green, grass-covered earth moving under me as I passed over a rocky beach and flew out over the water. I could tell my time was almost up, so I reached back, wrapped my fingers around the pilot chute, and pulled. Instantly, it grabbed the air and flew away as my descent slowed. I hadn't counted during the freefall, so I didn't have any idea how long a delay I had taken, but my gut had steered me right. My feet touched down in the middle of the grass landing area, where the emotions of the moment finally caught up with me. I bundled my canopy in my arms and sat by a few big boulders to be alone for a little while. I needed a moment to process what I had just experienced. After a while, I looked up as a large shadow covered me. It was Bubba, and I watched as he made a perfect landing on the grass. I yelled over to him, "CONGRATULATIONS!" He looked tired, but I could see excitement in his eyes.

This routine of hiking and jumping continued for a week. We woke up early, put on rain gear, hiked, got rained on, then waited at the exit for the weather to clear to hopefully do a jump. If the rain didn't stop, we had to make the epic hike back down the mountain, which was sometimes more treacherous than the hike up. Some days we would get two jumps, but most days we would get one. The weather in Norway was challenging, and a lot of our time was spent sitting in the big white house at the camping area, watching old BASE-jumping videos people had left behind. By day nine, my record of BASE jumps had gone from six to twelve. It was slow going, but even with all the sitting around in the rain and hiking in the mud, it was the most fun I'd had in my entire life.

On day nine, I decided to do something special. The first footage I had seen of BASE jumping was of a man doing a gainer off a cliff in France. A gainer is when you look out from the edge like you are going to do a normal jump, but then do a forward-moving backflip instead of just stepping off. In diving, they call it a "reverse flip." Seeing that this was the jump that had inspired me to come to Kjerag, I felt like I had to do a gainer. Todd and Anne took us to Exit Point 6 this time. The exit was flat—a great place to practice running exits. Todd asked me what kind of jump I wanted to do, expecting me to say either a running or poised exit.

"I'm gonna try my first gainer," I told him with a grin. He shook his head and gave me a look that said, "Of course you are."

"I've never even tried that myself," he said. "I'm not sure how to instruct you. Some of my friends like to do them, and they said all you need to do is push your hips toward the horizon as you jump off."

"Is it easier to do it at a run, or from a standing position?"

He shrugged. "Running is probably easier since you'll have the momentum to take you away from the cliff. That'll make it less likely to hit your head." He paused, then added, "Don't hit your head."

Todd's advice made sense, so I said, "Okay, I am ready to go." He wished me good luck and I started my five-second countdown. As I reached one, I started running towards the edge and jumped out, pushing my hips to the sky and—nothing happened. I was in dead air, stuck on my back, watching the cliff rushing by in an odd direction. Time felt distorted and I couldn't tell how long I was falling on my back. I finally flipped over by doing a half-twist to my left, which meant I was now facing the cliff wall. I wasn't sure how close to impact I was. I watched as the wall roared past my face at an increasing rate of speed. I dropped my left shoulder to execute what felt like a slow, flat turn away from the wall. I ended the turn as I faced away from the granite wall of death, then put my arms to my side, straightened my legs, and tracked for dear life. I ended up getting all the way to the beach before deploying, then landed in the main grass landing area, which came as a surprise considering how crappy my exit started.

Shortly after I set down, Ed landed next to me and instantly made fun of my horrible first attempt at a gainer.

"I've never seen someone spin their arms like that," he said through a fit of laughter. "Like you were rolling up the windows on a car in a rainstorm!" He windmilled his arms as he cackled.

I informed him he should play a little game called Hide-and-Go-Fuck-Yourself, but laughed right along with him.

We were both still laughing our asses off when the men in our safety boat started screaming at us. They yelled, "RUN DOWN THE BEACH NOW!!!" over and over, then sped off as fast as the tiny dinghy with a one-horsepower engine could go. Ed told me his knees weren't good enough to run over boulders and that I should just go. So, I started running with no idea what I was running for, other than it must be something bad.

Coming over a hill of boulders, I saw a man lying face-down in about a foot of water on the shore. His canopy was spread out around him, floating in the water like a menacing jellyfish. I knew right away, *This man is dead*. I started sprinting and watched as the boat ran aground. The two men jumped out, grabbing the dead man and flipping him onto his back. One of the men started hitting the obviously drowned man in the chest as hard as he could while yelling something in Norwegian. I couldn't understand any of it. During my training to become a scuba-diving instructor, I had taken medic first-aid, so I knew what this man was doing wasn't helpful.

As I got to the men, I pushed the Norwegian off the drowned man and told him, "You are not helping, you are hurting!" I could see the Norwegian was panicking and desperately trying to wake the man up. I looked down and recognized that it was the Englishman, Tony. I had been jumping with him all week and hadn't spoken to him much. His skin was purple and lacerations crisscrossed his face. His left arm and left leg were both twisted in unnatural ways, obviously broken in multiple places. I checked to see if he was breathing. He was not, and it looked like he hadn't been breathing for quite a while. I estimated that the run had taken me at least six minutes, and I had no idea how long he had been face-down in the water before the boat guys started yelling, but I knew it was way too long to be without air. I checked for a heartbeat and, miraculously, felt one. It was light, but he did have a pulse. I pinched his nose and lifted his chin, tilting his head back to clear the airway, and gave him a single, deep rescue breath. Tony instantly vomited blood, bile, and saltwater into my mouth. I gagged and instinctively pulled my head back, tilting his head to the side as he continued to evacuate the contents of his lungs and stomach across the shallow rocks. He remained unconscious, but began shallow, labored breathing.

After a few stressful minutes, Anne landed next to us, dumped her gear, and took over the situation. Anne was a registered nurse and by far the most qualified person to deal with the situation. She asked me to help her remove Tony's equipment and took special care not to move him too much. I did my best to lend a hand without getting in her way. The men brought us a rescue backboard from the small dinghy, and with their help, we all picked Tony up and strapped him to the backboard. We had to be cautious during this process because we didn't know if he had a neck or back injury. Then we moved him out of the water and wrapped him in a space blanket from an emergency kit on the safety boat.

As we finished tucking the crackling blanket around Tony, we heard a chopper off in the distance; the safety boat had sent out a rescue call. In moments, the chopper landed close by and the paramedics rushed toward us. They did a few more things to stabilize the situation, then everyone helped carry Tony to the chopper and loaded him on board. The paramedics warned us to keep low and stay clear of the tail rotor to avoid getting chopped to bits. Once Tony was loaded, the paramedics jumped back in the chopper and took off for the hospital. The entire thing, from me finding Tony to the chopper taking off, took less than twenty minutes. I was shocked at the speed and efficiency of those professionals.

Later, we found out Tony had a dislocated shoulder, a broken femur, and a crushed heel on his left side, as well as head trauma and superficial lacerations on his face. He had not been breathing for almost eight minutes by the time I got to him, but the cold waters of Norway had slowed his heartrate down, so the damage to his brain was minimal. It took some time, but Tony eventually made a full recovery.

Several factors led to Tony's accident. As I mentioned, people tend to avoid landing in saltwater with their gear. Tony had not read the windsock correctly and accidentally set up his landing approach downwind. Landing downwind means having a great deal of speed as you set down. Tony's landing zone had uneven ground and basketball-sized boulders, which usually translate into broken bones. Sometimes, when inexperienced jumpers find themselves close to the ground and heading downwind, they panic and do something called "hook turn," which is when a pilot aggressively pulls a toggle towards the ground and makes the canopy turn sharply. Then the pilot swings out to the side and the canopy dives to the ground. If you don't have enough altitude for the canopy to recover, the pilot can make contact with the ground at the same time as the canopy, usually leading to serious injury or even death. In Tony's case, he got away with only serious injury, but all he had to do to avoid that was do a gentle turnout towards the water and he would have landed wet, but safe. But in his panic, Tony made an aggressive hook turn that forced him into the ground at high speed in one foot of water. This ended up breaking him in multiple places, and his gear still got wet anyway.

Later that evening, when we got back to the schoolhouse, everyone was a little quieter than usual. I hadn't had much time to think about my failed gainer, but I decided to see what had gone wrong. Todd had taken a video of my jump and I thought I could learn something from watching it. I felt like I had been trapped on my back for over eight seconds and didn't think I could have messed it up any worse. Todd told me he didn't think I was on my back that long and thought I had recovered quickly. We got out the video and watched it. It looked horrible, for sure. Seeing myself flailing in the air, trapped on my back, and waving my arms around was not pretty. But I timed the moment and realized something interesting. From the time my feet left the cliff to the time I was facing away, my tracking was less than four seconds. I couldn't believe it. But then it dawned on me that I had screwed that gainer up as badly as possible and still recovered in four seconds. After watching that video, I realized I could do gainers off any object with at least a four-second delay. My mistake showed me that I had more margin for error than I had previously thought.

The next day, the group got together and headed back up the mountain, but Bubba opted to stay back and take a little break after what had happened with Tony. Between those two absences, our little group felt pretty sparse. The rest of us made it to Exit Point 6 in well under two hours, which was a record for us as lazy Americans. Anne had to keep reminding everyone she was from New Zealand so she didn't get mistaken for one of us, but I noticed she got winded just as often. As we geared up once more, Todd asked if I was going for another gainer.

"I sure am," I told him. "But this time I'm doing it from a standing position. I think that will make it easier for me." Todd wished me luck and I moved into position, planted my feet, and threw my first perfect gainer off the edge. It felt amazing, and I celebrated all the way down. From that point forward, I didn't do another flat jump. All I wanted to do was acrobatics. Every single jump I did for the rest of the trip, and for the next couple years, had a flip of some kind thrown in somewhere.

To me, that was my first real BASE-jumping trip, and it foreshadowed a lot of what was to come. Life is like a sine wave—it has ups and downs that follow a similar trajectory. I feel the goal of most normal people is to live a life with a nice balance, where the highs and lows stay within a reasonable parameter over the longest time frame possible. BASE jumping is anything but balanced or reasonable. It follows a similar structure of ups and downs, but the ups are just way higher, and the downs are way lower, with a much shorter timeline.

Tony's accident gave me a glimpse of just how low BASE jumping can get. My reality shifted from a high level of excitement—laughing with a new buddy—to instant darkness at seeing a drowned man lying face-down in the waters of Kjerag. That's the risk-and-reward aspect of BASE jumping: exhilarating highs and mind-crushing lows.

CHAPTER ELEVEN

ARCO, ITALY, AND THE FRENCH CONNECTION

One day, I was training at Perris Skydive when I saw a flyer for a new company called Dream Up. The flyer was promoting a trip to jump off Angel Falls in Venezuela, the highest waterfall on planet Earth with a 3,200-foot vertical drop. A man by the name of Tom Sanders had been taking people on trips to jump the waterfall for years, but his trips were super expensive: over $5,000 to do one jump, and that didn't even include airfare. Anyone could tell you that's an excessive amount of money. Dream Up was advertising the trip for $2,000 with as many jumps as we could do in three days for $200 each. The expensive part was getting the chopper to the location, but once it was there, ferrying people from the landing area to the top of the waterfall was quick and inexpensive. The offer sounded too good to be true, but I wrote down the email address and sent a message the moment I got home. Within a few hours, I got a response with where to send my money to secure the spot, and they also included a lot of information about Angel Falls and what the trip would entail. I informed my parents that I was going to need to take time off work to go BASE jumping in Venezuela, and they said, "Sounds good, Jeb. Have fun and be careful."

I responded with, "I will be as careful as a person can be when jumping off the highest waterfall in the world."

Within a few months, every slot was filled and the trip sold out. About two weeks before the trip was scheduled to go, I got an email with all the other jumpers CC'd on the message. The list of jumpers was impressive. I was new to the sport, but even I recognized a few of the names as some of the most respected jumpers on the planet.

The two names that stood out were Slim and Yuri, literal living legends at the time. The email explained that the helicopter we were going to use somehow crashed in the jungle, so the company that owned it was going to need to bring in a different chopper, but the cost would almost double. Francois, the owner of Dream Up, said he felt this was extortion, so he was going to cancel the trip and refund everyone's money. He went on to say he was sorry for the late cancellation, and he knew people had already paid for plane tickets that couldn't be refunded. He explained his company was new and he didn't want to start off this way, so he wanted to make up for this inconvenience by offering a completely free guided tour to BASE-jumping sights across Italy and Switzerland. I was bummed but understood completely; what are you going to do about a helicopter crashing in the jungle, right? So, I responded that I had already taken the time off work and would love to meet up with him in Europe. I only had sixteen BASE jumps and was looking to gather more experience, so to me, this was still good news. I thought getting to jump multiple objects in Europe might be better than just a few off a single object in Venezuela. And a free guided tour through Italy and Switzerland sounded great to my novice ears.

Francois and I started communicating in private emails and set up a time to meet at the Geneva Airport in Switzerland. The best time of year to jump Angel Falls in Venezuela is February, but that is definitely not the best time of year to jump in Europe. I was new and didn't know this. A few weeks later, I was standing at a baggage carousel in Geneva, watching strangers' bags go around in circles as I waited for mine to appear. Thirty minutes went by and one of my bags finally showed up—the one with my clothes. Great, now all I needed was my bag with my BASE gear in it. An hour went by, and all the people that were on my plane had left. I started to worry that my gear had been lost, so I headed over to the baggage desk and found a huge waiting line; it looked like I wasn't the only one missing bags from the flight. It took me another hour before I was able to talk to a representative. My concern grew with every passing moment because I had only spoken to Francois via email and didn't have any other way to contact him. Cell phones were still a rare thing at the time, and I didn't have one, nor did I have his phone number, so it wouldn't have helped anyway. When I finally got help, I explained what my bag looked like and filled out a few forms. They were able to locate the bag while I was standing there, but they wouldn't be able to get it to Geneva until the next day. I informed them I was being picked up by a friend and we would be driving to Italy that night. They explained it wasn't a problem and would forward my bag wherever I wanted; I just had to let them know where I was going to be. At that moment, I didn't know the answer to where I'd be, so they gave me a phone number and a case number. They told me to contact them once I knew my location and they would send the bag along. I was pretty stressed out; without my BASE gear, this trip was pointless. I was there to jump, and I needed that bag to do it.

By the time I made it through customs, it had taken over three and a half hours, and I couldn't see Francois anywhere. I was trying to figure out where I could get internet access so I could write him when a man walked up to me and asked in a strong French accent if I was Jeb Corliss. It was Francois.

I responded, "Yes, thank you so much for waiting." I explained the airline had lost my bag of gear and told me it wouldn't show up until the next day. He informed me we couldn't wait for it; Yuri and a friend were going to be meeting us in Arco, Italy, the next day, and we had to get moving. This three-hour delay meant we were behind schedule and might not be able to get to Arco in time to check into a hotel.

I asked Francois if I should have them send the bag to Arco and he said, "No, there isn't an airport anywhere near there. We will have to have them send it to Rome." After meeting with Yuri in Arco, Francois' plan was to take us all to Rome and try to do some jumps there. I was a bit pissed because it meant I wouldn't be able to jump in Arco, but he assured me after Rome we would head back to Arco for more jumping. Francois let me borrow his cell phone, and I called the number the airline had given me, gave them my case number, and told them to forward my bag to Rome. I then followed Francois through the airport to the parking lot, where he had a tiny European car. It was so small I thought it was meant as a joke; the thing looked like a roller skate with an engine. I shoved myself inside, feeling like a circus clown.

Francois was an interesting guy. He was about five feet, nine inches tall, thin, and wore glasses. He had an odd haircut that made him look a little like a nerdy computer programmer. He was stereotypically French in his attitude towards Americans, and I just smiled at his incredibly rude statements. For some reason, he also felt that all important things done in history had either been done in France or by French people. I found him super amusing, though, and his personality had me laughing out loud. I'm not sure if he thought I was laughing with him or at him, but I don't think it mattered to him either way since I was American.

During the drive from Geneva to Arco, Francois pointed out BASE jumps along the way, explaining how it was way too cold with too much snow to jump any of them right now. He explained that this time of year wasn't ideal for jumping in Europe and that was why we needed to head as far south as we could if we wanted to get any jumps in. I kind of felt like this information would have been better to get a few weeks earlier, before I decided to make this trip, but here I was, just excited to be traveling with the possibility of getting any jumps at all. By the time we got to Arco, it was too late to check into any hotels, which surprised me a little because I had never dealt with this issue before. Why wouldn't there be someone to check you in after 9:00 p.m., like every hotel I had ever been in before? We ended up having to sleep in his tiny car that night, which was not the most comfortable of arrangements. I am six feet, three inches tall and his car was built for smaller human beings. The engineers who designed that vehicle definitely didn't consider that someone might want to sleep in it.

The next morning, after freezing our balls off all night and getting basically no sleep at all, we found a hotel and checked in. Francois told me he had my money from the Angel Falls trip with him and, if I wanted, he could just cover all the costs of this trip and then he would give me the balance at the end. He explained it would just be easier because I wouldn't have to visit banks all the time and pay high exchange rates and fees. It seemed to make sense and I felt it would make everything much easier, so I agreed. (This actually turned out to be the smartest thing I did that whole trip, and it will become clear why later.) After checking in, we headed to a small breakfast place to meet with Yuri and his buddy, Mike.

Yuri was a Russian with a talent for computers and a love for skydiving. He came from a family of jumpers and had several jumps before he was even born. His mother had made a name for herself in Russia as a test jumper back in the sixties and seventies and jumped while she was pregnant with him. Yuri did his first skydives outside his mother's belly when he was only thirteen years old, and his first BASE jumps at twenty, so he had a big head start on me.

While living in Russia, he used to frequent the first computer forums dedicated to the sport of skydiving. There, he started an online friendship with a man who worked at the World Bank. He was coming to visit Moscow on business and wanted to do a few jumps. Yuri showed him around and did some skydives, and they became friends in the real world. The man liked Yuri and offered him a job in Washington, DC, working in the IT department. That was how Yuri earned his living and got the freedom to travel around the world BASE jumping, which is when I met him. Yuri was the first true friend I made in BASE jumping. I respected him immensely. To me, he was the best BASE jumper in the world at that time, and I felt like I had so much to learn from him. If I had questions, he was the one I would ask for years to come.

This was the only trip I would end up taking with Mike, and I didn't get to know him very well. He was good friends with Yuri, and they would travel together from time to time. He was a doctor from Kentucky, and he struck me as a true southern boy. A super-friendly nice guy. I remember him telling me the first thing he did with new canopies was put them in the washing machine. He didn't like packing new canopies, which I found strange. I thought, *Why not just buy used gear then?* But I was starting to realize BASE jumping had a diverse group of people who came from many different walks of life, each with their own host of idiosyncrasies.

As we ate breakfast, we discussed our plans and I told Yuri about my gear being sent to Rome. Yuri had a friend there that knew of a few possible objects we could jump in the city. The decision was made to jump in Arco that day and the next morning. We would then head to Rome to do a little sightseeing, pick up my gear, and hook up with Yuri's friend, Simone, who would hopefully show us around.

After finishing breakfast, everyone—except me—got their gear, and we drove to a small cafeteria across the street from the landing area under Brento, a four-thousand-foot cliff on the outskirts of Arco, Italy. It has a massive overhang for about ten seconds. After that comes a huge ledge leading to hills covered with large trees. You couldn't take long delays, even though the cliff was huge, and you would have to open your parachute high in order to make it to the landing zone. We drove in separate cars because we needed two shuttle cars to do this jump. We left one car at the cafe and then drove the second car up small streets snaking up the back of the mountain. There was a place we could park in the forest at the trailhead of a forty-minute hike to the exit point. After the jump, a couple jumpers would get in the car parked at the cafe and drive back up to get the other car while everyone else packed. This shuttling of cars was time consuming and not ideal, but it was the most efficient way to do the jump back then.

As we got to the landing area, we noticed that clouds covered Brento's entire face. These conditions made it impossible to jump, but Yuri and Francois both felt it might clear by the time they drove up and did the hike. They handed me a walkie talkie so I could watch the conditions and give them updates from the ground. As they drove away, I went into the cafe to order a hot chocolate. When I walked through the door, the first thing I noticed were pictures on the back wall of people BASE jumping Brento. I ordered, paid, then sat at a booth with my back to the wall, looking out the window at the enormous cliff across the street. I wished I was hiking up with everyone else. It was upsetting to realize I had come all this way and couldn't jump because the airline had lost my gear. It's funny: when you're young, you always feel like you're missing out on things. I felt this was my only chance to do this, and the opportunity had been stolen from me by an evil baggage handler. Little did I know, I would come back to this place many times over the next twenty years and would do hundreds of jumps from this location.

After a few hours of sitting, I heard Yuri's voice over the walkie asking, "Jeb, how are the clouds looking? We are in a total whiteout up here and can't see anything."

I walked outside, looked up at the wall, and said, "The clouds are about halfway down the vertical part of the wall."

Yuri responded, "That sounds jumpable to me. Just to double-check, the lower half of the vertical part of the wall is clear, correct?"

"Yes, the lower half is clear."

He went on, "We're going to gear up now. If anything changes, let us know immediately."

After about twenty more minutes, Yuri came back on the walkie, "I am ready to jump. Have the conditions changed?"

I informed him, "No, they are the same; the upper half of the vertical wall is covered in cloud."

"See you soon," he said, and I didn't hear anything again. The next thing I saw was an open canopy lining up to land. As Yuri landed, I ran over to him, and he grabbed the walkie to tell the rest of the group conditions were good and they would leave the cloud after about six seconds in freefall.

"Wait," I said, "how did you know you were flying away from the wall if you couldn't see anything in the cloud?"

He said, "I could see a shadow of yellow behind me from the cliff. That helped keep me oriented while I was in the whiteout." I remember thinking, *He's insane and that's not something I ever want to try*. It would be way too easy to become disoriented like that. If you went head-down on exit and ended up on your back, it could go bad in an instant. But his method had seemed to work out for him that day, and the rest of the guys didn't seem to mind, either. They all jumped, and they were all fine.

That evening, talking over pizza, we saw that a weather system was moving over Arco the next day, making another jump unlikely. So, everyone decided we would head to Rome the next morning. Over dinner, Francois offered the same deal to Yuri and Mike that he had offered me. He would pay their bills on the trip and give them the balance once the trip was over. I could see this made Yuri uncomfortable. Yuri responded with, "No, thank you. I will pay my own way and you can just transfer the money to my bank account."

Francois responded, "No problem," and didn't mention it again. But this interaction gave me an uneasy feeling and I got a sense that Francois might be trying to rip me off in some way. It was too hard for me to keep a proper accounting of what was being spent, but I decided I would just make sure to spend as much as I could to ensure that I got my money's worth.

The next day, we packed up all our stuff and drove to Rome. The first order of business for me when entering Rome was to call and check on my bag. The airline informed me it had arrived, so I could pick it up whenever I wanted. This made me happy because that meant my gear hadn't been completely lost and I'd have it again soon. Francois took me to deal with my gear while Yuri and Mike went to meet Yuri's local connection, Simone. Simone was one of the more experienced Italian BASE jumpers at the time and had data on pretty much every jump Italy had to offer in the late nineties.

After getting my bag, we met everyone for lunch to talk about our next move. Simone only had one jump in Rome that was possible on such short notice. It was a 280-foot freestanding gas tower. When I heard how high it was, I lost interest immediately. I didn't come all this way to jump off super low shit I could do back in the US; I was here for big walls and told them I could be ground crew for them.

We spent the rest of the day doing normal tourist stuff, seeing the Colosseum, Pantheon, Vatican, and so forth. I will say, seeing the Vatican was impressive. Being in the main chamber of Saint Paul's Cathedral, looking at 365-foot-high ceilings that were built over 340 years ago was amazing. You could see how people might believe it took a higher power to create something of that magnitude back then. The edifice wasn't just summoned up with a large amount of coins, either; it had been built with human suffering and death, and war and Catholic conquest for generations. It stood upon inquisitions that spanned the surface of the planet, bathed in the blood of sycophants and nonbelievers alike. That was the feeling I had standing in this building. Everything was made of marble, gold, and ivory. The number of priceless artifacts on display was staggering; so many resources just sitting around for decoration. It was a shocking experience, and I don't think I saw it in quite the same way as the people around me.

That evening, everyone went to jump the gas tower and I ground-crewed. After everyone landed, we went to dinner and made plans to head back up to northern Italy to spend more time jumping Arco. Simone told us about another jump that had just opened a few weeks before. It was called Campione and was named after the town it towered over. He told us it was a one-thousand-foot cliff and probably one of the most beautiful jumps in all of Italy. It overlooks a beautiful lake, and with a good track, you can deploy over the water. The town is classic old Italy and striking to look at. Yuri took down all the details. Simone told us to be careful, though, because with the last group that jumped, one of the jumpers got a 180 and ended up hitting the wall and getting stuck on a ledge about 300 feet off the ground. This triggered a rescue that shut down the only road in and out of town, which upset the locals in a serious way, as you can imagine. Simone told us not to talk about BASE jumping while we were in public and, when we jumped, to leave quickly.

As we drove back to Arco the next day, I was starting to get excited about the jump. Yuri told us some of his Russian friends had just arrived in Arco and were waiting for us. Mike called them the "Russian Mafia," and I wasn't sure if he was kidding or being serious. I asked Yuri if they were really mafia, and Yuri said, "Everyone in Russia is related to mafia in one way or another these days." Again, I wasn't sure if he was being serious. When we got there, sure enough, a van filled with Russians was waiting for us.

They joined us for my first trip to jump Brento. We did the hike, got to the top, and started gearing up. As I was putting my rig on, I saw one of the Russians pull something strange out of his bag. It looked kind of like a wetsuit with wings sewn between the arms and legs. I asked Yuri what it was, and he said it was a homemade wingsuit inspired by Patrick de Gayardon. I had seen pictures of them in magazines, but this was my first time seeing one in person. I had only seen them jumped from aircraft on TV and didn't know people were jumping them from cliffs at this point. I decided I didn't want to jump just yet; I wanted to see the wingsuit guy go first.

He walked up to the edge, counted down from five to one in Russian, and stepped off the edge. At first, it looked like he was just falling straight down like normal, but after about four seconds, you could tell he was moving forward a little. Then at about six seconds, he was really moving forward. Everyone made little sounds of amazement at how far he was flying. After about twelve seconds, which was when most people would have pulled, he was still going strong and had flown farther from the wall than any of us had ever seen before. Yuri lost his mind and started yelling, "It looks like a jet version of hang gliding!" over and over. The wingsuit guy took about a thirty second delay before pulling, which was the longest delay any of us had ever seen before. Yuri and I looked at each other and I said, "Where did he get that suit? I need one right now." We all did our jumps and, after landing, started talking about how to get wingsuits of our own. The excitement I had been feeling about doing my first jump off Brento had just become overshadowed by this new, amazing technology that made everything else seem almost pointless by comparison. We could all see it was the future of BASE jumping and would lead to a revolution in the sport. That wingsuit was going to change the way we looked at cliffs, landing areas, and possibilities.

This was an exciting time. It felt like we had found a new horizon that no one even knew was there—a whole new sport with all kinds of possibilities. It must have been what it felt like when boats were discovered; suddenly you could go places humans had never been and discover things people didn't even know existed. It was a mind-expanding experience. There is a quote by Oliver Wendell Holmes that expresses this idea perfectly: "Man's mind, once stretched by a new idea, never regains its original dimensions." At this point in history, man had climbed all the highest mountains, discovered all the new lands, been to the bottom of the deepest oceans, and even walked on the surface of the moon. Finding new horizons to explore had become nearly impossible, but the wingsuits could open up new methods to experience the world in ways humans hadn't even realized were possible yet.

CHAPTER TWELVE

THE POORLY PLANNED EXPEDITION

We spent about ten days jumping with the Russians before Yuri and Mike had to head back to the real world to start working again. We spent most of that time jumping Arco and Campione, with many close calls and general mayhem at every turn. Francois had a 180 at Campione and came inches from a cliff strike where he used the words, "Oh fuck" to describe the situation. I laughed that someone so French, who disliked all things American, didn't use French words in his brush with his own mortality. Yuri had a super low pull that almost put him in the water. I had a landing where my canopy hung up on a street sign that made me fall hard, hyperextending my left ring finger so badly I couldn't bend it properly for almost three months. But all in all, it was a fun and successful trip.

One evening after Yuri and Mike left, Francois and I were eating dinner with the rest of the Russians in a little pizzeria at the bottom of the cliff in Campione. As we ate, Francois and I discussed what we should do next. I still had two weeks left on my trip and we were getting a bit bored jumping the same two objects every day. Francois called friends in Magland, France, and Lauterbrunnen, Switzerland, to see if the conditions had improved enough to do some jumping in either location. Both friends said no; the winter was exceptionally harsh and both locations were having record amounts of snowfall, making conditions unsafe for jumping.

The look on Francois' face told me he was fed up, and he said, "Jeb, I think I am just going to drive home and get back to work."

I responded, "No way, dude. I still have two weeks left on my trip. I have no way to get around and I came out here to jump with you." He tried to convince me that I had the Russians to jump with now and I no longer needed him. I didn't feel comfortable with that idea, seeing as I still wasn't sure if Yuri was joking about them being Russian mafia or not. I didn't really want to play around with that, so I suggested that we go to Angel Falls.

Francois looked at me with a puzzled look on his face. He said, "Jeb, we are in Italy right now. Angel Falls is in Venezuela. That is on the other side of the planet."

I said, "So? How much could a plane ticket to Venezuela cost? You still have my money, right? We could use it to buy tickets and do the trip."

Francois tried to explain: "But Jeb, the helicopter crashed; we have no way to get on top of the waterfall."

"Let's drive to Paris, France, tonight and get on a plane to Caracas. From there, we can catch a bus to Ciudad Bolívar and then catch a cab to the closest airport. Once we get to the airport, we find a pilot and pay him to fly us over the waterfall. Once we're over the waterfall, we hand the pilot another hundred bucks and just jump out of the plane, landing on top of the waterfall. Once on top, we can repack our gear, jump off Angel Falls, and land in the jungle below. We can then hike four kilometers to the main river, put all our stuff in waterproof bags, and use them to float fifty kilometers downstream to Canaima, where we can catch a flight back to civilization."

He got a big smile on his face and said, "Okay, let's do it." We asked for our check and started getting ready to leave, but the Russians who had been sitting at the table with us and listening to our conversation were looking at us in confusion.

Dan, the leader of the group, said in a strong Russian accent, "Wait, what are you doing?" He had listened to our brief conversation and asked, "Are you guys really going to go to Angel Falls right now?"

We both looked at him and, almost in unison, said, "Yes, we are." Dan just started clapping with a grin that split his face from ear to ear. He expressed how truly insane this idea was and how totally unprepared we were, and he loved it. He couldn't believe that was the extent of our planning. Honestly, if I had put any more thought into it, I probably wouldn't have done it. It was the fact I knew so little about what we were getting ourselves into that I even considered something like this. You must remember, I only had 150 skydives and about twenty-eight BASE jumps at this time. I didn't even know what I didn't know, and that made me dangerous to myself and those around me.

Francois and I stood up, said goodbye to our new Russian friends, paid our bill, and headed to Francois' car. As we drove through the night from Campione, Italy, to Paris, France, Francois called and arranged our tickets to Caracas. We got to Paris and spent the day acquiring the waterproof bags to hold our gear. We knew they had tourist boats that went upriver to take people on tours of the waterfall, but depending on rainfall, the river sometimes didn't have enough water for the boats to make it to the base of the falls. We had to prepare for the eventuality of floating downstream, and the waterproof bags would allow us to do just that.

As we were going around Paris, looking for waterproof bags, Francois took me to see the Eiffel Tower. I told him I had been dreaming about jumping it for years.

"Maybe fifty people have jumped from the top," he told me. "It is nine hundred feet high, and the safest level to jump from with easy access. But the Eiffel Tower has three levels in total. The bottom level, known as Level One, is one hundred eighty feet high. I know one person who jumped from there, but he had a bad landing and broke both his legs."

"What about Level Two?" I asked.

"Level Two is four hundred twenty feet high," he explained, "and no one has ever jumped from it."

That got my attention. "Take me to Level Two," I told him.

With a shrug, Francois led the way, giving me a tour of how someone might go about jumping from Level Two. He showed me the stairwells I would need to use, the way to climb out to get to the exit, and where to pull my parachute so I would avoid hitting the first platform during the opening surge.

"If you wait to pull until you are passing the first platform," he went on, "you will have just enough altitude to get your parachute open and land. You do not want to open too early because you could hit the first platform, and that would be *fin* for you."

I knew right then I needed to do this jump. "Are you going to jump it?" I asked him.

"I am not sure," Francois replied. "It has such a small margin for error and getting away is close to impossible."

"Why's that?"

"There is a police station at the bottom of the tower, and they would catch me for sure. I don't think it's worth it for me; I only enjoy figuring things out. If you want to do it, you can, but I suggest you get more experience first."

The next day, we boarded a plane for Venezuela. Once we landed, we went straight to the bus terminal to catch a ride to Ciudad Bolívar. We ended up getting to the bus terminal late at night with no more buses leaving until the next morning. Francois, overseeing the money, decided we were going to do this trip "super ghetto cheap."

That meant sleeping outside the bus terminal. I thought that was a bit excessive on the not-spending-money scale, but didn't argue. I just put my two duffle bags on the trash-covered ground so I could use them as a bed. I lay on top of them with my arms through the handles to prevent people from stealing them if I fell asleep. This was not a nice area; it was located in a rundown part of town, and the people around us looked like they were living in desperate circumstances. They all had puzzled expressions that said, "What the hell are you guys doing here?" They could tell we didn't belong there.

Somehow, I ended up sleeping through the night. I woke with a jerk as buses started showing up early in the morning. My body felt heavy as I tried to stand, and my back was tweaked from sleeping on a lumpy surface. I wiped the sleep from my eyes as I walked over to get tickets for what would be a twelve-hour bus ride. The bus stopped in little villages along the way, where locals came to the windows selling food. That was how Francois and I ate. The food turned out to be delicious, and it was so cheap it almost seemed free. I wanted to give the people tips, but Francois got upset, saying Americans ruin everywhere they go by over-tipping. He seemed to think tipping made locals in poor areas try to take advantage of tourists, but I felt it was nice to help people who were obviously trying hard to earn a living. We argued about this the entire trip, and I still disagree with him.

When we got to Ciudad Bolívar, we stepped off the bus and directly into a cab. Francois directed the driver to the nearest airport, which was only fifteen minutes away. As the cab was pulling up to the airport, we saw a pilot putting gas in a small Cessna 182. We paid the cab driver and walked over to the pilot. Francois, in his broken Spanish, asked how much it would cost to fly us over Angel Falls so we could take some pictures. The pilot said, "Twenty-five US dollars each" in Spanish. Francois and I looked at each other with massive smiles. We asked if we could leave first thing in the morning, and the pilot nodded yes. We told him we would see him at 8:00 a.m.

Francois suggested we get the cheapest hotel room possible and leave most of our stuff there while we did the expedition. He suggested we take only our BASE gear, waterproof bags, and the clothes on our backs. He had a little fanny pack that he used to carry water-purifying tablets, a water bottle, and a white chocolate Toblerone. We were not expecting to take more than a single day to drop in, repack, jump, hike to the main river, and then float downstream. He thought it might take eight to ten hours, max. He had been to Angel Falls before, so he had an idea of what we needed to do.

Francois found us a hotel that cost about four US dollars a night. As we walked into the room, I instantly regretted letting him make that decision. I have never in my life seen a more horrifying hotel room. It didn't have a bathroom—you had to go outside for that, and you had to share it with six other rooms. When I went to try and use it, I couldn't believe what I saw. It looked like someone had taken a sledgehammer to the porcelain toilet and crushed it. Shit was smeared all over the floor, walls, and ceiling, and it smelled like death. Our actual room wasn't much better. It was so dirty we might as well have been sleeping on the street outside. There was zero chance I was going to sleep in, on, or near the bed. I could actually see bugs crawling all over it. I decided the dirty floor was a better option for sleeping.

I looked at Francois and was like, "Come on, dude. We can afford to stay somewhere nicer than this." He explained we may have to stay in Canaima for a few days after we jumped the falls. They didn't have daily flights out and we didn't know how much rooms would cost there. It was a tourist spot, which meant it could be expensive. So, he suggested we just sleep with our clothes on for the few hours we were in Ciudad Bolívar and then we could leave our bags with the people at the front desk while we're gone. I didn't feel like arguing, so I just went along with it. But I will say: I have never traveled with a bigger cheapskate than Francois.

Next morning, we got up early and headed to the airport. We only took our BASE gear hidden in waterproof bags, Francois' fanny pack, a TRV-900 mini DV camera to capture the trip, and the clothes on our backs. The pilot was waiting for us with his Cessna 182 ready to go, so we got on board and he started the engine. We rolled down the runway, and within a few moments, we were flying over jungle. The jungle was sparse at first, but the longer we flew, the denser it became. As we got closer to Angel Falls, we started seeing the unique table-top mountains called "tepui" that have made the Canaima National Park famous. Angel Falls itself launches over the edge of one of these Tepuis. We entered a cloud bank and couldn't see anything for quite a while, but, as we emerged, there it was: Angel Falls.

It was hard to understand how a waterfall could be so huge. It's over 3,000 feet tall, dropping from an orangish-red flat-topped mountain surrounded by emerald-green jungle as far as the eye can see. It was an impressive sight to behold. The pilot started doing close passes of the waterfall, so we asked him to fly higher. He didn't seem to understand why we would want to go higher. He asked us if we wanted to film the falls and Francois responded, "Yes, but we want to get footage from higher above the waterfall." The pilot nodded and started gaining altitude. While he was busy doing that, Francois and I geared up. We tried our best to do it in a way that wouldn't get his attention.

After we both had all our gear on, Francois took out a hundred-dollar bill and tapped the pilot on the shoulder with it. The pilot took one look at the money, and a confused look spread across his face. He glanced back to ask what the money was for, then he saw me in full gear with a smile on my face. His confusion turned to shock as I unlocked the door, pressed my back against it, and pushed as hard as I could with my legs. This forced the door open just enough for me to slip out into the sky with a backflip. As I came through the flip, I got stable and pulled my parachute. The canopy opened with a crack. I looked down and saw I was floating over Angel Falls, but I didn't have much time—I needed to find a place to land. I saw a massive open field with some long grass and small bushes on it. It looked close to the waterfall, so that was what I aimed for. I set down in ankle-deep water. The entire area was swampy, mossy, mushy, grass. I was wearing Air Jordans, black jeans, and a cashmere sweater. This was not the correct jungle attire. My feet were instantly soaked and would stay that way for the rest of my time in the jungle.

I looked around and didn't see Francois. It was quiet—too quiet. A sinking feeling set in, and it began to dawn on me that I was alone. I had been so fixated that I hadn't really thought about what the consequences of doing this actually were. I had no way to communicate with the outside world. I didn't know if Francois had jumped, and even if he had jumped, I had no idea where he may have landed. My parents thought I was in Europe; if I died out here, they would never know what happened to me. It was a strange feeling. I had just dropped myself into one of the gnarliest jungles on planet Earth with nothing. No food, no water, no supplies, and worse, no knowledge of how to survive in a jungle.

I think the silence was the most unsettling thing. There was no sound: not a bug, not a bird, nothing—only my own breathing. I started calling out to Francois, trying to see if I could locate him. I gathered up my gear and put it in my stash bag, all the while yelling for Francois. It didn't take long before I heard a voice off in the distance. It was faint, but I could hear Francois yelling back. Hearing his voice brought a sigh of relief; at least I wasn't in this completely alone. I moved in the direction of his voice until he appeared, sloshing through the mush. We reunited and headed to higher ground to get out of the swamp, and hopefully find some dry rocks to pack our parachutes on. After we started hiking in the direction of the waterfall, we came to a gaping seventy-foot-drop into a crevasse. We tried to walk around it, then gradually realized we had landed on a small island of rock with a seventy-foot-deep moat around us. Our only way across was to climb down into the crevasse and up the other side.

This is when I noticed the first of the mosquitos. It must have taken them time to locate us, because once they found us, they never left. The silence from earlier was replaced with an ever-present high-pitched hum that quickly became maddening.

I could see that we were only about a football field away from where the waterfall should be, so I didn't think it would take long to get there. We found some vines growing into the crack in the earth and decided to use them to help us climb down into the crevasse. Once we got to the bottom, I saw it was filled with vegetation: bushes, high grass, vines, and plants of all varieties. I had never needed a machete more in my life. Trying to move from one side of the crevasse to the other was extremely difficult. The moment I stepped off the rock into the dense foliage, I was consumed by the jungle. It was almost like being immersed in water, stifling and claustrophobic. I felt like I couldn't move. Francois jumped in next to me and had the same experience. We felt a bit trapped and weren't sure what to do. I started digging with my bare hands, pulling the jungle apart a few inches at a time, and pushing a little bit forward. We dug like animals, burrowing through the jungle for what felt like hours. After endless digging, I got so tired and dehydrated that I felt like I couldn't move anymore. I just went limp and sagged against the jungle—it was so thick it held me upright.

Francois was next to me and asked, "What are you doing?"

"I'm over this, dude," I told him. "I'm about to pass out. I need water and I'm pretty sure I have heat stroke."

He said, "We need to keep moving. We can't stop here. We will get to water, but we have to get out of this crevasse before we can find it." I felt as though an overwhelming oppression was suffocating me, a feeling of being buried alive in the belly of the living jungle as it slowly digested me. It was the first time I wasn't sure if I was going to be able to make it. We were just at the beginning of this experience, and if the jungle was this heavy up here, what were the four kilometers going to be like at the bottom of the waterfall? It seemed utterly hopeless.

The heat and humidity were overwhelming, but Francois convinced me to keep pushing forward. Finally, after what felt like an eternity, we made it to the rock wall on the opposite side of the crevasse. As I climbed up onto the rock, pulling myself out of the jungle, I felt like I had sidestepped a slow death. The claustrophobic feeling subsided and I no longer felt like I was being drowned. Francois and I found vines winding up the cliff face towards the top of the wall. We used them to help us climb out of that pit of despair, and I breathed a sigh of relief. Francois was right behind me and we rested for about twenty minutes before going in search of water.

We were both dehydrated at this point. The exertion from digging through jungle in 96-degree heat with 98 percent humidity made us sweat out whatever water our bodies held. You can go for weeks without food, but you will die in less than three days without water. Francois looked for trees with exposed roots on the side of the closest hill. There, he found water dripping from a tree's root system.

"This is the safest water for us to drink," he explained. "We must stay away from stagnant water where insects lay their eggs. That is where those mosquitos feeding off us for the last few hours come from." Francois gathered the water in a plastic bottle and dropped a water-purifying tablet in. He handed me the bottle after the tablet dissolved and I drank half, then I handed it back to him. We repeated this multiple times. This process was time consuming, and we needed to get moving. It had taken us way longer than anticipated to travel the relatively short distance across the floor of the crevasse, and we still had no idea how much longer it would take to get to the actual waterfall.

It was already getting late, and the shadows were growing long when we found a place flat enough and dry enough to start packing our canopies. I usually use special packing tools, but I was unable to bring them along because they would have taken up too much space. So, I was forced to improvise using rocks. I used the rocks to hold the canopy in place where I would normally use clamps. They didn't work as well, so it was one of the worst pack jobs of my life.

When we were done, Francois pointed out, "Jeb, it's probably going to get dark before we make it to the exit point. We should find somewhere to sleep up here before we lose the light. It also looks like rain is coming, so we better get moving." Sure enough, he was right; the rain started shortly after we began hiking again. I had experienced hard rain before, but this was different. It came in such torrents that it didn't even seem like individual droplets. It came in sheets, almost like someone was dumping buckets over us. We were desperate to find shelter of some kind when Francois pointed out a cave off in the distance. The light was fading fast, which made it difficult to see, but we made it to the cave.

The cave was big enough to fit both of us easily. The ceiling was about six feet high, and it was probably ten feet in length and ten feet wide. In the middle was a flat rock at an angle that I decided to try and use as a bed. But as I got closer, I saw we were not the only things trying to get out of the rain. The entire cave was moving. Unidentifiable bugs of all kinds and sizes were crawling around everywhere. The mosquito bombardment intensified. We had a sleepless night getting eaten alive by various nasty insects. I tried putting my hands in the sleeves of my sweater and pulling it over my head to keep them out, but it was no use. It was miserable, to say the least.

The bugs didn't surprise me. I knew we were going to face them when entering the jungle, but what did surprise me was the cold. I had not expected the cold that came in the night. I thought we were entering a steamy, hot jungle environment and didn't think cold was going to be a factor. But, the top of Angel Falls is at 6,000 feet, and at night, in the pouring rain, the temperature dropped, and I froze my ass off. I was wet, covered in bugs, and freezing. The experience truly sucked donkey balls. Dirty, stinky donkey balls.

We woke up—or should I say we got up—as the first light came through the opening of the cave. It was an odd light, though, a defused light. The rain had stopped at some point in the night, but as we walked out of the cave, we were standing in a cloud. Deep, dark fog made the visibility about thirty feet at best.

I looked at Francois and said, "This is going to make finding the exit point difficult, isn't it?"

He said, "*Oui.*"

I heaved a sigh and cinched up my pack. "Then let's get moving," I told him.

We started hiking again, and within five minutes, we found a trail. As we crossed it, I looked at Francois and asked, "Do you think this could be the trail Tom Sanders uses when he does his expeditions up here?"

Francois said, "There is only one way to find out." So, we followed the trail in the direction we thought the waterfall should be. Sure enough, it led us directly to the waterfall and the exit point. We had finally gotten some luck. But there wasn't much we could do till the fog lifted. We could hear the raging water as it went over the falls but couldn't see it make its descent.

As Francois and I waited for the cloud we were trapped in to clear, a sense of dread began to take hold of me again. We sat there for over ten hours, just staring at each other. It slowly dawned on us how truly stupid this plan had been. Why did we think we could get this done in a single day? Why didn't we bring more supplies? This was one of the most incredible rain forests in the world. It could rain for weeks without end. We had already eaten our Toblerone, which was our only source of food. We started talking in a low, panicked way about what it would mean if the clouds boxed us in for days. We would need to have enough strength to hike through the jungle after we jumped. If the jungle below was anything like the jungle we had gone through the day before, it was going to take a lot of energy and time. We wouldn't be able to wait for long before we became too weak to actually do it. We started talking about opening our parachutes and using them as paragliders to run off the cliff. We could then use the compasses we had brought to navigate through the cloud, hopefully landing somewhere in the jungle below. This, of course, was a stupid idea and the planning of desperate people who had made a series of bad choices.

After a few more hours, we started thinking we were in real trouble, when a light broke through the clouds. The fog layer began dropping and the sun flooded the sky. We now saw blue above us and what looked like a sprawling valley filled with an ocean of rolling clouds.

The jungle appeared to breathe as the mist slipped over and through the trees. We could now clearly see the river rushing over the edge that created the highest waterfall on Earth. I looked out and saw a gap in the blanket of white where a spot of green poked through. It was a hole in the cloud bank, and it was moving right for us. Everything started happening at once. Francois and I frantically started gearing up. We were not sure how long this hole would last, and we didn't want to miss it. Within three minutes, we were both geared up and standing on the edge, watching for our one chance at escape.

As I looked over, I watched the clouds clear, and I saw Angel Falls from the exit point for the first time. It was magnificent. A massive rush of water falling for over 3,000 vertical feet into a jade-green valley. It was one of the most stunning scenes of my life. I looked down and pointed to a small, slightly different color of green and asked Francois, "Is that the landing area?"

He looked at where I was pointing and said, "Yes, that is where you need to land."

I asked him, "Are you ready?"

"I am ready when you are." I felt an overwhelming sense of urgency to get off that cliff as quickly as possible and rushed my countdown. In my haste, I didn't focus—I just stepped off.

As I entered freefall, I looked over and saw the waterfall off to my left. There was a rainbow suspended between me and the falls as my speed accelerated. I went head-down and began to flip onto my back. I decided to just go with it. I wasn't going to fight it. I started spinning my arms to try and get more momentum to continue the rotation into a front flip. As I came through the flip, I pushed my legs out and put my arms to my side, going into a track.

As I was falling and looking down the waterfall, I noticed something about Angel Falls I didn't know before. It's not just an overhanging cliff, it's also a C-shaped, vertical tube with an opening in front. The rock actually wraps around you on all sides. It was an odd-looking thing, and I only noticed it as I was falling inside it. My track was weak; I wasn't making it out of the tube area of the waterfall, but I had so much room that it didn't matter. I opened my parachute and started looking for the landing area. As I got closer, it became obvious this landing area was tiny—maybe only the size of four king-sized mattresses all laid down next to each other. I was setting myself up to land dead center, when I got hit by turbulence coming off the waterfall. I thought I was all good, but the turbulence swatted me out of the sky and dropped me in a tree about twenty feet tall on the outer edge of the landing zone.

I broke through most of the branches and ended up hanging with my toes about two feet from the ground. I was wondering how I was going to get down when I heard Francois stomping through the jungle, laughing.

As he got closer, I could see he was holding a camera, filming me as he laughed. He said, "Sorry, but I have to film this."

I told him, "Yes, this is super funny, but could you help me get out of these trees?"

After filming a bit more, he finally put the camera down and started helping me. I cut the canopy away and dropped to the ground, then took off the rig. We both climbed up in the tree to start working on getting my canopy out of the higher branches. It took us over an hour to get my gear down because my lines were wrapped around strong branches. We were trying to get the canopy clear without causing it too much damage. It was a delicate process.

Once we finally had all my equipment back in my stash bag, Francois informed me we had to get moving. It was already late in the day and the dark was not far away. We knew there was a tourist trail that led from the main river to the waterfall for day hikers. We would need to find it if we wanted to get through four kilometers of jungle while we still had light. We would need to walk along the river's edge, created by the falls, to avoid the dense jungle for as long as possible, making sure we followed the river down the valley far enough so that, when we pushed into the jungle, we would have the best chance of intersecting the trail that would lead us out. If we could find that trail, we knew it would be smooth sailing. Once it led us to the main river, we were hoping the water volume would be high enough for tourist boat traffic. At this point, we knew floating fifty kilometers downriver on waterproof bags was a silly idea. If we were forced to do that, we probably weren't going to make it.

We spent the better part of the day slipping, falling, and stumbling our way down the valley, trying to find a reasonable place to cross the river. We finally found a location that was relatively calm and waded across without much trouble, then continued directly into the jungle, perpendicular to the water like we had planned. Within minutes, we hit the tourist trail, and it was a glorious sight to see—big and well-manicured. This made the walk to the main river easy.

The sun was beginning to set as we got to the main river. We found a campsite and could tell people had just been there. We had missed them by maybe twenty minutes, max; their campfire coals were still smoking. We decided to stay there for the night and hoped they would come back the next morning. I took my shoes off for the first time since landing in the jungle. My feet had been wet for over thirty-eight hours straight and they were starting to hurt. I rinsed them off in the river and washed my socks, then put them on a rock in the waning sun, trying to dry them out, but with the humidity, it wasn't going to be effective. My feet were swollen and discolored. I noticed blisters were developing around each of my toenails, and when I touched one, it burst, causing pus to pour out. It was a truly disgusting thing to see, and it smelled even worse. Just to be clear, Air Jordans are not the best choice for hiking in jungles.

The camping area had a makeshift picnic table that worked perfectly as a bed to keep us off the jungle floor for the night. As I lay on the picnic table, looking up at the shadows of the trees in the dark above, I had one regret in planning this trip: I regretted not bringing insect repellent. We had been getting eaten alive by mosquitos, and those evil little monsters were the worst part of the whole experience. They were relentless, constantly biting, constantly humming in our ears—thousands of the little shits. I was lying there, wishing I had slipped a can of OFF in Francois' fanny pack, when he said something interesting. He looked over at me and said, "Jeb, I don't see you as an American anymore. People from the USA would never do something like this." He then rolled over and went to sleep. I guess, in his way, he was trying to give me a compliment, but it was one of the strangest things anyone has ever said to me.

The next morning, I woke up as sun beams made their way through the jungle canopy and shone in my face. Surprisingly, I was able to get some sleep that night; it had been much warmer than the night before and there had not been a single drop of rain. Also, we only had to deal with mosquitos and not all the other super creepy bugs from the cave the night earlier. I sat up and walked over to the river to see if my socks had dried. As I leaned down to touch them, feeling they were still quite damp, I saw several boats coming up the river, and they were filled with people. I yelled to Francois, informing him that boats were heading our way. I quickly put on my damp socks and shoes, which squished and squelched with each step, and rushed over to greet the arrival of the first people we had seen since dropping into the jungle.

Everyone was wearing bright orange life vests. They stepped out of their respective boats one by one and walked up the path in single-file lines towards the picnic table Francois and I had used as a bed the night before. We greeted each other with hellos as each one passed, till finally the two tour guides walked up to Francois and me.

"What are you doing here?" one asked in English.

"We are wildlife photographers," Francois said, showing them his camera. "We got dropped off here a few days ago to film frogs and birds."

They looked at us with an expression of bullshit, and the second guide said, "No, you aren't. No one gets left in this jungle without a guide." He pressed further and asked, "If you have been filming frogs and birds, can we see the footage?"

We informed him, "No, we aren't going to show you any of our footage, but we could use a ride back to Canaima." The two tour guides looked at each other and spoke in Spanish for a few seconds.

Finally, the first one said, "Give us twenty dollars each and we will give you a ride."

Francois started to argue, but I kicked him and said, "Shut up, Francois. Yes, twenty dollars each will be perfect. Any chance we could get some water and something to eat?"

They grinned and said, "Of course," and handed us both bottles of water.

Francois wanted to bargain on the price, but I pulled him aside and said, "Dude, don't be a dick. Twenty dollars each is a bargain."

He said, "Americans are ruining travel for everyone else." He felt the guides were taking advantage of us because twenty US dollars was a small fortune in that area.

I didn't give a shit and said, "We will pay them." The river guides walked back to the dugout canoes and grabbed some ice chests out of the boats. They proceeded to start a fire, took whole chickens out of the chests, and put them on long sticks that they stuck in the ground, angling them so the chickens hung over the fire. I had never been more excited to see food being prepared in my entire life. I was starving and the smell coming off those roasting birds made my mouth water. I watched in anticipation as they seasoned the birds with salt and spices; I couldn't wait to eat something. My attention shifted when I saw someone with a can of OFF bug repellent.

I ran over and asked, "Any chance I could use some of that?" They handed me the can and I sprayed myself with it. The mist from that can was heavenly; I didn't see another bug the rest of my time in the jungle. I felt so stupid for not bringing the single most obvious thing to a jungle filled with bugs.

When the food was finally finished, they gave us plates filled with freshly roasted chicken and corn on the cob. It's remarkable how true hunger makes food taste so much better. Eating that meal was an experience I will never forget. The flavor was like an explosion in my mouth with every bite. It was hands down the best meal I have ever had. The taste set off what felt like electrical pulses in my brain, and I could feel the energy surging into my body. The combination of dehydration, overexertion, extreme heat, and humidity had taken a toll on my body to the point I felt like I was starving. We ate, we camped, and we left, but I took with me a new appreciation for the dangers of the jungle—Francois and I had gotten away by the skin of our teeth, and we both knew it.

Spending three days and two nights in the jungle with no food and little water made me lose a total of twenty pounds. I went from 200 lbs. to 180 lbs., and that weight didn't come back for over four years.

CHAPTER THIRTEEN

MEETING McCONKEY

Francois and I got our lifesaving boat ride back to Canaima, and from there, slowly made our way back to France. I had a week left before I needed to fly home and Francois asked what I would like to do.

"I have to get back to work," he explained, "and start returning all the money I still owe the other jumpers from the cancelled expedition to Angel Falls. I'll do the math and let you know how much I still owe you, Jeb."

"Don't worry about it, man," I told him. "I got to jump Angel Falls, along with a couple other wonderful cliffs, and the experience was amazing. As far as I'm concerned, we're all good."

"Thank you, Jeb," Francois replied. "Truly kind of you. Where can I drop you off?"

"Well, is Magland jumpable in February?" This was the cliff I saw in that documentary all those years before that had inspired me to follow the path to the dark arts of BASE. In a way, following that path led me through and out of the valley of death that had imprisoned my mind during my teen years. I couldn't deny Magland's pull for much longer.

Francois called a few friends in the area and they told him Magland was cold and covered in snow, but people were still jumping it.

"It is possible," Francois said, "but it will be freezing and you do not have proper clothes. Don't repeat our mistake."

"Don't worry about it," I said with a grin. "I'll buy a jacket on the way to the cliff."

We spent a few nights at Francois' home in Paris to recharge before heading to Chamonix, the French town where the Magland cliff is located. As we drove, Francois asked, "Would you like to stop at McDonald's to get something to eat on the way?"

I said, "No, thank you, bro. I don't eat that shit."

He looked at me like I was insane and said, "You are not a true American." He then pulled over, and I was forced to order a Royale with cheese. He tried to convince me McDonald's was better in France, with higher quality food. He was wrong; it was just as gross as everywhere else, but sometimes it's better than going hungry, so I ate it.

We got to Magland pretty late, but Francois was able to check me into a hotel across the street from the actual landing area, directly under the jump, which meant I could do the jump and then walk across the street to my room. I wouldn't have a car, so I'd have to hitchhike to get to the top of the mountain, where the hike began. We sat in a little bar as Francois explained how to find the exit point.

"Once you reach the top of the hill," he said, sketching out his instructions on a little bar napkin, "stop at the first roundabout you see. Get out of the car and begin walking from there. When you see two jet ski rental shops side by side, walk between them into the forest—that's where the trail head begins. It's such a popular place to jump, so you will for sure see fresh tracks in the snow that will lead you straight to the jump. It's as easy as that."

I took the napkin, looked at his instructions, and shook his hand.

"Thank you, Francois," I said. Francois nodded and then left the little bar. That was the last time I ever saw him.

I woke up early the next morning and had some breakfast, then put on the new jacket I had just bought and the warmest clothes I owned, which consisted of two pairs of socks, my trusty Air Jordans, a pair of black jeans, two black t-shirts, and a cashmere sweater. This was completely inadequate for hiking in the French Alps in the dead of winter, as I would come to find out, but I thought I was overdressed at the time. I had not yet learned about sweat-wicking material and performance clothing.

I went outside and started walking up the road that led to the top of the mountain. As cars drove by, I put my hand out with my thumb up like I had seen in movies, but it didn't seem to work. No one was willing to stop. I walked for hours and must have climbed over 1,500 feet up the mountain before a brown Mercedes with two friendly German men finally pulled over and asked if I needed a ride. I was already freezing, and the cold, combined with the jungle rot that had set in on my feet from Angel Falls, was excruciating. Both men spoke English and asked me why I was walking up a mountain road in the middle of winter by myself. I told them I was heading up to BASE jump off a cliff and they looked at each other sideways, like they had just picked up a weirdo. They weren't completely wrong.

It didn't take long before the steep incline turned flat and we came to the first roundabout. I told them this was my stop and thanked them profusely for their help, said they were lifesavers, etc. They just shook their heads and continued on their way as I double-checked my napkin.

I started looking for jet ski rental shops. I was thinking, *Why would they rent jet skis in the mountains in winter?* I came to a couple snowmobile shops and realized Francois must have been talking about these. There were two of them side by side, and if I walked between them, I would be heading straight into the forest. I was sure this is what he had been talking about. Problem was, snowplows had pushed a mountain of snow between the buildings, making a pile about twenty feet high. I would have to climb over it to get to the other side. It was hard to climb, and my shoes filled with snow. As I crested its summit, my hands turned into blocks of ice, feeling more like they were burning than freezing. As I came down the other side, I didn't see any tracks in the snow—nothing. I was a bit worried because I was already freezing and wasn't sure how far I could go before it was too far to get back. Francois said it would take about fifteen minutes to walk to the exit point from there, so I decided I would search for that amount of time and turn around if I couldn't find it by then.

As I was walking, my feet went completely numb. The blisters and oozing pus froze solid. I couldn't feel them at all. I could feel my hands, but what I felt was only pain. It felt like burning hot needles were poking through the skin. After about twenty minutes of walking, I started feeling like I was in trouble. I became worried that I wouldn't be able to make it back to the beginning of this hike, and even if I did, I didn't think I would be able to get a ride back down the mountain. I knew I needed to find this exit point and jump; that was the only way I could get back to my hotel before freezing to death. I began questioning my life decisions, but then I saw a set of footprints in the snow off in the distance. I knew I could no longer make it back the way I came, so I followed the footprints deeper into the forest, slowly freezing with each step.

As I came around a bend, I saw the back of someone in a bright yellow ski jacket and ski pants. He was peeing in the snow, writing his name with the stream. It read, "Shane McConkey." The man heard me approaching and turned his head to look at me.

He said, "Hello, dude. How are you doing?" I thought, *Dude? This guy is American.* I responded with, "I am freezing my balls off. How about you?"

Finishing his stream, Shane said, "I'm up here filming a ski movie. Got some cameramen in the landing area."

Teeth chattering, I did my best to nod.

"Hey, man," he continued, eyeing my pack. "You want to jump first so my guys can practice filming? That way they won't screw it up when I do mine."

I told him, "N-n-no problem. I need to g-get off this mountain as f-fast as possible anyway. I am literally f-f-freezing to death."

He looked at what I was wearing and nodded his head, saying, "Not the best choice of clothes for the mountains in winter, amigo. Let's get you off this hill so you can warm up." We both geared up and walked to the exit together. Shane called down with his walkie and told his cameramen I would be jumping first, and to use me as practice.

They responded with a 10-4, and Shane said, "Whenever you're ready." I stood there for a moment with a somewhat nostalgic feeling in my chest. I couldn't believe that I was standing there doing the jump that inspired me to continue living. It was actually more special to me than I had anticipated. I became quite emotional, which wasn't something that happened often. I jumped off, throwing a gainer, then reached back and couldn't feel the handle. My hands were completely numb. Somehow, I was still able to get my worthless fingers around the pilot chute and threw it out. My parachute opened. I struggled in the air, putting my hands through the toggles I couldn't grasp, but somehow managed to land without hurting myself. I gathered up all my gear and ran as fast as I could across the street to my hotel. I went into my room, turned on a hot shower, and got in. Standing in the spray of hot water for nearly an hour, I felt the numbness slowly release its grip on me and seep out of my body.

That evening, I went down for dinner and saw Shane sitting at the bar with his film crew. As I walked in, he yelled for me to come have a drink with them. He asked what I wanted, and I told him water would be great. He looked at me like I was a bit odd, but said, "Okay." I sat down, and he asked me where I was from and what I was doing there. I told him a brief history of my life and he shared a brief history of his own. I found out he was a pro skier and he had just started BASE jumping. That was his twenty-fifth BASE jump, and I told him it had been my thirtieth. He was from Northern California and lived in the Tahoe area. I told him that I had just gotten back from Angel Falls a few days earlier. He and his crew got a strange look on their face and Shane said, "What did you just say?" So, I told them the story of what Francois and I did over the last week. They didn't believe me. I told them if they wanted, I could show them the video—it was up in my room.

They put their drinks down and said, "Take us to your room. We need to see this." He paid for the drinks, we walked up to my room, and I showed them the footage I had gotten in Venezuela.

After watching it, they all just sat there looking at me like I was an alien.

"I'll be damned," he said. "What do you do for a living, Jeb?"

"I'm a graphic artist working for my parents' insurance brokerage company."

"Huh," Shane said, giving me a serious look. "Is that what you want to be doing with your life?"

I said, "No, not really, but I need to make money so I can do the things I want to do."

"Listen, Jeb. That footage...you jumping, your story...it's special. The right kind of special—the kind that's worth money to the right people."

I hadn't thought in those terms at that point, so I kind of just changed the subject. I didn't know what to say and it kind of made me feel uncomfortable for some reason. We talked a bit longer and then said our goodnights, and that was how I met Shane McConkey. Only later did I come to find out he was a living legend in the freeskiing world.

CHAPTER FOURTEEN

IIRO THE MAGICIAN

On August 15, 1999, I was in Norway once again on my second trip to Kjerag, and I had learned from my previous adventure here that I needed to bring my own food. So, I came prepared with two duffle bags this time: one filled with clothes and BASE gear, the other filled with ramen noodles and Rice Crispy Treats. I was there to spend one month training my ass off every single day the weather would allow. I was focused like a laser on getting better at acrobatic BASE-jumping maneuvers, and this was the trip where I wanted to take my skills to the next level. I had no intention of talking to or dealing with other human beings. I just wanted to hike and jump.

Of course, that's not how life—or Norway, for that matter—works. You see, it rains all the damn time in Norway, and socializing with the other jumpers becomes a huge part of the experience, whether you like it or not, because everyone gets trapped indoors with little to do other than sit and talk. However, despite how boring that sounds, I ended up meeting a network of friends I would jump with for the rest of my life.

Yuri had shown up, so hanging out with him was unavoidable. I became good friends with a South African couple, John Van Schalkwyk and his wife Lienkie. They would feel pity for me during this trip and take me in like a small, wounded animal. I would also end up meeting a group of Australians and the legendary Dwaine Weston, but all of that will be the focus of future chapters. This chapter is about Iiro Seppänen and how we became best friends.

I had gotten a room in the white house at the only camping area in Lysebotn. It was kind of like a hostel where you had a small room with shared bathrooms. Most of the rooms were shared as well, but I was able to get a room to myself. During my time there, I tried to stay quiet, just keeping to myself as a tall Viking-looking dude with long blond hair came walking into the main common room. He was energetic and super social, showing people magic tricks, telling jokes, and handing out shots to everyone in sight. He filled whatever room he was in with positive energy. I was sitting in the corner when he walked up to me and introduced himself as Iiro. I responded in an awkward, antisocial manner, as was my custom in those days, not returning his outgoing nature. I wasn't good with people back then, and I'm still weird even now. He looked at me kind of how a dog looks at you when it's trying to understand what you said. He then walked away to talk to other people.

The next morning, a group of us all packed ourselves into a small van and rode to the top of the mountain to begin the first hike of the day. Iiro ended up sitting right next to me and again tried to talk to me. I replied to his questions with one-word answers and felt more awkward by the second; I just couldn't communicate well when it came to actual back-and-forth conversation. But Iiro wouldn't give up. I could see he really wanted to talk, even though I wasn't good at it.

We got out of the van and started hiking, and there was Iiro again, right next to me with more attempts at communication. I was off in my own little world thinking about the jump and not paying much attention when he said something that pulled me out of my trance.

"...how I ended up becoming good friends with Gena Davis and her goddaughter, Emily."

"Wait, what?" I asked, finally responding to the poor guy. "My little sister is best friends with Emely."

Iiro looked at me and asked, "Is your little sister named Scarlett?"

I stopped walking and said, "Yes..." in a dubious kind of way. "How do you know Scarlett?"

"Holy shit," he said with a big smile. "I knew it! I have been in your house. You have a massive white snake in your room, and you are Scarlett's big brother who wears nothing but black and BASE jumps."

"What?" I replied. He knew who I was.

"This one time, I bought Emily and Scarlett a bunch of alcohol, and you must be the brother who found it and threw it all away."

"Yep, that sounds like something I would do."

"Well, I'm going to have to kick your ass for wasting so much good alcohol." But then he gave me a wink. I was stunned and didn't know what to say. Somehow, halfway around the world, I bumped into a Finnish BASE jumper who not only knew my sister, but had actually been in my home. That was the link I needed to feel comfortable around him from then on. This is when Iiro and I really started talking.

I learned that Iiro had been practicing magic since he was ten years old and earning a living from it since he was fifteen. He was now twenty-four and had grown tired of how fake magic was. He felt it was just tricking people and he wanted to start doing something with more real-world consequences. BASE jumping wasn't an illusion and I think that excited him. He was trying to add real danger to his magic, but it was difficult to get it approved and people couldn't really tell the difference between what was real and what wasn't anyway. Iiro wanted to do something that, when people saw it, they knew it was real.

He seemed obsessed with things being real, including the people he surrounded himself with. He had zero tolerance for fake people who talked shit. If someone said something that couldn't be backed up with either actions or science, he became visibly annoyed. I always liked this about him. His extreme skepticism was even more vast than my own, which is saying something.

Iiro also has a huge heart—one of the biggest I have ever seen. He feels things deeply. He truly loves and cares about his friends and family. This heart has a flipside, though. If you piss him off, he can hate with a passion that burns just as hot. That's the thing about emotions: they can have both a light and a dark side. I tend to be a little more level and don't show emotion as often as he does, but the thing we have most in common is that we both like honesty.

In the beginning, I think this is what drew us to the dark art of BASE. It was a true test of oneself, with real-life consequences. If you made mistakes, you died, plain and simple. It wasn't a sport, and to call it one would be an insult. In many cases, sports are just games people play with each other, with made-up teams and made-up rules where people transport a small ball back and forth across a field. One team wins and one team loses—but who really cares? They all go on the next day, continuing to make millions of dollars. In BASE, you win if you live and you lose if you die. There's something pure about this idea. BASE is more of a philosophy, a way of seeing one's own mortality and accepting the inevitable fact that we are all going to die someday. Accepting this fact helps release us from the fears that hold us back in our lives. Understanding that our time is limited somehow makes that time more precious and helps give us purpose. It is a beacon of light that helps guide us through the dark recesses of our own minds.

I've noticed most of the BASE jumpers I've gotten to know have had demons in one way or another. It takes a special kind of mind to have the desire to jump off buildings. Facing death was a way for me to exorcise the demons that were ripping away at my mind, and I feel many other jumpers have used BASE in a similar way.

It's almost as though peeking under the hood of the reaper can help you see the meaning of life. It shows you what has true value and what doesn't, and helps you reevaluate your priorities and focus on what really matters.

Iiro and I would talk about philosophy and the reasons why we wanted to do the things we were doing. We were both driven in a similar direction, so we decided to start working together. By the end of that trip in Norway, we were already making plans to travel the world together, BASE jumping off everything in our path.

We both still needed a building to complete our BASE numbers. To get a BASE number, you had to jump off an object in each of the four fixed object categories. At least one Building, Antenna, Span (bridge), and Earth. Once you had done all four objects, you could submit for your BASE number. Iiro wanted to register and get his number, but I just wanted to jump all the different categories and didn't care about numbers. So, for our first trip, we decided New York City would be the logical choice to do our building jump. We didn't know which building yet, but we felt NY would be the best place to find a good one. After that, we would head to Niagara Falls on the Canadian side. I had located a building there called the Skylon Tower and heard its observation deck had a fence that was easy to climb over. If it all worked out, we could get two buildings in one trip.

Iiro was one of the first people I really connected with. I always felt like an outcast, which made me feel alone even when I wasn't. I didn't know there were people out there who saw things the way I did. My friendship with Iiro was the beginning of me understanding I wasn't alone.

Being around him also had the effect of making me feel comfortable around normal people. He was so outgoing and social that it became easier for me to follow his lead. I tend to talk at people instead of with them, and I'm more a storyteller than a conversationalist, and I often retell the same stories. Iiro helped soften this issue and made conversations flow more naturally just with his presence.

I had gone to Norway with the focus of jumping, but I found something far more important: I found friends, but I also learned that I could be a friend as well. I met people who saw life and the world in a similar way. There, I was surrounded by like-minded individuals I could finally relate to. It turned out the jumping on this trip was irrelevant, but the friendships I made impacted my life and would forever change its direction.

Iiro and I met up in Manhattan later that same year. He had a friend named Suzy who was in a foster family that had taken in Iiro's brother as part of a foreign exchange student program. Iiro had visited his brother during that time and became good friends with Suzy. Seeing she was local to NY and had a car, Iiro thought she would be perfect for our ground crew. We all met up with a local BASE jumper named Joe the second day we were in town to discuss possible objects for our first building. Joe told us about a construction site on Park Avenue, close to 60th, that would be perfect for us. He explained all we had to do was jump the fence, walk into the lower level of the construction project, find the stairwell, and then just walk up the stairs to the fortieth floor. They hadn't put the windows in on that level yet and it would be jumpable until they did. He said the building would only be jumpable for about two more weeks, so he wasn't worried about us burning the object down. We continued talking about life, other objects, and future trips, and after a few hours, we thanked Joe for the information and went on our merry way to begin preparing.

Around 1:00 a.m. later that same night, the weather was perfect, so we decided to pack up our gear and go take a look at our first building. It was easy to find since it was under construction with scaffolding covering the exterior. We could tell right away why Joe wasn't scared of us burning the object. Without the scaffolding, the building wasn't vertical. Each floor set back from the one below it, creating steps that went from floor to floor. Once the scaffolding came down, jumping would no longer be possible.

Suzy dropped us off on the corner, and we casually started walking towards the construction site with our stash bags on our backs. As we walked up, we saw an obvious place to get over the fence and looked around to see if anyone was looking. Surprisingly for NY, there wasn't anyone around at that moment, so we went for it. We used the scaffolding to pull ourselves up and over the fence. It took only a few seconds for us to be on the other side and hidden in the dark shadows cast by the building itself. I was terrified of getting busted, but having Iiro there made me feel better. I'm not sure I would have been able to do it alone. I think I was okay with the jumping part, but the trespassing and possible arrest made me nervous.

We walked around the construction site, looking for a stairwell. I was amazed at how much equipment was just lying around, because it didn't seem like their security was very good. It didn't take long to find the stairs, but I was unnerved to see that all the lights were on. That seemed odd and I was concerned workers were still there, but we kept moving forward. We climbed the stairs as fast as we could, and I fell into a kind of trance watching Iiro in front of me, putting one foot in front of the other, step by step.

I started to become detached again and felt like my senses were trapped in a tunnel. Everything came through muffled. Our steps echoed off walls, creating a ghostly sound in the distance that made us feel like something was following us. Time moved and warped, which made it difficult to track. Each floor was marked as we went by, but they passed like distant shadows in my mind. I saw floor eleven, but by the time I looked up again, we were already on the fortieth floor. I heard Iiro say, "We're here," and that pulled me out of my tunnel. Everything became clear, and I felt air coming into the open holes where windows should have been as we entered the room from the stairwell. Iiro and I walked over to the gaping hole in the side of the building and saw wood planks spanning from the window frame to the scaffolding. The construction workers would use these planks to move between the building and the scaffolding outside. Somewhere in my memory, an image flickered of a little boy standing on a similar plank and taking his first step across a pit full of pigs.

I licked my fingers and held them up to the breeze that was hitting us straight in the face. We had a headwind and Iiro asked if I thought it was okay to jump. It was weak, not even five miles per hour, so I said, "I don't think it will be a problem." So we started gearing up. Iiro wanted to jump first, and that made me happy—watching someone else pull off a successful jump right before yours makes you feel better. When we were ready, we stepped through the holes and placed our feet on the wooden planks. We then grabbed hold of the scaffolding and stood side by side as we looked at the forty-story vertical drop to Park Avenue.

We had given Suzy a call about ten minutes earlier while gearing up and told her to get ready. Now that we were standing with our toes hanging over the edge, Iiro took out a walkie and asked, "Are you in position?"

Suzy replied, "Yes, and it's all clear. You can jump when you're ready."

Iiro keyed the walkie again and said, "Ten seconds." He looked at me and said, "Have a good one, Jeb," then stepped off the building with perfect body positioning. I watched him fall for three seconds before letting go of his pilot chute. His parachute opened with a crack as Iiro had a perfect on-heading opening.

I thought, *Nice, that was perfect!* but then something strange happened. Iiro's canopy had a violent, left-handed 180-degree turn and faced him back into the building. A second violent turn, this time 90 degrees to the right, sent him flying straight down Park Avenue in the opposite direction of where we were supposed to land. His canopy shuttered and vibrated in a way I had never seen before, and suddenly he was heading into oncoming traffic. It didn't look like he had much control as he hit the asphalt at high speed, narrowly missing getting hit by cab head-on, which would have killed him instantly. I watched from the fortieth floor as Iiro pounded the asphalt and rolled. He jumped to his feet, pulled his canopy in, and started running as fast as he could. I watched him run down a side street, and he was gone.

I didn't know what to make of what I had just seen, but it was now my turn to jump and I had to get moving. I leaned forward, took a deep breath, and pushed off. I fell towards the earth, watching scaffolding pass by my feet as buildings rose up beneath me. It was almost like falling into a manmade cavern. I pulled and my parachute had a perfect on-heading opening, just like Iiro's. I released my brakes, turned right, and landed on Park Avenue, then pulled in my gear and moved down 60th Street like we had planned. I found an alley way with no people around, so I put all my gear in a stash bag and grabbed my walkie.

"Is Iiro okay?" I asked, trying not to panic.

Iiro's voice came through loud and clear: "I'm fine, Jeb. We're just a few blocks away. Come meet us." When I got there, Iiro was bleeding a little from some scrapes, but they weren't bad. I asked him what happened, and he said he had no idea, but we should talk about it back at the hotel.

Once we got there, Iiro pulled his gear out of the stash bag and we started inspecting it. He told me that he had an on-heading opening, but when he went to release his toggles, the left one got hung up on something. When I looked at the riser with the hung-up toggle, I could see what went wrong. Iiro was jumping a rig called a Hummit. It was off-brand and, to this day, I have only seen two of them in use. Iiro's was the first. BASE rigs at the time had special toggles called "zoo toggles." They used a small metal pin that went through a loop and a metal ring, locking the toggle to the riser in a secure way during the opening sequence on slider-down jumps. The concept was designed to clear a malfunction known as a "line over," but in Iiro's case, and in the case of this badly designed set of zoo toggles, the metal pin somehow got pulled into the metal ring and then bent, locking it in place forever. No matter how much pressure Iiro used, the toggle would never release. When Iiro went to release his toggles, the right toggle released but the left toggle hung up. This put him in that violent left turn, and before he realized what was going on, it had him facing the building. He had to pull the right toggle all the way down to get the canopy to turn away from the building and then keep it pulled down to fly somewhat straight. Every time he would try to get the left toggle off, the pressure would stall the canopy, making it collapse and vibrate in an unnatural way. He barely had any control, and that was why he almost hit the cab. I was astonished he had walked away from something like that.

I told Iiro he needed to buy a different rig ASAP, but for the time being, I had an extra pair of zoo toggles from Basic Research he could borrow. I had to cut the old zoo toggles off the rig in order to release it from the metal ring. The toggles on the Hummit rig were the worst-designed toggles I have ever seen, and how they didn't kill people with those things, I'll never know. They almost cost me my friend's life.

The next night, the winds came up and jumping wasn't going to be possible, so we all decided to go see a movie. It was September 1999, and *Fight Club* had just been released. Iiro, Suzy, and I went to see it without having any idea what we were about to witness. It turned out to be one of the single most impactful films I have ever experienced. The philosophy that was woven into that cinematic masterpiece seemed to mirror what I was feeling at the time. The quotes, "This is your life and it's ending one minute at a time," and "The things you own end up owning you," just resonated with me as maxims for my life. The idea of "having to lose everything before you are free to do anything" impacted me. I felt that, when dealing with my depression, the rock-bottom idea mirrored what I had experienced. When you hit rock-bottom, there is nowhere to go but up. I felt I had burned my life down so I could resurrect as something else. BASE jumping felt like it mirrored the *Fight Club* ideology. Iiro, Suzy, and I all loved that movie, and it still resonates with me to this day.

The weather got better the next day, so I wanted to get another building jump in before heading up to Niagara Falls. My parents use to stay in the Palace Hotel for work a lot, so I had been in the rooms many times. On one of my trips visiting them in NY, I got a chance to see the locks on the windows used to keep people from opening them. I could see the locks would be simple to remove—all you needed was a pair of needle-nose pliers. Because of this knowledge, Iiro and I decided to check into the Palace Hotel to give that jump a try. We checked in and got a room on the fiftieth floor. Once we unpacked our bags, we began working on the window locks, but they turned out to be trickier than I expected. We needed to get them off without damaging them so we could put them back on. We didn't want anyone to know what we had done because we wanted to be able to do it again. So, after a few hours of playing around with the locks, we were finally able to get them off. We decided to do the jump at 3:00 a.m. to have the least amount of traffic possible. Our landing area was going to be W 50th Street next to St. Patrick's Cathedral. The road was narrow and the sidewalks were covered with trees, awnings, and streetlights. There was enough space to fit a canopy, but just barely.

When 3:00 a.m. came and the traffic had died down to a trickle, Iiro and I started mentally preparing as we geared up. I was terrified yet again, and I began to wonder if this feeling of horror would ever go away. It seemed like with every new jump, the fear elevated and attacked my mind in some new, sadistic way. I wasn't sure why the feeling was becoming so overwhelming, but as I was going through these emotions, Iiro decided I was jumping first this time.

Even without the locks, the window still only opened about two and a half feet, meaning I was going to have to slide out the window backwards, holding onto the top of the window frame with my fingers as my toes clung to the bottom. I would then have to figure out how to turn around. I didn't like this idea, but it was the only way. As I slid out and crouched in this uncomfortable position, I noticed the building was smooth on the outside without any ledges or places to get a handhold. As I was hanging out the window in this squatting position, my toes straining inside my shoes and my fingers gripped with all their might, I could feel the window flexing with the pressure. If the window was to shatter, it would send me falling on my back to the street, completely out of control and in exponentially more danger of dying. There have only been two jumps in my BASE-jumping career that were so scary they made me shake uncontrollably, where the fear was so extreme my entire body convulsed from my toes to my fingertips. This was one of those jumps. Pulling this off meant going through a series of awkward movements, but they were so unnatural that it's hard to explain. I had to hook the heel of my right foot to the window frame as I gripped the top of the frame with the fingers on my right hand, then twist and turn while releasing one set of toes, pin my arm against the building, and—you know what? It's too complex. Suffice to say, I had to contort my body like a circus freak doing some odd high-altitude show with no one watching. By the time I got myself turned around, I was in a near panic. I felt like I was about to fall with every move I made. My heart was racing and I was on the edge of a breaking point. The window felt like it was going to give way at any second and jettison me into open space followed by shards of glass. The shaking became so powerful I felt like I was going to lose my grip from the sheer vibration of my own body. I was now crouched like a gargoyle looking down at the massive gothic church across the street. Few humans have seen Saint Patrick's Cathedral from that vantage point, and it felt terrifying.

Iiro had been watching this struggle and was beginning to feel uneasy about this jump. Once I had gotten myself in position, there was no getting back inside the building. That was it. I had to jump now. I was starting to lose my grip, so I told Iiro, "I am jumping in five seconds."

I counted down and pushed off as best I could from my heels. I looked down and watched Madison Avenue moving slowly towards me. I saw the tops of the spires from the cathedral across the street below me, then in front of me, and then disappear above me. I felt like the city was swallowing me as I opened my parachute. Once under canopy, my chosen landing area looked tiny and congested. But I turned left down Madison and then turned right onto E 50th Street. The sidewalk on both my right and left had obstacles I needed to avoid hitting, so I set down in the middle of the street as tree branches brushed the top of my canopy. I ran out my landing, turned around, and pulled in my canopy. I stuffed it in my stash bag and quickly walked down the street, taking a left hand turn on 5th Avenue. I jumped in the first cab I found and asked them to drive me to Central Park.

As I sat in the back of the cab, I took off my rig and stuffed it in the stash bag. The cabbie looked at me through the rearview mirror and I could tell he was wondering what I was doing. I pulled the drawstring, sealing everything inside. As the cab stopped at the park, I paid him and got out of the car. I then walked a few blocks and waved down another cab. I told them to take me back to the Palace Hotel. I felt this would make it difficult for my movement to be tracked by anyone who might have seen what happened. Maybe I've seen too many spy movies, but it worked.

When I got back to the hotel, Iiro was still contemplating if he was going to do the jump or not. He asked me what I thought, and I said, "This is the goddamn scariest thing I have ever done." This wasn't actually true—the 260-foot antenna I jumped was way more frightening, but every time I scare the shit out of myself, it always feels like the scariest thing ever. Iiro didn't like the idea of sliding out the window backwards and having to go through what he saw me do. Plus, Iiro was bigger than me and weighed more, so the chances of the window breaking and sending him into an uncontrolled fall were higher. He decided there were other buildings to jump and this one wasn't for him. He took his gear off and we decided to head for Niagara Falls and the Skylon Tower the next day. After my big-top experience, I couldn't blame him.

The next day, we slept in and checked out late. The night before had exhausted us, and it was going to be a long drive to Canada. Like I said earlier, the Skylon Tower was located on the Canadian side of Niagara Falls, so we were going to be doing our next building in a foreign land, meaning this trip would make three buildings in two countries for me. Iiro was also excited to get another building, and we loved the look of this one. It was going to be a four-hundred-foot jump from an observation deck that made the building look like a giant mushroom. The unique shape of this structure meant you would get significant separation from the building after exit, making it about as safe as any building could be. It was also a tourist attraction, so you could buy tickets to the roof. This made me feel like the jump was basically legal. This was a gray area, and I didn't know if it had been tested yet, but logically, it seemed to make sense. I had never heard of any law prohibiting a person from jumping off a building with a parachute, and if we didn't trespass, what could they possibly charge us with?

We found a hotel within walking distance of the building, checked in, and then went on a quick scouting mission. We bought tickets to the observation deck so we could see what the security was like. Turned out security was light; the only thing they had was a small fence that was about shoulder high. A child could have climbed over it with little effort. We didn't see any guards in the observation deck area. We were able to find a wall close to the fence that we could use to hide from an obvious security camera as we geared up. Once we were geared up, it would take us less than a minute to get from the wall to over the fence. The cameras would see us do this, but there was no way they could respond in time to stop us from jumping.

This was going to be easy. You could tell they weren't set up to stop people like us. So, we headed down to look for possible landing areas. I noticed the building was on top of a large hill that went down to an observation point for Niagara Falls. If we opened high enough, we could fly down the hill and land quite far away from the Skylon Tower itself. I thought that would be a great place to land because people down there probably wouldn't have seen where we came from, and if anyone asked, I could just say I jumped from a plane. It was also a good place to walk back to our hotel from, so I decided that was where I was going to land. I told Iiro my plan, but he didn't seem convinced it was the best place. He wasn't sure he could fly that far and would just figure it out under canopy.

It was windy, so we had to burn some time. We ended up going to a museum close by with memorabilia of people doing different kinds of stunts over and around Niagara Falls through the years—everything from people tightrope walking across the waterfall to riding barrels over it. There were exhibits with old photos of women standing next to the barrels they used to ride over the edge of the falls. They even had one of the actual barrels on display. As I stood next to the barrel, I visualized someone putting themselves inside this claustrophobic device to go over a 175-foot waterfall and thought, *Those women were badass.* Niagara Falls was a place where people had been doing hardcore things to test themselves for generations. It was a place of power that seemed to inspire people.

The next morning, I woke up feeling anxious. There is something about the anticipation of doing a new jump. The fear seems to start somewhere deep in your belly. But I know it's really an illusion. A trick of the mind. The real origin is located in your head, sending out sensations to tickle you in odd places. Once we saw the wind had died and the weather conditions were perfect, we set the plan into motion. We grabbed our stash bags with our gear inside and headed for the building, and Suzy was with us acting as a camerawoman. We bought our tickets. No one asked to see what was in our bags and we went straight to the observation deck without anyone giving us a second glance.

Once on the observation deck, we were alone. It must have been off-season, because it felt like a ghost town up there. But the less eyes watching, the better. We went behind the wall and leisurely put on our gear. Once ready, we walked a short distance and started climbing over the fence. It took less than thirty seconds before we were standing at the exit point and looking out over Niagara Falls. I was going to try to film Iiro's jump, so he looked over at me and asked if I was ready. I wasn't, but for some reason I felt rushed, like we needed to get off that building right away, so I said yes. He started counting down and, as he reached one, I hesitated as he jumped. I followed but jumped a bit late and too head-high. I ended up deploying as I was rotating onto my back. My parachute opened, but I was upset with myself because I had missed the shot. This upset feeling melted away as I looked over my shoulder and saw Niagara Falls for what felt like the first time. I had looked at it earlier but hadn't truly seen it for how magnificent it was. From this vantage point, flying towards it, I finally grasped how vast and awe-inspiring it was. The landing area I had chosen was its main viewing point. Flying directly towards it from above made me feel like a bird witnessing this natural wonder in all its glory. I felt like I could finally, really see it with more than just my eyes.

I skimmed the tops of trees as I set down in a park across the street from the falls. No one was around, so I proceeded to slowly get my gear together without feeling any need to rush. I put the bag on my back and just started walking towards the hotel. Then it dawned on me: Iiro was nowhere to be seen, but I figured he must have picked a different place to land while under canopy. I walked up a trail between some trees that took me back to the top of the hill where Skylon Tower stood. I walked past the building without a care in the world.

As I started crossing its parking lot on my way back to the hotel, a man in a suit started walking from the Tower to meet me. I figured he was a security guard and considered running, but I decided that if I ran, I would be admitting guilt. If it was a security guard, I would just deny it was me. If he had video and could prove it was me, then I would make the argument I didn't break any laws and I was justified in using a parachute system instead of their dangerous elevator system.

As the security guard got to me, he held up a hand and said, "Stop right there. Don't try running away. The police are on their way and you are in big trouble."

I smiled and said, "Really? What exactly am I in trouble for?"

"You're in trouble for jumping off our building."

"What makes you think it was me?" I said, smiling wider.

He got irritated, "Don't even try it. We have you on multiple cameras."

My smile grew larger and I said, "Okay, I still don't see what's wrong with that."

This seemed to make him angry, and he raised his voice. "You're going down for stunting."

I burst out laughing and asked, "Did you just make that up?"

He blew up and yelled, "Just wait till the police get here and we'll see if you still think this is funny!"

The police showed up a few minutes later, and things did get a little more serious.

A police car pulled up in front of where I was standing, and an officer opened his door and stepped out right next to me. He asked, "You aren't going to try and run away, are you?"

I smiled at him, "Sir, I didn't run away from that guy, so I am definitely not going to try and run away from you."

He smiled and began questioning me. He asked, "Do you have any drugs or weapons of any kind on you?"

I replied with, "No."

"Do you have any form of identification with you?"

I reached in my pocket and handed him my driver's license. I was prepared for this possibility and knew I would need my ID.

He went on, "Do you mind if I put your bag in the trunk of my car?"

I nodded, "That is not a problem, by all means."

The security guard didn't like what he was seeing, so he began yelling at high volume that he wanted to press charges to the full extent of the law. At this point, the officer was facing me with his back to the guard. The officer looked at me and rolled his eyes in an exaggerated manner, then asked me, "Sir, would you mind sitting in the back of my car while I deal with this gentleman?"

"No problem." I took a couple of steps and sat down in the car. The officer left the door open and walked a short distance away with the security guard. As they were talking, I could tell the security guard was livid.

The police officer looked over at me multiple times with a smile and a look that said, "What's wrong with this guy?"

After about five minutes, another police car pulled up and the officer walked back over to me. He grabbed my bag and put it in the trunk of the new police car. He then asked me politely if I would please get in the other car. As I got in, he leaned over and said, "I'm going to have this officer drive you to the other side of the parking lot—away from this guy—and we will process you over there." I wasn't sure what was going on, but I could tell this officer did not like that security guard at all.

The officer driving the second car was a female, and I noticed she was kind of shaking as she drove. I wasn't sure if it was from anger, but it was noticeable. From out of nowhere she suddenly burst out, "What you did was *amazing!* I just watched the security videos of what you guys did, and it has to be one of the coolest things I have ever seen!"

I was shocked to hear this come out of her mouth. She then said something I will never forget because it was so odd. She exclaimed, "My boyfriend is a pussy compared to you." That took me by surprise, and I didn't know how to respond. This was not what I was expecting to hear sitting in the back of a police car. She parked the car and turned to look at me, then began asking me about skydiving and where would be the best place to learn. She explained she had always dreamed of skydiving ever since she was a little girl. I told her I didn't know of any good places in Canada, but Perris Valley Skydiving in California was a great place to take lessons. I was feeling uncomfortable at this point and didn't know what to say.

After a little while, the first officer showed up again and began questioning me about Iiro. He wanted to know who my friend was, and I told him I didn't know the other jumper.

He asked, "How is that possible seeing you two jumped the building together?"

I responded, "We met online and coordinated to meet on this day at a certain time. We never used names and I don't know who he is."

He kept pushing, and I slipped a little. I said, "All I know is he's from Finland."

I'm not sure why I said that, but I knew the instant I did, I shouldn't have. He informed me the other jumper had run away from the police and they were searching for him. I said, "I'm sorry but there isn't much I can help you with. I don't know the guy."

At that moment, a car pulled up and a man stepped out with a press badge. This guy had been listening to a police scanner and had heard what was going on. He started asking the police officer for more information. As he did, I slipped deeper into the police car. The reporter saw me do this and began shooting questions at me.

I just responded, "I would prefer it if you didn't write about this in the paper, please."

The officer smiled at me and asked, "Why wouldn't you want this in the paper?"

I told him, "This isn't good in the BASE-jumping community, and other jumpers are going to be upset with me."

He just kept smiling, "So let me get this straight. You jumped off a building and don't even want people to know you did it?

"Pretty much," I replied. "I was just trying to fly."

The officer motioned with his hand, "Get out of the car and come take a picture with me." He put his arm around me when the reporter took our picture. The officer then took out his book of tickets and said to the reporter, "Take a picture of me pretending to write this man a ticket."

He started laughing, and the female officer got out of her car and stood next to him. He looked at her and asked, "So, what do you think we should charge him with?"

She shrugged her shoulders. "I don't know, this is pretty serious."

He winked at me and said, "I'll tell you what: I'm going to write you a ticket for mischief. It's about a sixty-dollar fine."

With a surprised expression on my face, I said, "Sixty dollars!"

He said, "Don't worry, that's in Canadian dollars. It's like twenty-five US dollars."

I got a huge smile and asked, "If I give you sixty US dollars, can I go jump again?"

He shook his head. "Please don't. That security guard is a total dick and I don't want to have to deal with him again."

I burst out laughing and he asked if he could give me a ride somewhere. I told him my hotel was just at the end of the parking lot and he said, "Jump in. I'll give you a ride." He drove me to the front of the hotel and, as I was getting out, he said, "Have a lovely day." I thanked him and he drove off. The experience was surreal.

When I opened the door to my hotel room, everything was gone. All my clothes, bags, toiletries...everything. The room was empty and looked like whoever had gathered everything up had done it in a hurry. I realized I had left my wallet and passport in my bag in the room, so I had no way to get home. I had nothing. I took out my walkie and hoped Iiro was somewhere close.

I pressed the button and said, "Iiro, are you anywhere nearby?"

Within seconds, the walkie squawked back, "We're outside. Come out now."

I walked out front and, sure enough, our car was there waiting for me. Iiro was behind the wheel with Suzy in the passenger seat. Iiro looked frantic and said, "Get in the car."

The moment I got in, he sped off like we had just robbed a bank. He asked me what I had told the police. Apparently, he and Suzy had been watching me from across the way being interrogated by the cops and he was worried what I told them.

"They asked me who my friend was," I said, "and I told them I didn't know him. I told them we met online and coordinated everything from there." I then explained how I accidentally let it slip that he was from Finland. With this, Iiro got pissed.

He yelled, "You told them I was from Finland? What is wrong with you? Why did you do that?"

I said, "Sorry, it just kind of slipped out."

Iiro was furious. "Shit. We have to get out of this country—now. What did they charge you with?"

"They gave me a ticket for mischief, and it was around a twenty-five US dollar fine."

"Wait, what?" He looked, shocked. "Shit, I threw my gear away and ran. My gear cost over three thousand dollars."

"Why did you drop your gear and run?"

Iiro went on to explain in detail what happened on his jump. While under canopy, he decided to land in the parking lot right in front of the Skylon Tower. As he was setting down, he saw two police cars pulling into the parking lot. His first reaction was that no police officer was ever going to take him alive, so he just dropped his shit and started hot footing it in the opposite direction. The police gave chase. Iiro came to a ten-foot drop-off, so he hung from it and dropped, hoping the police wouldn't be able to follow with their car. He hit the ground hard and twisted his ankle a little. He thought he had given them the slip, but as he went about twenty paces, he saw two more cop cars come around the bend, so he started running again, this time on a twisted ankle. He saw some train tracks with a train coming, so he timed it so he would cross the tracks and the train would cut off his path from the pursuing fuzz.

While the police were trying to find a way around the train, Iiro found some bushes and jumped in to hide. He waited there for a while—until he was sure he had lost them. He then snuck his way around the backstreets to get to the hotel. Eventually, he got to the room, took all his clothes off, jumped in bed, and pretended to sleep, just in case police officers knocked on the door. His heart was racing a million miles a second, so it would have been funny if they had knocked on the door, because Iiro would have been sweating like he had just run a three-hundred-yard dash. But after a little while, no one came knocking, so he packed up the room as fast as possible and threw everything in the car. As he was pulling out of the hotel, Suzy came walking up, so she got in the car, too. She told Iiro she had seen me talking to the police as she walked from the Skylon back to the hotel. Together they found a place across the parking lot where they could see me being interrogated. They watched the whole thing as the police talked to me and then drove me to the hotel and let me out.

As Iiro finished telling the story, he became visibly upset about leaving his gear behind. He began to realize the cops didn't give a shit about us jumping and were only chasing him because he was running away. He was also irritated I had said he was from Finland, and I think this still upsets him to this day. He asked us if we thought his gear might still be where he had dropped it. I thought the likelihood of the police leaving it was small, but Suzy chimed in, "I can go take a look. I didn't jump, so they can't really do anything to me." Iiro was a bit paranoid that if his gear was still there, the police might be staking it out, ready to ambush. She said, "Don't worry, if they gave Jeb something equivalent to a parking ticket, I should be fine."

We drove back to the area, and she went to investigate. About ten minutes later, Suzy walked up with Iiro's stash bag slung over her shoulder and motioned for him to open the trunk. She dropped it inside and closed it with a thud. She got in the car, Iiro started it up, and as we headed for the border, he asked, "Was it just sitting there?"

Suzy responded, "It was in the middle of the parking lot with your pilot chute blowing in the wind. There wasn't a single person in sight." Both Iiro and I looked at each other like, "What the fuck?"

As we got to the border, Iiro started getting worried again. He felt me telling them he was from Finland was going to send up a red flag when his passport was scanned. The border patrol took all our passports and walked back into their office. Iiro was visibly concerned. I didn't think it was going to be a big deal. If the police just left his gear blowing in the wind, why would they go to the trouble of notifying the border of a possible Finnish BASE jumper crossing into America? After a few minutes, the border patrol came back out, handed us our passports, told us to have a nice day, and waved us through the checkpoint.

That was my first trip with Iiro, and it somehow cemented our friendship forever.

CHAPTER FIFTEEN

SOUTH AFRICA

On the same trip I met Iiro in Norway, I also met a man named John Van Schalkwyk and his wife, Lienkie. They both worked for the police force in South Africa. John was a member of something called the Special Task Force that had originally been developed to deal with the large drug cartels the normal police couldn't handle. In South Africa, the cartels had tanks and military-grade firepower, so the government had to create a division of the police that could handle that kind of combat. Lienkie worked in a rape unit. She was a sketch artist and would help victims identify their attackers. They were an intense couple of people with some of the most horrifying stories I have ever heard. Their stories of crime in South Africa were on a level I hadn't seen even in the most hardcore Hollywood movies.

I remember walking into a room where John was talking with another jumper named Ferrel. Ferrel was from Australia, was covered in tattoos, and had dreadlocks down to his butt. The name Ferrel was fitting because he did look like the little feral kid from the movie *Road Warrior* with Mel Gibson.

John asked Ferrel what he did for a living, and without skipping a beat, Ferrel responded, "I'm a drug dealer, mate."

John smiled, "That's interesting. Back home in Africa, I kill drug dealers for a living. Why don't you tell me what you really do?"

Ferrel looked him dead in the eye. "I already told you: I'm a drug dealer and we are way outside your jurisdiction."

John burst out laughing and said, "Fair enough."

That is the funny thing about BASE jumping: it brings in all walks of life. Police, special forces, Russian mafia, PHDs, lawyers, writers, people who wash dishes... everyone. It's interesting watching different kinds of people come together who ordinarily wouldn't interact with each other in everyday life.

The first week I was in Norway, John and Lienkie didn't speak to me, but they were watching me all the time. I wasn't sure if I made them uncomfortable, but they seemed concerned when I was around. On one rainy day, Lienkie came up to me and asked why I only ate noodles and rice crispy treats. I told her I was on a tight budget and that was all I had brought with me. She explained, "That is very unhealthy. John and I would like to invite you to have dinner with us so you can eat something nutritious." I smiled and thanked her; at that point I needed some real food.

That evening, Lienkie and John made burgers and potatoes, and after a few weeks of ramen, it all tasted amazing. John started telling me magical stories about how South Africa had become a playground for BASE jumping. He talked about it like it was some kind of Candyland. He told me that if I went there, he had legal buildings, bridges, cliffs, and even antennas for us to jump together. He knew all the laws since he was part of the police force, and explained BASE jumping was so new in Africa that no regulations had been put in place yet; we could pretty much do whatever we wanted. As he went into detail about all the different jumps they had, from Table Mountain to seven-hundred-foot bridges, I stopped him mid-sentence and said, "John, you had me at 'legal BASE jumping.' I am coming. You just tell me when and I'm there."

He explained the best time of year was February: that was their summer and the best chance for good weather. He said he would pick me up at the airport and I could stay at his house. We could spend six weeks just traveling around, BASE jumping off anything and everything we found. This, of course, was music to my ears. It sounded like an amazing adventure, and it had been a dream of mine to visit Africa since I was a child watching wildlife documentaries.

Yuri was sitting close by and overheard our conversation, so he came over to ask if he could come along. The idea of legal BASE jumping, especially off buildings, was impossible for any jumper to ignore, and we all sat together making plans for February of 2000.

A few months later, shortly after I finished my NY trip with Iiro, I was sitting in my living room watching a show called *Real TV*. It was a clip show where people would send in-home videos of accidents or wild vacations. At the end of the show, it had an email address where you could send short descriptions of the footage you had for licensing. I wrote the email address down because I thought maybe my footage from Angel Falls might be interesting to them. My trip to Africa was only a few days away at this point, but I thought I might as well send them a short summary of the footage I had with the story behind the trip. I sent off the email thinking maybe I would hear from them when I got back from my Africa trip. But within thirty minutes, my phone rang and the voice on the other end informed me he was a producer from *Real TV* and would like to see the footage I had. I informed him I was leaving for Africa in two days and didn't have time to deal with that at the moment. I told him we could talk when I got back from my trip. He asked me how long I was going to be gone and I told him six weeks. He then said something that was a mistake.

He said, "That's too far away. We have sweeps week coming and we need this footage before you go."

Now, I didn't know much about TV back then, but I had heard of sweeps week and I knew it was big deal. For him to mention that during this call meant my footage was important and he felt it would get good ratings.

This let me know it had real value. He then asked what my address was and said, "I am sending a courier to your house right now. Have a VHS tape of the footage ready. He should be there in sixty minutes."

Sure enough, fifty-five minutes later, there was a knock on my door, so I handed the man the tape and he was off. A little over an hour later, I got another call from the same man, who said, "We want to license this footage. How much do you want for it?"

I didn't have any idea what it was worth, so I asked him what they usually paid for good footage, and he responded with, "For good footage, we usually spend about five hundred dollars."

As I heard this number, I just hung up the phone. Within seconds, the phone rang again, and as I picked it up, I heard him ask, "Did you just hang up on me?"

I said, "Listen, don't waste my time. I won't even talk to you for five hundred dollars."

"Okay," he said in surprise. "Why don't you tell me what you want then?"

I had no idea what it was worth, so I just made some shit up. "I will take twenty-five hundred dollars per edited minute with non-exclusive rights."

He responded with, "Wow, that's a lot of money. I can't clear that kind of cash. I will have to talk to the executive producer and get back to you."

"No problem, but I'm leaving for Africa the day after tomorrow, so you better hurry if you want it before I go."

The next morning, I got a call bright and early from the same producer. He started the call by saying twenty-five hundred per edited minute was too expensive.

I got annoyed. "Then why are you calling me?"

He said, "The executive producer is interested in what you are doing in South

Africa. If you are willing to license us this story, plus bring back three more stories from Africa, we would be willing to pay you a twenty-five-thousand-dollar flat fee."

This was an odd proposal; twenty-five hundred dollars per edited minute was too much, but he just offered me twenty-five thousand for footage I hadn't even gotten yet?

I responded, "No, I have no idea what's going to happen in Africa, so this deal will just be for the Angel Falls story. We can talk about Africa when I get back."

He asked, "How about we give you four thousand dollars for Angel Falls and we get to use as much of the footage as we want?"

I got pissed, "How about if you say any other number than twenty-five hundred per edited minute, we stop talking?"

He took a deep breath that I could hear over the phone and said, "God, you're so difficult. Okay, fine, we will pay you. We'll be at your house at eight a.m. tomorrow morning to film an interview before you leave for your flight. Have the footage on a mini DV tape ready for us to take after the interview."

That was my first time getting paid for BASE jumping and the beginning of my career. From that point forward, I was able to license footage from almost every BASE trip I took. I became a professional BASE jumper with only 150 skydives and thirty BASE jumps. Looking back now, I see how crazy this was. For someone with that level of experience to become a professional is ludicrous. That would be like becoming a surgeon when you haven't even graduated high school yet. But I guess I wasn't getting paid for being a great BASE jumper—I was getting paid because I was good at telling a story. Throughout my career, I have noticed it's been my ability to express myself and my motivations in interviews that has gotten me the work. In the end, I've been earning a living in the entertainment industry, not the BASE-jumping or skydiving industries.

The next day, I did my interview and handed them a mini DV tape with all the raw footage. I then stepped into a cab and headed for LAX to catch my flight to Cape Town, South Africa. The flight was long and had a six-hour layover in London. I am six feet, two and a half inches tall, so there was no chance I could sleep in those cramped coach seats. The entire trip, from my house to John's, took over forty hours door to door. It was a brutal flight, and I was destroyed when I arrived. Yuri had gotten there the day before and was raring to go as I walked in the house. I was there just long enough to drop my bags in one of John's spare rooms before leaving to jump Table Mountain.

The top of Table Mountain is 3,558 feet above sea level and, from a distance, looks flat—hence how it got its name. At this time in history, it had two exit points. One was called the Lookout, and it had a five-second rock drop overlooking Cape

Town proper, and people only jumped it slider-down with no more than three-second delays. It had a large ledge system that you would fly over after deploying. The second jump was also a slider-down jump called Blue Roulette and was located on the back side of the mountain facing Camps Bay, giving you an amazing view of the ocean. In the year 2000, Table Mountain had only been jumped by a handful of people, but with John's help, they had made a deal with the cable car company that managed the mountain to give BASE jumpers legal access and a discount on tickets. We paid half-price because we only needed to ride the cable car one way. You would show up at the ticket office, tell them you were a BASE jumper, and sign a book they had next to their desk. They would tell you to have a lovely day and you would go jump.

Once at the top of the cable car, it was a short ten-minute walk to a beautiful lookout where tourists could view Cape Town. This is where we would start our descent to the exit point. The climb down was easy and only took another five minutes or so. You would come to a flat granite slab about the size of two king-sized mattresses, and on this slab was a crack that, if you followed it to the end, would take you directly over the edge of a 500-foot vertical cliff. This was the first jump Yuri, John, and I would do together in South Africa. John had also invited his friends Karl, an underwater welder for deep sea oil rigs, Moose, an extreme sports filmmaker, and Sean, an author, to jump with us. As I stood at the exit, John told me this cliff wasn't good for acrobatics and he asked me not to do any flips of any kind.

"No problem, bro," I said with a smile.

Karl looked down and noticed my shoes weren't tied and pointed this out to me. I looked at him and said, "Not an issue; I have never jumped with my shoes tied."

He looked at me with a grin and said, "Okay, if you say so." I then proceeded to throw a double reverse flip off the cliff. As I pulled, the force of opening was so strong that I watched both my shoes get ejected off my feet and go into freefall. I thought, *Shit, of course this had to happen right after Karl pointed that out.* I was now going to have to land on hot black asphalt—that had been melting in the South African sun—with nothing but socks on. As I touched down, the ground started scorching my feet. I grabbed my canopy and ran to the closest tree with shade. I felt like a dumbass as everyone landed next to me. Each one pointed out the fact my shoes had fallen off. They also mocked me by noting how hot the asphalt must be.

The next thing I needed to do that day was buy a new pair of shoes. Turned out they didn't have any completely black shoes anywhere. We went to three different stores, and I couldn't find my style anywhere. I finally found a pair of mostly black running shoes, but there was a truly unacceptable amount of white on them. John told me we could get a black sharpie and I could make them as black as I wanted later. The struggles a person goes through when they have mental issues.

Over the next few weeks, we ended up jumping Table Mountain a lot, along with a few buildings and bridges. I did thirty jumps off twelve different objects. It was an exciting time and about to get even better. John told us his friend Sean knew a helicopter pilot who would be willing to fly us to the top of a special set of cliffs called Milner. They were unique because they were stacked on top of each other. The lower cliff was over 900 feet tall and had an overhang of eighty feet. That meant if it rained and you were standing next to the wall, you wouldn't get wet. The cliff on top was over 1,600 feet high and had an overhang of over ninety feet. From the air, those cliffs looked like a giant had taken a massive ice cream scooper and dug rock out from the side of the mountain. The top cliff had a huge ledge that led to the lower cliff, so most BASE jumps done at this location involved doing a double jump. They would jump the top cliff, land on the ledge between the two cliffs, repack, and then jump the lower wall. But Yuri and I had just gotten the first commercially available wingsuits from a company called Birdman, so we had a different idea.

I had only gotten the suit a few weeks before my trip to Africa, so I didn't get much time to jump with it. I ended up only doing five skydives with it at my home DZ in Perris, California. It was the first of the modern ram air wing suits Skydive Perris had seen, and when I went to manifest for my first skydive with it, they asked me where I thought I should get out of the plane. I thought that was an interesting question to ask, seeing how I only had 150 skydives and no idea what I was doing.

But I asked, "How about I jump after the tandems?"

They answered, "Okay, sounds good."

My first jumps felt stable enough and I figured if I found a cliff high enough in Africa, I would try it out.

We all debated if a wingsuit pilot could jump the first cliff and have enough altitude to fly over the ledge connecting the two jumps into one. I was excited at the prospect and decided it was going to be my goal for the trip. We all packed up our gear and John took me to a sporting goods store to get a sleeping bag and some camping supplies. The helicopter was going to fly us to the Milner gorge and shuttle us from the bottom to the top of the mountain for the first day. We would camp that night. In the morning, the chopper would leave, and we would have to hike to jump the second day. We would spend one more night and then do an eleven-mile hike out of the gorge the morning of the third day.

We headed to a heliport close to Table Mountain to start the journey and loaded up the chopper with as much gear as it could carry, then took off with John, Yuri, Sean, and myself. The flight was fast, only taking about forty-five minutes to land at the base of the lower cliff. The site was something special, almost like an image out the Book of Genesis. If there were ever an Eden, this is how I would picture it. The cliff towering over our heads had a massive waterfall that hit the ground over one hundred feet away from the wall. Where it hit was a green oasis with white lilies poking out of a beautiful green background. It was truly stunning. Off in the distance, you could see and hear baboons howling at each other while climbing up the smaller cliffs. It's exactly how you would imagine a great African adventure should begin.

We got a good look at the cliffs from the air as we flew into the gorge and were surprised how large the ledge was. We had never heard of anyone attempting a flight like this anywhere in the world. Yuri was sure he could make it, but I wasn't. My wingsuit experience was limited and I knew I should have done more skydives in the suit before even thinking of attempting a flight like this. But I was a bit too busy actually doing stuff to let a little thing like not knowing what I was doing to stand in my way.

We put all our camping gear under the overhang next to the cliff behind the waterfall to keep it safe during our day of jumping. Yuri and I put our wingsuits on our BASE rigs and then placed them in our stash bags. We would gear up on top. The pilot asked us if we were ready, and we gave him the thumbs-up. We all loaded into the chopper as the rotors began to turn. The pilot lifted off, ascending in small circles so he wouldn't hit the cliffs that surrounded us. I was told earlier that he would land at the top of the mountain where we would then do a sixty-foot rappel to a small area where we could gear up. We would then do a second ten-foot rappel to get to the actual exit point. But as we got close to the top, I noticed the pilot started flying directly into the face of the cliff. I wasn't sure what he was doing, but I saw a small ledge jetting out from the wall. As I watched the pilot slowly inch his way closer, I thought, *No way is he going to try and drop us off there—it's too small for a helicopter.* It looked like the rotors would hit the cliff if he tried. But sure enough, that is exactly what he was doing. He slid the Jet Ranger in sideways and placed about one inch of skid on the little ledge poking away from the cliff face. The rotors were spinning inches from solid rock. He told me to open the door and get out. I was taken by surprise but did what he said. I opened my door and, as I looked down to put my right foot on the skid, I saw a 1,600-foot vertical drop beneath me. The skid was barely touching the ledge. If I slipped as I stepped out, I would have fallen to my death. I took my left foot and placed it on the firm rock before quickly removing my right foot off the heli skid. I then lay down on the ledge, getting as low as possible, as I watched the rotors spin dangerously close to the cliff. I felt like they could make contact at any second, ripping the helicopter from the sky and causing a violent crash that would send metal flying in all directions at high speed.

As this image was flashing in my mind, I watched the pilot spin the chopper around in place so the other guys could get out from the other side. I felt the pressure from the powerful rotor wash over me as he repositioned. It felt like I was going to be blown off the ledge at any moment. As he finished repositioning, the others stepped out of the chopper one by one and hunkered down next to me. After the last one was lying down on the ledge, I watched the chopper lurch up and bank over till it looked like the helicopter was almost flying upside down. I had never seen a helicopter do anything like that before and I knew this pilot was insane.

But we made it.

As the sound of the chopper faded away Yuri, John, Sean, and I all looked at each other with a wide-eyed gaze that expressed the sheer terror of what had just happened. I looked at Yuri and said, "His rotor blades were so close to striking the cliff as you guys were getting out. I was sure he was going to clip the cliff and kill all of us." Yuri just nodded with a crazy grin on his face.

It was totally silent now and the air was calm. We still had the short ten-foot rappel to get to the tiny four-by-eight-foot ledge we would jump from, so everyone geared up in silence. Yuri was the first to hook into a fixed rope with a belay device and step over the edge to slide down to the exit. I went next, followed by John, then Sean.

The exit point was crowded with the four of us standing side by side, perched on a small flake of rock poking off an enormous cliff face. Yuri and I were looking at the distance we would have to fly to make it over the ledge to the second lower cliff. It looked like a long flight, and it was hard to say if we could make it. I noticed a deep crack in the ledge to our left that ran its entire length and let out at the landing area. I thought if my flight didn't go well and I could see I wasn't going to make it over the ledge, I might be able to make a left turn and fly into that crack to give me a little more altitude; it was a possible out if everything went bad. It was hard to judge how wide the crack was from where I was standing, but I felt it could be an option. I told Yuri about it, and he said, "Just fly over the second ledge. That crack is too narrow. You wouldn't want to open a parachute inside that thing. If you don't feel like you're going to make it, just open your parachute. You will need to make that call early, though."

I responded, "Okay," but internally thought, *Nope, I'm going for that crack if I get too low.*

Yuri went first. I watched him perform a perfect exit and a strong flight. He was a natural in the original Birdman wingsuit. He looked like a little fighter jet rocketing across the sky, and he easily made it over the ledge and flew into the gorge beyond. It looked like he had taken over a forty-five second delay, which was insane at the time.

It gave me confidence to see someone else do it first, but I only had five skydives in the suit and I shouldn't have been doing my first wingsuit BASE jump with something so technical. Also, my plan of flying into the crack if things went wrong was a stupid idea, but I was starting to become known for surviving stupid ideas.

I took a few deep breaths and closed my eyes for a moment, and when I reopened them, I felt calm, centered. I stepped off the cliff and was in freefall. It felt like zero gravity for just an instant when I began to feel the air move around my body, filling the fabric between my arms and legs. As the speed increased, the suit inflated with more pressure, generating forward movement as the sensations of actual flight became acute. I aimed for the shortest point between me and the edge of the ledge that led to another 900 feet of valuable altitude. I focused everything I had on making it to that point, but I realized I wasn't flying efficiently enough to get there. I could see that if I kept on this trajectory, I was going to impact well before I would make it to the edge. I looked left and saw the crack much closer now. I could make it there, but wasn't sure how wide it was or if I would get enough altitude to make it out of the crack before I needed to deploy.

With a split-second decision, I banked left and went for it. I covered the distance to enter the crack rapidly, and before I knew it, I was slipping over the lip and banking right, sliding in between solid rock on both my left and right sides. The sensation of flying underground was extraordinary. I had never seen or even dreamed of anything quite like it. I could see the end of the crack coming and knew I was going to make it, but for some reason, I didn't want it to stop. I wished the crack would go on even farther. As I came out the end, I flew over the landing area, and pulled, getting a perfect on-heading opening. I landed right next to Yuri and he was ecstatic. He was jumping up and down, not just at the fact he made it over the ledge for the first time in history, but also at watching me come up short and turn left into the crack. We could tell this was something special and we had just glimpsed the future. Without knowing it and without doing it on purpose, I had done one of the earliest proximity flights in a wingsuit.

The idea of proximity flying wouldn't really be seen by people until three years later, when Loïc Jean-Albert would do a now-famous flight five feet off a snow slope next to skiers in the Swiss Alps. This flight showed the world what was possible and sparked the proximity flying movement that dominates BASE jumping to this day. We didn't have the cameras or budget to film what I did in Africa in the year 2000, and what video we had was grainy and far away. Plus, what I did wasn't planned; I misjudged a flight and almost killed myself. Loïc's was the first planned, executed, and properly filmed proximity flight, giving him the title as the father of proximity flying.

We all did three jumps each that day, trying to get as many jumps as we could while we had the helicopter. Once the chopper left, we were going to have to hike for each jump we did, which was going to take a lot of effort. Hiking in the heat of the South African summer can be brutal, which I learned firsthand on our second day.

The chopper had left and we all decided to hike to the top of the second cliff at first light. John said the hike usually took a little over two and a half hours. We grabbed our gear and put as much water as we could carry in our stash bags. It's a delicate balance to conserve weight but still have everything you need to make it to the top. We started hiking up through the same crack I had flown inside the day before. From this vantage point, it looked even narrower than I had thought it was.

We were smart to leave so early because it meant we would have shade for the first half of the hike. By the time we crested the top of the crack, we got hit by the full force of the African sun. I learned that day why wearing black all the time just isn't practical. After hiking in almost 100-degree heat for over an hour in direct sunlight, wearing all black, I started having issues. It started with a slight headache. Then a tremor in my hands. I became extremely thirsty, which made me finish my water rapidly. After another thirty minutes, my vision began to blur. From there it accelerated quickly. I became severely fatigued and started stumbling. I eventually sat down and couldn't get back up. At this point, John and the guys could tell I was in trouble. I was overheating and suffering from serious heatstroke. We were too high up the mountain for them to carry me back down. Everyone else eventually ran out of water, which didn't help. We had no cell service, so there was no way to call in a rescue.

John noticed a cave close by and felt it would be good to get me out of the sun. By the time the guys had carried me to the cave, I had gone blind. I could no longer see and was shivering uncontrollably. At the time, I thought you shivered only when you were cold, but apparently you can shiver during heatstroke, too. My mind was shutting down and I couldn't think properly. In the cave was a mossy area from a natural spring that ran through this mountain to create the massive waterfall, leaving pockets of moisture even during the hottest droughts. I ended up lying in this pocket for over an hour. Getting out of the sun and being in the damp cave helped cool down my core temperature. Slowly, my vision came back, the shivering stopped, and I was able to sit up on my own.

John, Yuri, and Sean weren't sure what to do. They could see I was improving but I was still weak. We were almost at the top and going back down would be way more difficult than jumping. They felt if they could just get me to the top, I would have a much better chance surviving a jump than I would trying to make it back down the mountain in my weakened condition. After another thirty minutes, John asked if I thought I could walk again. I stood up, putting my hand on the rock above my head, and took a tentative step. I almost fell and John caught me. He asked Yuri to come over and had me put one arm around him and one arm around Yuri.

Sean took my gear and we started walking up the mountain that way. The sun had moved lower in the sky and the temperature had dropped. We were so close to the exit point that it only took another thirty minutes to get to the rappel site. John asked me if I had the strength to rappel and I told him I was feeling a lot better. The rest and cooling down in the cave had helped a lot but my head was still groggy. I was so tired, all I wanted to do was fall asleep.

They helped me hook into the rope with my belay device and I was able to do the multiple rappels down to the exit point. I felt like I was going to pass out about three different times as I did it, but I got there. I unhooked and leaned against the cliff, waiting for them to get to me. Once they did, I said, "Guys, I am just going to go. I have to get off this mountain right now." They agreed, and I jumped. I had a weak flight and I pulled high, but I made it to the landing area and put my gear away. I went to the camp, drank as much water as my belly could hold, then lay on the ground and fell asleep. That was the end of my jumping at Milner. The next day we began the eleven-mile hike out and back to civilization.

After we returned to Cape Town, Yuri had run out of time and had to head back to the USA to work. We dropped him at the airport, and I was sad to see him go. I wasn't sure if I'd ever see him again. BASE jumping seemed to kill people so often that it was never a given that any of us would be alive much longer. Goodbye moments became emotional for me, even though I never showed it. I really hoped I would get to see Yuri again, and I told him we needed to plan another trip together soon.

So far, it had been an exciting three weeks, but I still had three more weeks to go. John and I started planning what to do next. John had work to do in Durban and asked me if I wanted to come along with him. He tried to sell me on the idea by saying, "Jeb, I have a few buildings, antennas, and a waterfall we can jump when I finish my work."

Of course, I said, "Yes, I would love to jump all of those things," and the next day we were on a flight to Durban.

We got there, checked into a hotel, and got hit by bad weather. For the first few days, all I did was follow John around to his different meetings, but I started getting a bit antsy by the third day. John saw this and said, "It's too windy for jumping buildings and antennas, but we should go check out Howick Falls. It drops into a gorge and might be protected from the wind." Howick Falls is a 310-foot waterfall located in the KwaZulu-Natal on the Umgeni River. I thought this sounded like a splendid idea.

John asked if I was okay with him picking up his friend, Rat, a South African skydiver who John was teaching to BASE jump at the time. He thought it would be a good jump for his new student, seeing as it had a water landing and should be safer than most other 300-foot cliffs. John introduced me to Rat, who seemed like a nice enough guy. I wasn't sure where his nickname came from, but I wasn't going to be a Judgy McJudger about it.

We all loaded into the rental car and went for a little road trip to see if the waterfall was jumpable. The winds seemed calm as we pulled up, so we got out and headed over to an outlook to get our first full view of the waterfall. I noticed the water volume rushing over its edge was immense. I looked at John and asked if that was normal. I felt even though the winds seemed calm, the water volume itself could create turbulence that might be an issue during deployment. John looked at the waterfall thoughtfully and responded with, "You won't know till you go over and drop some wind indicators. If the wind indicators tell you there's too much turbulence, don't jump." I thought that was fair enough, so Rat and I grabbed our gear out of the car and headed toward the exit point.

To get there, Rat and I would have to cross the river at the top of the falls. This was daunting because the river was moving a lot of water. John would stay at the lookout and film our jump from the side so we could get some footage.

As Rat and I crossed the river, I could feel it tugging at my legs with a powerful force. A few different times, I felt as though it might sweep my legs out from under me and drag me over the falls, but I kept my footing. We made it to the other side with a sigh of relief. It was a short walk from there to the vertical ledge that put the falls to our left. As I stood there, I was surprised how close the exit point was to the waterfall and I could sense the power raging over its lip. I had a few small paper wind indicators in my pocket, and I started dropping them to see how the water was moving the air around it. To my surprise, they went straight down with barely any movement at all. It didn't seem right for them to have that little reaction to such a massive rush of water in such close proximity, but I thought, *Wind indicators don't lie.*

I started going through a quick risk evaluation of the jump. I figured if I had an on-heading opening, I would be fine. If my parachute opened with a 90-degree off-heading to the right, I would be okay. Even if I got a full 180-degree off-head facing back into the wall, I felt I could still back the canopy up and just drop right in the water.

The only thing I was concerned about was my parachute opening with a 90-degree left turn and facing the waterfall itself. If that were to happen, I knew there would be a good chance I would hit a wall of water and collapse my canopy. I would then impact the pool at the bottom of the falls hard. But it was water, so I didn't think it would kill me...probably. I'd get seriously injured, but I didn't feel it would be fatal. I started thinking about the risk-versus-reward ratio of a jump like this. Would I get enough pleasure for the amount of risk I was taking? I then wondered how many 90 lefts I had gotten in the last sixty jumps. I could only remember about three and decided the pleasure outweighed the risk of serious injury, so I was going for it.

I looked over at Rat and told him I was going to jump in ten seconds. I waved my hands over my head to signal John I was about to go, then stood there with the raging waterfall to my left. I took a deep breath, counted down, "Three, two, one...see ya," and stepped off the cliff. As I jumped, I launched asymmetrically, accidentally dropping my left shoulder. I may have unknowingly manifested that bad opening. I was thinking, *Don't get a 90 left, don't get a 90 left,* and by doing so, I may have given myself a 90 left. As my left shoulder dropped, it loaded the left side of my canopy first, which made that side inflate first. This caused a surging opening directly towards the falls. As my parachute opened, I grabbed the right rear riser of my canopy and pulled as hard as I could; the canopy responded by turning me away from the waterfall. For a split second, I thought I had made it, but then I felt water touching my feet. I have found that when fear passes a certain level, my perception of time becomes distorted. It slows to a crawl; seconds can feel like minutes. In that moment, I could feel water moving past my feet and up my knees, and the unnerving chill of it spreading across my back. The water pulled me in, snatched up the canopy, collapsed it, and forced me through to the back of the cascade. I was freefalling behind the waterfall. Below, a big ledge of jagged rock was rising up in what felt like slow motion. I impacted the ledge in a sitting position, and the blow was so severe I instantly knew it had broken my spine.

There are no words in any language to express the magnitude of pain that shot through me; I couldn't believe a human body could hit something that hard and continue to live. I toppled forward, colliding with a second outcropping of rocks, first with my legs and then my chest. I hyperextended my right knee, then cracked my sternum, along with most of my ribs. I fell for what felt like ages, seized with pain, and plummeted into the water headfirst. Luckily, the water beneath the falls was deep and free of rocks, otherwise I would have surely died. The sheer force of the water sent me hurtling down. I was enveloped by agony and suffering in what felt like a watery grave. The first thought that entered my mind as I felt the current dragging me under was: *Am I paralyzed?* I knew my back was shattered—I just didn't know how badly. I started trying to wiggle my toes; I could feel them sliding next to each other as they moved up and down. A sensation of relief surged through me. I wasn't paralyzed. With that, I thought, *I'll be able to BASE jump again.* That's how obsessed I had become with jumping: even in that moment, drowning under a waterfall after being completely destroyed, the only thing I cared about was if I could jump again.

Quickly, my mind shifted into another gear. It became about survival. When you're faced with life-threatening accidents with no one there to help, it's up to you to figure things out. You become goal oriented. What do you need to do at that exact moment to not die? First thing I needed was air. Without air, I would die in the next few moments, so my goal was to get my head above water to breathe. Problem was, I couldn't move very well. All the broken bones and pain made movement close to impossible. Luckily for me, I was positively buoyant at the time, so I slowly drifted towards the surface without having to move much. As my face broke the surface, I tried to take a breath, but breathing was difficult with a broken sternum and ribs. I gasped for air, but very little made it into my lungs before I was forced back under the turbulent water. I would pop up, get a small gulp of air, then get pushed back down. This happened over and over, but I was able to get just enough to keep me conscious as the current pushed me towards shore.

Bobbing into the shallows, my movement was limited by my injuries. I watched my canopy float past me and get hung up on some rocks about six feet away. I lay there staring at it, trying to come to grips with my situation. As I did, I started noticing the cold. Howling wind blew over me from the plunge pool of Howick Falls. The cold grew more intense with each passing moment, so I began to shiver. The shivering created vibrations through my broken bones, sending shooting spikes of pain across my entire body. I was lying on jagged rock that felt like stone daggers ripping through my flesh with every tremor.

I focused on the canopy just out of my reach. I knew if I could get that canopy, I could wrap myself with it and defend against the harsh, cold wind generated by the monstrous waterfall. I tried with all my might to stand up. Every muscle tensed as I tried to will my body to move, but nothing happened. I couldn't even raise myself an inch off the ground—I was helpless. All I wanted was to get to that canopy. I knew it could ease my suffering and potentially save my life. I tried to reach out with my mind and draw it towards me, but it wouldn't budge.

As I lay there trying to use the Force, I felt something crawling on me. I didn't know what it was, but I could feel it moving. Then I felt another one, this time crawling across my lower back. I saw something scurry by my face but wasn't sure what it was. There were about a dozen of them crawling all over me before I finally understood they were golf-ball-sized crabs. The first impact behind the waterfall had torn a large hole in my pants and opened a gaping wound in my left butt cheek, which was pouring blood in the water and attracting the crabs. They were all moving towards the open wound, and this was the moment they began eating me alive. They had small mouths, so it was going to take a long time for them to completely consume me, but it was still psychologically terrorizing to be helpless and have little animals eat you. I would not call the experience habit-forming, and I would suggest avoiding this in your own life if at all possible. The sensation of being eaten was unforgettably disturbing. Pain became all there was. I could think of nothing else. It was all encompassing as little bites of flesh left my body.

I lay helpless in the water for over an hour before John was able to make it to me. It took him all that time to call in a rescue and hike the trail down the gorge to where I was. It was unfortunately too late in the day for a helicopter rescue, so I would have to be carried out by hand. As John got to me, I could see the relief in his eyes when he saw I was still alive. I hadn't been moving, so they weren't sure if I had survived. He went to pull me out of the water, but I told him my back was broken, so we decided to wait for the rescue team. I asked him to please get the crabs off me, which he did. I then asked him to please bring me the canopy and wrap me with it. It was difficult to communicate because I was in the jet-wash coming off the waterfall and the sound was deafening. But he was able to understand what I needed. After John wrapped me in my canopy, he squatted down in front of me. I reached out from under the canopy and grabbed his ankle. I held on, squeezing it as pain spasms rocketed through my body. It was the only warmth I could feel at the time.

It took another two hours in this position before the rescue team finally made it to us. By this time, the sun had long disappeared and it was pitch dark. Crabs had found their way into the canopy and had continued eating me bite by bite, but I had lost all ability to even care. As the head paramedic got to me, John unwrapped me from the canopy. The paramedic started asking me questions and examining me.

I gave him a basic rundown of where all my pain was when he said, "Don't worry; I am going to give you some morphine for the pain."

"No drugs," I told him.

He looked at me like I was completely insane and said, "Sir, you are going to need medication for pain. We will have to carry you out of here and it will take around six hours to do so. During those six hours, we will probably bounce you off every rock along the way. You are going to need something to deal with the pain."

I repeated, "No drugs."

He now looked annoyed and said, "You have to give me a good reason why you're refusing the pain medication or I'm going to administer it anyway."

"At this moment, I can feel what's wrong with me; so when I see the doctor, I can tell them what hurts. If you give me drugs, I will no longer be able to explain what's wrong. I did this to myself, and I deserve to have this experience with a sober mind. I earned this pain, and I will learn more from that pain than I will from being sedated."

He looked at me like I was a lunatic and said, "Okay, tell me that in six hours," and they began to prepare me for transport.

Six men lifted me at the same time and laid me on a backboard. They then strapped my legs, arms, belly, and head down so I couldn't move at all. They placed the backboard in a bright orange, plastic sled with sets of handles on each side. They added more straps, securing the backboard to the sled, then three men on each side of the sled all lifted me together. There were three groups of six men in the rescue party and they would take turns in rotation. As one group would get tired, another group would take over. All for my mistake.

As we approached the raging river that Howick Falls spawned, I could see lights shining on a series of ropes and pulleys spanning the rapids. The concern they had was dropping me in the river and the current dragging me away. It wouldn't take long for me to drown in those rapids, so they hooked the sled to the ropes and pulley system they had set up. They then slowly started crossing the river with me. From my vantage point, it was dark, but their headlamps illuminated what was directly over my face. I was looking up at the rope system they had installed, admiring their intricate work, when I suddenly found myself cut off from air—I was underwater. It was frightening and disorienting to be strapped down, unable to move, as I was plunged beneath rapids without knowing when I may resurface. I remember trying to shake my head and failing. The next thing I knew, I was gasping for air as my face broke the surface and, within a few moments, I was under again. This continued all the way across till we got to the riverbank on the other side. It was an extreme version of unintentional waterboarding. I was relieved when this stage of the process was over, until one of the rescue workers slipped and accidentally placed his hand on my broken sternum, putting his full body weight on me.

All I could do was gasp, "You have to be kidding." It felt like someone had driven a stake through my chest, directly into my heart. He apologized and I knew it wasn't his fault. I had created this shitty situation, not him. I deserved everything I was experiencing, and I was thankful these amazing men were trying to save my life. But man, did that hurt like a bitch.

The paramedic wasn't joking: they did bounce me off almost every big rock along the trail. With every impact, the sensation of nails being driven through my skin into my bones was present. Just when I thought I had maxed out on the level of pain a human could feel, a new wave would strike me. The pain just kept ratcheting up more and more, till finally my body tensed uncontrollably against the restraints. My

back arched and strained with all the force my body could muster. The paramedic from earlier saw what was happening and asked them to put the sled down.

He leaned in close and told me, "You need to stop doing that right now."

I responded, "I'm not doing anything; I have no control over this."

"This could paralyze you if the breaks in your back are unstable. I have a muscle relaxer that I can inject you with that will stop this. It won't affect the pain, but it will stop the muscle contractions."

At that moment, all my fight was gone. "Do whatever you need to do. I'm beyond caring at this point."

He injected me with something; I have no idea what, but the muscle contractions did stop. I don't think he was lying about the pain relief, either, because my pain seemed to be unaffected and continued like an electrical current running from my flesh to my bones.

Nine hours after impacting the waterfall, I finally made it to an ambulance. They took me out of the sled and placed me on what felt like soft floating heaven. This amazing gurney was soft, dry, and warm. This alone took my pain from 100 percent to about 80 percent; compared to what I had been going through, this was almost pleasure.

John poked his head into the ambulance door and asked, "How are you feeling, buddy?"

I told him, "I've had better days," and he laughed.

With a huge grin on his face he asked, "Would you like to see the video?"

"Are you crazy?" I said with a smile. "Of course I would." He got out my TRV900, opened the little screen, and started playing my accident for me as I lay in the ambulance waiting to head to the hospital.

John and I had a conversation earlier in the trip where we had talked about what to do if an accident happened. I told him "No matter what happens to me, you keep filming, always." People tend to turn cameras off or put them down when things go wrong. To me, this is a mistake. People need to see the accidents, too. Not just successful jumps. That isn't real life. In real life, things tend to go wrong. In real life, mistakes are made, and with BASE, those mistakes have serious consequences. I wanted everyone to see the good, bad, and ugly of what we do. So, when this accident happened, John took what I had said to heart and he filmed it all. Everything from the jump to impact to drifting to the riverbank. He never took the camera off me. I didn't know it at the time, but this was going to be the most important footage ever taken of me and would become the foundation of my entire professional career. In the meantime, though, it just hurt.

The ambulance took me to the closest hospital in a town called Pietermaritzburg.

I was brought directly to the ICU, where they began taking X-rays and MRIs of my back and chest area. As I was resting in a lovely warm bed with blankets taken from a hot dryer to help with my hyperthermia, a doctor finally walked in.

He had a wide smile and introduced himself as my doctor, then started joking around and said, "I bet you will never do anything like that again."

I responded with, "The only two things that will prevent me from BASE jumping are quadriplegia or death."

He replied with a toothy grin, "Looks like you will be jumping again, then."

He proceeded to go over the damage I had sustained. Turns out I had compression fractured my C1 vertebrae and sacrum. I broke my tailbone, shifting it 45 degrees inward. I had hyperextended my right knee and broken my sternum, along with multiple ribs in both the chest and my back areas. (I had also broken my left foot, but they didn't catch that until weeks later when I got up to walk for the first time.) He told me the injuries were not that bad considering the accident. He said I would have a 100 percent recovery in the short term, and the full recovery would take about six months or so. But he went on to say the compression fractures in my spine were a degenerating condition, and if I lived past forty, it would be something that would come back to haunt me.

I smiled and said, "There is a zero percent chance I'm living past thirty, so that won't be a problem."

He smiled again, shook his head, and said, "If you keep doing this sport, I concur: living past thirty is highly unlikely."

This was my first serious injury, and I believe it saved my life (despite how backwards that sounds). It's one thing to be told what you are doing is dangerous; it's another to experience what that word actually means. When people tell you how dangerous BASE jumping is, you feel like you understand what they're saying, but as you watch friends get hurt and die, you begin to realize it's way worse than you thought. You think, *Okay, now I get it,* but you still have no clue. Nothing gives you a better understanding of your own mortality than getting destroyed yourself. The pain, the suffering, the sensation of dying slowly and alone as you're being eaten by animals. The lying on your back for weeks on end, unable to move, just staring at a ceiling. Only after you have been through this can you truly grasp the sheer magnitude of the consequences of the choices you made. This experience is what changed my perspective and gave me a better understanding of what was truly at stake, a greater respect for my life, and a clearer picture of what I was doing. It also helped me put things into perspective and forced me to reevaluate my priorities.

I have to say, the single greatest lesson I learned from this experience had to do with bed pans. If there were a hell, it would involve the bed pan in some way. For the first few weeks I was stuck in a South African hospital, the bed pan was my nemesis. I would lay in bed trying to hold it as long as I could. I dreaded ringing that little bell for the nurse to come help me poop. I would stare at the bathroom across the room, wishing I could just get up and walk in there by myself. The pain from holding it in would become so strong that eventually I'd have to ring the bell. The nurse would come in and I'd tell her how sorry I was. She would smile, but I could tell she was not excited to be doing this part of her job. It was gross and mortifying. She would help raise me off the bed so she could slide the pan under my butt. Because my back was broken, this was a painful experience that made me constipated, which made it take forever and cause even greater pain. And the nurse would have to stay with me, just trying to hold me in position long enough to get the job done. When I was finished, she would then have to help clean me, and it was always a disgusting process. The smell and the feeling of poo all over me was horrible. It was such an upsetting experience for me that it helped change the way I saw life; any day you don't need help going to the bathroom is a good day.

People tend to take these simple things for granted, because, from their experience, that's just the way things are supposed to be. Once those simple things are taken away, you truly begin to understand how magical your own body is and how all its inner workings are special. I now wake up every morning with a smile on my face as I make my journey to the bathroom by myself. Being alone in the bathroom has become one of the single greatest joys I could ask for, and I get to do it every single day. Going from a suicidal person to someone just stoked to take a poo is something powerful, and I don't think I could have come to this understanding without this experience.

After breaking myself in South Africa, I shifted the way I approached BASE jumping, too. I became more cautious. I started looking at BASE jumping like it was a dark force trying to kill me. I knew I was playing with odds. Even if I did everything right, it could still kill me. So, I needed to make better decisions so I could push the odds more in my favor. I understood BASE jumping would always have risk, but if I trained hard, if I didn't always push it to the very edge of my abilities, and if I gave myself more margin for error, then I could shift the odds in the direction of success.

This was the beginning of my darker outlook on BASE. Up to this point, I had seen BASE jumping as the light that guided me through the darker parts of my mind and helped me find my life. This was my first glimpse of how the light also had dark, and they were equal in power.

I was finally able to travel home after six weeks in the hospital. They had given me a thoracic spine protector that locked my back in place for travel and for walking to the bathroom. My friend Shawn told me it made me look like Skeletor from *He-Man*. The doctor had told my insurance I needed to lie flat for the flight home. The insurance company didn't feel first class would be flat enough, so they bought nine seats on a commercial airliner and strapped a stretcher, with me on it, across the top of them.

They also sent two paramedics to help transport me back to the USA from Africa. The paramedics showed up, introduced themselves, and placed me on the stretcher, then we were on our way. I was moved from my hospital to the airport via ambulance. I had to be taken through a special security screening and was loaded from the back of the aircraft before anyone else was allowed on the plane. The process of attaching me to the top of nine seats was crazy, and when I pointed out that it seemed like overkill, they said when it comes to broken backs, they don't take any chances. I told them the breaks were stable, but it didn't matter at that point. As people loaded the plane, I got a lot of strange looks. Once we landed in LA, I was transported to a hospital in Compton. They placed me in a private room, and as the paramedics were about to leave, one of them leaned over and whispered in my ear, "Get out of this hospital as soon as possible. This is a bad place." She then walked out the door, and I thought, *Great, isn't this just lovely.*

Turned out the healthcare in South Africa eclipsed what we have in the USA on almost every level. Not only was the South African hospital cleaner, more friendly, and more efficient, but my entire six-week stay, with all my meals, rescue, X-rays, MRIs, so on and so forth, cost less than one night in the hospital in the USA. When we finally got the bills, I was shocked at how much healthcare providers scam injured people in the United States. Getting injured is a costly endeavor when you live in the Land of the Free. We are free to pay crazy amounts of money in insurance premiums, and then when it comes time for them to cover you, they do everything in their power not to pay. It's a sobering experience to face this fact, yet it's only getting worse by the year.

At the time, I had no way of knowing it, but while writing this down, I realized something important. When I was on the riverbank being eaten by crabs, I felt like my life was over and I would be lucky if I ever got to BASE jump again. I thought I had just experienced the absolute worst-case scenario. After weeks in the hospital eating crappy food and pooping in bed pans, I didn't see how things could have been more horrible. I had made a huge mistake and was suffering the consequences. This was an accident that would have made any sane person stop. They would have said, "Okay, that's it. This activity is stupid. I was lucky to have survived, but I need to do something else with my life." But my mind didn't work that way. Even with all the pain and suffering, I never contemplated giving up. I was obsessed and stopping was unthinkable. The only reason I even cared about getting better was so I could jump again. For me, rehab would have been pointless if it weren't for BASE.

It turned out this was not the worst thing that could have ever happened to me. My BASE-jumping career probably wouldn't have happened without it. This experience became a defining moment for me. Somehow I took the lemons this jump handed me and squeezed them into sweet lemonade. A few days after getting home from the hospital in Compton, I gave my new contact at *Real TV* a call and told him all about my trip. He got excited and told me the Angel Falls piece we did together was a major success. He sent a courier over to grab a VHS copy of the footage from Africa, and a few days later he bought three more stories from my trip. The waterfall accident was going to be the *pièce de résistance*. I had already set my price, so we didn't even talk about money this time—they knew what I charged.

I think it's important to point out that at this point in BASE-jumping history, most jumpers gave their footage away for free. If news or media outlets asked for footage, most jumpers just gave it to them without question, which made selling footage a difficult business. Why would people pay for something they could get for free? But this accident gave me something others didn't have and couldn't replicate. The story was powerful, and I ended up selling the waterfall footage over and over to different TV programs for more than a decade. When *Real TV* ended, all the producers I worked with moved on to other shows. I started getting calls from those producers as they moved from position to position. One producer actually licensed the waterfall accident five different times for five different shows. By the fifth time, I asked him, "Aren't you bored of this footage yet?"

He responded with, "Nope. Every new show is a new audience, and the story is amazing. People love watching other people get destroyed, but what they love even more is watching that same person stand back up and continue. They love the comeback story."

Every time I sold the accident footage, I would also end up selling all the other footage no one wanted to buy. The stuff the other jumpers would give away for free. The producers needed it to show the comeback. This is how I set up relationships with producers all over the world, and it led to 99 percent of my paid work. So, in an odd way, I owe my freedom of traveling the world and being my own boss to hitting that waterfall. Had it not been for that accident, I probably never would have been able to earn a living from BASE jumping. I would have had to work a normal job to cover bills, and I would have ended up with a completely different life. It's odd how the things I thought were the worst turned out to be some of the best experiences of my life. This particular one helped make it possible for me to live my dreams. It's strange how my career began with a career-ending injury.

After doing the interviews for the three stories, I was paid for all three at the same time, which made for a large check. I went to my parents and told Barry I no longer wanted to do graphic art for his company. He asked me what I was planning on doing for money because he wasn't going to be paying for everything. I showed him the check from *Real TV* and said, "I think I want to try and make a living from BASE jumping."

He looked at the check and said, "Okay. As long as you can pay your bills, then by all means, chase your dream." I thanked him, and as I left the room, I could see a life unchained laid out in front of me.

CHAPTER SIXTEEN

CONNECTING WITH REALITY

During my movie theater projection days, I spent a lot of time with my friend, KC. He loved the ganja and would smoke from the time he woke up to the time he went to sleep. One evening, he tried to convince me I needed to try some of his weed.

I told him, "I'm good, bro. You should be happy I don't smoke: more weed for you."

He said, "Jeb, you just don't get it, man. When you smoke weed, it makes a Double Western Bacon Cheeseburger taste sooooooo gooooood."

"Dude, I don't want a Double Western Bacon Cheeseburger to taste so good. I want bad food to taste bad and good food to taste good and I want to be able to discern the difference between the two. The last thing I want is to ingest a substance that makes mediocrity amazing. I think boredom is important. You need it to motivate you to get up off the couch and go out in the world to do something with your life. I don't want the most amazing thing I did last weekend to be sitting on my couch staring at the ceiling."

He didn't seem to understand what I was trying to say, but that was okay—he didn't have to. I wasn't trying to convince him not to smoke weed. I was just explaining why I wasn't interested in doing it.

BASE jumping—and extreme sports in general—tends to draw in sensation-seeking individuals, and a lot of them like experimenting with drugs of all kinds. I'm a bit of an oddity in my world for not finding them interesting. Personally, I want to experience things for what they really are, not what I would like them to be. I feel that's the entire point of life in the first place. Not just for humans, but for every living thing that has developed senses. Sight, smell, taste, touch, hearing, sonar in the case of dolphins, so on and so forth. These senses are how living things experience the reality that exists outside themselves. We have billions of years of evolution fine tuning these senses to help us connect to our surroundings. I will always trust billions of years of evolution over some hippy mixing up acid in their bathtub to show me what reality is. I have always felt psychedelic drugs are not opening doors to some alternate reality; they are just causing distortion, making everything harder to understand. Reality is constant; it does not change. What you change when taking drugs is your perception of that reality.

Imagine you are just a brain trapped in a skull. Your only windows to the outside world are your senses. LSD, mushrooms, molly, DMT—take your pick. All they do is put little colored gels over your windows so you see the light coming in with distortion. They don't give you a better understanding of what's real—they just fuck up your ability to perceive things properly.

Drug users love pointing to people like the Beatles or Steve Jobs and saying drugs made them creative. They infer that, without the drugs, we wouldn't have iPhones, or the beautiful art created by artists. I disagree. We will never know what these people experimenting with drugs could have accomplished without them. Maybe their art would have been worse, maybe it would have been better. But we do know one thing about these people: they were geniuses. It seems that some forms of genius tend to be attracted to using drugs. But in most cases, I think these people still would have been geniuses even without the drugs. I'm willing to bet they still would have done creative and amazing things no matter what. If you feel the drugs were responsible for these people's genius or even their creativity, then why isn't every drug user a genius or a super-creative artist? The majority of people I have met traveling the world use mind-altering drugs in one form or another. But, for every story like the Beatles or Steve Jobs, there are literally thousands of people who don't do shit except become strung out or mentally damaged. I feel these genius people who used drugs were actually operating at a disadvantage. I feel they succeeded in spite of the drugs, not because of them. You take Einstein and put him on LSD and he will still be way smarter than you or I. But he would be a weakened version of himself. He may still have done amazing things and come up with amazing math explaining our universe, but if he did, it was because he was a genius and not because he took drugs.

Every single time I have been around people using shrooms, acid, weed, alcohol, whatever, I have noticed one thing: they all became less intelligent while under the influence. Many lose simple motor function and find balance difficult. Most couldn't or shouldn't operate a motor vehicle. What's even more interesting is many of them think they are operating at a more optimal level. It's fascinating how their perception of their own abilities becomes so skewed in the opposite of what's actually taking place. To a sober mind, they are clearly handicapping themselves, but they can't seem to understand this while trapped in their own drug-induced delirium. If they were to film themselves and watch it later, they may get a glimpse and realize what a truly weakened state they have placed themselves in. Even still, there's just no getting through to some people.

The way people evaluate risk is always interesting to me. I describe it like this: imagine there was a pill that made you stupid. Imagine it slowed your reaction time and dropped your IQ, making it hard to think rationally or abstractly. This pill would make operating a motor vehicle dangerous, increasing your risk of crashing and dying. Now, imagine surrounding yourself with the single most dangerous predator the Earth has ever known and then taking that stupid pill. This is what most humans do every time they go to a bar and get drunk. Most people don't even think twice about doing this. They actually do this for fun and call it unwinding.

Humans are, hands down, the most evil, dangerous predators this planet has ever seen. Humans are responsible for murder, rape, theft, and just downright horrible things done to other human beings, period. Yet so many people are willing to surround themselves with strangers and then get totally shitfaced drunk. I have always found this to be insane, yet people tend to look at me like I am a lunatic and seem to think I take unreasonable risks because I like to dive with sharks and jump off cliffs with parachutes. I would get in the water with a great white shark any day over getting drunk in a bar surrounded by strangers. Without a doubt, sharks are safer on every level. If you just look at the statistics and hard facts, you'll see this is the truth. About twenty-five people die from shark attacks worldwide each year, and that's with millions of people entering the oceans daily. Also, there are shark dives around the world where people pay to pour blood and get in the water with sharks in their most pissed-off, agitated state. Shark diving without cages is common worldwide. Even with all this going on, the number of people being killed by sharks is tiny. If you made a list of things that kill people most often, sharks would be near the bottom of that list. Death by shark would be below things like coconuts, cows, spiders, snakes, mosquitos, and vending machine accidents. People say, "Well, that isn't fair. There are more people using vending machines than there are people around sharks." Fine, let's do an apples-to-apples comparison: the water that sharks live in kills more people in one week than the sharks that live in that exact same water all year round.

How many people do you think die every single day from alcohol-related accidents? Because it's a hell of a lot more than people dying from sharks.

I constantly have people tell me, "If you haven't tried it, you have no idea what you are talking about."

To this I say, "One of the things that makes humans unique is our ability to learn from watching others." So, as I watch a person sitting on a couch, tripping on acid, thinking a condor is ripping through the ceiling trying to eat them, I have a better understanding of what's going on than they do. Their mind is distorted and they have blurred the line between dream and reality. They are no longer capable of having an objective understanding of what's really happening to them. Whereas I, being sober, can see there is no condor trying to eat them, and this is all just a construct of their own mind. Also, I have experienced drugs my entire life. First, I got to watch my father smoke weed throughout my childhood. I'm not sure I have ever seen my father *not* stoned in one way or another. I got to watch all his friends. I got to watch my sisters and most of their friends as I grew up. I am also in extreme sports, where 99.999999 percent of the participants use drugs in one form or another. I literally have a lifetime of experiencing what drugs do to people over long periods of time, and these experiences have made me not want to do them.

Having said this, I do still believe most drugs should be legal. I feel people should have a right to make their own choices with their minds and bodies. Just like I should have every right to abstain from their use if I so choose. I guess it's like this: you should have every right to smoke a cigarette if you choose, but I should have a right not to smoke that cigarette. If you and I are sharing the same room with the same air, then your right to smoke that cigarette ends until you are either alone or with other people who want to share that smoke. This same principle applies to drinking as well. You should have every right to drink alcohol as long as you aren't getting behind the wheel of a car and crashing into me or my family. Hard drugs would work similarly. You should have every right to take them, but if you become an addict and lose control of your life, I shouldn't have to deal with you breaking into my house and stealing my shit to help support your drug habit. That is the sad thing about many of these substances—it starts out as a choice, but over time, it becomes an addiction. Once it reaches that point, it's no longer a choice. It seems logical to state that the only true choice a person can make to ensure they maintain the power to choose is to never use substances in the first place.

People tend to ask me why I don't like to use painkillers. Usually, it's doctors asking me this question because they are the ones prescribing and I'm the one refusing the prescriptions. Now, I have to be clear: I use medication when it fixes a problem, but I do not take pills that just cover up symptoms. That is at the root of why. Pain is a signal something is wrong. You need to listen to it, not try to cover it up. I will use one of my broken ankles to illustrate this concept.

I was jumping off a building in Malaysia and got a 180-degree off-heading opening with like twists. I ended up impacting the building, breaking both my ankles and cracking my hip. I was rushed off to the hospital, where the doctor instantly informed me that he was going to give me morphine.

"No, thank you," I replied. "I'm fine. Please just go ahead and put the cast on my ankle." The X-rays had shown no surgery was needed and only my left foot needed a cast. He informed me that pain was bad for me and I needed to take the morphine.

I said, "I am fine. Just put the cast on."

He kept pushing and I informed him I only needed to say no once and said to stop pressuring me. He said, "Fine," then began preparing a cast. As he was putting the cast on, the pain in my ankle went from a two to a ten.

I told him, "Excuse me, but you have placed the cast on wrong and you need to take it off and redo it."

He said, "No, sir, you need to take the pain killers."

"Take the cast off right now and put it on the right way."

His face turned red and I could tell he was pissed, but he took the cast off anyway. As he did, we both could see the cast had a lump that was pushing directly against the place where the bone was broken, causing the excessive pain.

As he saw this, he apologized. I told him, "That is exactly why I don't use pain medication. The pain is there to tell me when something is wrong."

Pain tells you important information about what's going on in your body. When I have a broken ankle, the pain is what keeps me from walking on it. Without the pain, I would walk around and just hurt myself more. When I lie in bed with a broken ankle, the pain tells me how to position it. If you don't hold it in the proper position for healing, it causes more pain. So, the pain helps you adjust the position and healing comes much faster. I have injured myself a lot over my twenty-year BASE-jumping career, and I have spent over three years of it recovering from injuries that I have sustained. One thing I always hear from doctors and physical therapists is that I am a rapid healer, and they always seem to question why. I really do feel it's because I don't use painkillers and just listen to my body. I use pain to help me know how hard to push and when I am ready to do more. It's as simple as that.

There is one other reason I don't like the idea of using pain medication during a traumatic accident or in the recovery process. I choose to do dangerous things that have serious consequences for making mistakes. When I make a mistake, I feel I must be punished or I will not learn from it. My pain has taught me more than my pleasure ever could. When I make a mistake, I earn whatever comes next and I do not want to distort that experience. Pain is part of life, and I am in a constant state of practicing mental toughness, both physically and mentally. These experiences give me an opportunity to test myself to see how much I can take. They make me grow as a human being.

Now, like I said earlier, I must be clear here. I absolutely use medications that fix problems; I just don't use substances that cover up symptoms. If I have a bacterial infection, I will use antibiotics to kill the infection. I also have a hypothyroid condition and take thyroid medication every single day. I will also use Novocain when getting cavities filled and I have no problem being put under with anesthesia for surgery. I also know there are people with true mental disorders who can and do benefit from medication, bipolar disorder being just one example. Again, to be super clear: I am all for doing things that fix problems. I am just against things that cover up symptoms.

I also have never liked the term "adrenaline junky." I see it as a dismissive term from people trying to categorize action sports athletes with drug addicts. "Normal" people can't see themselves doing these extreme activities, so they label the person who does them as either insane or addicted to some drug-like substance called adrenaline. I see drug use as almost exactly opposite to people doing extreme activities, and this is why:

You would never call an astronaut an adrenaline junkie. What they do causes adrenaline for sure, but that is not their motivation for doing what they do. An astronaut has set a goal that's trying to push the human species forward. A junkie is motivated only by the feeling. The junkie injects a drug into their system with no other goal than getting a rush or a feeling of euphoria. An astronaut is trying to accomplish a complex goal, and however that goal makes them feel is irrelevant. The only thing that matters is accomplishing the objective. Astronauts do their work almost in spite of things like adrenaline, not because of them.

I feel that many action sports athletes fit into this category. They are goal-oriented and more about high-performance human achievement. I have listened to many interviews and notice when they are asked questions like, "Why do you do this?" many find it difficult to answer. They say things like, "I do it for the rush," or, "Because it's fun," not realizing they're failing to answer the question. All they're doing is talking about a feeling. Lots of things are fun, but what makes this fun? Why are you willing to risk injury or death to do this particular activity? If they would take the time to truly analyze themselves, I think they would come to understand it's about doing things other human beings are incapable of doing. It's about training their minds and bodies so they can perform at optimal levels and push what the human species is capable of. They are trying to connect to the reality that exists outside themselves.

From what I have seen, most drug addicts seem to be trying to escape reality.

They usually seem to suffer from pain, either mental or physical or both, and are just trying to numb what hurts. They don't like the reality in which they live, so they try to alter it to become something more pleasant. In my experience, people doing extreme activities have completely different sets of motivations. Instead of retreating from pain or fear, they actually seem to seek it out. (I can't really speak for others here because everyone has their own motivation for doing things, so I will speak from my own experience and what my motivations have become.)

I am constantly trying to connect to the external reality in which I exist. When you perform an activity that you know can kill you, something special happens in the brain. This is something you can't fake. Your mind knows you are in real danger. You enter a state that goes by many different names. Some call it "the now" or "flow state." Others call it "fight or flight" or "time distortion." Whatever name people label it with, what they are really talking about is the body understanding that it needs to do something with precision correctly in the next few moments or something bad will happen. Once the mind enters this state, it releases everything your body has in order to operate at optimum levels. Your senses become heightened—sight, smell, taste, touch, hearing, and a few others we don't fully understand yet, become supercharged, connecting you to reality at the highest levels possible. This true high-level connection to the environment helps you perform the task at hand. That connection to reality is the entire point of existence. We are here to experience reality for what it actually is, not what we would like it to be.

CHAPTER SEVENTEEN

THE ISRAELI DOCTOR AND THE CAVE OF SWALLOWS

South Africa ended up leading to my next adventure. While jumping with John and Yuri off a series of bridges on the N2 freeway, we ran into an Israeli BASE jumper named Omer Mei-Dan. He was a medical student and, in his time off, he filmed extreme sports TV shows. He was traveling with a cameraman at the time and was super friendly. While at the bridge, we struck up a conversation and I liked him right away. I told him about an awesome jump in Mexico called *Sótano de las Golondrinas*— The Cave of Swallows—a 1,200-feet-deep cave, and how much I wanted to go jump into it. He was intrigued and asked me questions for over an hour about the location. I told him what I knew, which wasn't much, and we swapped contact information. After that, he drove away and I didn't really expect to hear from him again.

Shortly after selling the South African footage to *Real TV*, I got an email from Omer. It said he was planning an expedition to the cave in Mexico and he wanted to know if I would come along. He had gotten a winch system to pull us out after we jumped and had worked out all the logistics. He said the expedition would be for Israeli National Geographic and they would cover all the costs. All I had to do was get myself to Mexico City in two weeks.

This was only two and a half months since my accident at Howick Falls, and I was still in a lot of pain. I wasn't sure if my body could handle something like this, so before answering Omer, I went to the doctor to get his opinion. I told him what I wanted to do, and he said, "The breaks in your back are stable. It takes about six weeks for them to be as strong as they are going to be. But there is other trauma in the area that takes longer to heal, and you will feel great pain and discomfort if you choose to do this."

I asked, "Could this damage my back if I have a bad opening?"

He said, "If it would damage a healthy back then it would certainly damage your back, but if it wouldn't damage a healthy back then you should be fine. It's just going to be uncomfortable."

That was all I needed to hear.

A couple weeks later, I met Omer and his two cameramen, Yuron and Barak, in Mexico City. From there we headed to San Luis Potosi, the closest town to the Cave of Swallows. We spent the next few days scouting the cave and preparing for the jump.

One evening while eating dinner, Omer asked if I was going to Europe for the summer and if I had any fun jumps planned. I told him I was going to be jumping in Norway again and then head to France to jump the Eiffel Tower. I explained how a buddy of mine had shown me how you could jump from the second platform through the tower's center, which, to my knowledge, had never been done before. He instantly sat up a little taller in his chair and said, "I would love to do that jump with you."

My reply was, "The more the merrier. You are welcome to come along if you like." So, we spent the next few hours planning logistics. Omer decided he was going to meet me in Norway, and we would travel together for the entire summer, jumping across Europe.

The next morning, we got to the cave bright and early to start setting up ropes and anchors so that Omer could repel into the cave and set up markers for the landing area. As we arrived, we heard an odd sound growing from the depths of the cave. At first, I wasn't sure what I was hearing, but as I got closer and looked over the edge, I understood what it was. Hundreds of thousands of white-collared swifts were flying in circles as they rose up from deep inside the cave. It looked like a gigantic tornado of birds all chirping and screeching as they jockeyed for position to exit the cave and find food for the day. As I leaned over, looking into that massive sinkhole, birds started rocketing past my head at extreme speeds. It frightened me, because if one were to hit me going that fast, it could cause serious damage. I had never seen a flock of birds spinning in a vortex, all moving as one, and it filled me with a sense of awe.

It took hours for all the birds to leave the cave. I had never seen that many animals in one place before. I could feel the surge of life in my core, and I began to understand how magnificent this world truly was. The reality of what I was witnessing made every fairytale I had ever heard seem small and insignificant. I was witnessing something in the real world that had more power than any made-up fantasy ever could.

Standing there, on the edge of a 1,200-feet-deep cave, watching hundreds of thousands of birds rising up and flying by at breakneck speed, being enveloped by the sound and moving air, I had an epiphany. This whole idea of connecting with nature and seeing it through the eyes of birds became all too clear. I was about to experience this cave the way birds did. It felt like we were growing beyond being human, evolving into something new. Since the beginning of human consciousness, once we became aware of ourselves and other living things, we would look up at birds and dream about what it would be like to do what they do. The freedom of flight has been a consuming desire since the onset of our ability to think.

We must evolve. If we do not evolve, we'll become stagnant as a species and die off. It's the ones pushing the boundaries of what's humanly possible who lead this charge. Sure, some die here and there, but how many squirrels do you think died trying to learn how to fly? How many hundreds of thousands of years of squirrels jumping from tree to tree did it take for them to evolve the ability to truly glide? Humans are special: we can evolve more rapidly using our minds to develop technology that make jumps in evolution happen more rapidly. We went from dreaming of gliding like flying squirrels to actually doing it in a few short decades, and without having to morph our bodies.

People constantly ask, "What is the point of doing these kinds of activities? What social good could it possibly do?" I respond with, "What is the point of anything any of us do, ever? Why wake up in the morning? What is the point of eating food, drinking water, breathing air? Why do you exist?" I feel people pushing the boundaries of human capabilities is the single most important thing anyone can do. Without curious, adventurous people climbing imposing mountain ranges and getting in little wooden boats to cross vast oceans in search of new lands, our species would never have left our huts in Sub-Saharan Africa. Without people putting themselves in little metal tubes and blasting into outer space, we would have no chance for long-term survival in the universe. If we don't leave this planet and find planets outside our solar system to explore and colonize, our species will die with our sun in time. Adventure and exploration are the only things that truly matter. We need people willing to risk and sacrifice their lives in the pursuit of evolution. Without them, our species will go extinct for sure.

Many people do not understand why someone would risk their own life. They can't see the bigger picture that the person taking the risk sees. If you are reading this and you're one of these people questioning why someone would take risks with their life, all I can say is: I hope you one day find something you are so passionate about that you are willing to give your life to it. Because only then will you truly understand what it meant to live in the first place. Your life isn't important—what you do with that life is.

Now, back to trying to figure out how to jump into a cave filled with birds. We had to wait till all the birds left the cave before the locals gave us permission to jump. This made sense, because at the end of the day, this cave was the birds' home, and their safety was more important than us jumping. We would wait as long as it took for the birds to vacate the premises.

This time wasn't wasted though: Omer used it to rappel into the cave and set everything up. It would also be the first test of our winch system, which was man-powered and meant we needed to hire locals to help us pull people out. Two men would stand on opposite sides of the winch, each holding a hand crank. They would work in unison, spinning the cranks to pull the rope through the system. It ended up taking over three hours to pull Omer up from the cave floor, which was way longer than expected and was a difficult process besides. It dawned on us that we weren't going to get many jumps. We would be lucky to get one jump each, maybe two if we pushed it. By this time, the birds had all finally left the cave and it was time to get ready for the first jump. It was decided I would go first so I could film Omer's jump from inside the cave and get his landing. I decided I would do a double reverse flip, which was an acrobatic maneuver I had been working on.

As I stood on the exit point, looking into the cave was unnerving. Usually, you are worried about getting an off-heading where your parachute opens facing the object you just jumped from. But in this case, no matter what direction your parachute opened, you would be facing a wall of rock. You were surrounded by it. From the top, it didn't look like you would have any room to maneuver a canopy. It was also much darker than I expected. I couldn't see the bottom of the cave, so it gave the illusion that I was jumping into a bottomless pit. I called out, "Ten seconds!" and got ready to jump. As I stepped off, I pushed my hips up towards the horizon, grabbed my knees, and started flipping. As I came out of the flips, I saw a green parrot about a foot from my face go by at high speed. I opened my canopy and, sure enough, there was a cliff right in front of me. I turned and again saw a cliff right in front of me. No matter where I turned, there was a cliff, but the deeper I got the more open it became. The landing area was large and Omer had placed a long sheet of white plastic to mark its center. The ground was soft and spongy, covered in moss and bird shit. As I landed, I let out an echoing scream of excitement, and instantly the walkie cracked with Omer telling me not you yell. The locals said it scares the birds. I apologized and put my gear away. I then found a rock to sit on to wait for Omer. After about twenty minutes, Omer came on the walkie to tell me he was ready to jump and would be exiting in one minute. I turned the camera on and aimed it at the opening of the cave over 1,200 feet above my head.

He jumped and I filmed him all the way to his landing. We both had great jumps, but now came the scary part: the sketchy, ghetto winch ride to the top. Omer went first so I could film him being pulled up from the bottom. It was the slowest process I had ever been a part of. For long periods it didn't even look like he was moving. It was like watching grass grow or paint dry. But then something beautiful happened. The sun moved directly over the top of the cave and an almost angelic beam of light came piercing into the cavern. The shaft of light slowly moved down the wall of the cave until it was directly over Omer, and it looked like he was being beamed up to a spaceship. The sun started heating up the cave floor and an ominous-looking fog drifted up. It was one of the most stunning scenes my eyes had witnessed. I took out the camera and filmed as much as I could. I am sad that the technology of mini DV cameras at the time were so bad. The footage couldn't capture how magical the visual was—only my own eyes could translate such beauty.

After almost four hours, Omer was finally out of the cave, and I could see them lowering the rope back in for me. Once it hit the bottom of the cave floor, I walked over and tied a figure-eight knot to the harness I had brought along for just this occasion. I called up on the walkie and told them I was ready to go. Gradually, I felt tension on the harness as it pulled me up inch by inch in an excruciatingly slow process. My back hurt the instant my full weight was supported by the harness, and I knew this was going to be an unpleasant experience. After about an hour and a half, I heard Omer come on the radio speaking Hebrew. The cameramen responded, also in Hebrew. The winch stopped and I felt the rope slip as I fell about five feet. I got on the walkie and asked, "What's wrong?" There was no response. I asked again. Still no response.

After about twenty minutes of dangling there in silence, I heard Omer's voice saying, "Jeb, everything is fine. We just had to put in a few more anchors. When we are finished, we will start pulling you up again." I ended up sitting without moving for over an hour. Finally, I heard the walkie crack with a little more Hebrew, which concerned me because I knew they didn't want me to know what they were saying. But the rope started moving again.

After almost five hours hanging in a harness on a rope, I was pulled over the lip of the cave. As I reached up and grabbed Omer's hand, I looked over and noticed all the new anchor points. There must have been at least six new ones. I also noticed that the giant rock that Omer had originally anchored to had moved about ten feet and was now much closer to the cave's opening. I asked Omer if that rock had slid while they were pulling me out and he said, "Yes, your fat American ass made this several-ton rock slide all this way, and if we didn't add new anchors, it was going to fall into the cave. You would have fallen to your death, and then the rock would have dropped on top of you, burying you right were you impacted."

"Lovely," I said. "So that's why you guys were talking in Hebrew. I knew something bad was happening."

Omer laughed and gave me a pat on the back as we turned to walk away, but I couldn't help imagining being buried under that boulder in the Cave of Swallows.

CHAPTER EIGHTEEN

CIRCUS CIRCUS

A few days after I got home from my Mexico trip with Omer, I got a message from Iiro inviting me to come to Vegas to jump off the Stratosphere Casino with him. I had never been to Vegas before and felt this could be a cool way to see the city. I was never a good tourist. I loved traveling with a purpose and having a mission of some kind. Looking at old buildings or art in some museum wasn't enough to motivate me in those days. Things like BASE jumping, surfing, climbing, and scuba diving are activities that motivate you to get up off the couch and out into the world to do something with your life. I love things that push me into living. So, I responded to Iiro's invitation with, "Of course I want to come."

I was still dating my first girlfriend, Michelle, at the time, so she came along with us. This would be her first time experiencing what I did in person. She had seen the videos for years now, but being part of the process is something different. She would work as our ground crew, which meant filming and keeping an eye out for security—and being ready to respond if something went wrong.

Iiro, Michelle, and I all checked into the Circus Circus Hotel and Casino on the Vegas strip. It was a rundown, gross kind of place, but the price was reasonable, and we didn't plan on spending much time in the room. As we pulled into the parking lot, Iiro and I looked up and wondered if we could find access to the roof and maybe do a warmup jump. After dropping our stuff in the room, Iiro asked if we should go up the stairs to see if we could access the roof somehow. I agreed, and we were out the door within five minutes.

213

We found the stairwell and made it to the roof quickly. As we got to the door, there was a big sign that read, "Alarm Will Sound If Door is Opened."

Iiro asked, "What if we gear up right here, push the door open, and then just jump off the building before anyone has time to respond?"

As I was thinking about this plan, I looked over his shoulder and saw a metal ventilation system that let air in from the roof. I noticed the grate had long vertical shutters that could be opened and closed. A few of the shutters were missing and it looked like you could slip right between them with little effort. I pointed over Iiro's shoulder and, turning his head to look, he saw what I was pointing at right away. I walked over and pulled myself up and through the vent in less than ten seconds. Iiro followed and we suddenly found ourselves standing on the roof of Circus Circus.

We walked to the edge of the building and saw the parking structure where we had left our car right under us. We knew this corner of the building would be perfect for jumping, and we could land across the way next to a smaller hotel behind the Circus Circus. Michelle could position herself on the roof of the parking structure directly underneath us, giving her a perfect vantage point to film our jumps.

"Should we contact the local Vegas jumpers?" Iiro asked. Technically, it was the right thing to do. There was a pretty good chance the locals were jumping this building. That vent hadn't gotten broken like that by itself, but it seemed like something a jumper might do. Iiro had met a local jumper named Chris while drinking in a bar on a previous trip and decided to give him a call to find out if Chris knew anything about people jumping this building.

Chris had no idea if people were jumping Circus Circus, but he was keen to do it with us if we would have him. We felt the more the merrier, so we told him to meet us at 1:00 a.m. We wanted it to be as quiet as possible, and jumping in the middle of the night would keep the number of witnesses to a minimum.

We told Michelle the plan, and she seemed scared. Shortly after 1:00 a.m., she would leave the room and head to the top of the parking structure where we had parked our car with a video camera and a walkie talkie. She would go to the corner closest to the Circus Circus and contact us when she was in position. We would then leave the room, head for the roof, gear up, and give her a five-minute call when we were ready to jump. She would then turn the camera on and begin filming. Her location would give her the perfect vantage point to film us and give her a clear view of everything around. She could also warn us if there was any security walking on the ground. We told her that, after we jumped, if anyone approached her and asked if she knew us to say, "No, I have no idea who they are. I saw people jumping and happened to have my camcorder with me, so I started filming." We repeated, "It's important you tell people you don't know us."

She said, "No problem," and seemed to understand.

At 12:55 a.m., there was a knock on our door. Chris came inside and we told him the plan. Iiro and I had moved our car to the parking lot of the hotel across the street where we were going to land. Iiro would jump first and get in the driver's seat of the car. Chris would go second and get in the passenger side of the vehicle. I would jump last and get in the backseat. Iiro would then drive us around the Vegas strip until we got the all-clear from Michelle.

Once the explanations were done and everyone understood, we set the plan in motion. Michelle went first, and it took her about fifteen minutes to get into position and give us the call. We left the room, heading to the stairs and making it to the roof in less than ten minutes. I went through the vent opening first and Iiro handed all the gear to me. Iiro and Chris came through next. As we stood next to the vent on the roof, we saw a camera pointed at the door. We weren't sure if the camera was activated when the door was opened, but just in case the camera was always active and had a wide angle, we decided to move away as quickly as possible. We walked to the edge of the building and used our walkie to call down to Michelle and ask if the coast was clear. She responded, "I don't see a single person anywhere. Nobody's around right now." Iiro and I looked at each other and nodded. This was good news: it was even quieter than we could have hoped for. Less people equaled less chance of being seen.

The air was still—that's one thing I've noticed about all the building jumps I have done. Wind is always such an issue when jumping in urban environments, so I only ever did them with zero wind conditions. Because of this, the air always felt dead and added an eerie quality to an already intense situation. The Circus Circus is only 300 feet tall, and there was a smaller structure under us, so Chris took out his pilot chute to go handheld. Iiro decided to go stowed, which was considered pushing it at the time because pilot chutes were known to hesitate and could cause accidents on objects this low. He noticed I wasn't getting my pilot chute out either and asked if I was going stowed, too. I told him I was going to do a gainer. Now, by today's standards this is pretty common, but at the time, this was unacceptable. To compound the insanity of doing a reverse flip from a 300-foot building was the fact I had zero formal acrobatic training and had only done a handful from very high cliffs. It's hard to grasp the level of insanity a person would have to possess to do something like this. Iiro and the local both looked at me like I had just told them I was going to shoot myself in the head with a shotgun, but they didn't ask any further questions.

We called down to Michelle on the walkie and asked if the coast was clear. She responded, "Everything is clear and there's no one in sight." We gave her a one-minute call and she said, "I am ready and filming."

Iiro stepped up on the ledge and looked down. I heard him take a deep breath and he counted down, three, two, one, and stepped off with perfect body position. He threw his pilot chute and it opened with a slight off-heading to the left. He grabbed a right rear riser and pulled hard. This caused an over-correction to the right, and he had to make another adjustment to the left. There wasn't enough altitude, so he hit the parking structure Michelle was standing on maybe six feet from the ground.

From where I was standing, it looked like he hit hard, but he stood up quickly and ran to the car, so I thought he couldn't be hurt too badly. Chris stepped up and jumped off seconds later. I watched his parachute open with a perfect on-heading and he landed right next to the car, perfectly. I stood up on the edge, took a deep breath to steady myself, and stepped off into a nice, laid-out reverse flip.

As I came through, I pulled and had a perfect on-heading opening, too. By the time I landed, Chris was in the car and everyone was ready to roll. I quickly pulled all my gear in and jumped in the backseat. Iiro put his foot on the gas and we left the parking lot in great haste.

As we pulled onto the Vegas strip, Iiro looked over his shoulder and said, "Guys, I think I need to go to the hospital."

I asked, "What are you talking about?" I then looked from the backseat and saw that his leg was bleeding.

"I'm pretty sure my leg is broken," he said.

He then told me to contact Michelle and ask if she had gotten the shot. I smiled because, you know, priorities.

I got the walkie and pushed the button to ask, "Michelle, how did the footage turn out?"

"I can't talk right now," she replied.

I thought that was an odd answer so I asked, "What do you mean you can't talk right now?"

A male voice came back on the walkie saying, "Sir, we have your girlfriend. You and your friends better come turn yourselves in."

I threw the walkie on the seat next to me like somehow the security guard was going to grab me through the device.

Iiro yelled, "Shit, they got her." I knew right away what I was going to have to do.

I said, "Iiro, turn around and take me back to the hotel. I need to get Michelle."

"Do you want me to come with you?" he asked.

I told him, "No, you go to the hospital and get your leg looked at. There is no reason for all of us to get in trouble. I'll deal with this."

Iiro turned the car around and dropped me at the front entrance of Circus Circus.

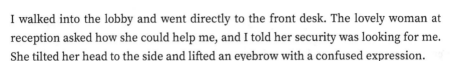

I walked into the lobby and went directly to the front desk. The lovely woman at reception asked how she could help me, and I told her security was looking for me. She tilted her head to the side and lifted an eyebrow with a confused expression.

I noticed the look and said, "I just jumped off the building with a parachute, and your security has my girlfriend in custody."

She picked up the phone next to her and pushed a few numbers, and within minutes, a security guard walked in the front door with a bicycle and asked me to follow him. I followed him through the casino to a hidden door that took me to a place you don't normally see when visiting the establishment. They have their own little city behind those walls. He took me to an area with interrogation rooms and temporary holding cells. Michele was sitting in one of them with a look on her face that could kill. She didn't seem happy to see me, which I thought was understandable. The guard opened the door and asked me to sit with her while we waited for the police to arrive. I went in the room and sat next to her.

To call her angry would be an understatement of epic proportions. She started unloading on me, so I just sat and listened. When she was done expressing how upset she was, I asked her, "What happened? How did they know you were with us?"

She calmed down almost instantly and said, "A bicycle security guard was on the floor beneath me in the parking structure. When the first parachute opened, he heard it, and his first reaction was to go to the top of the structure to see what was going on. That's when he saw me filming. He came straight for me and, as you were landing, he asked me if I knew you guys. I didn't know what to do, so I said yes."

I looked at her with disbelief. "Michelle, I told you to say you didn't know us."

She said, "I was scared, and it just came out. It didn't matter anyway because as he was talking to me, you came on the walkie asking if I had gotten the shot, so there was no way out of it."

She was right; that was a bad move on my part. I took a deep breath and said, "Sorry for getting you into this." There wasn't anything to say beyond that—this was my fault, not hers.

We sat in silence for a little while until the same security guard came walking back in. He sat at a little desk across the room and asked me to come talk with him.

As I sat in a chair across the desk from him, he began to speak. "You are in a lot of trouble, sir."

I responded with, "What exactly am I in trouble for?"

He thought for a moment, then told me, "You were trespassing on private property."

I slowly took my room key out of my pocket, placed it on the table between us, and said, "No, I am a paying customer."

He narrowed his eyes and, with a tight little smile, he said, "Okay, so you want to play that game. Well, by jumping off our building, you were endangering our other customers, and that is reckless endangerment. That is a much bigger offense."

A large grin spread across my face, "No, I was not being reckless. You see, before jumping I looked down and there were no people underneath me. I also looked in my landing area and there were no people there, either. I also looked at the space between where I was jumping and where I was landing, and that was also clear. The only person that was in any danger was me. I can also prove all of this in a court of law. I was wearing a camera on my head and filmed the entire thing. So, if you want to go to war with me over nothing, let's roll."

With that, he was finished with the conversation, so he stood up and said, "Let's see how you feel about things when the police get here."

I went back to sit with Michelle, and we ended up waiting for three hours until the police arrived. When the officer showed up, he walked into the interrogation room and asked me for my driver's license. I handed it to him, and he walked into the hall, where he handed the license to another officer. That officer left for about ten minutes.

While he was gone, I heard the original officer talking with the security guard, saying, "What would you like me to charge him with? Breaking and exiting? There is no such thing." They all started laughing. When the officer with my ID returned, he told everyone, "This guy has no warrants." The original officer walked back into the room, followed by the security guard. He handed me back my ID, looked at the security guard, and said, "This man has done nothing wrong. I can't charge him with anything." Turning to me, he said, "Have a lovely morning," and walked out the door.

You could tell the security guard was annoyed as he looked at me and said, "Well, maybe he can't do anything to you, but we can." He placed me against the wall and took my picture with a Polaroid camera. He took my fingerprints, then had me read and sign a piece of paper that informed me I was permanently banned from the Circus Circus and all other affiliated casinos.

I smiled and said, "That sounds totally reasonable." He then handed us over to another security guard and told him, "Escort these two to their room to get their stuff. Their stay here is over."

While walking to our room the new security guard said something strange: "I think what you did was hot." I wasn't sure what he meant by that, but he continued with, "What you guys did was soooooo amazing. Don't worry; the security from Circus Circus is never going to remember who you are." He then winked at me with a huge smile. I thanked him and was pretty sure I understood what he was telling me.

Michelle and I gathered up all our bags, along with Iiro's stuff, too. We walked

downstairs, loaded our things into a cab, and started searching for a new casino/ hotel to stay at. I wasn't sure if it was still in effect, but supposedly, I was now banned from three of them. I didn't feel like testing what the last security guard had said, so we checked casinos that weren't on the banned list from Circus Circus. We got a room in the Stratosphere but had to wait in the lobby till 10:00 a.m. before we could check in. It had been a long night with no sleep, and we were exhausted.

While waiting for our room, I was finally able to contact Iiro. I asked him how he was, and he said, "My ankle's broken, but it's not bad. I will have to keep weight off it for six weeks or so."

He then went on to explain how, before going to the hospital, he and Chris decided to stop by a strip club for a few hours just to make sure the cops weren't searching for him at the hospitals. He knew I had loose lips from our Niagara Falls jump, so he had to make sure I hadn't given him up. Iiro had an odd sense of humor, but it made me laugh.

Iiro spent the next few days taking Michelle and me to different Vegas shows. I had never seen a show before, so it was interesting to experience how big the productions in Las Vegas were. We watched Blue Man Group, Cirque du Soleil's *Mystère*, and a unique show called De La Guarda that was in a temporary installation outside the Rio Casino. Iiro had opened my eyes to a whole new type of entertainment, and I was fascinated by all the performances. I always thought going to shows would be lame, but he showed me there was more to life than BASE jumping and sharks.

CHAPTER NINETEEN

THE EIFFEL TOWER

About a month after Vegas, I was getting on another plane to travel back to Norway and meet up with Omer and Yuri at Kjerag. We were going to start the trip there, do a little training, then head for Italy and France, and finally finish up in Omer's home country of Israel. Yuri was only interested in the Kjerag and Italy portions of the trip. We asked him if he wanted to jump the Eiffel Tower with us, but he'd be busy with work at the time. So, we jumped with Yuri, training wingsuits for a few weeks. Once we were finished with the Italian part of the jumping, Yuri went on his way, and Omer and I continued on to Paris.

We met up with Omer's cameramen, Yuron and Barak—the same guys he used in Mexico—and a new local camera operator I had never met. We immediately began planning for what would be Omer and my first high-profile BASE jump: a landmark with high levels of security. To make it somewhat legal, we would buy tickets and jump it during the day. We would be coordinating four different cameramen in four separate locations around the Eiffel Tower. We would need to do a lot of recon in order to figure out the best way to get through security and the best places to position our cameramen. This project required a lot of moving parts.

We traveled to the Eiffel Tower on three separate days. We bought our tickets and scouted all the possible camera positions both on the tower and beneath it. We figured out the best way to move from the ground level to the exit point with our equipment undetected. We checked to see what the earliest time we could enter the tower was and when the fewest number of people would be around the landing area. We saw there was a police station located at the foot of the south pillar, only a few hundred feet from where we were going to touch down. This meant escape was highly unlikely. We would jump and instantly be captured by the police.

I planned to use the same strategy I used at Skylon Tower and Circus Circus. When we got captured, I would act like everything was legal and we weren't doing anything wrong. We would have people controlling our landing area, ensuring it would be clear of people so no one else's life would be placed at risk. This would show we weren't being reckless, so it would be difficult for them to charge us with endangerment. Aside from that, I wasn't sure what they could charge us with. I did some research and couldn't find any laws against what we were going to do, so I felt we had a pretty good chance of getting away with a fine of some kind. Omer wasn't so sure about my approach.

He said, "I am going to run for it as long as the police don't see me. If they see me, then I will stop running so they can't charge me with evasion."

I agreed to do something similar. I would walk away quickly until I made eye contact with the authorities. Once they saw that I saw them, I wouldn't put up any resistance.

Back at the hotel, we all started discussing what kinds of jumps Omer and I were going to do. We had learned from our scouting trip that we would be jumping from the bottom of the second platform at about 340 feet. We would then have to wait to deploy our parachutes until we passed the first platform at 180 feet. If we pulled too early, we could impact the first platform during the opening surge of our canopies. The other problem was if we pulled too late, our parachutes wouldn't have enough time to open before impacting the ground at a high rate of speed. There would be about a 1.5 second window where we could deploy our parachutes and land safely.

Omer's main cameraman, Barak, looked at me and asked, "Jeb, what are you planning on doing?" They all knew I was obsessed with doing acrobatics and he was concerned I might try something crazy.

I told him, "I'm going to do a double reverse flip, timing it so that I will be coming out of my second rotation right as I'm passing the first platform."

Barak looked at Omer with an expression that said, "Are you going to do something about this?" He then looked at me and asked, "Why would you do something like that? Isn't this complicated and dangerous enough without having to throw flips into it?"

I looked at him and said, "I have been training to do this for the last year. I found a bridge in Oregon that was three hundred and twenty feet tall and I did double reverse flips over and over again, filming them from every angle to get the timing down just perfect. All the low-altitude acrobatics I've done were in preparation for this jump. My goal isn't to just jump the Eiffel Tower; my goal is to jump it like no one has ever jumped it before." Everyone expressed their concerns but knew they could do nothing to change my mind.

It was decided I would jump first and Omer would film my exit. Barak would be on the first platform and film us passing by him in freefall as we deployed our parachutes. Yuron would be in the landing area, controlling the crowd and capturing our landings. The local cameraman Omer had hired would be across the park, filming from a distance to get a wide shot with the entire Eiffel Tower in frame. Everything was in place, and all we had to do was wait for the weather to be perfect.

We didn't have to wait long. The next day, we woke up to zero wind and clear skies. We gathered all our gear together and moved as a unit towards the Eiffel Tower. We set the cameramen in their positions across the park from the tower and made sure their walkies were working. We then moved for the tower with Barak and Yuron capturing our every move on film. As we walked by the police station at the southern leg of the tower, Yuron walked off in another direction while we headed for the stairs. We had bought tickets the day before to avoid as many Eiffel Tower employees as possible on the day of the jump. We had noticed during our scouting days that the security was softest at the entrance to the stairs. For some reason, they looked at bags much closer when we tried to use the elevators. Today there was no one around. It was early and the tourists must have still been sleeping. This was the quietest we had seen the Eiffel Tower in the last five days.

We started climbing the stairs and the fear began to build. I felt as though I was being pulled through the back of my body and was no longer connected to it. That familiar feeling, as though I was in a tunnel with all sound muffled, came back. My vision narrowed. I could only hear my own breathing. With my heart pumping, I felt my mind short circuiting. Suddenly, we were there. Omer frantically started gearing up. I could hear him telling me to hurry up. I was gearing up but was completely detached from what was happening. I was gripped by fear. It washed over me and clouded all my actions. It was like a virus flowing through my veins, pumping into every cell. A small family came walking up the stairs—a father with a boy and girl.

The girl said, "Daddy, what are they doing?"

He grabbed her by the hand and kept moving with a look of concern in his eyes. For a brief instant, I wondered what he saw when he looked at us, but there wasn't time to consider further.

I stepped over the rail and began to climb through the iron I-beams, trying to get to the exit point quickly. Once we climbed into the ironworks of the structure, no one could stop us. No security on Earth would be willing to go where we were heading. This jump would happen. My mind did not like what it knew was coming.

I started shaking uncontrollably. I was shaking so badly that it became hard to hold onto the iron as I was climbing. My body was rejecting what I was doing, desperately trying to stop me. I got to the exit point and was in Omer's way. He asked me to move so I shuffled over to the right a little. He called Barak and asked if he was in position.

Barak responded with, "I am ready and filming."

Omer checked in with all the other cameramen and they were all filming. He looked at me and asked, "Jeb, are you ready?"

"Yes," I responded automatically.

But I was lying; I wasn't ready. I didn't want to do this. I was shaking so hard I could feel my teeth rattling in my head. I told myself to stop shaking. I tried reasoning with myself, explaining how this wasn't helping the situation and was only making things worse. But fear can't always be controlled with rational thought. I was in danger of being overwhelmed. My mind was on the edge of shutting down completely. I took a deep breath, trying to center myself. The fear was rising like an unstoppable wave about to crash over me. I closed my eyes and took a series of deep breaths; it felt like a switch got flicked in my head and everything started calming down. There was no coming back now. I had committed to this fully and was ready to accept my fate. It had been a good life and I was ready to die.

I opened my eyes and said, "Ten seconds."

Omer repeated this into the walkie talkie.

I counted down, "Three, two, one," and stepped off into a double reverse flip. I was engulfed by iron beams all around me as I flipped, seeing ground, iron, ground, iron. I pulled as I came out of my second rotation. My parachute opened with a bang and five seconds later, I was sliding on asphalt for a landing.

As I turned to look back up, I heard Omer's canopy slam open just as I saw him sitting upright in his harness. He landed about forty feet away and yelled, "Come on, Jeb, let's get moving!"

Over Omer's shoulder, I saw a female security guard moving towards us. She walked to me and, before a word could leave her mouth, I wrapped my arms around her with a huge hug and said, "I'm alive! I'm still alive!"

She got a smile on her face and responded in a thick French accent, "Yes, you are alive, and now you're going to jail."

I started laughing in an almost maniacal way and told her, "I don't care."

Omer walked over to us and said, "Jeb, she is only a security guard; we don't have to stay here. We can go."

"Why would I go anywhere?" I asked him. "I didn't do anything wrong. If she would like me to speak with the police, then I will."

Omer looked at me like I had serious psychological issues and said, "Okay, Jeb.

Let's see where this goes."

The French police moved quickly, reaching us in less than five minutes. They only spoke French so there wasn't a lot of talking. They motioned for us to follow them, so we did. They walked us to a police car, put us in the back, and drove us to the station. They placed us in what looked like an empty waiting room with all our gear and motioned for us to stay there. After about twenty minutes, a detective in plain clothes walked into the room. Apparently, he was the only one on staff that day who could speak any English at all. Communication was difficult, but we were able to get our points across to each other.

He asked us, "Why did you jump off the Eiffel Tower today?"

"Because it's an extremely fun thing to do," I replied.

He gave me the side eye and, in a thick French accent and with broken English, asked, "You know this is not permitted, correct?"

I said, "No, I had no idea. I didn't see any signs saying this wasn't permitted."

He gave me a dubious look and asked, "So, if we had posted a sign saying you are not allowed to jump off the Eiffel Tower, you would not have jumped?"

I smiled and responded with, "Of course I wouldn't have. I would never break the law on purpose."

His calm demeanor broke, and he burst out laughing. He then said, "That was a good answer."

Just then, a female police officer, also in plain clothing, walked into the room. She said something to her associate in French, and Omer looked at me with concern. When she left the room, I asked the officer what she had said.

He told me, "We are trying to find something to charge you with. We have laws about skydiving into Paris from aircraft, but we are finding it difficult to find something that fits what you did. We are calling different judges, but so far we have nothing." He then winked at me and walked out of the room.

About an hour went by before he came back. This is where the communication broke down and, to this day, I don't fully understand what he said, but what I gathered was, they were going to hold on to our gear till we came back to speak with a judge in six weeks. I told him we were leaving France in three days, and he smiled. He explained we weren't being charged with any crimes, but they were going to hold on to our gear for a little while and if we wanted it back, we would have to come back to France to get it from the judge. It seemed to me this was their way of punishing us. They couldn't charge us with anything, but they could make life difficult by forcing us to spend money coming back to France to deal with getting our gear back. Omer wasn't happy about this at all, but I didn't care. I felt it was a small price to pay for a permit to BASE jump the Eiffel Tower. They could keep my gear. I had a second rig waiting for me back at the hotel, anyway. Omer swore he would come back to France to get his rig; he wasn't going to let them keep it. I figured he would probably get over it after a few weeks, but they let us walk free either way.

Omer and I traveled together for a few more weeks in his home country of Israel. I found this part of the trip intriguing. I had never been anywhere quite like Israel. The trip started with me landing in Tel Aviv, and as I was going through customs, I got separated from Omer. They took me to a small room and grilled me for two hours, asking me questions unlike anything I had experienced before. I was treated like a suspected terrorist.

"You guys do this with everyone who comes to visit your country?" I asked.

"This is a random selection," was their only reply, but I felt like this couldn't be a normal line of questioning. By the time I was finally released, Omer had begun to worry. When I saw him, I apologized and explained where I'd been. He told me it was pretty normal and not to worry about it.

"That's normal?" I blurted out. "Really?" Omer just shrugged as we left the airport.

Over the next few days, I noticed strange things. Everywhere we went, there were teenaged soldiers, both male and female, carrying assault weapons. When we went into a McDonald's, we had to go through metal detectors. At the mall, they checked our car for bombs. I had never been somewhere with such high levels of security in such basic locations. It gave the place a strange aura that is hard to put into words. It made me feel uneasy even though Omer kept telling me it was normal and there was nothing to worry about. It sure didn't feel normal to me.

One day, we went to a mall because Omer had to buy something. As we were walking, I noticed something strange. I was looking around and felt like I had somehow passed into a different dimension where everyone was super smoking hot. Usually when I travel, I would say I find about 5 percent of the population in any given country attractive. But here, over 90 percent of the people looked like models. Just a simple mall, nothing special about it, filled with some of the most attractive human beings I had ever seen in my life. I grabbed Omer by the shoulder and said, "Dude, what the hell is going on? Is there a model convention in this place? Why is everyone so damn hot?"

He looked around and said, "It's always like this. This is nothing special."

I was like, "Bullshit nothing special. These are the best-looking humans I have ever seen. This is unbelievable."

Omer shrugged his shoulders and moved on. I had always heard how beautiful the women were in Brazil, but they have nothing on Israel. Don't get me wrong, there are some truly beautiful women in Brazil, too, but maybe 6 percent are attractive in my eyes. Israel was on a different level, and to this day, I have seen nothing like it anywhere else in the world. If you're on the lookout for beautiful people, try Israel first.

After a few days, Omer decided to take me to Jerusalem because he felt it was an important place to see at least once in a person's lifetime. I am not religious, so I didn't feel all that excited about going, but since it was important to him, I went along. As we drove into Jerusalem, I was awestruck by how stunning the city was. I have never been a fan of cities located in the desert, but every manmade structure was covered in Jerusalem stone, whether it was a skyscraper or a small house. This made for such a striking visual, and I have never seen a picture that truly captures the beauty of this place. As we got closer to the old city surrounded by ancient walls of stone, I was again surprised. I could just feel how old this place was. As I walked into the old city and moved through the different quarters, the place gave me a sense of moving back through time. The markets were colorful and reminded me of what it must have been like shopping over 1,000 years ago.

It was surprising to me that old Jerusalem has four distinct quarters, three of which are dedicated to different religions: the Christian Quarter, the Jewish Quarter, and the Muslim Quarter. This all in such a tiny space. You can feel an almost explosive energy as you walk through the different areas. Everywhere you look, there is military with fully automatic weapons. The religious tension in the air is so strong you can cut it with a knife.

We walked by the Wailing Wall and Omer explained how people write prayers on small pieces of paper and stick them into the cracks in hopes they will be answered. Watching all the devout believers bobbing their heads with their mouths moving in silent prayer was a sight to see. I have always been fascinated by religious belief, and this was a new level of commitment to behold. It felt like being on another planet. I usually don't share my thoughts on the subject unless asked, but I couldn't help wondering what reality those people live in.

The trip ended with Omer showing me the lowest BASE jump on Earth. It was on the outer rim of the Dead Sea, and the jump was 1,000 feet below sea level. Omer had jumped it and was proud to hold that record. I was impressed; it was a sketchy place. I had no desire to do the jump myself. It's not often that I turn down an opportunity to jump something.

CHAPTER TWENTY

TIM THE STUNTMAN

On a balmy spring day, I was training at Skydive Perris when a lovely English gentleman walked up and introduced himself. He informed me his name was Tim and he was training to become a stuntman. He had overheard me talking about BASE jumping and was interested in learning more about it. After talking for a bit, he asked if he could come along the next time I went to Auburn Bridge. He already owned some BASE gear and was being mentored by Mike Muskat. Mike was a well-known jumper at the time, and Tim described him as having the courage of a top X Games competitor but the body of an eighty-year-old broken man with bad knees.

Tim's dry English humor made me laugh hard, so I said, "No problem. I would love to have you come along next time I go."

Tim and I ended up doing a few Auburn trips together before something came up and I needed to ask him to do me a favor.

"What do you need, Jeb?" he asked.

"I have an idea of how to get past security on every building in downtown LA."

Tim gave me an inquisitive glance and sad, "Go on..."

"All buildings in LA that are over twenty stories high have helicopter landing pads on their roofs. Something to do with fire codes. Class B airspace begins at twenty-five hundred feet over the city, meaning it's legal to fly a small plane over downtown as long as you stay below that altitude but at least a thousand feet above the tops of the buildings. So there's a small corridor that a Cessna 182 could fly through without setting off any alarms at air traffic control. Now, if I use that corridor, I can step out of an aircraft and land on any helipad I want. Then I just repack my gear and jump the building."

A large smile spread across Tim's face and he asked, "What do you need me to do?"

My question was, "Would you be willing to do ground crew for me and pick me up after I jump the Arco building?"

His grin grew even bigger and he asked, "Why the Arco building?"

I told him I had already flown over LA with a friend and taken pictures of all the roofs. I had decided on the Arco building because it had by far the largest helipad with the least number of obstacles to avoid in the dark. I explained I wanted to do the jump at around 3:00 a.m., when the city would be sleeping. It took him about two seconds to say yes, then we started planning the project in greater detail.

We drove to the building to walk the landing area, keeping an eye out for power lines and security cameras. We decided West 4th Street would make the best landing zone; it was big with no wires crossing it, so it won by default. We also knew that at 3:00 a.m., there would be little to no traffic. 4th also had large sidewalks, meaning I could land on one of them if the need arose.

After scouting the ground, it just became a matter of waiting for a no-wind evening and we would be ready to go. I had a pilot friend—who will remain nameless—who was willing to let me step out of his aircraft. I promised that if I was captured, I would tell the police I was BASE jumping the building, and when they asked how I go on top, I would say the security had left the door unlocked, so I just walked up the stairs to the roof. There would be no way for them to know an airplane was involved unless I told them.

It took a few weeks till the weather was perfect. Everyone was on-call and would be ready to move at a moment's notice. The day finally came where I saw zero- to five-mile-per-hour wind in downtown LA. I called my pilot, and he confirmed the positive weather report. The jump was on.

I then called Tim and told him, "Tonight's the night. Are you still able to come?"

"Yes," he responded, "but I have a good friend who's a big-time stunt coordinator. Would it be okay for me to bring him along so he can see what we do in real life?"

"Absolutely," I said, "as long as he keeps quiet and doesn't tell anyone." I trusted Tim and, if he said the guy was cool, then I had zero problems with it.

Tim and his buddy drove to LA to wait for me as I drove to the Hawthorn Airport to meet with my pilot. I parked my car and walked to the hangars where Mr. X was pre-checking the aircraft. He informed me he was scared but excited.

"I can relate to those feelings," I told him. "I feel quite a bit of a panic rising myself. Sometimes I come up with ideas that are quite terrifying." I asked him if he had a private place to put my gear on and he pointed to a small hangar, so I went in and started gearing up.

It's odd how there are different levels of fear. The lead-up to doing something really dangerous and scary tends to cloud my mind. It gives me this odd feeling of being trapped in glass. It seems to muffle sound and distort images and memory. There is a small internal voice that always seems to be trying to convince me not to do whatever it is I'm thinking about doing. It racks my mind with doubt and indecision. Through training, I have learned how to quiet this little voice. Or maybe "ignore" is a better word for it, because I still hear it whispering in the back of my mind even to this day. No matter how much I suppress my fear, it's always there.

As I walked to the aircraft, I felt a familiar disconnection like I was almost floating towards the aircraft. I got in, closed the door, and buckled my seatbelt. Mr. X fired up the plane and started doing some more pre-flight checks as I just zoned out and tried to keep my fear under control. He asked me if I was ready, and I nodded yes. I tend to have a blank expression during these kinds of things, and I'm pretty sure most people find it hard to read what's going through my mind. If they knew how shit-scared I was, I don't think they would have the confidence to let me do the crazy-ass shit I do. Mr. X was convinced I knew what I was doing, and he had 100 percent confidence I would be fine. I, on the other hand, was shitting my pants and felt like I was walking down the green mile to an electric chair. People always say it must be nice not fearing anything, and I always look at them and say, "What makes you think I don't fear anything? I'm exactly as scared as you would be jumping off a 1,000-foot building. I am not superhuman; I have the same fear every other human has. It takes courage to do things that scare you. I can't stop feeling fear; I just do these things scared."

As we approached downtown LA in our small corridor of airspace, the sky was clear. I could see every little light of every little building. It was beautiful. The city is amazing by air at night. All the red taillights from cars driving up and down the 405 Freeway and breaking off onto smaller side roads look like blood running through veins, like the city's a living, breathing creature. As we started flying over downtown, I noted how close the roofs of all the buildings looked. It felt like I could reach out and touch them. As we flew over the Arco building, I looked down and noticed something odd: the lights were on.

I looked at Mr. X and said, "Do you see that?"

He responded with, "Yes, I sure do."

"Why do you think it's the only roof with lights on?" I asked.

"I have no idea, Jeb. Should we abort?" I tried to look closer for movement of any kind, but the roof looked completely clear.

I said, "No, we aren't going to abort. The conditions are perfect; I'm going for it."

Mr. X said, "Okay, I'm going to head north for two miles and turn back around, giving you a straight shot at the building. When I'm a half mile out, I will let you know, and you can open the door and get yourself in position. When you see your building under you, just drop out. And good luck, Jeb."

I nodded and started getting myself ready. I took off my seatbelt and did a double check of all my gear. As the pilot turned in for the final run, the fear ratcheted up to the next level and I started feeling nauseous.

This is where things got even more quiet. I became more detached. The muffled walls of glass around me got thicker and the small voice telling me not to do this became more frantic. Calling it a voice may not be the right description. It's more like a feeling without words, like every cell in your body is rejecting the choices you're trying to make and overriding your mind.

Mr. X told me, "We are a half mile out; open the door." I could only open the door about a foot before the wind from the forward movement of the plane gave too much wind resistance for me to push it any farther. I had to squat in the door frame, pushing it open with my back and wedging my body in the frame to keep it open. I looked down between my legs at the drop beneath me as buildings passed one by one. I saw the roof of my building and, with one final motion, my legs pushed with all their might, squeezing me out the door.

The glass clouding my mind shattered.

The next level of fear is when you go against all your instincts and do what every cell in your body is screaming for you not to do. At this level, your mind goes, "Goddamn it! I told you not to do this, but you did it anyway, you silly son of a bitch! Now we're going to have to deal with this crap!"

My body released everything it had to heighten my senses as much as it possibly could so I would be able to survive the next few moments. All adrenaline, all endorphins, everything dropped all at once. The hyper-sensitivity kicked in and I became the best version of myself, operating at the highest levels of efficiency. I fell backwards out of the airplane as the air cushioned my fall. I did one backflip and, as my belly faced back towards Earth, I saw the building underneath me coming up at high speed. I pulled my parachute and it opened with monstrous force. I looked down and started setting up to land on a small helicopter landing pad on the roof of a 700-foot-tall building. I set up perfectly but misjudged the wind a little.

I overshot the helipad by about a foot, landing on its side but still on the roof. As my parachute fell, landing right in front of me, I began doing a little victory dance... until I heard someone coming up from my left side.

A voice that sounded concerned said, "What are you doing up here?"

I looked over to see a man approaching me with his hands held up in front of him.

My first thought was, *Shit, I am so busted,* but I responded with, "Nothing."

He stopped walking towards me and said, "What do you mean, nothing? You're doing something—you just landed on the roof with a parachute."

I decided to just tell him exactly what I was doing. I said, "Listen, I jumped from an airplane so I could land on this building, repack my parachute, and then BASE jump it."

The expression on the guy's face changed from confusion to awe. He said, "That is pretty cool, but there's no way I can let you do that. I am going to get in so much trouble."

I looked him right in the eye as I pointed and said, "See that building across the street?"

Tracking my gesture, he said, "Yes."

I explained, "I jumped off that building."

He smiled and I could tell he understood what I was saying. He thought for a moment, then said, "Okay, tell you what: I need to finish up some work over there. You go pack your stuff, and when you're done, come let me know. I want to see this."

I asked, "What are you doing for work at three a.m. on the roof of a building?"

"I'm setting up the equipment to wash the windows for tomorrow morning," he said.

I smiled and said, "Seems totally reasonable. It shouldn't take me more than forty-five minutes to pack my gear. I'll let you know when I'm ready to jump."

He said, "Perfect," and was off to finish up his work.

I called down to Tim on my walkie talkie to make sure he was in position. He asked me how my landing was and I told him it wasn't a problem, but there was a window washer up here. He responded with, "Are you busted?"

"No, he's cool. And he wants to watch the jump."

Tim said, "Really?"

"Yes, really. I think we're all good. It will take me about forty-five minutes to pack. I'll give you a five-minute call when I'm geared up and ready to jump." I put the radio down and put a small headlamp on so I could pack in the dark shadows next to the helipad.

About fifteen minutes into my pack job, I heard something strange. It was a sound I couldn't really place, but it was getting louder. As I looked to my right, a police helicopter rose up over the edge of the building and flew directly over where I was packing. I jumped forward, placing my body over my canopy to keep the rotor wash from blowing my pack job apart. Luckily for me, everything I own is black;

233

I blended into the roof like a ninja. But the helicopter was now hovering over the helipad, right next to where I'd been packing. It shone a light on the helipad for some reason. I was sure I was busted. I knew they were going to land, step out, and arrest me on the spot. But then the spotlight went out and the helicopter flew back over me on its way across the street, where it landed on a distant building.

I was lying there in shock as my walkie talkie went off with Tim on the other end. All he said was, "Are you busted?"

I grabbed the walkie and said, "No, the police in the helicopter didn't see me." Tim couldn't believe it. He had just seen a police chopper fly over the roof of the building I was packing on and shine its spotlight on what he imagined was me. But nope, I hadn't been seen. I told him I had about thirty more minutes till I was done packing and I would let him know when I was finished.

When I was finally done packing, I went ahead and geared up. I let Tim know I was about five minutes out and then went to look for the window washing guy. I walked over to where I had last seen him and, sure enough, he was still there organizing equipment.

I told him I was ready to go. He closed his toolbox and said, "I'm ready."

As we walked to the corner of the building, he said, "Hey, can I ask you for a favor?"

I looked at him and said, "Sure. What would you like?"

He responded, "My buddy is never gonna believe this happened. Would you mind if I call him, and you leave him a message on his machine just telling him I am not making this up?"

"No problem," I said, "but I'm not sure that will help him believe you. I could just be some guy you met in a bar." He called his friend and it went straight to voice mail, which wasn't a surprise given how early it was. He handed me the phone and I left a short message, then handed back his phone and we continued to the edge of the building. I had selected a corner facing West 4th Street with Tim parked right under me. There was a four-and-half-foot wall I had to climb on. The window washer put his arms on it, leaning against it and looking over the edge.

As I stood on the corner of this wall with my toes hanging over the side, the window washer looked up at me with wide eyes and said, "Man, I don't know about you, but I'm terrified right now."

I looked down at him and said, "What the hell are you scared of? I'm the one jumping off the building."

He said, "I don't know, I'm just really scared." I nodded and called down to Tim, telling him ten seconds. I put the walkie away and pushed off hard, doing a double reverse flip. As I came out of the second flip, I looked down and waited a few more moments, enjoying the view of the ground rising up to meet me as I dropped into the center of the city. I opened my parachute, lined up, and landed next to Tim's car. I quickly gathered up all my gear and opened the door to the backseat, jumping in as fast as I could so we could leave the area.

As I got in, Tim stepped on the gas and we were moving fast. I asked Tim if he was able to get any footage of the jump and he said, "No, I couldn't see anything. All your gear is black and I couldn't see you till after you got below streetlight level." I took this as a good thing because it meant fewer people would have been able to see what was going on, and my exposure to prying eyes had been limited. Chances for repeating this style of jumping and successfully getting away would be high. Tim introduced me to his friend, and we moved on.

I'm pretty sure this jump was done early in the year 2001. At the time, I thought I had found the keys to all the buildings in LA with this technique, but the logistics of jumping like this were complicated and took way too many people to pull off. The risk to the pilots was high and it was difficult to convince them to repeat after doing it once. The novelty wore off quickly and the pilots didn't see any real benefit for them, which I totally understood. I came to the obvious conclusion the risk was too high for everyone involved, so it was a fun one-off experience. I never ended up doing it again.

But this led to Tim and I becoming lifelong friends. He told me after doing this jump that he knew a lot of people who talked about doing big things, but few actually went through with doing them. He really liked the fact I decided to do something with such a high level of risk and then just went out and did it. He seemed to like the fact I walked the walk after talking the talk.

Tim became one of my early BASE-jumping travel buddies. We traveled all over the world together, doing some of the earliest wingsuit BASE jumps. He even made a little documentary about one of our trips to Norway, talking about the connection jumpers felt with one another.

Tim was always an inspirational person to me. His story is one I like to share with people when trying to illustrate how a person can do anything if they have enough determination. Whenever someone tells me they can't do something in the entertainment industry because Hollywood is all about connections and who you know, I tell them Tim's story. Here it is:

Tim was in the Royal Navy during the first Gulf War. He was an EOD diver, which stands for Explosive Ordinance Disposal. When that war ended and his time in the Navy was complete, he wasn't quite sure what he wanted to do with his future, so he went on a walkabout through Australia for a year. He worked a bunch of odd jobs along his travels to make ends meet. Things like picking plumbs in orchards. Pearl diving in the Perth area. Teaching windsurfing to tourists. He even spent some time working at an amusement park. During this period moving around doing odd jobs, he decided what he really wanted to do was move to the United States and become a stuntman. At the time, he wasn't sure what a stuntman's job really was, but he decided it looked like a fun way to make a living and he was pretty sure he would be good at it. So, without knowing anyone or anything, he took the little money he had saved up, bought a plane ticket, and flew to LA. He landed at LAX and found a cheap hostel to stay at on Paloma Boulevard, right on the Venice Boardwalk.

Tim knew he needed to work in order to have money, because his savings wouldn't last long, so he got a job scraping the bottom of boats in the Marina del Rey harbor. His diving experience in the Navy helped him get the job, but honestly, to call him overqualified is an understatement to the extreme. He didn't know a single soul in LA and had no idea how to become a stuntman. So, he decided to go to Universal Studios and watch the live *Miami Vice* show. He thought he might be able to wait outside the exit after the show for the stunt performers to come out and maybe get a few tips on how to get started.

Tim paid for his admission, watched the show, and then waited where he thought they might come out. Sure enough, after a little while, he recognized one of the performers approaching. He went right up to him and introduced himself, "Hi, my name is Tim, and I used to be an EOD diver in the Royal Navy. I'm interested in becoming a stuntman and would love any pointers you could give me on where to begin."

The stunt performer looked at Tim and said, "I hear this all the time. My only advice to you is pick a different job. There are ten thousand people in Hollywood calling themselves stuntmen, and only about two hundred of them are actually making a living from doing it. It's easier to become an actor and there's way more money in it. Stunt work really isn't something you want to do, trust me."

The performer then turned and walked away. The strange thing is, this was music to Tim's ears. He loved the idea of stuntmen being an elite group of individuals where only a few could make it. One of the things he loved about becoming an EOD diver was watching others wash out while he had the endurance to keep going. Tim had a strong mind and he loved testing himself to see how far he could go. If everyone could do it then it wasn't something he was interested in. Now more determined than ever, he waited for another stuntman to walk out.

Sure enough, a few moments later another man came down the path who he recognized from the show. Tim said, "Excuse me, sir. My name is Tim, and I was an EOD diver in the Royal Navy. I'm interested in becoming a stuntman. Would you have any advice on where I could begin training for stunt work?"

The man looked at Tim and repeated what the first guy said almost word for word, then turned and walked away. Again, Tim wasn't fazed by this and just waited for another one.

This process repeated itself a few more times until finally a man walked up to Tim and said, "Hey, buddy. I've been hearing what everyone is telling you. It's true: there are ten thousand stuntmen and only two hundred of them are making a living doing this, but there is no reason why you can't be one of those two hundred people. I've set up a small training facility at my home, and for fifty bucks an hour, I would be willing to teach you what I know. Right now, I have six p.m. on Thursday nights available. If you'd like to learn a few things, this could be a good way to get started."

This excited Tim immensely, but he had a few problems. First, fifty bucks an hour was a small fortune for him at the time. With the kind of money he was earning scraping boats, it was going to be challenging to come up with that each week. Also, Tim didn't own a car, and when he looked up the guy's address, he found out he lived in North Hollywood. That was over twenty miles from the hostel Tim was staying at. He would need to figure out transportation with a non-existent budget. When Tim got home, he noticed one of the other hostel dwellers had a bicycle. Tim ended up working out a deal to use this bike Thursday nights to get to his lessons. It was the only transportation he could afford at the time.

Tim rode a borrowed bicycle every Thursday night twenty miles each way to train in North Hollywood with his mentor. He did this for almost a year while scraping the bottom of boats for his survival. The amount of money Tim ended up paying this man amounted to a small fortune in proportion to what he was earning. On one Thursday evening, riding the borrowed bike back from training, a woman pulled out in front of Tim with her car. Tim had no time to stop and impacted the front of her car, sending him over the handlebars and across the hood. He hit the pavement on the other side with force but was able to transfer the energy into a roll and came up on his feet with minor scrapes and bruises. Tim's borrowed ride was destroyed and he now had to replace it, which was a financial catastrophe for Tim at the time. This was obviously a difficult period in Tim's life, but I love how he never wavered in his determination to reach his ultimate goal of becoming a stuntman, no matter how hard it got.

Tim became good friends with the stuntman from the live *Miami Vice* show, and one day his buddy told him the show was going to have an audition. He told Tim, "You should come and audition, buddy. I think you'd have a good chance of getting this job." Tim had spent the last year training his balls off with this guy, and if he felt Tim had a chance, well, he might as well go for it.

The timing was perfect because Tim had just gotten his green card. He had been working hard on it with his boss at the harbor to ensure he could work in the country legally. That green card was the last barrier to him being able to work in stunts. So, he said, "Yes, just tell me the day and time and I'll be there."

Tim found a ride to the audition and showed up exactly where he was told to be, but as he walked in, his heart sank. There had to be over two hundred people there for the audition and they all looked way more prepared than Tim. They all had headshots and resumes showing the work they had done; plus, they all seemed to know each other from having worked together before. Tim had no experience and felt like he had already failed. They were taking people into the audition ten at a time while everyone else waited in a large room together. Tim felt like he was about to make a fool of himself, so he decided to walk out. He left, feeling like it was hopeless and he had just wasted a ton of his time. But as he was leaving, he saw an opening that gave him a view of the auditions going on in the next room. He stopped and began watching closely to see what was happening. He noticed his competitors were struggling through the audition, and he began to realize the man he met outside this very room a year earlier had been training him for this exact audition. Every day he had ridden that bike to North Hollywood was a day training for this; he just wasn't aware that's what was going on. As he watched the other people struggle with mini ramps, fight choreography, and air rams, Tim knew he was going to get this job. He walked back to the room feeling much better and waited to be called in for the audition. Sure enough, when the audition was over, they called his name. Tim had gotten his first job as a Hollywood stuntman.

From there, he met the people and made the contacts he would use to build his career. Tim eventually became one of the founding fathers of Brand X, the biggest, most powerful stunt group in Hollywood. This was a man who quite literally made the American dream come true, and his story has impressed me from its earliest stages. Here is a man who built himself up through hard work and determination, never giving up and never making excuses for why things weren't working out. He showed me that if a person wants something badly enough, they will find a way to make it happen. If it's not important to them, they will find an excuse to fail. Tim never looked for excuses, he just found solutions.

CHAPTER TWENTY-ONE

THE PSILOCYBIN SOLUTION

In the late nineties, there were a group of Australian BASE jumpers pushing the boundaries of the sport to levels no one believed possible. They were taking risks that no rational mind could comprehend. No one understood how they could push so hard, so often, without dying. The two biggest names coming out of Oz were Slim and Dwain. I had seen them in passing all over the world for years before I finally got the chance to know them on a personal level. But once I did, we became good friends, and they would change me in ways I still don't fully understand.

Slim and Dwain moved from Australia to the USA in the early 2000s to a sprawling house in Portland, Oregon, owned by a man named Nick, aka "Dr. Death." Nick was a doctor who specialized in doing autopsies for the FBI and was a mega-fan of all things BASE-related. Slim moved in first and was working on finishing a degree in forestry. Dwain moved in a year later after hearing Slim's stories of how epic the BASE jumping was in the area. Slim would tell Dwain about how they had more legal BASE sites than they did jumpers. This was perfect for them, seeing how they were so focused on jumping as much as possible to improve their already impressive skills.

Dwain and Slim had become the driving force of the slider-down acrobatic movement—but before going any further, I need to take a moment to explain what that means. A slider is something jumpers use to slow down the opening of parachutes. If you are falling at terminal velocity (120 mph) and try to open a parachute without a slider, you would go from 120 mph to zero almost instantly.

That rapid deceleration would damage your body and/or your equipment, so the slider was developed to slow down the opening process. Think of it as an air brake that holds the parachute closed until the speed decreases to safe levels. Only then does the slider come down the lines and allow the parachute to fully inflate. Sliders are used on jumps where you have enough altitude to take delays longer than four seconds. After four seconds, the human body builds enough speed that you need a braking system to slow down openings. But if you are jumping low objects, usually under 600 feet, you can only take short delays in the zero- to three-second range. In this case, you wouldn't want or need a slider because your body is still traveling at relatively slow speeds towards the ground.

When doing slider-down jumps, having a symmetrical body position is key to having an on-heading opening, meaning the parachute opens facing away from the object you have just jumped from. Any asymmetry can cause off-heading openings, smashing the pilot right back into the object they jumped from. To do acrobatics from low objects, slider-down is considered extremely dangerous. You have to complete the acrobatic maneuver within three seconds, making sure you are belly-to-earth with perfect body symmetry. Any mistakes could result in serious injury or death. In the late nineties to early 2000s, this was the most hardcore technical form of BASE jumping, and Slim and Dwain were on the bleeding edge of this discipline.

They are the ones who inspired me to begin incorporating more complicated acrobatic maneuvers into my jumping. I was doing gainers, but they showed me I could do twisting, too. I liked the challenge and it seemed way more interesting than just stepping off a fixed object. Wingsuits were still in their infancy and more of a novelty at this point. I saw their potential, but my focus, along with the rest of the sport, was on low-altitude acrobatics at this point. Over 95 percent of my jumping revolved around training this discipline, so when I got a chance to go on a trip where I could jump with the godfathers of the movement, I got super excited.

Yuri invited me and a new friend of mine named Karin on a trip to jump with the Portland crew in early 2001. Karin is a third-generation Japanese American woman with a Valley Girl accent who also just so happens to be a world champion skydiver with over 5,000 jumps. Yuri, Karin, and I planned to meet up with the Portland crew and I would finally get a chance to jump with my heroes.

When we showed up at Nick's house, Yuri introduced me to him first. Nick was an odd fellow with an almost manic look about him. His hair was wild and he reminded me of an insane version of Hunter S. Thompson, which is saying a lot because Hunter S. Thompson was batshit crazy. As I talked to Nick, I had this overwhelming sense that I was talking to a man on heavy mind-altering drugs. He was friendly, though, but in an uncomfortable kind of way. He had gotten the nick name "Dr. Death" because he had an obsession with dying. He had gotten into jumping because he had done an autopsy on a skydiver who had impacted the ground without a parachute. He found the damage so interesting that he felt compelled to try it himself.

Nick also liked to collect things from the bodies he performed autopsies on. Years later, Dwain would tell me creepy stories of how Nick had a small jar of baby hands that he would clip from the fetuses of deceased pregnant women. I didn't believe the stories until many years later when I actually got a chance to see the little jar with my own eyes. To call Nick odd would be an understatement of monumental proportions. He also liked to BASE jump in drag. He would dress up in high heels, fishnet stockings, and crop tops to jump off buildings. He liked to explain how there was nothing more hardcore than the idea of being caught by the police while dressed like a woman. I admit that I'm weird, but I've got nothing on Nick.

After meeting Dr. Death, Yuri introduced me to a towering, hilarious, thin man wearing a salsa dancing outfit. It looked completely out of place because he was gangly and as white as a human being could be. The outfit almost looked like a Halloween costume on him. He spoke with a thick Australian accent and introduced himself as Slim. He was on his way to do a salsa competition, which I later found out was another passion of his. This man loved dancing almost as much as he loved BASE jumping. Slim would end up hitting a low cliff in Australia that would permanently cripple him a few years later. He would break both his femurs, his back in about eight places, his hips, and most of his ribs. He would flatline twice on his way to the hospital and he would need two blood transfusions before being in the clear. It would take him over a year to recover enough to start BASE jumping again, but he would never fully recover and would walk with a noticeable limp for the rest of his life. The odd thing is, even though he ended up being barely able to walk, he was still able to salsa dance, and when he danced, you could hardly notice his disability. Slim and I ended up doing many BASE trips together becoming good friends before he later died. In this moment, though, he was vibrant and smiling as he danced around the room.

I was then introduced to a rather small fellow with a strange bowl cut hairdo. He had an almost-feminine lisp to his voice and I was shocked to find out this bird-framed fellow was Dwain. I had been expecting to meet the single most hardcore human being to have ever lived, but this dude was not what I was expecting. However, looks can be deceiving and, as the saying goes, you should never judge a book by its cover. Dwain didn't look hardcore, but he was definitely pathologically insane. He would constantly do jumps with less than a second of margin for error.

He would jump in horrible weather conditions, and even I walked away from multiple jumps he did because they were just too risky. We would be sitting there arguing about the wind being too strong and he would just jump off. I'd watch his canopy collapse and the wind throw him around like a ragdoll. After landing in some horribly uncontrolled ways, he would then call up to me on the walkie saying, "The conditions are fine. Jump, you pussy."

I would call back on the walkie saying, "Nope, not interested. You are way better than me and if I try this, I'll die for sure."

Dwain was the most competitive person I have ever met. He would constantly try and push others beyond not only their comfort zone but way beyond what was reasonable. Lucky for me, I didn't give a shit about competing with anyone, so I would just do what I was doing; Dwain had little to no influence on my safety protocol. I knew what it was like to get seriously injured and I didn't have anything to prove to anyone, but I feel like Dwain was always trying to prove something to everyone else. This meant he had a huge red button on his chest that people could push. I felt all anyone had to do was call him a pussy and he would jump off just about anything, anywhere. I have never seen someone so willing to do such dangerous things for so little reward.

That evening, after Slim got back from his dancing competition, we all sat down for dinner. I sat next to Slim and Dwain sat next to Karin. As people ordered drinks, I ordered water. Slim looked at me and asked if I drank alcohol. I informed him that I didn't drink and never would. He asked if I smoked weed or took any other drugs and I said, "No, and I would rather shoot myself in the head with a shotgun then ever use them."

Slim smiled and said, "Wow, you aren't even a little on the fence about that subject, are you?"

I smiled back and said, "No, not even a little bit."

Slim then went on to say something else I found interesting. He said, "Jeb, as you walked up, I knew who you were without ever having seen a picture of you. You have the stereotypical BASE jumper look. From the shaved head to the dark sunglasses to the black clothes. If the word BASE jumper were in the dictionary, they would have a picture of you in the description."

"I've been dressing like this since I was twelve years old," I told him, "long before I even knew what BASE jumping was. I guess it must be in my DNA."

Karin and I had been friends for a couple of years at this point, having done a few BASE trips together, but mostly through skydiving at Perris. When we got to Portland, she took an instant liking to Dwain, and they became inseparable. By the end of the trip, they had already started planning their next trip together. It didn't take long before they were in a relationship and Dwain eventually moved in with Karin at her home in Orange County.

Karin's relationship with Dwain is how I became friends with him. We talked a bit during this trip, but I wouldn't say we became friends right away. As I've said before, I'm socially awkward and I don't make friends easily. I need to spend quite a bit of time around a person and really get to know them before I feel comfortable enough to interact. Dwain would come down to Southern CA regularly to see Karin, and that's how I got to know him. When they moved in together, we spent even more time around each other. We would go see movies and jump at the drop zone. We did many BASE trips together, and sometimes other members of the Portland crew would come along on the journeys with us.

On my first trip to Lauterbrunnen, Switzerland, in the summer of 2002, both Karin and Dwain joined the journey. Dwain brought Nick (Dr. Death) along as well and we tried to hit the ground running when we got there. The weather was challenging, though, making jumping difficult the first few days, but Dwain and I decided we weren't going to let a little thing like rain stop us. Nick and Karin hung back because they were not interested in getting wet and muddy. Dwain took me for my first jump in the valley to a beautiful 1,000-foot waterfall visible from the center of town. Dwain and I had a fun jump, but the best part of the experience was just doing a nice hike together where we had time to talk about life. He was an intelligent human being, and it was nice to talk about our motivations for doing the things we were doing. He was also the most knowledgeable person on the planet about BASE jumping, and he took my education on the subject to the next level.

When the weather cleared, we began hiking and jumping the different exit points around the valley with the whole group. On day four, Karin, Dwain, Nick, and I went to Le Moose, an exit point on the far side of Lauterbrunnen. I was going to jump my new SkyFlyer, the cutting edge of wingsuit technology at the time. My goal was to fly over a ledge system, across a road, over a river, and past a tree line. This location was used as a measure of wingsuit performance at the time. I counted down, jumped off, and started flying.

I made it over the ledges and tree line easily and watched the road come and go, but as I was crossing the river, I noticed I was a bit low. The SkyFlyer was a crappy wingsuit by modern standards, and I wasn't flying it well, either. I made it over the river but saw there was a powerline that I didn't want to deploy on top of, so I kept flying. By the time I had gotten enough distance over the powerline, I pulled too low. I had less than a four-second canopy ride and landed without even touching my toggles. This was not one of my best moments in the sport. I had cut it way too close.

If I had had any kind of hesitation on deployment, I would have died.

Later that evening, we were all sitting at dinner together. Nick gave me a talking-to about not pushing so hard. He told me, "Jeb, I know you're experienced and already know what I'm about to say, but you need to give yourself more margin. We love you and don't want to see you die from pushing so hard." I told him I agreed. I had made a mistake and would try harder to give myself more space. Funny thing about this sport is it draws you towards the line that separates life from death. People tend to push themselves to get as close to this line as possible while trying their best not to cross it. Unfortunately, that line is invisible, so you usually don't know exactly where it is until you've already stepped over it.

The conversation covered many topics that evening, but one important thing I remember was Nick telling me he had always dreamed of owning a Jaguar sports car. He told me how he had stopped in France for a few days on his way to Switzerland and stayed with a French jumper while he was there. They had gotten into a conversation about sports cars, and Nick had expressed his love for Jaguars. The French jumper went off on what pieces of shit cars they were, which upset Nick. He didn't understand how the French jumper had so little social awareness and didn't seem to understand that crapping on another person's dream, no matter how big or small, was rude. I asked him, "If you like Jaguars so much, why don't you buy one?"

Nick told me something that didn't resonate at the time, but the next day it would have a huge impact on the way I looked at life. He told me, "I still have student loans I need to pay off from medical school and a large mortgage on my house. I wouldn't feel right spending money on an expensive car until I've paid off my debt."

I responded, "Bro, you never know how long you're going to live. If owning a Jaguar is a dream, make it come true now."

Nick said, "No, I need to be responsible."

He then changed subjects and told me about how he, Dwain, and Slim had formed a BASE-jumping team to compete at Bridge Day in West Virginia. The team was called "Psilocybin Solution." He said, "We're looking for a fourth and would love for you to join us."

I was flattered but said, "Thank you for thinking of me, bro, but I'm not a competitive person. Even if I was, I don't like the idea of competing in something like BASE jumping. Competing in things that can kill you just doesn't seem reasonable to me." I was tempted, though—being part of a team with two of my heroes would have been amazing.

The next morning, everyone was heading up to jump a different exit called "The Nose II." My back was a bit sore from my low pull and hard landing from the day before, so I decided to just sleep in and maybe do a jump later in the day if I felt better. When I woke up, I turned on my walkie talkie and called to see where people were and how the first jump of the day had gone. Karin called me back and said, "Nick had a one-eighty, hit the wall, got cocooned in his canopy, and bounced down the ledge system for over seven hundred feet. He's dead, Jeb. We're in the middle of recovering his body from the wall right now." I could tell she was in shock with the almost robotic way she had conveyed the information. I got a strange empty feeling that spread from my chest to my stomach, like a void had opened up inside me.

It's odd the kinds of thoughts that enter your mind at a moment like this. The first thing I thought was, *His lucky charm bag didn't work out for him.* Nick used to carry a bag filled with objects that he thought brought him luck; he wouldn't jump without it. I have zero superstitions, so I always seem to notice when other people do. I can't help wondering why they think these things will help them, especially when it comes to dying.

The second and far more profound thing that came to my mind was, *Nick never got to own a Jaguar.* It seems silly because it's a material thing and who really gives a shit, right? But different things matter to different people. He dreamed of owning that car. I could see it in his eyes as he talked about it, and he decided to put it off for some distant time in the future where he might be debt-free. I decided right then I was never going to put something off for the future if I really wanted it. If I wanted to do something or if I wanted to buy something, I would just do it. I knew I was doing dangerous things and death was always right around the corner, so I would never wait to turn one of my dreams into a reality. I was going to decide what I wanted to do and then do it. Once that goal was accomplished, then I would choose a new goal or dream and make that happen, too. This was how I would live my life. I was going to live every single day like it was my last on Earth, because it very well could be.

The one fundamental difference between Nick's dream and the things I dreamed about was that I felt money was evil and I wasn't that interested in material things. I was much more interested in life experiences. Not saying one is better or worse than another, just saying mine was different. At that time, I felt if I died with even one penny in the bank, then I had failed at life. I would spend every dime I had. I wouldn't waste my life gathering material shit that was left behind after death. My retirement program was to die. I felt living past thirty was an impossibility with the types of dreams I wanted to turn into realities. This line of reasoning became the philosophical foundation for the way I lived my life through my mid-twenties to mid-thirties. At thirty-five, I had a profound shift in the way I saw life and money... but we'll get into that later.

Nick's death had one major factor: he was an experienced slider-down BASE jumper with over 500 jumps—which was a lot at the time—but he was a novice when it came to slider-up jumping. From the jumps I had witnessed him doing all week, his track wasn't good enough for this location. Tracking is when a person puts their legs together and their arms down to their sides. They become flat as a board and can then angle their bodies so they slide across wind generated by falling towards the Earth at high speed. This is how people fly away from big cliffs after they have jumped off them. In hindsight, I see that Nick hadn't spent anywhere near enough time training basic tracking skills in the skydiving environment, and that's what killed him.

The cliffs in Lauterbrunnen have large ledge systems that a jumper must track over in order to survive. If a jumper is not able to track over the ledges, he will impact them at a high rate of speed and die. In 2002, Lauterbrunnen was considered a highly technical location to jump. Nick had shown that his track was subpar and needed work while we were at Le Moose, which was a more forgiving exit point, and Nick probably should have stayed on that side of the valley and worked on his tracking skills more. But he was with Dwain, and Dwain tended to push people outside their comfort zone. I'm not sure Nick was aware of how weak his tracking skills were or how important those skills would be once he headed over to the Nose jumps. Nick also seemed to rely heavily on luck. His little bag filled with lucky charms made me feel uncomfortable; it showed a lack of realism about the situations he was putting himself in. He wouldn't jump without this lucky bag, but personally, I feel he should have spent way more time training his skills on safer jumps and less time on superstitions.

Nick's death was unfortunate and impacted everyone in the group. We all wished we had paid closer attention to his tracking issues over the days leading up to his accident. I learned I needed to be more vocal when seeing people pushing beyond their skill level. The irony of the conversation we had the night before his death—where he told me not to push so hard when I should have been telling him the exact same thing—is palpable.

Despite what happened on our Swiss trip, Dwain and I started spending more time together. Our friendship grew and he became a mentor to me. I respected his skill and he inspired me to train harder, approaching the sport with more of an athlete's mentality. He convinced me to start training with high divers. In one season of BASE jumping in 2002, I did about 300 jumps. You could do 300 exits into the swimming pool, practicing different acrobatic maneuvers, in a week. The progression in acrobatic skills in the pool was exponentially faster than with BASE jumping. Dwain had realized early on that using high diving training in the pool could help him surpass other jumpers rapidly. I didn't care so much about being better than other jumpers, but I did like the challenge of learning complicated acrobatic dives, and it seemed like a new way to push myself. I liked the idea of training for specific maneuvers and then executing them on different objects around the world.

Dwain and I went on trips together where he would train his advanced acrobatic skills, and I was always impressed to see what he could pull off. My acrobatics were rudimentary compared to his, but I would do the best I could. Once I began doing high diving training at USC, my skills grew rapidly. I began spreading my jumps almost equally between acrobatics and wingsuit flying. Dwain's focus was almost 99.9 percent acrobatics and maybe 0.1 percent wingsuits; he just didn't like them very much. Dwain wasn't interested in skydiving, and in order to understand wingsuits, you needed to skydive them a lot. Because he didn't want to do that, Dwain just jumped them off cliffs, and that made him struggle. In the early years, the suits were difficult to fly efficiently, and without skydiving, you couldn't properly learn this skill. Every time I saw Dwain jump a wingsuit, he would potato chip (rock side to side), and it always seemed to me he was on the edge of losing control. Dwain had become accustomed to being at the apex of BASE and didn't seem to like the idea of going back to being a student, so he just kind of ignored training with wingsuits altogether.

One day, almost a year after Nick's death, I got a call from a man named Troy, who owned an energy drink brand called GoFast. Troy told me about an event they would be sponsoring at the New River Gorge Bridge in Colorado, the highest suspension bridge in the world in 2003. He said he was going to invite the fifty best BASE jumpers from around the world and asked if I would be interested in attending.

"I'd be honored," I told him.

"Excellent," Troy responded. "Do you think you'd be able to fly a wingsuit under the bridge if we can get permits for you to jump from a plane?"

"Yes, I can absolutely fly under that bridge. No problem."

He said, "Great. I'll work on the permits and get back to you, but if you don't hear from me in time, bring your wingsuit just in case." We hung up, and I was excited. Events like this were rare and it was awesome that I was considered one of the top fifty BASE jumpers from around the world. I wasn't sure I agreed with that assessment but was happy to be invited all the same.

Dwain called and told me he had been asked to go to the games as well. He then asked if I would let him shoot videos of my jumps. He said he didn't feel like doing acrobatics for the event but would rather work on his filming skills and wanted to use me as his subject. I was super stoked. The legend of acrobatic BASE jumping wanted to use his jumps to film me doing acrobatics. As a side motive, he also wanted to break into the filming and licensing business of BASE. I was already earning pretty good money from licensing footage, and I think Dwain wanted to start working his way into earning money that way, too.

A few weeks later, Dwain and I showed up in Colorado for the first GoFast Games at the New River Gorge Bridge. When I got to the location, I went to sign in and saw Troy standing at the entrance. We greeted each other and the first thing I asked was, "Were you able to get permission for me to fly under the bridge?"

Troy said, "No, it doesn't look like we can get approval for this year. I'm going to try and secure it for next year, though."

I was a bit bummed but totally understood. Getting approval for these kinds of things is difficult. We talked a bit longer and then I headed off to start getting ready for the event. Dwain was in the packing area getting his gear in order when I showed up. I walked over to him, and he asked me what I wanted to do for the first jump. I decided to do a handstand, cut through, triple reverse to warm things up. I did the jump and he captured it perfectly. We kept jumping over and over, working on different maneuvers and camera angles, for the next three days.

Finally, on the last day for the last jump, I decided I was going to go for my full twisting triple reverse. That was the most difficult acrobatic maneuver I could do at the time; I was only successful about 75 percent of the time when trying it. The event was coming to a close and the time was getting late, so I decided to go look for Dwain, but couldn't seem to find him anywhere. I asked around but no one had seen him. As I checked the packing area, I saw Dwain in a corner putting his wingsuit on his BASE rig.

I walked up to him and asked, "What are you doing, Dwain? I thought you wanted to film me doing the full twisting triple."

He responded with, "Jeb, we got permission to fly wingsuits from the plane. You will fly under the bridge, and I'm going to fly over it."

That shocked me a little, so I said, "What are you talking about? Why didn't anyone tell me this information?" I then thought to myself, *Why are you on this load? Wingsuits aren't your thing.*

He could tell by the look on my face I was concerned, and he said, "Jeb, don't worry. I'm going to fly high over the bridge. I won't come any closer than two hundred feet."

I didn't say anything in reply but I was thinking, *Well, you might be okay if you fly high over the bridge, but why the hell would you want to?*

That just didn't seem like Dwain. There was a crowd with all the best jumpers in the world watching. Flying 200 feet over the bridge didn't seem like something

Dwain would want to do, but he had been chill the entire event. I thought maybe he just wanted to try and get better footage of me flying under the bridge. I wasn't sure what was going on and it confused me. It seemed out of character for Dwain, and it gave me an uneasy feeling, but there wasn't much I could do. It wasn't my call, and how could I tell the greatest BASE jumper to ever walk the face of Earth what he should or shouldn't do?

I quickly put my wingsuit on my rig and we loaded into a pickup truck that drove us to a small nearby airport. Dwain and I loaded into the aircraft with another jumper named Robin. He also had a wingsuit on, and I asked what he was going to do. He said the same thing Dwain did: "I'm going to fly over the bridge high and pull over the top of the gorge. I just want to take a look at the bridge from above." Robin was a more conservative jumper and what he said made a bit more sense based on his personality. I didn't have any doubts he would do exactly what he said he was going to do.

As we sat in the aircraft heading to altitude, Dwain seemed nervous; it was odd seeing him act this way. I had been on a lot of scary jumps with him and had never seen him be like this before. His wrist-mounted altimeter didn't seem to be working and he said, "I think I'm going to need to get a new battery when we get back to California." I pointed out he wouldn't need it right now because this was more a BASE jump from an aircraft than a skydive and he nodded, acknowledging he knew he didn't need it for this jump. As we got to exit altitude, he seemed to get even more nervous. I noticed it but didn't understand why. This jump didn't seem to be all that scary. We had plenty of altitude, and if he was going to fly 200 feet over the bridge, it was pretty much a skydive for him.

As we moved to the door and started spotting where to exit the aircraft, he grabbed me by my hand, squeezing it hard, and yelled in my ear, "Jeb, whatever happens, happens." I looked at him, puzzled by what he said, and shook my head in an uncomfortable way, not understanding what he meant by that. He was acting weird.

The pilot asked us to please fold up our wings when we left the airplane—he was worried we may hit the tail, which is a concern for some pilots, and rightly so. So, both Dwain and I exited with our wings shut down and did a little tumble out the door before opening them back up and flying. I didn't see much of Dwain during my flight towards the bridge; only a split second when I exited the aircraft out of my peripheral above me, but that was it. I became hyper-focused on the bridge under me. It was far below and we had gotten out a little too close. I realized I would have to shut my wings down to lose some altitude. After dumping about 1,000 feet of altitude, I could see my line coming into view, so I opened up my wings again. I wanted to fly as close to the bottom of the bridge as possible in order to conserve as much altitude as I could. I would then use that altitude to fly far under the bridge and deep into the gorge. As I was powering up underneath the bridge, I saw something I didn't understand at the time: Dwain's parachute deploying right in front of me.

My first thought was, *Why is he deploying there?* I had to take evasive action and swerve to miss him. As I flew to his right, missing him by only a few feet, I noticed there was other stuff floating in the air all around us. I didn't understand what all this debris was. As I weaved my way through the objects spiraling around me, I wondered if people were throwing stuff off the bridge, but I had to block all of these thoughts out of my mind. I was now deep in a narrow gorge flying a wingsuit and I had to concentrate. I just kept flying for as long as I could before I finally opened my parachute. I turned my canopy back towards the bridge and landed gently on train tracks at the bottom of the gorge. As I landed, I looked up and saw that I had flown way further under the bridge than I had thought possible. I became excited and felt like the jump couldn't have gone any more perfectly. This amazing sensation of joy rushed through my body, giving me an experience of absolute joy. That feeling wouldn't last long, though.

I looked up and saw Dwain's canopy drifting towards the cliff on the opposite side of the gorge. His canopy, with him under it, impacted the cliff with shattering force and I yelled, "Holy shit, Dwain just had a cliff strike!"

A woman standing close to where I landed said, "No, Jeb. Dwain hit the bridge and he is dead." I looked over towards where she was standing and noticed a severed leg lying between us. I looked down towards my hands and saw that my wingsuit was covered in blood. I went into shock. BASE jumping can have this way of making you feel the highest of highs and then, within seconds, it can bring you crashing back down to levels lower than anything you could ever imagine. I had just completed a jump no one had ever attempted before and executed it flawlessly. I landed and felt a surge of absolute joy. A few moments later, I realized my friend had just been severed in half right in front of my eyes, and a shockwave ripped through my mind, leaving damage that could never be repaired.

I felt disbelief and denial, repeating over and over, "This is impossible, this is impossible." I couldn't understand how he had hit the bridge. I didn't think a person could hit that bridge without *wanting* to hit that bridge. I don't know how I got back up to the deck of the bridge, because everything was a blur. I was stumbling around in a deep dark fog, not really understanding what was going on. I remember standing next to Jimmy, one of the organizers of the event and a good friend. We weren't talking; we were just standing there next to one another when, out of nowhere, I suddenly dropped to my knees and started crying. I put my head down with my eyes closed and sobbed silently. Jimmy put his hand on my shoulder as I had a miniature breakdown. I didn't know what to do or what to think. My brain couldn't process what was going on. After a period of time—I have no idea how long because time was distorted and my brain was short-circuiting—I got back on my feet and dried my tears. It was the first and last time I would cry for the dead in this activity.

We walked over to where Dwain had hit a guard railing, just below his waist at over 100 mph. His impact was so hard he had bent steel and broken supports under the bridge. There were over 200 people standing on the bridge watching as Dwain had his accident, and it was filmed from six different camera angles. We watched the footage to try and figure out what had gone wrong. How could he have made such a horrible miscalculation? As we watched the footage from each camera angle, I became convinced he had been trying to fly through a small hole between a support cable and the steel railing. No one questioned me at the time because everyone was in shock. But over time and after many viewings of the footage, we all came to realize Dwain had just fucked up. He was an amazing acrobatic BASE jumper, but he was a shitty wingsuit pilot. He hadn't put in the level of training needed to attempt a close flyby of a fixed object. He lied to the organizers, and he lied to me, in order to get on the load. If he had done what he said he was going to do, which was fly 200 feet over the bridge, he would have been fine. If he had told us he was going to try and skim the bridge by five feet, he would never have been allowed on that aircraft. He lied to us, and he lied to himself, and now he was dead.

About a week later, I woke up early in the morning on a crisp autumn day. As I got up, my toes bumped a small box sitting at the foot of my bed. This box contained the ashes of my good friend, Dwain Weston. I picked it up with my left hand and examined it. As I turned it from side to side, I was surprised at how light the box was. How did an entire human body fit in something so small? Only one week earlier, he and I had been planning a surfing trip to Indonesia. We were talking about the next summer and what countries we were going to visit on our next BASE tour. Now, standing in my room alone, I had the surreal realization that all these plans were never going to happen. A life had come to an end with one mistake, one miscalculation. Dwain had done over 1,400 BASE jumps without so much as a scratch. Now he was in a box, and this was the day of his memorial.

Karin called it "Dwain's Celebration of Life" and wanted to do it on the beach in front of my parent's house in Malibu. Dwain loved surfing and had almost as much passion for it as he did BASE jumping, so it seemed fitting. Later that day, after all Dwain's friends and family (the ones in the United States, anyway) showed up, we all got on our boards and paddled out in the surf beyond the breaking waves to dump some of his ashes. The rest would be saved and distributed to his friends to spread on all his favorite BASE sites around the world. Once everyone was past the breakers, we all got in a circle, facing each other. A handful of ashes were handed out to each person, and with a classic BASE countdown, we all threw his ashes in the air and watched as the wind took them away. I was carrying the bag containing Dwain's ashes and decided to keep some of them. As I was paddling back, I caught a small wave and rode it to shore, giving my buddy his last wave.

I didn't jump for almost six months after Dwain's death. It was the first time since I was sixteen that I questioned if BASE jumping was really worth dying for. I went into a depression and felt I was losing direction. One day as I sat by myself on the beach, looking out over the sea where we had thrown Dwain's ashes, a thought came to me: death doesn't always happen the day your life seeps out of you. There is another form of death that can happen to a living person and, in many cases, it's far worse. If someone completely gives up on their dreams, effectively turning their back on the things that truly matter to them, they can lose purpose, and without purpose, what would be the point of existing in the first place?

I thought, *Okay, I can quit BASE jumping. I can stop riding motorcycles, climbing, diving with sharks, doing anything considered dangerous, and you know what? I will still die. There is nothing I can do to change that. Death is inevitable.* There is a Russian saying I have grown to love that roughly translates to, "Don't drink, don't smoke, still die." I don't drink or smoke, but the idea still rings true. I could stop doing the things that bring me happiness and I might live a bit longer, but would it be a life I was interested in living? I have always been wired in an odd way. My mind has seemed incapable of just being happy or content. I needed purpose, a reason to wake up in the morning, a reason to eat food and breathe air. I needed a reason to exist. BASE jumping somehow became that reason. It was the driving force that had pulled me kicking and screaming through almost a decade of time. BASE had burned the demons ripping away at my mind and turned them to ash. That ash became the soil that my life sprouted from. I came to understand I didn't truly have a choice. There was nothing else I could do. To give up was unthinkable; to give up was to die right away. Maybe not a physical death at that moment, but a psychological death that would have led to a life not worth living.

I had to come to terms with what happened to Dwain. He had brought the fearlessness of the world's best acrobatic BASE jumper to wingsuiting. Problem was, his skills in acrobatics did not transfer over to the new discipline. Wingsuit BASE has almost nothing to do with aerial acrobatics. They are two completely different skillsets. Dwain was so smart when it came to his training regimen in acrobatics, or the way he would progress from pool training to safe object, to complicated object. He understood safe progression and how important it was to prepare. It's sad he didn't bring that same level of dedication to training wingsuits. It's also sad that he always wanted to one-up everyone around him. BASE is not an activity where being competitive is a good thing, because competing at something that can kill you is stupid. The only person a BASE jumper should be competing with is themselves. They should be in a constant competition to be a better person today than they were yesterday. Besides, why try to be better than others in an activity where the concept of "best" is arbitrary?

This is going to sound trite, but Dwain died doing what he loved; it wasn't a tragedy. He didn't die from cancer or getting hit by a car. He didn't walk into a room and fall on the ground from a brain aneurysm turning him off like a switch. He made conscious decisions, knowing exactly what the risks were, and he was willing to accept those risks like a man. He lived his life on his own terms. I am sure Dwain wouldn't have wanted to die any other way. He had a somewhat sick sense of humor, and he was a bit of a sociopath, so dying in front of a crowd in a truly gruesome way would have brought him great joy. He really was that weird. He and I had many conversations where he made it clear that, if he died and it was captured on camera, he wanted the world to see it. It was a special kind of crazy, and anyone who knew him either loved him or hated him for it.

Dwain died on October 5, 2003. On October 5th the following year, I found myself with the last living member of Team Psilocybin Solution: Slim. He and I were jumping the Jin Mao in Shanghai China for a huge live event that aired on CCTV across all of Asia and had over 100,000 spectators clogging the city streets below. We were joined by the best BASE jumpers the world had to offer.

Early in the day, we had a briefing where they informed us of their safety regulations and asked what kind of jumps each of us were planning on doing. They explained how the building was high but covered in sharp spikes. If anyone had an off-heading opening and hit this building, they could get skewered, which may upset some of the spectators. Because of this, they wanted us to be as conservative as possible to ensure a positive experience for everyone involved. They asked us to give detailed plans on our every move, then they would say yes or no depending on how complex the jump was and the skill level of the particular jumper. As they got to me, the lead organizer paused, took a deep breath, and, in an almost nervous way, asked what I was planning. I said, "I'm going to do a double twisting quad front."

He took another deep breath, shook his head, and said, "I don't even know what that is...but whatever," and quickly moved on to the next jumper.

At this point, I had become known as one of the better acrobatic BASE jumpers still left alive. The double twisting quad front was by far my most difficult maneuver, and I was only able to pull it off about 50 percent of the time. In my mind, that was a completely reasonable success ratio, but looking back on it with the way I see things now, I can see I was completely irrational and borderline stupid. Actually, there isn't anything borderline about it—I was being stupid, plain and simple.

They asked Slim what he was planning, and he informed them he would be exiting with a wingsuit to try and get the most separation he could from the building. It had been a couple years since his cliff strike left him permanently disabled. His limp had not improved and he could no longer push off with his toes. This meant he couldn't physically jump out and away from the object. He shouldn't have been BASE jumping off a building this technical, but he was a living legend and no one was going to tell him what he could or couldn't do. He felt that because he couldn't push off anymore, the wingsuit would give him the necessary distance to deal with an off-heading opening if one occurred. I don't think he realized how disabled he really was; not only were his legs badly damaged but he also suffered from weakness in his upper body. Not fully understanding this is what got him in the end.

After everyone submitted what they were planning, we were then given our exit order. The producers of the show gave us a rundown of how the show was going to move along based on the time of day. Everything was meticulously coordinated down to the second. Each person was to take no longer than one minute at the exit point, and they would be told exactly when to jump with a countdown. All footage from each jumper was to be gathered in the landing area so it could be broadcast to the live viewers. The jumpers would be lined up at least twenty minutes before their turn to jump.

At around 2:00 p.m. that day, my time came up and I walked out on the platform. I looked down and, for the first time, I saw the immense crowd that had gather to witness the day's festivities. I was blown away at how many people were crowding the city streets; I had never seen that many people all gathered in one place before. It was a sight to behold. Quickly after stepping into position, I was given my countdown and I moved my toes to the edge of the steel grade platform they had built specifically for this event. A giant crane supporting a camera buzzed around over my head. There was so much going on all around me that it became overwhelming to the senses. As they counted down, I tried to focus on the complicated acrobatic maneuver I was about to perform. The countdown hit zero and I pushed off as hard as I could. I went through the full double twists with two simultaneous laid-out front flips. I then tucked up and completed two more forward rotations. I felt the maneuver was sloppy, but I had done what I'd set out to do. I ended up doing the jump three times that day and cleaned it up a bit by the last one.

After landing my last jump of the day, I was feeling pretty good with my performance when I looked up and saw something upsetting: it was Slim, and he was in trouble. He had flown his wingsuit from the building as planned and had a good flight that gave him great distance from the building, but on deployment, he got a terrible set of line twists. The line twists had spun up so far that he couldn't reach above them, making his canopy uncontrollable. He tried to grab the line twists and climb above them, but because of his previous injuries, he no longer had the upper-body strength. His canopy had turned downwind on its own and Slim was under the canopy facing the wrong direction. I watch him struggle as the canopy impacted the roof of a nearby building. I couldn't see what happened after he disappeared past the roof, but I could tell he hit with force and would have injuries. Rescue services scrambled to get to him, but it still took time. After what felt like ages, I watched as they carried Slim past me in a jog towards a waiting ambulance. Six paramedics were holding what looked like a white sheet with Slim hanging in the middle like a hammock. Within that sheet, there was no movement at all.

Slim had impacted the roof of the building while flying backwards under his canopy. He was trapped under line twists that he didn't have the power to climb above. He hit an air-conditioning unit directly on the back of his head where it met the spine. He was pronounced brain dead at the hospital and needed to be placed on life support machines to keep his vital organs working. He would have died that day, but his family wanted him kept on life support until they could arrive to say goodbye. His wife and parents showed up a few days later to watch as doctors unplugged one of the most wonderful human beings to ever grace this planet with his presence. Within moments, Slim was gone.

In three years, we lost every member of Team Psilocybin Solution: one each year starting in 2002. Shortly after that, the Australian BASE scene lost four more of their ranks in less than a year. The crazy Australians, who no one could understand how they were surviving, finally came crashing down all at once. It was the collapse of an entire movement, and it was sad on a level that words could never express. But it reinforced the old saying about pilots: "There are old pilots and there are bold pilots, but there are no old bold pilots."

CHAPTER TWENTY-TWO

JOURNEY TO THE CENTER

In 2003, I was contacted by a producer named Brent. He was working on a series for the Outdoor network called *Fearless*. Each episode would focus on an icon of a sport and try to tell their life story in a one-hour documentary. I told him using the word "icon" to describe me was a very loose use of the term, but I was flattered to even be considered for the project. I said I would be happy to do the project as long as the production could afford to pay a licensing fee of $2,500 per edited minute with non-exclusive rights for my archive of footage. I was earning my living from jumping and wasn't interested in unpaid projects at that time. He said my prices were a bit expensive, but he thought he could find the money in the budget somewhere.

We ended up working together on the project for a few months, doing interviews and telling the story of BASE jumping from my perspective. When it was almost complete, I got a frantic call from Brent telling me he was sorry. I asked him what he was sorry for, and he said, "Jeb, I'm only the producer for your episode. There's another producer who oversees all the episodes, and when he saw what I was paying you, he lost his shit. He told me we don't have that much money in the licensing budget. I tried to explain I was going to grab the money from my graphics/visual effects budget, but he informed me the budget doesn't work that way and we needed that money for different episodes. I told him you were not going to negotiate your rates and the show is already in the can. He told me he's going to call you to get you to come down on your rates. You should expect a call from him soon. Just know I don't have anything to do with this and I told him he shouldn't call you."

I laughed and said, "No problem, bro. He can call and I'll tell him what I told you on day one: I don't negotiate my rates."

Sure enough, a few hours later, I received a call from some producer saying he worked with Brent. He started out by telling me they didn't have the money in their budget to pay me the amount promised. He then told me they were using footage from the Kennedy assassination for only a fraction of what I was charging.

I stopped him right there and said, "Okay, wait one minute. First off, I don't give a shit what you're paying for the Kennedy assassination. That footage has been seen thousands of times on thousands of shows. Second, I told you guys what my rates were before we began, and they were agreed to. I do not negotiate my prices, ever. Third, you are insulting me now. You need to realize how much it has cost me to gather this library of footage. Think about what it would cost you to get permits to jump from the Eiffel Tower. What, fifty thousand? A hundred thousand? Assuming you could even get them. Then think about hiring a camera crew and all the plane tickets, hotel costs, food and catering, etc., etc. The stuntman you would hire to do the actual jump would cost anywhere from five to ten grand per jump. Think of what it would cost to permit the Golden Gate Bridge or the Patron's Towers or any of the other hundreds of jumps in that library. Or let's talk about me impacting a waterfall and getting eaten alive by animals. You couldn't recreate that even if you wanted to. You know what? We can go ahead and call this off right now. I don't care about this show, and we don't have to do this."

He quickly realized he had fucked up and apologized profusely. He then did something odd. He said, "Okay, I understand. How about we work a deal where we pay a flat rate of twenty thousand dollars to use as much footage as we want?"

I smiled to myself and said, "Alright, I'll take that deal, mostly because there's no way Brent's going to use that much of my footage. I suggest you talk with Brent before making this deal, though. I know he wants to license footage from other BASE jumpers, and if you blow your entire budget on me, he won't be able to get footage from anyone else."

The guy seemed like he wasn't sure what to do after that and said, "Okay. I will call you back after talking to Brent." It was funny; he had called trying to talk me down on my rates and ended up trying to pay me more. It was an interesting negotiation tactic.

The show completed airing on December 14, 2004, on the Outdoor Life Network. (Later, it would air internationally on the National Geographic Channel as well.) I loved the way it turned out and Brent became a good friend in the process. A few months later, Brent told me he was tired of working in Hollywood and needed to change his life's direction. He explained he had felt somewhat inspired by working

with me and loved the free spirit BASE jumpers embodied. He expressed interest in working with me on whatever my next project would be.

I told him he was in luck because I had a friend named Paul Fortun from Norway, and he had sent me an interesting photograph of a man walking on a tightrope across a massive 2,000-foot-deep cave in China. I was thinking about going there to make a documentary about BASE jumping into its depths. I told Brent that if he was interested, we could use a director/editor for the project. Our budget was going to be low, but excitement was guaranteed. He instantly said, "Yes, I'm interested!" so we began the process of putting everything together.

I contacted my buddy Iiro to help with producing the project. Iiro had been a professional magician and had produced many TV specials over the years. He's also an incredibly organized individual and has a powerful work ethic. He also was the single most social human being I had ever met and had contacts located all over the world. When I told Iiro about the project, he said yes before I even finished explaining what we were going to do. Iiro and I had similar ways of seeing production and we loved working together.

I then called Paul to see if he would be interested in helping with the project. I let him know we were planning on going to the cave he had discovered deep in the heart of China to make a documentary, and asked if he would like to come along and be one of the three jumpers featured in the film. Paul said "Absolutely! Just tell me when and where to show up."

For the third jumper, I asked an Australian that went by the name of Douggs. He was probably the single best all-around BASE jumper in the world (still left alive anyway). But more important than being a good jumper, he was a super colorful character who was great on camera and would add an interesting dynamic to the project. Douggs was covered in tattoos and piercings and had a massive pink mohawk that stood out in a crowd. His outrageous style would be an extreme contrast to the people at our destination.

We had been told only two groups of westerners had ever visited this remote part of China before. The mountain people who lived in this region didn't even speak Chinese in its traditional sense, so our interpreters would have trouble communicating in the region. I had met two female government officials when I was working on the Jin Mao live show the year before. They had told me if I ever wanted to do projects in China to contact them and they could help me get the proper government approval. That made them the next phone call I made. I told them what our plan was and asked if it was possible to get permits for a project like this. They said, "No problem, but it will take a few months." I was happy to hear this because pre-production would take us a few months anyway.

Once pre-production was complete and we had our permits in hand, we all got on planes headed for China. Iiro, Brent, a camera assistant named Trevor, and I flew together from LA. Paul flew in from Norway and Douggs traveled from Australia. We also had two cameramen fly in from Cape Town, South Africa: Moose and his camera assistant. Moose had made a documentary about Iiro and me a few years earlier, leading to a strong friendship. Moose also happened to be an extremely talented filmmaker and mountain rescue climber—the perfect combination for a project like this. We all met in Beijing and filming began the moment we touched down. Brent directed the production but learned quickly that Moose was a powerful asset. Their cooperation turned into a dream team and the footage they captured together was nothing short of amazing.

It's funny how, when you're working on a production, you can get permission to do things that authorities would never let you do otherwise. We went to an ancient Chinese acrobat circus and, as we walked in, there were signs everywhere saying "No Filming" in both Chinese and English. We went to the person selling tickets and explained we were filming a documentary and would love permission to film the performance. Phone calls were made, and the head of the circus came down and told our interpreters it would be no problem at all. We then filmed the entire production and were asked backstage to do interviews with all the performers. It was a lovely experience that would never have happened otherwise.

The next day, we started the long journey to the cave called Xiaozhai Tiankeng, also known as the "Heavenly Pit." The location was remote and there were no airports anywhere near the small village close to the cave. The closest airport was located next to the largest dam project in the world. They called it the Three Rivers Dam Project and they were damming the Yangtze River in order to produce hydroelectric power. The dam was also meant to stop major flooding that had plagued the region for generations, killing thousands of people. When we saw the dam, it was hard to believe humans could build something so colossal. I had seen and even BASE jumped off many dams at this point, but none of them had been this huge. It went on as far as the eye could see and was an obvious engineering marvel. It wasn't complete yet, but they had these huge concrete slopes with water level indicators coming up the sides, showing where the water was going to rise to after the dam was finished. It was crazy to see how much of the valley would be intentionally flooded. It was one of the biggest relocations of population in history, with over five million people needing to be moved to other parts of China.

This was where we boarded a boat called "Mr. Dragon." It had gotten its name because it literally looked like a giant dragon floating on the water. It would take us two days floating upriver to a town called Fengjie. The river boat ride was slow moving but beautiful. The banks of the Yangtze were covered in emerald-green canopies of jungle and, at times, the river would narrow to where the boat could barely fit between towering cliff faces. As jumpers, we saw potential exit points everywhere we looked. It seemed like you could exit a different cliff every single day for years without ever repeating a jump. The sky was always cloaked in a gray fog that blotted out the sun and clung to the sides of jagged peaks. It was a beautiful landscape that didn't seem real.

When we got to Fengjie, we loaded into 4x4s and started a twelve-hour drive to Xiaozhai (which literally translates to "little village"), the closest civilization to the Heavenly Pit. The Chinese government built a staircase into the cave with over 2,800 steps in order to attract tourists to the region. That also turned out to be the reason they gave us permits to film our documentary there: the government hoped it would bring international tourists and their money to the area.

As we made the drive, we could see they were building up the infrastructure to be able to handle large amounts of visitors. We were probably going to be the last expedition that needed to drive on dirt roads and take boats to this area. The next year, they were planning on opening a new airport that would unlock the region to international tourists, and the location would be forever changed.

We felt privileged to see the place before all that happened. The people were simple and life seemed to be as it had been for hundreds of years. People worked in fields, growing food with homemade tools. We saw children, maybe six or seven years old, carrying crops back to their homes. One of the houses we saw had livestock living under it to help keep the home warm in the winter. It was the first time I'd ever seen a home heating system like that. People were kind and would ask us in for tea everywhere we went. If we stopped in a restaurant, every single person would turn their chair around and watch us eat our food. Even the cooks would come out of the kitchens and watch us. It was almost like we were aliens from another planet. They were fascinated by us being there and they didn't even know why we were there.

As we approached Xiaozhai, we saw two looming cliffs spiking out of the earth with farms and crops tucked underneath them. They were so striking the team decided to take a closer look. On closer inspection, we knew they could be jumped if we could find a way to climb them. Our interpreters asked a local farmer if he knew how to get on top of the cliffs and he responded, "Of course." He walked up there all the time for exercise and to look at the valley. We asked him if he would guide us up and he grabbed a walking stick and started walking. We asked him if he could wait for us to grab some gear and we went back to the 4x4s to get our camera gear and rigs.

The hike was easier than we expected. The locals had made a nicely groomed trail all the way to the top, so it was more of a stroll than an actual hike. As we got there, it was decided I would go first. This would be my first sighted location, meaning it was the first time I was going to jump an object before anyone else ever had. If you sight a location, you get to name it. For some jumpers, this is the holy grail of jumping. Some people dedicate their entire BASE careers to jumping off new objects first and naming them. That wasn't really my thing, but I couldn't deny there was something special about sighting a location for my first time.

As they set up the cameras, we did a couple rock drops to judge how tall the cliff was and make sure it was vertical. We determined it was close to 700 feet tall and it was overhanging. By the time the cameras were in place and rolling, I was already geared up and ready to jump. I looked out over the peaceful valley with farms and crops below me and thought to myself, *If I ever get old, I would love to live in a place like this.* I then stepped off and flew over the little valley. Douggs and Paul followed shortly after, and when the camera crew made it back down, we regrouped and made our next plan.

We decided to check out the landing area of the larger cliff across the valley. The hike turned out to be longer and deeper into the valley then we had expected. Also, the cliff was much taller in person. The valley narrowed as the two cliffs on each side squeezed it, and that tight space made for an awful landing area. We were going to have to land flying back into the base of the taller cliff on a dirt talus that was steeper than 50 degrees. The walking path was carved into it in switchbacks, and the hope was to just hit the talus at some point and then slide down it till we hit one of the dugout trail sections. Douggs is an Australian, and Australia is known for having some of the worst landing areas on Earth. He was worried by what he saw and said this was by far the worst landing area he had ever contemplated landing on. But it was doable, so we set about finding a way to get on top.

Lucky for us, the same farmer who had shown us to the top of the first cliff also knew how to get on top of this one, which ended up being even easier to climb than the smaller one. There was a road that went up the back that had just been completed earlier that year, so we could just drive up and then it would only be a flat ten-minute walk to the edge.

We packed our gear and headed up for another jump. Once we got to the exit, random local people started showing up, seemingly from nowhere. At first, there were just a couple adults with their children. Then ten more families showed up, then thirty. It became concerning because there wasn't much space on the edge of the cliff and people began doing unsafe things. They started scooting to the edge without any protection and we had to have the interpreters tell them to step back, especially the children. It was over 2,000 feet straight down and a fall would be fatal for sure. Everyone wanted to see us jump off the cliff but didn't seem to care about their own safety. Trying to control the crowd became scary—way scarier than the actual jump was. But the interpreters eventually talked some reason into the crowd and people backed off. Some of the locals found sturdy trees to hold onto and stayed back from the edge. This helped us relax a bit more and we were finally able to focus on filming.

Douggs was the first to jump this time and took an extended delay. His track was so good he probably could have hit the other side of the valley had he wanted to. I jumped second and threw a nice, slow, laid-out gainer, followed by Paul, who also crushed a massive tracking jump. The landing area wasn't as tricky as it looked from the ground. I just lined up at the middle of the talus, hit it, and slid down to the closest part of the switchback trail. Douggs decided to name his cliff "Big Kahuna," so I named my cliff "Little Kahuna," seeing as they were directly across from one another.

We then headed to Xiaozhai to check into our hotel and get some much-needed rest after a long journey and opening two brand new cliffs. To call our hotel rustic would be a nice way of putting it. They were in the process of building a new hotel that would support the new wave of tourists the local community was hoping would come with the new airport, but for now we were in a small building decaying with age. But after almost four days of non-stop travel, it was a lovely thing to just be able to take a warm shower and sleep in clean sheets.

The next morning, we woke up, packed our gear, ate a small breakfast, and headed to the Heavenly Pit to finally see it with our own eyes. As we approached, the sky was its usual gray color and the fog was thicker than it had been the last few days. We were a bit concerned we wouldn't be able to see the 2,000-foot drop into the earth. Fog banks rolled through like thick clouds scraping across the ground. After parking the cars, we began walking on a well-groomed pathway towards our final goal. As we caught sight of the chasm, we were instantly awestruck by how vast it was—much bigger than we had imagined. Pictures couldn't illustrate the magnitude of what this place was; it was so enormous that whole cities could fit inside it. On the edges, we noticed cave systems all along the top rim, and it turned out the caves were used as dwellings by locals hundreds of years earlier. They used long boards to bridge the gaps between them and then pull the boards in to protect themselves from bandits and thieves. I found this information fascinating because the vertical drops were just insane, and it must have been a frightening place to live during that period.

We started walking down the path to the bottom to scout for possible landing areas and could tell this was going to take a long time. We had to maneuver over

2,800 steps and descend over 2,000 vertical feet into the depths of the earth. After what seemed like hours of putting one foot in front of the other, we finally made it to the bottom. As we looked up, we began to get a true grasp of what we were about to face. There was a 1,000-foot spire that rose up from the bottom of the cavern, and two 1,000-foot waterfalls cascading through any possible flight paths. A raging river ran across the bottom with class-death rapids, and if we somehow fell in, we would be sucked underground for over four days before we popped out on the backside of the mountain and ejected over a 900-foot cliff into the valley. We were informed they had black venomous snakes with poison that would eat your flesh if they bit you. If we got injured down here, we would have to be carried up the 2,800 steps by hand, and it would take about two days before we could get to a decent hospital. There were no good landing areas; everything was covered by steep, jagged boulders. The best thing we could find was a somewhat-smooth piece of ground next to a set of stairs, about two king-sized mattresses long and set at a 45-degree angle. It was small, steep, and if you missed it, you were going to get hurt.

After seeing all the obstacles to avoid and the unforgiving terrain, we were pretty sure someone was going to get hurt. I gave us about a 60 percent chance that someone was going to get at least a broken ankle, and in this place, it was guaranteed to be bad. If the break were to be compound and an artery were severed, it would mean almost certain death.

We all looked at each other and understood how serious the situation was. The jump was going to be the easy part; the challenge would be landing without getting broken. You could see the fear on everyone's faces and could almost feel an electricity in the air.

The hike back out was more difficult than the hike in. It took well over an hour to climb all the stairs, and by the time we made it, we were exhausted. We headed to a restaurant to get some food and talk about what we were all going to do the next day. We decided if the weather was good, we were just going to get this done ASAP. We knew we would need to do at least three jumps each in order to get all the different camera angles needed to tell the story properly, which was a tall order that only increased the risk. While we were traveling to the location, we were all excited to do as many jumps as we possibly could, but after seeing the landing area, we wanted to finish this as fast as possible with as few jumps as we could get away with.

This was my first time being an executive producer for a documentary. I had felt the pressure from high-risk jumps before, but producing created a whole new group of challenges that I had never dealt with before. I had also never felt the enormous pressure that comes along with financial risk. I thought I understood what taking risks meant, but this showed me there are levels of risk you can't understand till you have experienced them. This could cause my financial ruin, along with physical destruction.

Something else dawned on me during this production. When I was a child, maybe only five or six, my grandparents would ask me what I wanted to be when I grew up. I would always tell them I wanted to be a zoologist. They would get a funny look on their faces and ask if I even knew what that was. I would tell them, "Zoologists film animals." I would tell people I wanted to be a zoologist until around the sixth grade; then, for some reason, I stopped saying it.

While making *Journey to the Center*, I realized what I had meant all those years ago: I wanted to be a documentary filmmaker. I used to love watching National Geographic documentaries about animals in Africa. Whenever they would show the people making the documentaries, they always called them zoologists. It dawned on me hiking out of that cave I had somehow fallen into doing what I had dreamed of doing since I was little. I just didn't have the words to explain myself as a child, or even the cognitive ability to truly grasp what was so compelling about the documentaries I saw. In a strange twist of fate, here I was producing my first documentary. Then I remembered I had already made three documentaries before this and hadn't even realized that's what I was doing. The motivation for BASE jumping was slowly transforming into something else: I was becoming way more interested in the storytelling aspect of the sport than I was in doing the actual jumps.

The next morning, everyone woke up and quietly prepared all the equipment we were going to need for the day's filming. Douggs, Paul, and I were focused on our BASE gear and the climbing gear we were going to use to slide out to the center of the cable suspended over the cave. This cable was put in place to break a tightrope world record a few years earlier; it spanned over 1,760 feet. Our jumps would not be possible without this cable in place. The walls of the cave weren't completely vertical, and there were two stages to the sinkhole. The top section was much wider, and the cliffs were only vertical for a few hundred feet. Then there was a second section that was smaller, making it look like a hole inside a hole. The only way to get enough altitude was to slide out to the middle of the cable and drop from there. A lot of what makes BASE jumping scary is the exposure. Sometimes it's nice to have something to lean against or hold onto, like rocks or trees. Dropping from a cable suspended over a 2,000-foot drop makes a person feel exposed and intensifies the fear factor for some jumpers.

In order to slide out on this cable, we would need to attach large carabiners to special slings that would hook through the harnesses of our BASE rigs and then attach those carabiners to the cable. Once we tested the rigging to ensure it would support our weight, we would slide out to what we felt was the center, then drop an orange to get a gauge on how far from the lower hole's walls we actually were.

One of our camera operators had extensive climbing experience and was supposed to be the one to come out and film us from the cable, but once he saw the cable and saw how long it was, he raised some valid and somewhat scary points. He was afraid the cable was not tested or designed to hold the weight of four large men. The cable itself must have weighed thousands of pounds, and once you combined its weight with ours, he wasn't sure it would be able to support all of us. His second fear was about us moving along the cable while dragging our carabiners. He felt it would send vibrations down the cable that could build speed and start oscillating like a sine wave, possibly building up enough energy to snap the cable. If we were on the cable as it snapped, we would all ride that cable to the ground at high speed because our parachute wouldn't be able to deploy while we were attached to it.

Still, the cable looked plenty sturdy to us. Douggs, Paul, and I all had no problem taking the risk—we were going for it no matter what.

The camera operator said, "I'm sorry, but I'm not willing to put my life on the line without having more information on the cable and how much weight it's rated for."

Lucky for us, Iiro was there. Being the crazy-ass BASE jumper he was made him think the same way we did. He said, "No problem; I'll just take over and film you guys."

I smiled and said, "Iiro, that's what I love about you. I can always count on you to do insane things to make a project work." Iiro has balls of steel, but lucky for him, we wouldn't need him until the second jump. On the first one it would just be Douggs, Paul, and me, which would give Iiro a chance to see if it would at least hold our weight before he had to give it a go himself.

It was finally time to start gearing up. All the cameras began rolling. We were terrified. It was so scary that I thought there was a 50/50 chance Paul wasn't even going to jump. He was the most conservative jumper in the group and I felt this was a bit too dangerous for his speed. I knew Douggs and I were jumping but felt we had a 60 percent chance of getting totally fucked-up when we did. Paul hooked into the cable first and tested to make sure he would be able to release the hook before sliding out further. Once he was sure he'd be able to release himself, he started sliding out over the abyss. I hooked in second and did the same test, making sure I'd be able to release the carabiner before pushing out over the big drop.

Then Douggs hooked in, but he seemed to be struggling a little. I asked him if he was okay and he said, "No, man. This is very uncomfortable."

"Do you still want to go?" I asked.

He responded with, "Let's just get moving, I want to get off this cable as soon as possible." So, we started pulling ourselves out along the massive cable.

As we started moving faster, sure enough, the cable started oscillating and the sound was terrifying. The vibrations traveled all the way to the end of the cable, then returned and hit us like a wave. Those vibrations hurt our hands, and it's impossible to describe the sound. But the faster we moved, the worse it got.

I could hear Douggs behind me, his breathing deep and loud, like he was suffocating. His panic was rising. I felt my heart beating against my ribs so hard I was sure it added to the vibrations, like it was trying to break through and escape from my body. Paul was silent; I heard nothing from him but slow, controlled movements towards the center of the cable. His face showed no emotion and it was impossible for me to get a read on what he was feeling, but everything seemed stretched thin.

As we approached what I thought was the center, Paul suddenly stopped and said, "I think this is where we need to drop." He took out the orange and we all watched as he dropped it into the cave.

It fell uncomfortably close to the wall and I said, "Let's move another fifty feet." Both Douggs and Paul agreed, so we moved across and then stopped again. I said, "I am going to drop from here." The exit order would be me first, Paul second, and Douggs last. Just before detaching from the cable, I looked at Douggs and said, "Bro, I think you need to get a bit closer to me."

He was going to be the cameraman for the first jump and he responded, "No, I can't move any farther, Jeb, I'm sorry but I'm done."

I could see he was completely gripped with fear, sweating profusely and breathing like he was suffocating in quicksand. I decided I didn't want to get in his headspace, so I just nodded and started focusing on my jump. I brought my legs up and wrapped them around the cable, then let go of the cable with my right hand and detached my carabiner, wrapping it up through the chest strap of my rig and clipping it to the main lift webbing on my left side. This was to prevent it from flying up and smashing into my face during deployment. I unlocked my legs and hung under the cable with only my ten fingers grasping cold, shaking steel. I took a series of deep breaths and kicked my feet forward. I initiated a swing and kicked my legs back and forth a few times as the momentum built more and more. I waited till my legs swung directly out in front of me before I let go and started a full twisting quad reverse. It was one of my more complex acrobatic maneuvers and I wanted to perform it here.

The acrobatic maneuver felt clean and smooth. As I came out of the twist and flips, I stabilized my body, orienting myself belly-to-earth, and watched as the ledge of the inner, smaller section of cave approached and passed. I could see the waterfall in front of me and the giant spire off to my left. I also saw the river, but noticed the water level was much lower today; the rapids didn't look as deadly as they had the day before. My parachute opened and I looked for the small patch of semi-smooth-but-steep ground we had decided to use as a landing area. From that height it looked crazy small, but I focused on it like my life depended on it. For such a tremendous cave, my flight pattern was very restricted. The spire and waterfall made the space smaller than I had expected, but I was still able to line up and make the tiny landing area. It was a no-wind landing and I hit pretty hard, but was completely uninjured. The relief I felt once my feet were safely on the ground is hard to explain, but the residual effects from the jump made my hands shake. I lifted them up and noticed a slight tremor in them.

Paul and Douggs would later explain that my swinging exit had put a super violent oscillation in the cable that made them lurch around. They said it took what felt like ages for the line to calm down enough before Paul could finally detach from the cable and exit. When I watched the footage of Paul exiting the cable, I was impressed. He seemed cool as a cucumber, and you couldn't tell he was scared at all, like it was just another day chilling by the pool. He hung with his knees up to his chest and exited on his back, just watching the cable fly away as he dropped into the center of the Earth on his back. He landed right next to me and started screaming. The pure, unfettered joy that spread across his face was a beautiful thing to witness. If you could call the level of joy a normal person would feel while riding, let's say a rollercoaster, something like a bonfire on the beach, then at this moment, Paul's level of joy was like an erupting volcano.

Douggs was now left all alone on the cable and he was by far, without a doubt, the most horrified of the three of us. We were all scared, but Douggs wears his fear on his face and in his breath. You can literally feel his fear just by watching him. I haven't seen many people manifest that much horror and then still do the very thing that was causing their visible trauma. In the documentary, you can hear his breathing, but unfortunately, during the sound mix it somehow got quieted down. In the cut before the sound mixer got ahold of it, you could really feel the true terror that was raging in Douggs—his breath was that of a suffocating human about to take his last gasp of air before death. He had all kinds of plans to do complex acrobatic maneuvers, but once he was there faced with the true fear, he decided to just do a gainer and chill. He dropped, executed a flawless gainer, and then landed between Paul and me. He hit the landing area hard, so I was worried he had injured himself and asked if he was okay. He didn't respond right away, so I asked again. He said, "I'm all good. Just give me a minute." He needed a few moments to pull himself together before the cameraman was able to start asking him post-jump questions.

Once we were all safely on the ground and had successfully completed the first jump, we were ecstatic. That feeling didn't last long, though. We were in the middle of a production and needed to hike out of the hole now, repack our gear, and do it two more times. It seemed almost silly to have to put ourselves through all of that again, but that's how production is. You need different camera angles, meaning you need to do everything multiple times even if you don't really want to. Lucky for us, the second time wasn't anywhere near as bad as the first. We all felt more comfortable and none of us were as scared as we were the first time. We again landed safely and hiked out a second time.

We went for the third jump, but Paul said, "Guys, I'm done. Two jumps were more than enough for me and I don't want to jump this anymore." Douggs and I totally understood; we didn't want to jump anymore, either, but someone had to finish the production, so we dressed Iiro in Paul's clothes so he could get footage of me from the opposite side and get a shot of Douggs exiting as well. This would camouflage Iiro so people wouldn't be able to tell it wasn't Paul on the long shot. We completed the final jump and, to our great relief, again landed safely. With this, the jumping portion of the trip was complete. Now all we had left were interviews, filming B roll, and side stories to add color to the documentary, things like outdoor markets and general Chinese culture from the area. Piece of cake.

That evening, everyone except me wanted to celebrate. I'm not much of a partier and, as far as I was concerned, we were still working, but I went along because I simply had no other choice. The group bought a bunch of fireworks, which in China you can buy year-round and pretty much everywhere. The Chinese love their fireworks and use them to celebrate everything from babies being born to people getting married to the opening of every business you can imagine. Many Chinese are superstitious and feel fireworks also ward off evil spirits, but don't get me started on that.

The group started drinking a bit on the early side and got sloppy before it even got dark. By the time the sun had gone down enough to light fireworks, the group was in a full drunken swing. I was kind of sitting back watching the mayhem unfold, but seeing how the Chinese love fireworks so much, I didn't feel it would be too big of an issue. But the sheer magnitude and crazy amounts of fireworks the group let off brought the attention of the police. The group got shut down, but not before Douggs had lit a roman candle that exploded in the wrong direction, sending flames and debris directly at his nutsack. That was my cue to head back to the hotel and go to bed; I had a strong feeling it was only going to get worse from there, and as I found out the next morning, it did.

Apparently, the group went out to a karaoke bar and proceeded to get even more wasted. Douggs and Brent decided getting completely naked in public would be the logical thing to do in their drunken state. It didn't take long for the police to get called once again, but this time the police escorted the group back to the hotel to ensure they stopped making trouble. It kind of made me feel like I was dealing with children because we still had filming to do. I just wanted to get everything completed before we had to head home, and this wasn't helpful. The next day, the group woke up with hangovers and everyone seemed a bit out of it. No filming happened that day as we began our journey home. It ended up not being an issue, though, because we were able to get all the pickup shots we needed along the way during our several-day journey.

Once we got to Beijing, everyone was tired and ready to head home. Paul and Douggs would fly to Norway and Australia, respectively. Brent would carry all the footage we had captured back to the USA and begin the monumental job of going through all of it, digitizing it, and organizing everything to begin the editing process. Iiro and I would fly together back to LA, where we would meet up with Brent after a few days to talk about the post-process of the documentary.

In our first post-meeting, Iiro and I explained how we felt we needed a trailer to help sell the documentary to potential buyers. Brent stated that a trailer would equal a lot of extra work and he wasn't sure we needed it, so we decided to stick a pin in the idea for the time being and work on other action items.

The next day, I called Brent and reiterated that we needed the trailer. Brent agreed to make it because it might help him organize his thoughts to go through and build an idea of the story. It took a few weeks for him to complete the trailer, and when it was done, both Iiro and I thought it was a masterpiece; we absolutely loved it. After Iiro and I saw it, I called Brent to tell him how much we liked it. Brent said, "Thank you. It makes me happy you guys like it, but it was a lot of work to make, and I think we need to renegotiate our deal. This project is going to be a lot more work than I thought it was going to be."

I told him, "Okay, let me talk with Iiro and I will get back to you."

I instantly called Iiro and told him what Brent said. Iiro took this as Brent trying to extort money out of us and felt he was holding our film hostage. Iiro got angry and he told me he would take care of this. He hung up the phone to call Brent. The next thing I knew, I was getting a call from Brent telling me he would no longer work on the project because Iiro had just threatened to drown him in a lake if he didn't return our footage today. I said, "Are you sure that's what Iiro said? He must have been kidding; there's no way he was being serious. Come on, Brent, you know people get emotional and this is just a misunderstanding."

But Brent didn't care. He felt Iiro had stepped over a line, joking or not, and there was no way he was going to work with him any longer.

This turned into a serious issue. Brent was the editor of the entire project and a really talented human being. He knew all the footage and was also the director. The entire production was his brainchild and I didn't know what we were going to do without him. He wouldn't be easy to replace.

We spent months talking to director after director and just couldn't find one that was within our budget. We finally got a director interested, but right when he was going to sign the contracts, he got another, higher-paying job and backed out. We had to put the project on the backburner for a while till be we could find a new editor.

In the meantime, I went to Europe to train and gather more footage. While there, I got invited by my friend, Jens Hoffman, to a premier of a documentary I had helped work on a year earlier called *20 Seconds of Joy*. It was about my first BASE-jumping student, Karina Hollekim. She had gone on to become one of the first female sponsored Red Bull athletes from Norway. During an event in Switzerland, she got serious tension knots during a deployment that led to a high-speed impact with the ground, breaking her left femur in three places and her right femur in twenty-one places. The documentary was dark and somewhat depressing. I also came off crazier than usual in the documentary, but that wasn't Jens' fault. I am crazy, so it never shocks me to see myself looking crazy. Even though the documentary was sad to watch, I liked its style. I asked Jens if he was interested in helping me finish a documentary I had been working on, then told him what our budget was and gave him a short synopsis of the project. He quickly responded with, "Yes, Jeb. I would love to help you with this project."

I felt somewhat relieved because it had been a real challenge finding someone to replace Brent that we could afford. I sent Iiro a message that I had found a new director and said, "Don't threaten this one's life, okay?"

Iiro told me, "Don't worry, I'm feeling much better now." I smiled because I knew he had never meant any harm, he just felt Brent was trying to take advantage and that tended to make Iiro emotional. When Iiro gets emotional, he says aggressive and sometimes silly things. I try my best to think logically about everything and I really try not to let emotion make decisions for me, but Iiro wears his heart on his sleeve. Anyway, we had a new director, so the project could finally get finished.

I'll spare you all the boring details of doing post-production on a documentary, but there were months of editing, music, sound design, graphic design, titles, so on and so forth. When it was finally complete, we had a mini-premier for friends and family in a small theater and it felt good to finally have it done. We showed it and won a few small film festivals like X-Dance and The Banff Mountain Film Festival.

The Banff festival was our first time seeing the film in a theater with hundreds of strangers, and it was wonderful to hear and see the audience's reaction to something we had worked so hard to create. When we won the Best Mountain Film award, we were surprised. We were up against some amazing films and a few of them had big Hollywood directors behind them.

In the end, we licensed *Journey to the Center* to National Geographic International and it aired all around the world in over eighty countries. Even though we were able to license the film and it seemed like a success, we still found it hard to make money. We never ended up recouping what we had spent making it. The production just cost too much money and we learned an important lesson that changed the way we would conduct the business of making documentaries in the future. We realized working with sponsors to offset costs was the best plan moving forward. Production is expensive and documentaries don't pay well, but sponsors need marketing; they see productions like this in a different way. This would be the key to earning money from making these kinds of films in the future.

Win-win.

CHAPTER TWENTY-THREE

STUNT JUNKIES

On a regular day in 2005, with nothing out of the ordinary going on, my phone began to ring in my pocket. I was relaxing on a beach in Malibu as I pulled out my phone and answered, "Hello, how may I help you?"

A man I didn't know responded with, "Hello, my name is Jordan and I worked as a producer on *Real TV*. I helped produce the episode of you hitting the waterfall in South Africa and I would like to talk to you about a new TV series I'm working on about stunts."

Jordan went on to ask if I could give him three different stunt concepts I would like to perform. He told me he was talking to many stuntmen and would incorporate the best ideas in a pitch deck that he would then take to different networks to try and sell the show. If the show sold, he would then contact me and we would discuss what the next steps would be. I was intrigued, so I quickly broke down three different stunt ideas I had been thinking about for some time. He liked what I had to say and decided to put all three ideas in the pitch.

"I'll get back to you when I have more information to share," he said before hanging up.

About six months went by and I had all but forgotten about the phone call with Jordan when he finally called back, but this time he asked me something different.

He said, "Jeb, have you ever thought about hosting a TV show?"

"No," I replied, "and I have no interest in being a monkey with a microphone. I like actually doing things and right now I just want to BASE jump and fly wingsuits."

He said, "But what if you weren't a normal TV show host? What if you were more like a fly on the wall, backstage with the athletes just sitting and talking with them? No scripts, no voiceover, all one hundred percent real. Just getting to know the athletes and what makes them tick. Also, what if you could also do your sports while working on the show? You could do BASE jumping and wingsuit flying on the job. We would be able to get you permits to do bigger stunts than you could ever do without a show behind you."

I said, "No scripts, huh? Maybe without scripts it might be interesting. I'm pretty good at just talking off the top of my head with people, but I'm horrible at memorizing lines."

Jordan said, "No scripts. We're looking for unscripted, real content."

"Are you asking me to host your TV series concept?"

"Maybe," he said. "I'm just seeing if you would be interested right now."

I responded with, "Okay. If there are no scripts, no voiceover, and all I am is a guy who talks with the athletes to find out what makes them tick, that could be interesting. Also, I would have to do stunts, too. It's important for me to be able to keep BASE jumping."

He said, "Absolutely. That would be the entire point of having someone like you as the host. We would need to see you do stunts as well."

At this point in my life, I had begun doing more and more TV and commercial licensing of my footage, and Iiro suggested I get an agent to help out with the ever-increasing workload so I could focus more on the jumping and less on the negotiating. It's hard to negotiate on projects when you really want to do them. It's always best to have someone else be the bad guy when it comes to telling people how much things are going to cost. He introduced me to his agent, Sandi, who worked with the Gersh Agency. Iiro was always helpful when it came to the actual business side of things. I was always more an idea person and never really liked dealing with the business side of things.

Sandi was more than happy to help me with whatever deals came along, and it was somewhat serendipitous to meet her at this period in my career. Shortly after I signed on with her, Jordan called me again and said the show had been sold to Discovery and they wanted me to host it. They felt I would bring a high level of authenticity. They wanted to do twelve episodes with different iconic athletes, and for the final episode, they wanted me to do a massive stunt showing I wasn't just an ordinary TV show host. I gave him Sandi's contact info, and they began banging out the details for the contracts.

Everything was pretty standard, but Discovery asked for a seven-year contract. I felt that was way too long and asked for two years. They came back with a drop-dead four years, meaning that anything less than four years would be the end of negotiations and they would find someone else to host the show. My only drop-dead point in the contract was that I had to wear black, always. Sandi told me that if that wasn't in the contract, they would force me to wear color and she knew how much I would hate that. She was correct: being forced to wear color would be upsetting for me. I have discussed how I have serious mental problems, and this is one of the manifestations of my mental illness. When I do stunts doubling other people or am just an anonymous stunt guy, I don't have a problem wearing color if it pays enough. I am a whore that will do things I don't want to do for money at times. But I am an expensive whore, so I have to be paid a lot if it's something I really don't want to do. I'm sort of joking, but not really. If I'm being myself on camera, then who I am is a person who wears black all the time. If I'm acting or playing someone else, then I'm okay wearing color. I know this is weird to some people, but it's how my brain works.

The Discovery negotiations went back and forth for a few weeks, and during this time, Jordan asked me to come meet with one of the other executive producers named Perry Barnt. Jordan explained how Perry had been a producer on *X Factor* for years and was responsible for most of the show's high-level stunt concepts. I could tell Jordan had a lot of respect for Perry, so I was excited to meet him. I drove out to the valley to have lunch with the two of them, and the instant I met Perry, I loved him. He was a crusty old stunt guy who was about as straight-shooting as a human being could be. I felt like this was an informal audition over lunch. Perry wasn't sold on having me as a host for the show, and I could tell he was feeling me out to see if I was full of shit. Most of my stories seem outrageous and, if I hadn't lived them, I would think they were full of shit, too. Honestly, without the footage to back up my stories, no one would believe them and even I might question my memories. It just all seems so impossible, but it all happened.

Perry, Jordan, and I talked for a few hours, and by the end of it, I could tell Perry and I were going to be buddies. To this day, I respect this human being and would follow him anywhere. He's the type of stunt coordinator you can trust your life with, and if he said the stunt was going to work, then I would do it, period.

Contracts got completed and signed. We had a half-hour show on Discovery and I was the host. It was something I had never dreamed of, and I feel I may have been a little too young to grasp what it meant. I'm not talking too young in actual years on the planet, but more about being mentally young. I had the mind of a sixteen-year-old and had no clue what this meant or the impact it would have on my life. In 2006, all I cared about was my freedom and doing what I wanted, when I wanted. I was under the impression I would get lots of time off and could still BASE jump and do side projects. This impression existed because it's what I was told by the people trying to talk me into do the project. As it turned out, this couldn't have been further from the truth.

The first episode we did was about a man backflipping a quad over a moving train. I thought the concept was cool and was excited to get started. As I showed up on set the first day, they handed me a script with my name on it. I took it in my hand and said, "I was told there weren't going to be any scripts." I was informed the format had changed and now I was going to be required to give monologues for the opening of each episode. They wanted me to memorize three paragraphs of dialogue and then deliver it while standing on top of a train as a camera on a big jib arm swung around me. I said, "I have a mild case of dyslexia and my memory is horrible. This isn't what I do."

They looked at me and said, "Well, it's what you do now, so you better figure it out."

I went to talk to Perry about this and he said, "No problem, Jeb. We can do as many takes as you need to get it and you don't have to say it word for word. Just get an idea of the point we're trying to make and then make it your own." Over the next couple of hours, I tried to memorize the dialogue as best I could, but my brain just doesn't work that way. As I was getting ready to get on top of the train, Perry called out, "Makeup!"

I said, "Dude, I don't wear makeup."

He looked at me and said, "You have a bald head, and we can see the shine from space right now. We have to cut that down with a little powder." As the makeup person came over and started putting powder on my forehead, I felt super uncomfortable. It made my face feel like it was covered in dirt, and I absolutely hated it.

Freshly powdered and a little pissed, I climbed up the side of the train and got into position. I looked down and there had to be over thirty people there watching me. I got incredibly nervous and totally forgot everything I was supposed to say. I had to ask them to give me the script again and spent a few minutes trying to refresh my memory. I hid the script and we tried the first take. I got about three words in and forgot everything. This went on for over an hour and we did—no shit—eighty-plus takes. It was one of the most horrible experiences of my life, and you have to remember, I've been eaten alive by animals. I was like a fish out of water. I had never had to memorize dialogue and deliver it in public like this, and it made my brain short circuit. It was embarrassing and I knew I had made a huge mistake taking this job.

But the rest of the filming went smooth and felt natural. I knew I wouldn't have a problem just talking off the top of my head with the athletes, and the stunt was interesting, so it all felt real and genuine. But by the end of the day, I felt destroyed by the overwhelming amount of takes. That experience on top of the train was torture and I never wanted to do anything like that again. But I knew I had at least eleven more episodes to go, and if the show did well, I would have a second season of the same thing. This was an unpleasant prospect at the time, and I didn't know what I was going to do about it.

We finished filming episode one and I thought my work was done. The show was to have a one-week-on, one-week-off filming schedule. I thought in my one-week-off period that I'd have time to go jump and do the things I would usually do, but that didn't happen at all. As I was planning to head out on a BASE trip, I got a call saying they needed me to go to a sound studio in Hollywood to do voiceover for the first episode. I told them they must be mistaken because I was told I wasn't going to be the one doing the voiceover work.

They said, "Sorry, but the format has changed and you're doing the voiceover now." My patience was tested, but I got in my car and drove through traffic for an hour and a half to get to a voiceover studio off Melrose. I had no idea what the hell I was doing. I walked in and was escorted to a room behind glass with a microphone and an easel with a script sitting on it. I started looking through the script and it was immense. I heard a voice come into the room and it reminded me of the voice of God you hear in movies: very deep and very loud. It came from a man who was a producer from the New York office and would be the one directing me during my voice over sessions. I told him I had no experience with doing voiceover and had no idea what I was doing. He said it wasn't a problem—he would teach me.

The first voiceover session took over eight hours, and by the end, my brain felt fried. Again, I was horrible at this, and for some reason, when you are forced to do something you aren't any good at, your brain tends to burn. I drove home thinking, *What have I gotten myself into and how do I get out of it?* It then dawned on me: I was stuck in a four-year contract. I don't have the words to express how horrible this made me feel. I had agreed to something without having any idea what I was agreeing to, and now I was in too deep to get free.

This went on week after week, month after month, for almost a year. All that time off they had promised me never existed. Anytime I would make plans to do anything, I'd get called in for another voiceover session. I went on a little trip to Palm Springs for Valentine's Day with a girlfriend, and that morning, I got a call saying they needed voiceovers. I informed them I was in Palm Springs and they said, "No problem, we'll find a sound studio there." I ended up spending the entire time in a room by myself, listening to a disembodied voice direct me how to speak into a microphone. In that entire year, I didn't do a single BASE jump. I was at the peak of my athletic career and had given away the only thing I truly cared about. They took and took and it slowly started turning me against the show. I was young and my mind was still childish...and children sometimes act out.

The thing that kept me holding on was the fact that I would get to do a stunt of my own at the end. But as we approached the episode where I was supposed to do my stunt, something strange started happening. For some reason, all the stunts I wanted to do were impossible to get permits for. My stunts were high concept, but I found it strange how we never seemed to have trouble getting permits for the other athletes. We started contacting different buildings across the country, trying to get approval for BASE jumps, but not a single one would work with us. We had an idea where I would ride a jet ski off Niagara Falls, but when the producers called the city to try and get approval, the person on the other end of the phone laughed at them and said, "That will never happen, ever." I had been in a sport where you didn't need to ask for permission—you just did it—and this new barrier was infuriating me. Working in a system where you had to get permits just didn't seem conducive to the work I was trying to do. I was feeling stifled and imprisoned and every day seemed to only get worse.

They did dangle one carrot, though. We were coming up on episode eleven with an athlete named Bob Burnquist. He was a pro skater who specialized in a new discipline called the "mega ramp." For his show, he was going to set up a mega ramp on the edge of the Grand Canyon and launch himself off it into a BASE jump. Perry told me not to stress out; he knew I hadn't jumped in a while and he could see I was getting antsy. He told me I would get to BASE jump as much as I wanted during this episode.

This calmed me down and made me feel a bit better. I was getting used to the voiceovers, and the memorizing dialogue was getting easier, too. I still didn't like it, but I was able to get the openings in about six takes instead of eighty. It no longer felt like I was being tortured, just more of a mild annoyance. But I felt like I had been tricked into doing this job and wasn't sure why someone would want to do that. Why didn't they just hire an actor? Getting someone like me was like killing a fly with a flamethrower. They didn't need someone like me for this show and my skillset was too extreme for what they had me actually do.

The mega ramp episode finally came, and I made sure to bring all my BASE gear and wingsuits so I could finally get some training in. I was rusty and was going to need a lot of jumps to get back in the swing of things. On the first day, I asked Perry when I could get some jumps in and he said, "Jeb, just wait till we have Bob's stunt in the can and then, if the weather is still good, you can use whatever chopper time we have left to do some jumps." I felt impatient but I only had to wait a few more days, so we went to work filming the episode. Weather made things difficult the first few days, but by day three everything was perfect. Bob nailed his stunt and production was finished. Perry told me he would like me to do a flight from the helicopter in the wingsuit and buzz a camera position on the edge of the cliff with smoke. So, I geared up, talked to the helicopter pilot about exit altitude and distance from the edge, and we headed up. The pilot told me we were at the exact altitude and distance I had requested, but when I looked out, I felt like I was too far away. He assured me the numbers were accurate, so I jumped, feeling like it was just a practice jump anyway and I would have many more coming to adjust the line. As I left the chopper, I could tell instantly I was too far away to make it to the edge of the cliff, so I had to pull early.

On deployment, the smoke bracket went into the lower wing and burned it. This completely destroyed the wingsuit, meaning no more wingsuit jumps this trip. As I landed, I was pretty pissed off about what had just happened, but figured I would focus on BASE jumping the different cliffs. We still had over three hours of daylight, the conditions were perfect, and we had two hours of chopper time left. I thought I could probably get three or four more jumps with that time. I had hoped for multiple days of jumping and three times that number of jumps, but something was better than nothing.

I went to Perry and told him I was going to grab my second rig and jump the cliff across the gorge.

He looked at me with a concerned expression and said, "Jeb, Bob's stunt is over and no one has been hurt. We need to pull the plug now and head home."

I looked at him and said, "Bro, I need to train. We talked about this. I was promised I would get to do BASE jumping during this episode."

Perry responded, "Jeb, if you get hurt, the show will end. We can't risk that."

I looked at him and said, "You've made a huge mistake. You should have hired an actor for this job, not me." I then turned and walked away.

As I walked out the door, I called Sandi and said, "I'm done with this show. I'm not going to work again tomorrow."

She said, "Jeb, you need to take a deep breath and think about this. You are in a four-year contract, remember? If you don't show up for work tomorrow, you will be sued and you will lose. If this happens, they will really own you." I was infuriated: everything was out of my control and I felt like I had been tricked over and over. A few weeks earlier, I had gotten the news Discovery had picked the show up for a second season, meaning I had another year of this coming. I would only get a two-week break between seasons before filming would begin again, and for the second season, they wanted double the episodes.

I asked, "Okay, Sandi. I hear you. But during my time off, can I BASE jump?"

She responded with, "Yes, Jeb."

I said, "Okay, during my two-week vacation between seasons I'm going to go film a documentary about BASE jumping. I don't want to get one phone call from production. No voiceovers, no people trying to get in my way. I will not respond to anyone during this two-week period. Is this understood?"

She said, "Yes, I understand. No problem."

The next phone call I made was to Iiro Seppänen and I said, "Iiro, it's time to make a documentary about BASE jumping off the Empire State building, and we are going to call it *Fall of the Empire*." This name would come to have some irony in it.

Iiro responded, "When do you want to start?"

I said, "Right-fucking-now."

I can't go into much detail about what happened during this two-week period. You can google it for yourself if it interests you. I had to deal with many lawsuits and spent years of my life in and out of court. It took about six years to finally lay all of what happened at Empire to rest. It's a can of worms I don't want to reopen here. But to keep things simple, I got out of my contract with Discovery and was free to go back to BASE jumping whenever and however I wanted to.

I will say this: I was young and mentally unstable. It wasn't the right time in my life to host a TV show. I was at the peak of my BASE-jumping career, and for people to trick me into a contract that made jumping impossible was a bad thing. It would be like taking Tony Hawk at the peak of his skating career and telling him he can't ride skateboards anymore. That just won't go over well. I exploded and did things I shouldn't have done. The almost ironic twist is that now, at forty-five years old, it would be the perfect job at this stage of my life. But back then, I needed the next fifteen years to grow up and find my center. I needed to get BASE jumping out of my system.

I needed to die and be reborn.

CHAPTER TWENTY-FOUR

GRINDING THE CRACK

Three years later, after all the chaos from Empire finally died down, my friend Ueli Gegenschatz told me about a jump in a small Swiss town called Walenstadt. He told me of a magical place with a 5,000-foot-tall cliff and only a fifteen-minute hike to the exit point. At the time it sounded almost like a fairytale. How could something so big only be discovered now? BASE jumpers had been combing Switzerland for decades and it seemed impossible to me that something like this could still be undiscovered. He promised he would take me there so I could see it myself next time I came to Europe. Unfortunately, Ueli had an accident jumping a building a few months later for a Red Bull event. The building was low, winds were iffy, and he ended up clipping its corner and collapsing his canopy, which slammed him into the ground hard.

As medics got to him, he spoke his final words before losing consciousness and dropping into a coma. They were, "I'm sorry." Ueli was taken to the hospital and died a few days later from his injuries. I had lost a good friend and, far less importantly, I had also lost the chance at jumping Ueli's magical cliff.

In 2010, a video hit the internet from a secretive French BASE jumper only known as the Samurai. It was a short five-minute summary of jumps he had done from around the world earlier that year. The footage was some of the most incredible proximity flying anyone had seen. It went viral with millions of views overnight. When you read the comments, everyone was asking the same question: where was the jump at two minutes thirty-five seconds? The footage looked like he was flying at flat ground between trees and was just going to impact, but as he came through the trees, the ground opened up and he entered a massive crack in the earth. Nothing like it had ever been seen before and it set the wingsuit world on fire. Everyone was trying to figure out where it was. The Samurai took the video down after only a few days. When he posted it, I don't think he understood how many people were going to see it and how fast it was going to spread. But it was too late; once seen, it could no longer be unseen, and we were all going to find it eventually.

That summer, I did my annual trip to Lauterbrunnen, Switzerland, where I met my buddy, Jeff Nebelkopf. Jeff was the head designer for Tony Suits and had taken wingsuit designs to the next level. Tony Suits was owned and run by Tony Uragallo, who made free-fly suits and relative work suits for the skydiving industry. Jeff is the one who convinced him the world needed better wingsuits. Before Jeff and Tony started working together, wingsuits made tiny improvements in performance each year. Robert from Phoenix Fly had a ten-year plan to make small adjustments and slowly make the wings bigger over time. He wanted to make sure he always had a design for next year's model that would be slightly better than the one he was currently marketing.

Robert didn't have any real competition, so this approach worked well until Jeff and Tony started collaborating. When Tony and Jeff got together, they decided to just make the biggest wings they could put on a suit. They didn't care what next year's suit was going to be. They wanted to make the best performing suit right that instant. It created a boom in performance and new guys you never heard of started out-flying the pilots who'd been doing it for over a decade. The new suits were easier to fly and crushed all the suits that had come before with huge jumps in glide and speed. Jeff quickly became one of the best camera flyers around. I started hiring him for jobs and mentoring him in the business of filming and licensing footage.

When I saw Jeff in Lauterbrunnen, he was sitting with a man named Matt Gerdes. Jeff introduced me to Matt and my first impressions of the man were positive. He seemed super intelligent and knowledgeable about all things both BASE and life related. He worked in marketing for a company called Ozone that manufactured paragliders and speed wings. He was helping Jeff and Tony with marketing their suits and giving them feedback and advice on how to make their designs even better.

Matt and I started talking about the video of the Samurai and I expressed how much I wished I could find out where that jump was. Matt smiled with a grin that could only mean he knew exactly where it was. He informed me he had located it on Google Earth and it just so happened that they were heading that way the next day. He asked if I would like to come along to do a few jumps with him. I looked at Jeff with a shocked expression and said, "YES!!!"

I found out the jump was called "Sputnik" and had been opened by Ueli Gegenschatz. This was the jump Ueli had told me about before his fatal accident. To say I was ecstatic would be an understatement of epic proportions. I had no clue the jump Ueli was talking about was the same jump the Samurai had flown. The Swiss locals were protective of the location and tried to keep it top secret. Problem for them was that Matt and modern technology meant it could never be kept secret. Once the video was out, there was no stopping people from locating it. Matt noticed a lake in the background, and from the trees and type of grass cover, he knew it was in Switzerland. With just those few clues and Google, he was able to find the location with ease.

The next day, Jeff and I loaded into Matt's car and we all headed for a small town called Unterwasser. That was where the cable car would take people to the top of the mountain, mostly hikers in the summers and skiers in the winter. The ride up usually took about thirty minutes. Once you stepped out of the cable car, you would walk along a well-worn tourist trail for about fifteen minutes, where you would then see a much smaller, less-worn walking path veering off to the left that wrapped around closer to the edge. Following that, you'd come to a small relatively flat area where you could gear up and get your first true glimpse of the wall you'd be jumping.

The exit was named Sputnik, but the line we had come to fly had no name. It was just a gigantic crack in the mountain about two thirds of the way down, and you would have to fly about half a kilometer at a two-to-one glide ratio (that is two feet forward for every foot you fell) to get there. From our vantage point, it looked insane and didn't seem real. We stood there looking over the edge, trying to see exactly where the crack's entrance was and how far you would have to fly to get to its exit. We realized quickly that it wasn't a straight flight; it actually took a turn to the left as you entered, and that seemed scary. From where we were standing, the entrance looked particularly tiny. The Samurai line was no joke.

I wasn't sure I was going to be able to make it that far or fly into such a small opening. I had just gotten the new X Wing designed by Jeff and Tony, and didn't have that much experience flying it yet. But I could see there was an out if I got too low. I could fly at the crack and, as long as I aborted around 500 feet before its entrance, I could fly to the right and out into open air. This out gave me the margin for safety that made me feel okay about just going for it on my first run.

I asked Jeff what he thought, and he said "If you fly through it, I will follow you. If you bail right, I will follow you. Do whatever you need to do, and I will film it."

"Okay," I said, "let's do this."

At this point, fear had become so normal to me that I don't even know if I truly recognized it as fear anymore. I think the process of desensitizing yourself to fear has both good and bad qualities. Without this desensitization, you would be incapable of dealing with the ever-increasing risks you face in an activity like BASE jumping. As you push and grow in the sport, you keep crossing new horizons. With each crossing, the level increases. Your skill gets higher, which opens up new boundaries that you couldn't see from your old vantage point. As you push through these boundaries, you see even more off in the distance. You just keep leveling up over and over, and with each new higher level, you start to get a better picture of what's possible, and you grow toward it. But this constant pushing, constant expansion of the mind, constant desensitization of your senses, starts to make you lose touch with reality. Your priorities become unhinged. You become willing to sacrifice everything for things with little true value. You start losing your gauge of what you should and shouldn't do. You start doing things because you can, without truly analyzing if you should. This can become a vicious cycle that pushes many high-level action sports enthusiasts to their deaths.

Here I was, standing on the edge, looking off in the distance at a small crack in the earth. I was trying to visualize what I was about to do.

A calm came over me. Things became quiet. I asked Jeff if he was ready.

Jeff responded, "Ready when you are."

I started my countdown, "Three, two, one, see ya," and stepped off the edge with Jeff right behind me.

I began flying straight towards the crack. The jump was a bit of an optical illusion. I felt the crack was way too far away and there was no chance I could make it even if I was under an open parachute. But as I flew, the ground kept giving way underneath me. The terrain was much steeper than it looked from above. As I got closer, I could see the trees at both ends of the opening to the crack like goalposts. I saw I had just enough altitude to make it over the lip of the crack, so I aimed between the trees, which seemed impossibly tight. This was the point of no return. I was now committed to the line and there was no way to bail out now. I had no idea if Jeff was still following me, so I decided to focus on the left-hand banking turn that was coming up after I got through the goalpost trees. I punched through the trees and dug into the air with my suit to initiate a banking turn deeper into the crack.

The visual was unlike anything I have ever experienced. It was the first time I truly got the feeling of flying like a bird. As trees fired by at high speed, I went deeper into the guts of jagged, unforgiving rock, making small adjustments with my wings to keep me as centered as possible between the two walls on either side. I focused on the exit and held my breath as it approached, then punched out and was free. I cleared the crack and was flying out into open air. I looked over and saw Jeff flying off my left shoulder with a beaming smile on his face. We kept flying together for another few thousand feet before deploying over the town below. We both landed in a little park and hugged as our canopies touched the ground.

Jeff said, "I got the shot, Jeb! You got a little away from me at the entrance of the crack, but once we exited, I was able to catch up."

I said, "Don't worry about that, bro. Thank you for just being here with me." Somehow, I knew this was a special location unlike anywhere else in the world. This place was going to become the training ground that would take my proximity flying to the next level.

We packed and went for it again. The second jump didn't go as well as the first. I didn't have a good exit and I couldn't seem to get the suit flying. I saw I wasn't going to make it to the crack early on, so I bailed to the right and flew around the outer rim. As we landed, Jeff and I could tell this would be the last jump of the day and we'd have to head back to Lauterbrunnen. Matt was our ride and he needed to get back, but I really wanted to stay there and jump more. Matt offered to let me borrow his car so I could leave at my leisure, and he could find another way back to LB.

His offer surprised me and I didn't know what to say, but I told him, "Thank you, Matt, but there is no way I could take your car." It was an amazing gesture from a person I had just met, and I will never forget it. Matt's offer showed me I was being a little selfish, so I decided to postpone my jumps for now. We all loaded into Matt's car and headed back to LB together, but I knew I was going to be back in Walenstadt soon.

When I got back to LB, I gathered all the footage from Jeff's and my first jump through the crack and edited it together. I had set up a YouTube account and was using it as a place to upload demo reels of my footage to easily share with my network of producing partners around the globe. The account was new and only had a few followers, so I didn't expect people to actually watch videos on my page. It was originally just for sharing footage with the few people that might be interested in licensing. But within a few hours of uploading the footage, I got a direct message from a man named Christian Gubser. The message said he had watched my video and thought it was amazing. He extended an invitation, saying the next time I came to Walenstadt to please let him know and he would take time off work to help me in any way he could. He would drive for me, work ground crew, I could even stay at his house—pretty much whatever I needed. I wasn't sure what to think but felt if this guy was for real, I could definitely use his help. The logistics of the jump were quite complicated. The cable car was on one side of a mountain range called the Churfirsten and the landing area was on the opposite side. With a dedicated driver like Christian, I would be able to do more jumps faster. Without one, I would need multiple jumpers with multiple cars so we could take turns shuttling cars back and forth, which would be a total pain in the ass. There was also a train you could take, but it took almost three hours and was also a pain. I sent Christian a reply saying I would be heading back his way in a week and would love to meet him. If he could help me with rides from the landing area to the cable car after each jump, I would be eternally grateful. He wrote back and said he was taking off work right now and he would also get his brother Andy to come help, too. I was impressed by how friendly and excited he was. I felt with local help I could get at least double the number of jumps and maybe even some footage from the entrance to the crack.

A week later, I was checking into a hotel called the Star within walking distance of the cable car on the Unterwasser side of the jump. I didn't know at the time, but this was a small town with zero to do other then take the cable car to the top of the mountain. Later, Christian would explain how Walenstadt was better suited to extended stays. I had Christian's cell number and called him to coordinate my first jump. He told me he would be in the landing area with his brother when I landed, and he would then drive me around the mountain as many times as I wanted so I could jump as much as possible.

I did my first jump and landed right next to them, and we had our first meeting in person as I gathered up my chute. Christian was full of energy and smiling from ear to ear. I shook his hand as he introduced me to his brother, Andy, who also had a big smile on his face. Christian could speak English, but it was a bit broken. He did most of the talking because his brother's English was almost non-existent and he didn't feel comfortable speaking. But he smiled a lot and would speak through his brother as an interpreter. I could tell right away they were super happy, friendly people. We became friends on the spot, and during our drives around the mountain, they told me about their lives growing up in the area, which I found fascinating. Their lives were so foreign from my own experiences.

At the end of the first day of jumping, Christian and his brother took me to dinner at a local restaurant. As we sat down and ate local Swiss cuisine, I asked them if they could somehow get to the entrance of the crack and shoot some video from that location. They explained that the land was owned by a local farmer and the road was small with steep sections, making it hard to drive on. They said they would look into renting an ATV and see if they could get permission from the farmer to go there.

The next day, Christian called early and said they had sorted a quad and were on their way to the crack. They would film my first jump of the morning from the tree line at its entrance. After I did my flyby, Christian would then ride the quad back down the hill to his car to give me a ride around the mountain so I could do another jump. I was super impressed with how motivated they were to help me. It was an exciting time and it seemed they understood as much as I did how special this was;

we were working together to capture images of something people had never seen before.

I did my first jump, and as I flew towards the crack, I noticed Christian standing right at the entrance wearing a bright red shirt and holding a camera. I was surprised to see him standing right in my flight path and felt he had a lot of trust to do something like that. I flew directly over his head by about twenty feet and caught a glimpse of Andy hanging from a tree by the outer edge of the crack. Turned out Andy was a climber and understood how to rig ropes. He was also a damn good photographer and captured some of the most amazing stills of the flight. Between the two of them, they made the trip a huge success. I couldn't believe the footage we had gotten, which was groundbreaking at the time.

After our week together, I felt kind of sad having to leave Christian and Andy, but I told them I would be back the next year for sure and would stay for as long as I could. They asked me to give them at least one month's notice so they could request the time off work, because they didn't want to miss a single moment. I thought, *Damn, I love these guys.* They were just up for anything and were the most helpful human beings I had ever been around. Long story short, I really liked them.

The next summer as I was planning my trip to Europe, I got a call from a producer on a show called *20/20* on ABC. They informed me they were doing a special on people with extraordinary abilities and they were going to call it "Super Humans." The show was interested in following me to some part of the world and telling the story of proximity flying. I told them I knew just the place and sent them a small demo from the crack jumps I had done the year before.

They said, "Yes, that's exactly what we're looking for." We made plans and set up dates. I contacted Christian and told him about the show, asking if he and Andy would be willing to help out with the production by working as local guides.

He said, "Anything for you! What do you have in mind?" I told him I wanted him to get party balloons and attach a six-foot long string to them. I then wanted him to stand at the entrance to the crack while holding them over his head. I was going to fly five feet over his head, snatching the string of the balloons and pulling them from his hand. He got excited and said, "Yes, I would like to do this."

I thought this would be a great way to demonstrate how accurate we could be with a wingsuit. Nothing like it had ever been attempted and it was going to take a level of precision never before achieved with a wingsuit. But this was also going to be a dangerous stunt for Christian. He would be an integral part of this, no longer just a bystander watching from afar. His life was now on the line, just as much as mine. If I were to miscalculate, I could tackle him into a multiple-thousand-foot-deep crack in the earth at over 120 mph.

I showed up a few days early to get in some practice jumps before the *20/20* production crew arrived. I wanted to be sure I was fully prepared and would have the best chance of hitting my target. The day before production arrived, Christian brought the first set of party balloons for me to try and hit. As I was flying towards them, the wind blew hard up the crack and dropped the balloons too low; I felt if I hit them, I would also hit Christian. I flew over the tops of the balloons by about a foot and something interesting happened: the balloons got caught in an invisible wake vortex created by my suit. The balloons were ripped from Christian's hand and came spiraling after me into the crack. The shocking thing was how far they chased me, which was well over a hundred feet. I had never seen the power of the forces we were working with illustrated in such a visual way before, but it was awesome to see.

20/20 arrived and we got right into planning the production. We intended to do an early jump the next morning when the light was directly over the top of the crack, filling it to the brim with sunshine. The few days of practice had shown us exactly when this was. Christian would stand in the opening holding balloons and I was going to try and hit them. The crew would set up fixed camera positions using GoPro cameras leading into the crack and one big camera that would try to follow the action. Andy would rig himself to the side of the crack and shoot both stills and video. Christian and Andy had a local friend named Gian Autenrieth, who would give me a ride to the back of the mountain to catch the cable car.

Everyone got up bright and early the next morning. Christian, Andy, and the *20/20* cameramen headed up to the entrance of the crack. Gian picked me up and we headed for the back side of the mountain. As we were driving, Gian asked me if he could hike up to the exit point with me so he could see the jump. I said, "Of course you can." He seemed excited as we pulled into the parking lot and walked to the cable car station. We sat, patiently waiting for the cable car and talking about what was coming. The cable car showed up shortly after and we rode it to the top. We exited the cable car and did the short walk to the exit point, just talking about life along the way. As I was gearing up, I noticed that the wind was strong. I turned on my walkie talkie and asked Christian how the winds were at the entrance to the crack.

He said, "The winds are zero and the balloon is flying straight up. It's not moving at all." I was surprised, so I called our cameraman set up in the landing area and asked him what the winds were doing there.

He said the same thing: "Zero wind."

Something was odd; the wind at the exit was super strong, right on the edge of jumpable. I called Christian again because I just couldn't believe the wind could be so different just a few thousand feet lower.

He again confirmed, "Zero wind."

I thought about the situation for a few minutes. The wind at the exit scared me, but if there was no wind at the crack then shouldn't it be fine? I wasn't sure, but I decided to jump. Gian took out a small camera and started filming, so I turned on all my GoPros: I was wearing six at the time. I started making the traverse from the gearing-up area to the actual exit point. It was a small path that butted right up against the cliff with a thousand-foot vertical drop off. If you were to slip during the traverse, the resulting fall was certain death. Stuff like this always makes the process a bit nerve-wracking. I got to the exit and zipped up my suit. As I stood there, I could feel the wind shoving against me. I was worried: if I felt this amount of push standing on firm ground, what was it going to be like stepping off the cliff?

I called down on the walkie to tell everyone I was about one minute from jumping. I put the walkie away, took a few deep breaths, and said, "Ten seconds," to Gian so he knew I was ready to jump. I took another deep breath and counted down, "Three, two, one," and jumped.

Sure enough, the wind hit the back of my suit hard and sent me head-down. The feeling was uncomfortable and it made me swim a little, swinging my arms up and down like a flapping bird, but I quickly regained control. I started flying towards the crack while trying to keep as much altitude as I could. I wanted to come in high and dive at it. For the first few seconds of flight, there was heavy turbulence, and I was being bumped around badly. I wasn't sure if I would be able to fly into the crack. About thirty seconds into the flight, the turbulence went away completely and everything became calm. I was coming in with plenty of height and could see Christian and the balloons. The balloons were standing straight up with no movement at all, so I knew I could hit them safely. I started my dive towards my target and used a tree on the slope near the crack as a marker point. If I came in close and below the tip of that tree, I knew I would be on target and within striking distance of the balloons.

As I approached, everything slowed down and I became hyper-focused on my target. I was now coming in low over the grass hill leading to Christian. I could see my own shadow on the grass below and knew I couldn't be more than five feet off the ground. I could see Christian's face and saw the fear in his eyes as he started ducking into a crouch, pulling the balloons lower.

I tried to mentally tell him, *Don't pull the balloons lower, bro.*

Drawing closer, I saw Christian let the balloons go and jump out of the way with a yelp. The balloons floated over my head, but my left arm caught the string as I flew between them and Christian. He was now sliding across the ground, and I think he made the right call jumping out of the way. I was coming in hot and, if I made a mistake, I would have tackled him at 122.4 miles per hour (as measured with GPS) into the crack. I continued flying through the crack and out the other end. I deployed directly over the landing area and set down right next to the cameraman. I was giggling like a crazy person and the first words out of my mouth were, "I came extremely close on that one!"

A few hours later, I met up with Christian and Andy at a farm on the side of the mountain. We needed to get a few interviews done and it was my first time seeing Christian and his brother since the jump. Andy had been practicing his English in the year since we had first met and was able to communicate much better, which was good, because I hadn't spent much time practicing my Swiss German.

Andy walked up to me and, in broken English, said, "Jeb, you almost killed my brother." But he had a wide smile on his face, and I took it as a light-hearted, but kind of dark joke.

I said, "No way; he pulled the balloons lower, so I had to come in lower to get them." We all laughed, but in all honesty, I did almost kill the both of us. I wouldn't understand how close it was until many years later, but at the time, I thought I had total control and that there was zero chance I would have hit Christian had he stood his ground. But now, with the experiences I've had since that day, I'm pretty sure if he didn't jump out of the way, we would have both died.

A few months later, I was back home in Malibu when I got a message from Andy. He asked me if I remembered his friend Gian. He reminded me that the guy gave me a ride around the mountain on the day I flew through the balloons.

I said, "Yes, I remember him. Really nice guy."

Andy said, "Gian would like to use the footage from the day to edit a small video and wants to know if it would be okay."

"Sure," I replied. "As long as he doesn't try to monetize it, he's welcome to make an edit if he likes."

Andy assured me he just wanted to do it for fun and that was that. The footage had already aired on ABC's *20/20* and I thought they had done a good job on the piece. After that, I had pretty much forgot about it and moved on to my next project.

Another couple of months went by before I got an email from Gian this time. He wanted to Dropbox me the edit he had made. I downloaded the file and saw it was titled "Grinding the Crack." I thought the name was a bit suggestive, but witty. I watched the video and was impressed. I felt Gian had done an amazing job putting the footage together, and the song "Sail" from AWOLNATION was perfect. I sent him back a message asking him if it would be okay for me to post it to my YouTube page.

He said, "I would love you to post it, but won't AWOLNATION sue you?" My YouTube page was small and I didn't think many people would see the video, so I said, "Honestly, I don't think anyone will even notice it's there."

I had already posted videos flying through the crack, and for some reason, I didn't see this footage as all that different from what was already up. I posted the video without thinking much of it, but I could never have imagined what would happen next.

Within three days, that video got over three million views, totally crushing anything I had ever posted before. It went viral, averaging a million views a day for two weeks. The response was overwhelming, and I started getting calls from all over the world wanting to license the footage for different programs. It quickly became the most viewed wingsuit flight on the internet, period and would stay that way for eight years, ultimately reaching over thirty-four million views. It was a bit of a shock—I didn't understand what made it so different from other videos I had seen or posted. By this time, the crack had been flown by many people and the footage was everywhere. But thinking about it now, it may have gone viral because of Christian. I think him standing there holding those balloons helped people connect with the footage.

What I do is hard for people to relate to. Most people can't understand what they're seeing and could never imagine themselves doing it, so they dismiss it. But they can easily put themselves in Christian's shoes and ask themselves, "Could I have stood my ground? Would I have jumped out of the way?" Also, having Christian standing there gave perspective of how close I really was and how fast I was moving. You can see I hit the string between the balloon and Christian's head. The string was five feet long. You can see exactly how close I came, and I think this helped people understand the magnitude of what was going on and how serious the consequences would have been if we had made contact with each other. Lastly, I think the song was catchy and people liked it a lot. Even the name "Grinding the Crack" made people want to see what the video was about.

This viral video marked the beginning of a new chapter in my life, the precursor to the live megastunts with viewership in the hundreds of millions that were about to dominate the next decade of my existence.

CHAPTER TWENTY-FIVE

HEAVEN'S GATE SINGLE DRAGON

About a year before we found the crack, I returned home from a walk on the beach to an email sitting in my inbox. It was from my old friend, Paul Fortun, the man who had shown me the gigantic cave in China that became the documentary *Journey to the Center*. The subject line of the email was simple: "Do you think you could fly through this?" I opened up the email and there was a picture of a monstrous hole in the side of a mountain, located in the Hunan province of China. I opened Google and learned that its name in English was "Heaven's Gate," and it was located in Tianmen Mountain National Park in Zhangjiajie.

My response to Paul was simply, "I don't know, but I'm going to find out."

I instantly sent the picture with the information I had to Iiro and asked him if he thought this location would make for a good project. He wrote back saying he would make a few calls and see what he could find out, but it would take time. A few months later, I got a message from Iiro telling me he was going to the location with his good friend, Frank. Frank was a businessman from Beijing, China, and was well-connected with government officials. He could speak four languages fluently, and if anyone could get permission to do something like this, he was the man. But before Frank would commit to helping, he wanted to make sure there would be a way to finance the project.

In order to do so, he and Iiro would have to go to the location to meet with the local government and see what kinds of possibilities were there. Iiro said he would get back to me after their trip and we would discuss what they found out.

A few days after that conversation, Iiro called me and said, "Jeb, the mountain is controlled by a cable car company, and their business is tourism. They would love to do a massive live stunt for the media where large numbers of people could watch. But you are going to have to come here to check if this is even possible in the first place. There is a lot that will need to go into pulling something like this off, and we need to be one hundred percent sure this is something you can do before we commit to it."

"No problem," I said. "When do you guys need me there?"

A month later, I was on a plane to China. I had no idea what to expect but felt excited at the possibilities. No one had ever flown through a mountain before, and just a few years earlier, the idea would have been science fiction. Advances in wingsuit technology were changing what was possible.

I landed in Beijing and was picked up by Iiro, Frank, and Stefan Muller, who was an experienced BASE jumper living in the Beijing area and had agreed to help with the scout. Frank explained the journey ahead. We were going to catch a flight to a city about a ten-hour bus ride away from Zhangjiajie. We would arrive late at night, but a hotel had been booked and they would be waiting for us. The next day, we would meet with officials from the Tianmen Mountain Cable Car Company, and they would take us on a tour of Heaven's Gate.

The next morning over breakfast, two representatives from the cable car company, named Mr. Huilin Tian and Mr. Bo Xie, showed up and Frank introduced us. They didn't speak any English, but Frank interpreted on their behalf. They were two of the nicest human beings I have ever had the pleasure of spending time with, always smiling and helpful in ways that went beyond just doing their job. We finished breakfast and headed towards the cable car for our first journey up the mountain. The sky was gray and cloudy, and fog obscured our view, but on the drive, we noticed everything looked like it was under construction. Frank explained how the cable car company had big plans for the region and the city was growing fast. Everywhere we looked, new buildings were going up, and Mr. Bo Xie explained that, by this time next year, a magnificent new luxury hotel for visitors to Tianmen Mountain would be completed. The region was expanding at an exponential rate. Mr. Huilin Tian explained that Tianmen Mountain was a big draw for tourists from inside mainland China, kind of like the Grand Canyon in the USA. But where it was different from the Grand Canyon was not many people outside of China knew about it yet, which was something the cable car company would like to change. They wanted to do projects that would help draw the world's attention to the region, and they were hoping we could help them with that.

As we arrived at the station, Iiro, Frank, Mr Huilin Tain, Mr Bo Xie, and I were walked past all security and placed on the first gondola that appeared. Within a few short minutes, we were in the mountains. It was surprising how quickly we were out of the city and suddenly floating over small farms with people tending their crops. There was an eerie fog that blocked out all view of the city we left behind, like it was something we were supposed to forget. There was a small stream coming from higher up the mountain and we could see local people washing their clothes and taking baths in it.

About thirty minutes into the ride, we saw a big group of buildings in the middle of the jungle that looked traditional, and Mr. Bo Xie explained to Frank that it was the set for a live show that happened every night, with over one hundred performers, and during its finale, they would light up the entire mountain. We didn't truly understand the magnitude of what he was talking about till after we witnessed the show for ourselves a few days later, but it was spectacular on a level that's hard to express in writing without being there, and lighting up an entire mountain that size could only be achieved in a place like China.

Shortly after seeing the buildings, we came up and over a large hill and saw what looked like a set from the movie *Avatar*. It felt like we were being carried through the floating mountains of Pandora. The area was stunning, and I had never seen anything like it anywhere else on Earth. As a child, I had seen old paintings from China of towering cliffs jutting straight up in the air at odd angles with fog covering their lower sections, giving the illusion they were floating, but I always thought it was just an artist's creative vision. This was my first time seeing that it was all real, and for some reason, it felt like finding out Dr. Seuss had gotten all his made-up doodles from real places. The artists were just painting exactly what they were seeing, and seeing their true inspiration left me speechless.

All the cliffs were stacked on top of each other, which made it difficult to judge how high they were, and everything seemed to have spikes and spires. But the most striking visual was the humongous hole running though the side of the mountain. It looked strange and unnatural from every angle. I wondered what kind of forces could create something like this. It was a geological anomaly unlike anything I had ever seen. The pictures really didn't do it justice.

At this point, we came to a midway station and were instructed to get off. From there, we were going to need to catch a small bus that would drive us to the bottom of the cave and a torturous staircase with 999 stairs leading to its entrance. The road leading up to the cave also had ninety-nine switchback turns, which shows how superstitious the Chinese can be. In China, the number nine is lucky, so they try to incorporate it anywhere they can, and this road was no exception.

As we stood at the base of the stairs, looking up at the daunting climb in front of us, I was struck by the beauty of the area. I have always loved the jungle and big cliffs, and these were some of the sheerest walls I had seen all stacked on top of each other in a jungle setting. It really did look like a film set straight out of a fantasy movie. There were many locals dressed in traditional clothing working as tour guides. I noticed that all the tourists I could see appeared to be Chinese. We were the only westerners I saw the entire trip. As I was noticing this, Mr. Bo Xie explained to Frank that they were in the middle of drilling deep into the mountain to build an escalator so handicapped people and the elderly would be able to get to the cave, because currently, you had to be in relatively good shape to make the climb up that extremely long staircase. When he said this, I found it hard to visualize what he was talking about. What he was describing didn't seem possible. How could you drill into a mountain, thousands of feet up, and create an escalator system?

We started up, and it took us about thirty minutes of nonstop climbing to reach the top. Luckily, we had shade and it wasn't too hot. As I stood in the opening of that impressive natural arch called Heaven's Gate, its true size overwhelmed me. I could tell it was big; I just didn't know how big yet. Stefan took out a rangefinder and a GPS and we began taking measurements. I needed to know the exact dimensions of the cave to know if I could fly through it safely. We found out the cave was 360 feet tall, 100 feet wide, and 200 feet long with a slight bend in it. If I were to exit a helicopter and enter the cave at the top of the opening, I would need a 2.5 to 1 glide ratio (meaning I would need to fly 2.5 feet horizontally for every foot I dropped vertically) to get me to the bottom of the staircase and over the first cliff where I could deploy a parachute. I would be trapped in a no-pull zone for almost a kilometer. At this point, I had only just begun flying with GPS, and I knew I couldn't sustain a 2.5 to 1 for that distance. I was only flying a 2 to 1 at that point in my Stealth wingsuit from Phoenix-Fly. We did the measurements flying the opposite direction to see if the glide was more in line with my capabilities, and it turned out that all I needed to fly the other way was a 1.5 to 1. It was much steeper coming out the back side of the cave. Only problem with that was there was nowhere to land on the back side of the mountain. It was just super steep jungle with nothing but trees and cliffs.

After we ran the numbers, Frank and Iiro asked me if I thought it was possible.

I told them, "It's kind of possible. I'm not able to sustain the necessary glide to fly from the back side of the mountain to the front side right now. But I'm hoping the new wingsuits coming on the market in the next few months will have better glide ratios. Newer, more powerful suits, mixed with a lot of training, should make this possible by next year. In the worst-case scenario, I could always fly from the front side to the back side and just land in the trees. I've landed in a lot of trees in my years of jumping. It's not ideal, but it is doable."

When we walked back down the 999 stairs, Mr. Bo Xie asked through Frank if I wanted to do a jump from one of the cliffs next to the cave. Iiro and I looked up and weren't really sure how high the cliffs were. We knew the cave was only 360 feet tall and it looked like the cliffs were the same size from that perspective. Frank asked Mr. Bo Xie how high the biggest vertical cliff was, and he said 1000 feet. That was unbelievable to us. We thought he was exaggerating but said we would go up and do some measurements to see if we could find a cliff tall enough to get a suit started. Iiro and I both thought it was a waste of time, but we went ahead and made the trip to the top of the cave anyway.

Mr. Bo Xie took us on a walkway that skirted the edge of the highest vertical cliffs, and the views were impressive. Jagged spires of mountain stuck out of dense layers of fog with clouds moving above and below. The trail snaked back towards the jungle and our view of the edge was obscured by trees. After about thirty minutes of walking through forest and a rather interesting cave, we ended up close to the edge of the cliff again. I was impressed how they were able to build this network of walkways on the edge of these huge cliffs, because my danger senses were already starting to tingle at the back of my mind. Mr. Bo Xie suddenly announced we were close to the tallest vertical wall in the park, and through the trees, I could see the edge only about fifteen feet away. I decided to get off the path and go investigate. Mr. Bo Xie was concerned about me walking down to the edge without a harness and rope, but Frank explained I had the trees to hold onto and that this is how we scouted cliffs all the time. I felt no hesitation getting close to the edge with the trees to hold onto, and Mr. Bo Xie didn't object further as he watched me head out.

It only took me about one minute to get to the edge. As I looked over, I couldn't get a sense of how high it was. I felt like it was low, maybe 400 feet. I grabbed a big rock, took out my stopwatch, and timed how long it took for the rock to hit the ground. As I watched it fall, I was expecting it to hit in about four seconds, but it just kept falling. Six seconds, eight seconds, eleven seconds—impact. I couldn't believe my eyes. I yelled back, asking them to bring me some more rocks and my rangefinder. I dropped three more rocks and all three measured at eleven seconds to impact. I then used the rangefinder and it confirmed what the rocks had said: it was a 1,000-foot vertical drop.

Despite confirming the height through multiple methods, the measurements just didn't seem accurate. For some reason the cliff just didn't look that high. I had my rig with me, and the conditions were perfect, so I decided to do a jump and see what it was like. Mr. Bo Xie got an ultra-excited smile on his face and called down to make sure the traffic on the road would be stopped. He asked if I would like to have them clear some of the branches to give me a better exit and I said, "Yes, that would be nice." I pointed out a few branches that needed to go and he got his workers to clear them. No one in this area had ever seen a BASE jump before and the energy coming from the locals was palpable. They shared looks that were both curious and terrified. As I was gearing up, Mr. Bo Xie and the rest of his entourage that had been showing us the way started getting into position. Harnesses seemed to appear out of nowhere and they started rigging up so they could get as close to the edge as possible. They all seemed eager to watch this firsthand.

I geared up quickly, and by the time I had my wingsuit on, the branches had been cleared and everyone was in position ready to see the first flight from Tianmen Mountain. I stood at the edge in a fairly confined space with branches poking me in the back. I thought, *Man, I should have had them clear that branch, too,* when Mr. Bo Xie saw where I was looking, reached over, and pulled it away with his hand. I glanced back at him and smiled, nodding a thank-you as I turned back to look over the edge. I said, "Ten seconds," to give everyone a heads-up that I was about to jump. I did my usual countdown, "Three, two, one, see ya," and stepped off.

As my wings caught air and inflated, I realized just how high I was. This cliff was huge. I wanted to fly down and buzz a series of switchback roads directly under the exit point, but as I started diving towards them, I quickly understood I was way too high and couldn't actually dive straight down to them. I would have had to make a series of turns to burn altitude. Even though I knew the rock drops and rangefinder said it was a 1,000-foot vertical drop, I still didn't truly understand the overall altitude I was working with until after I was in freefall and could see how far away everything was. The flight was epic, and with every ledge I flew over, I gained more altitude. I flew around large pinnacles of rock, over roads, and it just kept on going.

Finally, I saw the cable car and instinctively knew I would need to fly under it to get to a large open area that would be perfect for deploying my parachute. As I flew under the cable car, I looked over and saw people's faces as I went by. The look of astonishment in their eyes made me giggle a little in my helmet. They looked so freaked out that it made me smile. I opened my chute and the space was tighter than I was expecting. I needed to move fast to unzip my arms or risk hitting trees on steep cliffs. Right under me was a long stretch of road that ended with a bridge. I decided it would be my best option. Most of the road had trees overhanging it, but the bridge was clear, so I felt that was my best option. The bad news was the bridge was narrow. If I was a little off to the left or right, I could easily miss and get hurt. I lined up and came in for a fast, no-wind landing on asphalt. I ran out the landing, but as I came to a stop at the center of the bridge, a small gust of wind grabbed my canopy and pulled it over the left side of the bridge. As this happened, I quickly pulled on my left brake line, collapsing the canopy and forcing air to escape out its nose. I then reeled the canopy in as fast as I could to keep it from pulling me over and off the side of the bridge.

When I had everything together, I gave the signal for them to let the traffic move again and I sat resting on the side of the bridge. My wingsuit flight was over 3,500 feet high. To have a jump this big, with a cable car to the top and a short hike to exit, was something special, and it dawned on me that maybe there would be more to this place than just flying through the cave. Within fifteen minutes, a small bus stopped in front of me and the driver motioned to get on. He then took me to the midway station, where I met up with Iiro and crew. They asked me how the jump went, and I explained this place was perfect. I could now see that everything here was jumpable. There had to be at least ten exits, maybe more. Mr. Bo Xie asked if it would be possible for me to jump from the cable car itself. I responded with, "Yes, of course I can." So, the next day I proceeded to jump from the cable car as well.

Once we knew the cave flight was possible and I could use the cliffs for training, we began talking about what the event would look like. Mr. Bo Xie explained they would like to do a two-hour live show and asked how long it would take from the time I left the helicopter, to flying through the cave, to landing on the bridge. I told him probably between two and three minutes. He asked if we could bring more jumpers to help extend the show and we said, "Absolutely." Mr. Bo Xie felt it would be good to have several exhibition jumps leading up to the cave flight with jumpers doing "big way" wingsuit (as in multiple wingsuit pilots exiting and flying formations) flights from the helicopter, jumps from the cliff, and people exiting from the cable car. We explained that would not be a problem, and it was decided right then and there we had a deal.

As Frank, Iiro, and I traveled back to Beijing, we talked about how we would finance the project. Frank said he could get soft money for hotels, food, local manpower, and local transportation from the cable car company, but we would need to find more sponsors for the event to pay for hard money costs like jumpers' fees, international flights, and production costs. Frank felt the cable car company would put in hard money, too, but not enough to pull off an event this large. So, he was going to check with his contacts and see what he could do, then talk to us in a few weeks when he had more information.

True to his word, a few weeks later, Frank sent an email asking to get on a conference call with Iiro and me. We set up a time and got on the call. Frank told us he had a friend at a high level with Chinese Red Bull. He had talked with his friend and explained the event and that we had partnered with the Tianmen Mountain Cable Car Company. His friend passed him down to people within the organization who dealt with sponsorships and events. Frank had gone into a meeting with these people, but they did not have a strong response. They told Frank that Chinese Red Bull was nothing like Austrian Red Bull. Chinese Red Bull didn't work with small, fringe extreme sports. They were more interested in spending their marketing budgets on Olympic sports like soccer and badminton. They also didn't think a relatively unknown American athlete doing a completely unknown sport that didn't even have a word to describe it in Chinese was going to be popular with a Chinese audience. They didn't feel many people would watch the event on TV and felt, if they were lucky, they could maybe get an audience of ten million. Which, by Chinese standards, was quite small. They only had a few channels and a population of over one billion people, so their expectations for our event were low. But their boss had informed them this was something they were going to support, so based on their idea of what the viewership would most likely be, they were willing to give $100,000 to the project and do some marketing for the event. This was a small amount of money for a project of this magnitude, and it would mean none of us would make any money in the end; it would be enough to pull off the project, but just barely. Frank, Iiro, and I felt it was worth doing the project in hopes that, if it went well, maybe we could do bigger projects with Red Bull China in the future. We all agreed we would do the project with a super small budget, and if we broke even, so be it.

That conversation was June 2010 and the project got slated to happen September 24th of 2011. This would give me little more than a year to train for the event and try to get my sustained glide ratios up to 2.5 to 1. I was also hoping the new wingsuit designs coming out in the next few months would have better performance and make this more reasonable.

Shortly after returning home from the scouting mission to Tianmen Mountain, my buddy Luigi Cani got an X-Wing from Tony Suits. I was still flying my Stealth from Phoenix Fly. Luigi and I had been flying wingsuits together for almost six years at this point, and because of my height, I always had a bit of an advantage flying with him. I would usually have to fly with my legs bent and wings collapsed to match his fall rate. On our first jump together with his new X-Wing, Luigi said, "Jeb, this is my first jump on the suit, so it probably won't fly that efficiently."

I said, "No problem, bro. I'll stay with you." We jumped and instantly Luigi pulled away from me at high speed. No matter how hard I pushed, I couldn't catch up to him. It was one of the more shocking things I had experienced when it came to advancements in wingsuit performance technology. We had flown our Stealths together the jump before and I had owned Luigi, easily flying around him at will.

But the instant he put the X-Wing on, I couldn't even get close to him.

When we landed, he asked, "What happened? I didn't see you anywhere."

"I couldn't keep up," I told him. "How hard were you pushing?"

Luigi said, "I wasn't pushing at all. I just jumped out and relaxed in the suit."

I called Jeff that night and ordered an X-Wing. It was rushed through production and I had it only a few weeks later. I did some skydiving with it and fell in love. I could feel a huge leap in performance and decided to take it to Europe and train with it as much as possible. This was the year I flew the crack for the first time, and it became the perfect location for me to do my training for the Heaven's Gate project in China.

By the end of that summer, I had the X-Wing dialed in but still couldn't sustain 2.5 to 1 for as long as I needed. I would get to 2.5 and even 2.7 here and there, but only in short bursts. I would need something more if I was going to pull off the cave flight with a safe margin.

As the summer of 2010 shifted into fall, Jeff told me Tony was about to release a new suit that could sustain over a 3 to 1 glide. He called it the Apache X, and it was going to revolutionize the wingsuit flying industry.

I told him, "The instant it's ready, you let me know." Sure enough, a month later, I received my first Apache X in the mail. I took it to the drop zone and jumped it from a plane with a friend. As I exited the aircraft, something odd happened: the suit just started veering left without me being able to do anything about it. It was a slow but uncontrollable turn. I had never had an issue like this before and wasn't sure what to do about it. I felt like the suit was about three inches too long and I couldn't push my toes far enough to stretch the suit completely. The wings were so big that they actually attached from the wrist down to the outside of the foot, meaning if you couldn't stretch your toes, you couldn't properly control the suit.

The jump was a bit scary, and when I landed, I needed to find a solution. I went to the rigging loft on the drop zone and talked to a rigger about my issue. He said he could take three inches off both booties and that should fix the problem. While he was doing this, I decided to look at the GPS data from the flight just to see what kind of glide I had gotten, even though the suit was out of control. As I imported the files, I saw that I had hit a glide ratio of 3 to 1 multiple times and was sustaining over 2.5 to 1 even without having control of the suit. I couldn't believe it.

I got the suit back from the rigger and got on the next plane I could find. I was a bit nervous jumping out because being out of control in a wingsuit is a horrible feeling. But I needed this suit to work, and I was pretty sure the problem was the suit being a bit too long. I jumped out, and sure enough, the suit was perfectly stable. I had 100 percent control, and what surprised me most about the suit is, even though it had huge wings, I barely felt any pressure on my arms at all. Usually after a wingsuit flight from 12,000 feet, my arms would be exhausted by pull time, but in the Apache X I barely noticed any fatigue. I landed and plugged in the GPS and was amazed that I had sustained 3 to 1 for almost the entire flight without even trying. I now knew that I could fly Heaven's Gate with a safe margin, and a feeling of relief washed over me.

I trained all that winter at my home drop zone in Perris, California, and the coming summer, I headed back to Europe to train at my new favorite location: the Crack. I was flying the Apache X when the *Grinding the Crack* video was filmed, and that was the training program I used for the Heaven's Gate project. I knew if I could hit that balloon, going through a 360-foot-tall, 100-foot-wide cave would be no problem at all.

I showed up in China feeling confident this project was going to happen without me getting hurt. I was told I would have a helicopter and a week of training leading up to the event. I felt if I could do at least four jumps a day for five days, I could easily work my way into the cave. I knew I had the precision and glide to pull it off. Now I just needed to figure out where to leave the chopper and find marker points to help lead me into the cave at the correct angle and altitude. There was a long, tight kill zone that started at the cave's entrance and ended at the bottom of a staircase where I would be able to go over a cliff, giving me the altitude needed to safely deploy a parachute. If I didn't judge the entrance correctly or sustain the 2.5 to 1 glide, I would die, and it would all be aired live.

Red Bull China and the Cable Car Company partnered with a Chinese TV network called Hunan TV. They were in charge of the live broadcast and would send the signal out with satellite trucks parked at the midway station. As I showed up in China, something happened Red Bull hadn't anticipated: media from all over the world started taking notice. In 2006, my run-in with the Empire State Building had made the media interested in me and what I would potentially do next. From that point forward, anytime I did anything, they would report on it. So, hundreds of reporters started showing up the week before the event. News stories started going out en masse and Red Bull China realized this was something bigger than they had anticipated. There was a snowball effect happening and Red Bull finally decided to start putting real money into the marketing side of things. I was never told exact amounts, but Frank estimated that Red Bull put over a million dollars in marketing once everything was said and done.

The woman we worked with at Red Bull was named Joan, and on my first day of training she walked with me to the exit point. The cable car company had built a large exit point made from scaffolding and plywood right on the edge where I had done the first jump the year before. I would use this platform for training and the rest of the team would use it for their exhibition jumps during the live show. As Joan and I climbed up the makeshift stairs, I could see she was nervous. She walked to the platform's edge while holding the scaffolding handrail with both hands. As she looked down the face of the 1,000-foot vertical drop, I could see a true sense of terror in her eyes; she was shaking from head to toe. I proceeded to put on my body armor and wingsuit. There were about eight other people on the platform with us, mostly workers for the cable car company, but also a few people from the press. As I walked up to the edge, I looked over at Joan and smiled.

She said, "Jeb, when Frank originally came to talk to us about this, I didn't truly understand what he was talking about. Right now, seeing you standing on that edge about to jump, I finally get it. This may be the single most frightening thing I have ever witnessed."

"This is just practice," I said with a grin. "You haven't seen anything yet." Then I stepped off the mountain and did my first training jump for the event.

As I returned to the platform for my second training jump, Joan was still standing there, shaking but smiling. I asked her how she was doing, and she said, "Jeb, I have never experienced anything like this. The feeling I had as you stepped off was a mixture of exhilaration and horror. I'm not sure I have the words in English to fully express my feelings. That girl standing over there started crying as you left."

I looked at the girl and recognized her as one of our interpreters. I asked her if she was okay, and she said, "Yes, I have always had dreams of flying. Watching you fly from this mountain overwhelmed me and I exploded with emotion."

Social situations are not my cup of tea, and I am still terrible at communicating with people under most circumstances. I didn't know how to respond to what was being said to me—I mean, what do you say to that kind of thing? I just smiled awkwardly and said, "Thank you," but inwardly I recognized the girl's dream as my own from so long ago. There I was, flying for both of us, but I couldn't verbalize my thoughts to her.

I geared up and jumped off the cliff as fast as I could: I needed to escape from the overwhelming emotions of the people around me. The way people were looking at me made me feel uncomfortable.

The next day, the other group of jumpers started showing up to begin their training for the event: Jeff Nebelkopf, Jokke Sommer, Matt Gerdes, Barry Holubeck, Joby Ogwin, Roberta Mancino, Chris "Douggs" McDougall, and Stefan Muller—a truly epic group of human beings. The format for the show had already been decided and they were going to do various styles of wingsuit flights from helicopters, the cable car, and the cliff I was using for training. As they got in, we gave a briefing of how the event was going to happen and the timing of the live show. Different jumpers were selected for each position, and everyone was made aware that training would begin the next morning at 9:00 a.m. sharp.

Frank pulled me aside and informed me we had a problem with the helicopter, explaining that we had gotten approval for the project the year before from the head general of the Chinese Air Force in the area. But with the press descending upon us like a tidal wave, the general had decided he no longer wanted to take responsibility for the project. He was concerned that if something went wrong, it would not be localized anymore, and the entire world would see it. He was concerned it would negatively impact his career and he was pulling the approval for the helicopter.

This was a serious issue because the stunt could not be done without a helicopter, and we now had hundreds of people working on this project. The live trucks were already in place and camera positions had already been installed. Red Bull China and Human TV were dumping vast amounts of resources into the project. Press releases had already been made and the unstoppable machine this thing had become was already in motion. There was no turning back at this point. Frank made it clear to the general that the decision had already been made a year earlier and it was too late to back out at this point. The general said he was sorry, but he wasn't going to stake the rest of his political life on this project, and if Frank was adamant that we had to move forward, then he would need to get more generals from other regions involved. He asked for at least ten different generals to clear the project in case something went wrong so that the fallout would be shared and not just fall on him.

I asked Frank if this was something that could be done. He looked at me with concern in his eyes and said, "I will try, Jeb, but this is not going to be easy." Frank spent the next four days struggling to get the necessary approval. On the morning before the event, Frank pulled off the impossible and got all the signatures for the project to move forward. Shortly after everything was cleared, we learned the helicopter was on its way. It had to be flown from far away, so it didn't show up till late in the afternoon. I knew I was in trouble. With all the negotiations and troubleshooting, I had not gotten the five days of training I had asked for. I was only going to get one to two jumps for training at this point and would then have to do the stunt live the next day. I told Frank and Iiro that I wasn't sure if I could pull the stunt off with so little training.

They said, "Jeb, your safety is the number one top priority. If you don't feel like you got enough training and you don't feel comfortable, don't do the stunt."

This made me feel a bit better, but I still felt an enormous amount of pressure. It's easy to say, "You don't have to do it," but when millions of people will be watching you live, it's hard to just walk away. I am a man of my word: when I say I am going to do something, I do it.

I decided to do my practice jumps and go from there. If they went well, I would go for it; if they didn't...well, I didn't want to think about that. I geared up in the parking lot of the main theater with the rest of the jumpers and waited for the helicopter to show up. As I heard it off in the distance, I began to get excited. These practice jumps were going to be crucial. The chopper landed and the pilots turned off the engine, then got out to talk with us about what we needed them to do. Frank translated, but the main pilot spoke pretty good English on his own. We used a large model of Heaven's Gate that the cable car company had built to show the pilot the angle we needed him to fly towards the backside of the cave. I explained I needed to be 2,000 feet above the cave's opening, and I wanted him to start the run up to the cave at least one mile out. I wanted him to fly the jump run at thirty knots because it made for the most comfortable exits.

He understood everything I said and responded, "This is pretty cool."

"You're right," I agreed, "this is pretty cool." He asked me how much time I needed, and I told him, "I'm ready when you are."

He jumped right back in the helicopter and fired it up. I got in and we started moving.

As we got to altitude, I got my first view of the cave from above. It looked so much smaller from up there. For the first practice jump, I wanted to get out close to the cave to ensure I would get over it. I really didn't want to land on the back side of the mountain. I couldn't see a landing area there and felt it was almost certain death if I didn't make it to the other side of the mountain. The pilot got us to the perfect altitude and flew exactly one mile away from the cave before turning around. He slowed down to thirty knots, and I started spotting from the aircraft, looking for landmarks underneath me that I could use to tell my distance from Heaven's Gate. I noticed a giant spire on our flight path and felt it would be a good marker point. As I watched the cave get closer, I felt like it was time to exit, so I did. The instant I left the helicopter, I noticed I was too high and way too close. I started diving the suit to try and get down closer. If I flew over the cave too high, it would have been a wasted practice jump, and I wasn't getting enough of them to allow for that. I couldn't seem to get down; the Apache X was great for glide but was terrible when it came to diving. I needed to go steeper, so I kept pushing the suit and it started getting unstable. I was still too high, and I tried to dive it even more, when suddenly, the suit let loose and flipped me on my back. I was now above the terrain, flat spinning on my back. I was losing altitude fast and I knew I needed to either recover or die. Somehow, I was able to flip the suit over within a hundred feet, and luckily, I still had the altitude to make it over the top of Heaven's Gate. I have had flat spins on my back while skydiving that have taken thousands of feet to recover from, so what just happened was miraculous. As I recovered, I looked down and saw that I was right over the top of the cave and was closing distance with the ground fast. I went over the top by about thirty feet and got a clear view of how close my practice jump had come to impact. I flew the rest of the way down and landed at the bridge. I pulled my canopy in and jumped in a car that was waiting for me. It drove me back to the parking lot, where the helicopter had already landed and was waiting for me to do a second jump. I took my wingsuit off the open rig and transferred it to a freshly packed rig. I handed the unpacked gear to Barry Holubeck, who began packing it right away. As I stepped on the helicopter, I knew I wasn't even close to being ready for this. I needed way more training. This next training jump was all I had left before doing it live in front of millions of people the next day.

We went to altitude, and I watched for the spire that I had decided to use as my marker. I saw it and got out farther away this time, but again I got out way too close and was having to do a steep dive that made the suit unstable. This time I stopped pushing it, though, and just allowed myself to fly over the top higher than I wanted. I landed below and knew I was fucked. Those two jumps told me I wasn't ready for this, not by a long shot. I had only been training the Apache X for glide and hadn't even thought about what it would mean to dive the suit. I now understood diving the suit steeply would equal death on this jump, and that was a serious problem.

That night, I explained my issues to Frank and Iiro. I told them I needed more practice and the jumps I had done that day only confirmed my worst fears. Iiro said, "Jeb, we are doing the best we can. We couldn't get the chopper until today, and if you don't think you are able to get enough practice, then don't do it."

Frank continued with, "Jeb, you have the chopper all day tomorrow. You can wake up at five a.m. and jump till eleven a.m. Take Barry and he can pack for you. Do as many jumps as you can in that time frame and see if it can be enough." I felt I could probably get about four jumps in that time frame, which sounded really good at that point. If I could figure out where to exit the helicopter with those jumps to get a smooth run up to the opening of the cave, then I should be able to do this. So, I agreed. I would get up at 5:00 a.m. and do as many jumps as possible before the live show began.

I didn't sleep much that night. I was super scared and my mind felt like it was on fire. I just couldn't turn my brain off no matter what I tried. I've noticed a lot of my fear comes from the anticipation of doing something, from trying to foresee all the possible things that can go wrong and trying to figure out how to solve each issue before it even happens. A lot of people think I have a negative approach to what I do because I'm always weighing the worst-case scenarios, but I disagree. I take what I do seriously and look at it like it's trying to kill me. The best way to describe it is:

imagine you knew that, in six months, you had to get into an octagon to fight. Now, if you thought you were going to be meeting a big bad man who wanted to rip your arms off and beat you to death with them, you would prepare in a serious way. You would probably work out five hours a day to put on muscle, you would eat healthy, and you would do whatever it took to prepare yourself to ensure you had the best chance to not get your ass totally killed. But, if you thought you were going into that octagon to have a tea party with children, you would have a completely different approach. You wouldn't do anything to prepare for it; you would just go have a tea party. That's why I've always been concerned when people are too optimistic and treat BASE jumping like it's all fun and games. BASE jumping is not a tea party—it's a big bad man who wants to kill you.

I knew I had to get up early, but each time I looked at the clock, another sleepless hour had passed by. It felt like torture. I didn't want to let myself and everyone else down. So many people had believed in me and were working so hard to make this happen. I was pissed I didn't get the training days or the jumps I felt I needed, but I was going to try the best I could with what I did have. At 4:30 a.m., I got up before the alarm even sounded. I got all my gear together and went downstairs.

Barry was standing there with our driver, and we quietly walked outside and got in the car. We were all dead-tired, so we headed towards the mountain in silence. As we got to the theater parking lot, we saw the helicopter pilots getting ready. I sluggishly put on my gear, feeling like I was wearing lead weights. It was an effort to just lift my arms. I headed for the helicopter and got in. The helicopter fired up and, before I knew it, I was at altitude looking out the door before the sun had even crested the horizon. It was still dark with just a faint glow from the sun peeking over the mountain. This time I was going to try to get out even further away, making it so I could fly straight without having to dive too steeply. I wanted to fly about twenty feet from the top. I looked for my spire that I used as a marker point and stepped out of the chopper directly above it.

Again, I could tell I was still too close, but this time I decided to try something different. Instead of diving at the cave, I would make a large S turn. I turned to the right at almost a ninety-degree angle and flew away from the cave, all the while keeping it in view. Once I felt I had burned off enough altitude, I turned back towards the cave and started flying. It worked perfectly; I now had the glide angle to fly exactly where I wanted to without the suit becoming unstable. I flew over the top of the cave by about twenty feet like I had planned and then dropped into the canyon after the opening of the cave. Success at last.

This was my first true training jump at Heaven's Gate and it made me feel much better. As I landed on the bridge, a feeling of relief washed over me. That one jump showed me I had control, and I knew I would be able to fly through that cave. My ride picked me up and took me back to the helicopter. I grabbed my second rig and transferred the wingsuit. Before I knew it, I was back over the spire and exiting the helicopter. This time, I judged the exit better and only had to do a small S turn to get myself on the proper trajectory. I could see my window through the cave and just decided to go for it. I flew through the cave, down the valley, under the cable car, and landed on the bridge. By this time, Frank had gotten to the landing area and he asked, "Jeb, did you just fly through the cave?"

I responded with, "Yes, I did, and I don't need any more practice jumps. I'm one hundred percent sure I can do this when the cameras are rolling." Frank smiled and sent me back to the hotel to rest—they wouldn't need me until 1:00 p.m. at the earliest.

When I got to the hotel, I decided to get some breakfast. Our hotel had a wonderful buffet right next to the lobby, and I had some noodles and a couple fried eggs with some fruit. Once I finished eating, I headed to my room to see if I could get a little rest. As I stepped in the elevator, my stomach started gurgling and an overwhelming sensation of having to go to the bathroom hit me like a ton of bricks. It was such a strong urge that I could tell I had a serious problem. I barely made it to the bathroom and was one second from pooping my pants. The food I had at breakfast went straight through me. I now had full-on diarrhea, and it dawned on me this was going to be a nightmare. I couldn't believe it. The bathroom on the mountain had some of the worst sanitation I had seen anywhere in the world. I actually had to hold my breath when using the toilet, and to have the "single dragon," as the other pilots had come to call it, was just not going to be pleasant. Plus, what was I going to do when I was on live TV, sitting in a helicopter for unknown periods of time? I just hoped it would move through my system quickly and be done with.

I ended up spending my entire time in the hotel on the toilet, and when it was time to walk downstairs, I grabbed as much toilet paper as I could carry because I knew I would need it. When I got in the car to take me to the event, I instantly had to go to the bathroom and knew I had to hold it for at least thirty minutes. It was a battle to hold myself together and I was sweating by the time I got there. When the car finally stopped, I opened the door and ran as fast as I could for a bathroom. As I stormed through the bathroom door, the smell hit me like a wall of funk. It brought tears to my eyes, and I had to take a few steps back outside to take a deep breath. I held it and went back into the dark room. The first stall I looked at was covered in smears of poo and I just couldn't go in there. The second one was a bit better, but China doesn't have toilets like we're used to in the west: they have holes in the ground that you squat over. I couldn't think about it too much since I had to get my pants down ASAP. As I was squatting there trying to do my business as fast as possible, I realized I was still holding my breath. Unfortunately for me, I couldn't hold it long enough and had to gasp for air—the smell was so foul I almost vomited. How had I gotten so unlucky right before doing the biggest stunt of my life?

Mission accomplished, I walked out of the bathroom and was greeted by Frank, who told me I needed to do a series of interviews for a group of reporters. All the major CCTV channels where there to witness the stunt live and they all wanted to ask questions before the event took place. So, for the next few hours, I went from one interview to the next. I had to take bathroom breaks in between each interview, but I finally made it through all their questions.

The show began and I couldn't believe how many camera positions there were: they had placed live cameras all over the mountain. It was a truly humongous production, unlike anything I had experienced. I was moved to the helicopter staging area where I yet again had to find a bathroom to repeat the horrors of the single dragon in extremely unsanitary conditions. When I got out, Frank told me the instant I landed I would need to hand the GoPro cameras I was wearing to a technician from Hunan TV. He pointed out the man and said, "He will be in your landing area. Just take off your cameras and give them to him. He'll rush them to the satellite truck, and they will use the footage to do recaps of the jump for the viewers at home."

The clock hit 3:00 p.m., and I was supposed to do the jump at exactly 3:30 p.m. I was told to gear up and get in the helicopter. The cable car company, along with Hunan TV, insisted I fly with a smoke canister attached to my foot so it would be easier to see me as I flew towards the cave. They also felt it would make the footage more spectacular. These smoke canisters are what the military uses to mark landing zones for helicopters so the pilots can see what the winds are doing. Skydivers and wingsuit pilots use them to track each other through the sky. I personally hate using smoke because it has a tendency to burn and destroy your equipment, but I agreed to put it on because I also understood I wear all black and that makes it difficult to see me when I'm thousands of feet away. Seeing this event was live and we had one shot at this, we needed to make sure the cameras on the ground could see me leave the helicopter and follow me through almost a mile-and-a-half flight.

I put all my gear on and strapped the smoke canister directly to my foot with gaffer's tape. I had tested one the day before to make sure it wouldn't set my shoe on fire. The canister said it was "cold smoke," but there is no such thing as cold smoke. The canister stayed a reasonable temperature where it attached to my shoe, but the bottom where the smoke came out shot flames and a black molten substance that would burn anything it touched. If I were to light the smoke and stay in the helicopter too long, it could set the helicopter on fire, so I'd have to light it and instantly exit. I had used smoke before, but usually the smoke would have a ring you pulled that would activate it. This smoke had a battery that you would have to attach wires to a positive and negative terminal. I had never seen smoke like it before and it seemed overly complicated. But it was what we had, and they wanted me to use it. Looking back, I probably should have been using it during the practice jumps, but I was too worried it would destroy my only wingsuit with Red Bull logos on it. I had burned many suits with smoke in the past and didn't want to risk it. This was the project where I learned you must always have at least two identical sets of gear in case one gets damaged.

I got in the helicopter all geared up with the smoke on my foot and the wires hanging out, ready to attach. We took off at about 3:15 p.m., giving us fifteen minutes to get into position for the jump. The pilot flew the exact same pattern that he had during the practice jumps and everything was perfect. I looked out the door and located the spire I had been using as my marker point. There was a haze in the air that made it more difficult to see, but I was able to make it out in the distance. I could see I was getting close to where I needed to jump and I looked back in the helicopter to start putting the wires on the smoke to activate it. I got one wire in place, and as I was fumbling around with the second wire, I accidentally made contact with the smoke. I knew it was too early to jump, but the smoke started going. I thought, *I'm in big trouble.* If I stayed in the chopper, it would fill with smoke and blind the pilots, and the canister would most likely start a fire. The helicopter was a Sikorsky with fancy flammable carpeting inside. I knew I had to jump out, but I also knew I was too far away from the cave to make it through. If I couldn't make it, I would have to land on the back side of the mountain; there was nowhere to land back there, just deadly 1000-foot-plus cliffs covered in trees. There was no time and no choice—I had to get out of the helicopter, and I had to get out now.

So I jumped.

When I looked forward to see where the mountain was, I knew I was fucked. There was no way I could make it to the cave. On my current trajectory, I would impact the staircase leading up to the entrance. I decided to open my parachute and start looking for a place to potentially land. As I opened, I became enraged. I looked around and saw no good options. My mind was trying to figure out if I could fly through the cave with the canopy, but I knew I wouldn't make it. I thought about trying to fly around the cave but could tell it wasn't possible. I looked for trees to land in, but they were all horrible options. I saw what looked like an avalanche of rocks that had taken out part of the jungle just underneath a walkway that led to the staircase to the cave. It was the only option. I couldn't tell how steep it was, but it was the only clear place I could set a canopy down, so I focused on it. As I got closer, I could see it was super steep and I wasn't sure if I would be able to stay where I landed or if I would slide backwards down the mountain for a thousand feet. It was too late to change my mind; that was where I had to hit. I flared and landed hard. I was able to stick right where I had set down, but I was in a precarious position. I screamed at the top of my lungs, "Fucking smoke!!!"

From the live TV production's perspective, they didn't know what to do. We had been telling the audience all day that if I landed on the back side of the mountain I was probably going to die. They had gone into great detail about how that side of the mountain was only cliffs and death, and it would be a worst-case scenario to land back there. The commentators didn't know what to say now. Everyone was dumbfounded. People watching on TV just saw them all look at each other with a shocked expression as Hunan TV cut the live feed and went to black. Within seconds, they put on a pre-recording of a Chinese version of *Dancing with the Stars*. People watching the program in China didn't understand what had happened. Everyone thought they had just seen an American die on live TV and it created hysteria. It went from being a live stunt on Hunan TV to becoming mainstream live news on all CCTV channels. When Hunan TV realized I was okay, they rushed to bring the live feed back online. This had turned into a live rescue now.

I was trapped on the side of the mountain as teams of rescue workers started repelling down to my position. I spent the time gathering up my gear and putting it in my stash bag. By the time they got to me, I was ready to move. They tried to put a harness on me, but I knew I didn't have time to deal with that. I knew I only had thirty minutes to get back to the helicopter to get another shot at doing the jump before the live broadcast would be over. I told the rescue team, "No, I don't need a harness. Let's just go." I grabbed the rope with both hands and started pulling myself up the side of the mountain. It wasn't vertical, so it wasn't that hard to climb as long as I had hold of the rope. The rescue team protested but I completely ignored them and just went as fast as I could. I made it to the walkway and started running. I got to the bottom of the stairs and began sprinting up them. I passed a reporter who asked if I was going to try again and I said, "I don't have time to talk; I need to move." As I got halfway up the 999 stairs, I felt like my heart was going to explode. I was carrying about thirty pounds of gear and my run turned into a walk in slow-motion. Moving upstairs without sleeping for two days and with a serious diarrhea problem wasn't fun. One of the rescue team was keeping pace with me and decided to grab my gear with my wingsuit attached. I protested but he wouldn't take no for an answer, so I let him have it. I told him to stay with me and we moved as fast as we could. As I got to the top of the stairs, I got a second wind and started moving faster. I ran through the cave and started running down the stairs. This was a race against time, and I needed to get to the helicopter now. More reporters tried to stop me and asked if I was going to try again. I responded in motion, "Sorry, don't have time to talk, must keep moving."

As I got close to the bottom of the stairs, I noticed I had lost the man carrying my wingsuit. Iiro was there and could see I was on the edge of losing my mind and asked what was wrong. I explained how someone had grabbed my wingsuit and was somewhere up the stairs with it. We started yelling for someone to call him on a walkie talkie, but no one knew who it was or what channel he was on. Douggs was standing there and said he would rush up and find him. Within about ten minutes, Douggs came running back down the stairs with the wingsuit in his hands. He handed it off to me and I rushed as fast as I could to a waiting car. I got in and we raced down the ninety-nine switchbacks at completely ludicrous speeds. Driving down swerving roads at high speed started making me feel car sick, and I thought I might throw up when the car came to a sudden stop.

We were there. The choppers blades were already spinning, and as I stepped out of the car, Barry handed me a freshly packed rig. I ran to the chopper, got on, and started attaching my wingsuit to the rig. I told the pilot we needed to hurry but he replied that there was air traffic and we were on a hold. I tried to explain the live broadcast was about to end and he said, "They have extended the live broadcast to give you the time you need to do the jump." His words were music to my ears and I was able to finally relax a bit. I lay back, took a deep breath, and cleared my mind. I felt like I had just run a marathon while people were hitting me with baseball bats, and I was destroyed both physically and mentally. But as I lay there, everything became quiet. Even though my heart was pounding out of my chest, I felt a calm come over me. I'm not sure how long we were sitting there on the asphalt before the helicopter took off, but as it did, the feeling was surreal. I felt a warm sensation all over my body that started in my core and seemed to work its way out to the ends of my toes and fingertips. I felt like I was glowing with energy. As we reached jumping altitude, the calm became more profound, almost like I was lying in bed meditating. As I looked out the helicopter door at the ground thousands of feet below me, I felt peace unlike anything I had ever experienced. I looked at the cave off in the distance and knew without question I was going to fly through it. I saw the spire I had been using as a marker and stepped out of the chopper to the waiting air. I could feel the wind filling my wings and felt it support my body. I could see I needed to burn a little altitude, so I did another S-turn, lining myself up perfectly for the cave.

As I flew towards the opening, I noticed a crowd of people completely filling the inside of the cave—hundreds of them. I had been told it was going to be cleared of people in case I had an accident, but I guess that safety protocol went out the window. I was close enough to see their eyes as I flew past at over 100 mph. I came out the other side of the cave and flew down the stairs with plenty of altitude to spare. I turned left over a series of roads and around a gigantic spire of rock, then saw the cable car. As I approached the cable car, I noticed my left foot had started to shake, then my right foot. The tremor spread to my arms, and I knew my energy was spent. I couldn't hold the pressure in the suit much longer: I had used up everything I had, and I was about to crash. I flew under the cable car, flared the suit, and deployed. I had a perfect opening and all I wanted was to get to the ground as fast as possible. I landed right in front of cameras with two Red Bull girls rushing out to hand me a drink. I did a small interview and, when the cameras turned away, I got down on my knees, put my head on the pavement and just stayed like that to recuperate some strength. I was done; I had no power left for anything else.

The next day, after sleeping for sixteen hours, I was doing interviews for countless news programs when Frank told me we had a special visitor: the head of Red Bull China had flown to Heaven's Gate to meet me in person and wanted to talk about what had happened the day before. Frank introduced me to a well-dressed woman and she congratulated me on the cave flight. I thanked her and she asked me how I thought it had gone.

I told her, "I'm still alive, so I think it went pretty good."

She said, "You have no idea how good."

She then explained that Hunan TV's live broadcast was picked up by most CCTV networks. It had become international news and countless news networks from around the world were doing thousands of stories about the feat. She said they had expected maybe ten million viewers would watch the event when she first talked with Frank about this project. But since yesterday, they had been trying to track the numbers from the event...and couldn't. It had ballooned beyond expectations and the real numbers were now impossible to calculate. She guessed that more than one hundred million people watched the event live, with further hundreds of millions of impressions from news outlets from all over the world. She explained it was the single most successful event in Red Bull China's history, which was a big deal because they worked with football (soccer in the USA) events, and this crushed their numbers with that extremely popular sport. She explained this was a phenomenon unlike anything they could have ever imagined, and if I ever wanted to do another project in China to please let them know. They would be happy to support anything I wanted to do.

I didn't truly understand what any of that meant at the time. I was just happy to have survived. But a year later when ABC decided to do a countdown of the greatest stunts of all time, leading up to Nick Wallenda walking across Niagara Falls, I was surprised to get a call. Producers from the show said my cave flight had been selected as a possible choice for the top twenty, and they wanted to interview me and get my take on the other contenders. I was shocked they were even considering me with names like Harry Houdini, Evel Knievel, Philippe Petit, and the list of iconic adventurers went on and on. I didn't know if it was appropriate for me to even speak about these people. They were all larger-than-life characters and I was just...me.

I showed up to the ABC studio, and they started asking me questions about all the different names on their list. I was as honest as I could be and didn't really know why they cared what I thought about these people. I was just a wingsuit pilot who did a stunt in China that was quite big there, but few people in the USA had seen it or knew anything about it. As far as I knew, it was just a blip on the radar in the western world. They told me as I was leaving that my stunt had been selected in the top twenty, which again took me by surprise.

"Out of that list of absolute legends," I said, "you really think my stunt belongs in the top twenty?"

The producer said, "Jeb, your stunt was unprecedented and had one of the largest live audiences of all time. It's hard to judge because China doesn't track numbers like we do here, but even so it was aired on most major networks in Asia both live and on the news to a potential audience of billions. That is something unique." Despite his insistence, I still didn't think it belonged in the same category as the people on that list, but I thanked him all the same.

A month or so later, I watched the ABC program *Megastunts: Highwire Over Niagara Falls* and saw the countdown. As it went from twenty to ten, I didn't see Heaven's Gate and wondered if they had changed their minds. As it when from ten to number two I couldn't believe they had lied to me. Why would they tell me I was going to be on the list if they weren't going to put me on it? I thought it was pretty lame to get my hopes up for nothing, but then they got to number one and I saw an image of me flying wingsuits—I was thunderstruck. I couldn't believe they had picked mine over everyone else as the single greatest megastunt of all time. I know this sounds stupid, but I had a real moment there on my couch. To be recognized for something you do is special, and I got a powerful feeling that brought me immense satisfaction and made me feel that it had all been worth it.

When I started BASE jumping, I never thought anyone would see the things I did. I was doing it because I had demons ripping away at my mind and I needed to figure out how to exorcise them before they killed me. When I found BASE jumping, it gave me a powerful outlet to channel rage and dark energy in a more positive direction. I was a depressed, dark, ticking time bomb just waiting to explode on large groups of people. I had serious psychological problems that I needed to work through, and this activity helped me face my innermost horrors. I felt the fear, the injuries, the pain, along with the feelings of euphoria, flight, joy, and unexplainable happiness that came from forcing myself to step off the edge over and over again and succeeding. The constant struggle, the constant shock therapy I subjected myself to, rewired my core programming. I would burn myself to the ground and rebuild better each time. I would hammer myself into oblivion, cracking my mind, melting it into molten liquid, and then reforming it the way I wanted—no, *needed to*. The strongest metal has been hammered the hardest and everything became about hammering myself. Training mental toughness was everything for me. I would not take pain pills; I would take pain. I would not shy away from fear; I would embrace it, let it flow through me, let it shape me.

What happened with Heaven's Gate somehow helped me come to terms with the fact I was getting better, that there might be more to what I was doing than just fighting and struggling with my own mind. Maybe there was more to this than just me. I had been so hyper-focused on myself and what I needed to do in order to survive my own mind that it had never dawned on me that what I was doing had an impact on other people's minds, too. Large numbers of people were now watching what I was doing. This was the first time I started getting out of my own head and started seeing the potential of what this could mean for other people. It was the beginning of seeing something more. Just a glimpse, almost a shimmering mirage off in the distance. It's sometimes hard getting out of your own head, and it took me time to see through myself.

But this was the beginning.

CHAPTER TWENTY-SIX

TABLE MOUNTAIN— THE IMPACT

I had been home from the Heaven's Gate project for about a month when I started planning my next trip with my new buddy, Joby. We had been training together over the last season and I told him I wanted to go back to South Africa to fly wingsuits from Table Mountain again. I explained it was going to be the ten-year anniversary of the day I almost died doing the first ever wingsuit flight from that mountain.

You need to understand the context of why this was significant, so I'll explain quickly. Yuri and I had been debating if flying a wingsuit from Table Mountain was possible since our first trip there together. Each year, we would stand on top of that mountain and wonder if the five-second rock drop would give us enough time to get a wingsuit started. In 2002, I was asked to participate in an action sports endurance race called "Extreme Air" that was being organized by my friend, Omer. Four teams from four countries with four competitors each. Think of an extreme version of Eco Challenge. While doing this event, I was asked by Moose—the same cameraman from *Journey to the Center*—if I was thinking about flying a wingsuit from the mountain. I told him, "Not really," but that was a lie. I only said that to him because I didn't want any pressure from cameras if I decided to do it.

After the event was over, I decided to go do a jump from the mountain with D-Dog, one of my teammates from the event. When we got to the exit point, I took my gear out of my stash bag and D-Dog noticed I had a wingsuit attached to my rig.

He asked me if I was going to fly it from this exit point and I said, "I'm not sure. I haven't made up my mind yet. I think I'll put it on and stand at the exit point. If I feel good, I'll jump. If I don't, I'll take it off."

He got a concerned expression on his face and said, "Maybe we should look for a better exit along this ridge. Something with a slightly longer rock drop?"

I said, "If you'd like to look for one, go ahead, but I think this exit is fine."

As I was gearing up, D-Dog went down the ridge dropping rocks, looking for something better. I put everything on slowly without knowing what I was going to do.

As I finished tightening my chest strap, D-Dog walked over and said, "Jeb, I think I found a better place for you to jump about two hundred feet that way." He pointed down the ridgeline. I agreed to walk over and take a look with him. When we got there, I picked up a large rock and looked over the edge, but there was a large outcropping blocking my view of the cliff. I took out my stopwatch and threw the rock in my hand just over the rocks obscuring my view. It instantly disappeared behind the ledge, but I did hear the rock hit seven seconds later. D-Dog said, "See? Bigger rock drop."

I responded with, "Yes, but we can't see the rock hit and the sound takes longer to get to us. I can't see what I'm jumping into, bro. I'm not sure this exit is better."

He said, "Jeb, this is a better exit. Hearing it at seven seconds is still better than seeing it at five seconds."

I decided to finish zipping up my suit and then scooted my feet as close as I could to the edge. I looked down to see where my angle of flight would take me if I was able to get the suit flying. I was in the first version of the SkyFlyer from Phoenix Fly, and by today's standards, it was a crappy wingsuit. I could see that my angle would take me low over the talus and I would have to deploy close to the ground. I saw a boulder field that would most likely become my landing area if I jumped. I handed D-Dog my stopwatch so he could time my flight; up to this point, the longest delay ever taken from Table Mountain was four seconds. I looked at D-Dog and said, "I'm going to exit, fly down that ledge, deploy low over that boulder field, and break both my legs."

Then I stepped off the mountain.

As I cleared the outcropping and saw this section of the cliff for the first time, I understood—too late—that I had just made a huge mistake. I was instantly too low to pull and had to fly to live. I was scraping down rock only a few feet away for what felt like ages.

I started yelling in my helmet, "FLY, FLY, FLY!" repeatedly. The sensation of imminent death surrounded me. I passed between two spires that were sticking up making a goal post. As I did, I got the impression of gaining altitude, but as I looked forward, I could see the terrain flatten out and I knew this was the most altitude I was ever going to have—I needed to pull right that second. I dumped, the canopy started inflating, and as it did, it stood me up, sending my legs out in front of me. With the canopy inflating behind me and my legs out in front of me, I impacted the ground with my slider still coming down the lines. I hit with so much force that it knocked the wind out of my lungs: I couldn't breathe. I was dazed and wasn't sure if I had been hurt. I lay there trying to catch my breath as I started looking around and saw that I had impacted the center of the boulder field I had seen from exit.

The boulders were much bigger than they had first appeared; they were the size of large cars all scattered and stacked on top of each other. Somehow, I had impacted on my back directly between two of them. I had also hit a small pile of sand just slightly larger than the size of my body. As I caught my breath, I stood up and started inspecting myself for broken bones. I ran my hands up and down my legs, feeling my arms, ribs, and back. Nothing hurt; somehow there wasn't any damage. I looked down at my thigh and saw a large stick that had rammed through my suit, tearing a gaping hole, but had somehow slid right by my skin, only causing a superficial scratch. I couldn't believe it. My cell phone rang, and D-Dog was frantic.

He shouted, "Are you okay, man? How badly are you injured?" From his perspective, he had seen me go into a deadly boulder field under a canopy that wasn't fully inflated.

I said, "I'm all good. No injuries."

D-Dog's disbelief came through the walkie. "Uh, are you sure you're okay? Did you hit your head or something?"

I told him, "No, I'm fine. I'm going to start walking back to the car and will meet you there."

He burst out laughing and said, "Okay, Jeb, but you may want to know your wingsuit flight just now was 24.7 seconds."

At the time, it was by far the longest delay anyone had ever taken on that mountain. As I walked back to the car, I decided I would never fly a wingsuit from Table Mountain again. I had survived on dumb luck, and the wingsuits, along with my skill, were not up to the task.

Even though this first flight from the mountain ten years earlier hadn't gone well, I had recently been seeing footage from newer pilots flying Table Mountain with modern suits and getting some amazing flights. It made me realize the flight was no longer quite as dangerous, and with the Apache, I felt I could now do it safely.

So, after I talked Joby into coming with me, I called Iiro and told him I was thinking about heading to South Africa sometime in January 2012 for a BASE-jumping trip, and I was wondering what he was up to around that time. He explained how he had been planning another trip to Africa himself. He wasn't sure when, but he knew Frank was also interested in doing a South Africa trip. He went on to say our buddy, Christian Schmidt, who had been the still photographer from the Heaven's Gate project, was usually in South Africa in January each year and he always rented a big beach house with extra rooms to crash in. I loved Christian; he was an amazing photographer/artist and was a super positive person to be around. He also surrounded himself with some of the hottest models on planet Earth, so that was a plus, too.

I could see it was already shaping up to be a fun group of people to travel with, so I started getting more organized. As I made plans, I got a call from a producer from *Real Sports* on HBO. He explained they wanted to do a show about emerging fringe sports like wingsuit proximity flying, and asked if I had any interesting trips coming up. I told him he was in luck because I was planning a trip to fly from Table Mountain, which had recently been declared as one of the New 7 Wonders of Nature, in South Africa in early January. I explained I had an event jumping off the Marina Bay Sands Resort in Singapore at the end of December and would head to Africa from there. He seemed interested and told me he would talk to everyone at the show and get back to me. Sure enough, a few days later, he called me back and said they were in. We hammered out exact dates and the ball got rolling.

I called Jeff Nebelkopft, who had become a great wingsuit cameraman and an even better friend, and told him HBO's *Real Sports* would be calling him for a job in South Africa. I let him know when we were getting there and said if he wanted to show up a bit early, we could do some training before the HBO crew arrived. He asked if he could bring his girlfriend, Tia, with him, and I said that was something he would have to work out with HBO. Jeff had become indispensable and was capable of following me with five cameras on his head. He also had an amazing eye for framing, and the fact he could frame an image while proximity flying a wingsuit was remarkable. He was my go-to cameraman for any and all projects I worked on.

Joby and I landed in Cape Town, South Africa, on January 6, 2012. We picked up our rental car and drove to a rental apartment on the west side of the mountain, about a thirty-minute drive from the cable car that would take us to the top of Table Mountain. Iiro and Frank had landed a few days before we got there and were staying in a hotel in the city center. Jeff showed up on the 8th with his girlfriend, Tia, the same day as the HBO crew. This gave Joby and I a few days to practice before the camera crew got there. It's always nice to do your first jumps without the pressure of filming. The flights were fun and uneventful. The Apache X had great starts and amazing glide, so the jump had gone from super hardcore to quite relaxing. I became comfortable right away—and I have a feeling this helped lead to my downfall.

I think what makes wingsuit proximity flying so dangerous is it feels easy: it lulls you into a false sense of security. It just doesn't have the same edge of fear that regular BASE jumping does. I would say proximity flying is like living a dream many of us had as children, where we would jump out of bed and fly around the room with total control. Whereas classic BASE jumping—without a wingsuit—is more like a chaotic nightmare of falling off a high object. One is more about an epic sensation of power and flight; the other is more about horror and how much fear can you take before you break. On a regular BASE jump, you are jumping off something and falling close to the structure you jumped from. You can't get much distance and that makes it terrifying. You know your parachute could open with an off-heading at any time, taking you right back into the object you're falling next to, and this knowledge makes you take everything dead serious. It creates a fear that permeates from your core and gives you a heightened sense of things that clears your focus. Most wingsuit proximity flights don't do the same thing. They do focus you, but in a different way. It's not a fear-based focus. There's a little bit of fear as you exit because a bad exit could lead to trouble, and there is a little fear on deployment because you might have to deal with getting line twists, but in general, you don't feel the same levels of fear in a wingsuit.

With proximity flying, you step off the object and the wings almost instantly fill with air. A sense of euphoria begins to take over and a joy fills your heart unlike anything words can describe—believe me, I've tried. You begin moving away from the object and a sense of total control overtakes you, making you think you can fly away whenever you want and giving you a dangerous kind of confidence, but you don't recognize it as such. You feel like you can fly behind waterfalls, in between trees, through small holes in rocks, and more. It feels like you could pick any leaf from any tree and touch it at will. You feel like a bird. But this feeling is false: we're not designed like birds. We're heavy. Our bones aren't hollow. We can't stop mid-flight like a bird can. Our vision doesn't work the same way as theirs. We can't just decide to land inches from the ground at will. What we're actually doing is gliding toward the ground at over 100 mph with no brakes, and all we can do is turn a little to avoid hitting things. To land, we have to deploy a parachute that needs over 300 feet of altitude to open safely. When we do deploy this parachute, we are tossing nylon and Dacron lines into high-speed wind and hoping they operate properly. We have minuscule margins for error, and when we make mistakes, they are often catastrophic. Since proximity flying has been introduced to BASE jumping, it has quickly taken over as the leading cause of death in the sport. Each year, about five times more people die in wingsuit accidents than any other discipline in BASE jumping. In my eyes, this lack of fear, combined with the almost hypnotic feeling proximity flying gives the pilot, is a strong contributing factor to why the death rate is so heavily skewed towards proximity flyers.

The odd thing is that, even with the overwhelming risk of death surrounding the activity, the numbers of people getting into it are growing. It seems like the only reason we haven't gone extinct is because more new blood gets infused each year, then gets bled out. It reminds me of moths. It's in the moth's nature to fly towards fire, not realizing or even seeing the possibility of danger. BASE jumpers are colorful moths being drawn toward a force that compels them, a feeling so powerful it's almost subconscious. Proximity flyers are like beautiful fluttering moths flying toward dazzling brilliance, unaware that all that light is coming from a raging inferno that can take them to their burning deaths.

The HBO crew showed up with a production team, ready to film for a few days. They only needed a few jumps to get the footage they were looking for and wanted to focus more on interviews and lifestyle shooting around Cape Town. I asked them if they had secured permits to film the BASE jumps on Table Mountain, and they said they were still working on it. It was our understanding that it was legal to BASE jump the mountain, but illegal to film it. That was information we had received from local producers and jumpers.

After my accident, we found out the legality of jumping Table Mountain was a more complicated subject. When I had started jumping it in 1999, it was 100 percent legal. My friend John was part of a special police force in South Africa and had established relations with the people running the cable car. He worked deals where we would get discounted tram tickets if we told them we were BASE jumpers and signed a little book to keep track of how many jumps were being done so they could start getting statistics on jumps vs. accidents. I'm not sure exactly what happened, but sometime in 1998, Table Mountain became a national park. There were a few years where people doing activities on the mountain, such as climbing, paragliding, rappelling, hiking, so on and so forth, had to put forward paperwork to establish their activity's existence. Any activity being done before the park was established would be grandfathered in and would continue to be permitted as long as it didn't have a negative impact on nature. John had started the process of putting the paperwork through the proper channels to ensure BASE jumping didn't get banned. He knew the sport had troubles in national parks all over the world and he was trying to avoid the same thing happening there. Unfortunately for BASE jumping, John got busy; he went to Iraq to fight as a government contractor, so the proper paperwork never got all the way through the bureaucratic process. From what I was told by the jumpers of the time, the newly appointed park rangers just turned a blind eye to us. Kind of a "don't ask/don't tell" policy. They didn't get involved as long as no one filmed commercial projects.

This is where HBO comes in. They had been hitting walls at every turn trying to get this permit. One night in the hotel bar, one of the producers struck up a conversation with a local man and the subject of the permit issue came up. Turned out the local man was in production in Cape Town and told the HBO producer that he could easily get him a filming permit for the mountain. The next morning, the producer told me we were all good: we had the permits we needed and could start filming ASAP. I was on probation at the time (long story), and the only stipulation the judge had given me was that I couldn't do any illegal BASE jumps. So, I was sensitive about this subject. The probation was a remnant of the Empire incident I couldn't talk about earlier.

We had already made plans to do interviews on the beach and capture B roll footage all over Cape Town, but an odd thing started happening throughout the day: I was getting recognized everywhere we went. Every single time we showed up in a new location, someone would stop me and ask if I was Jeb Corliss. Each time it happened, I'd look at them and ask, "How do you know my name?" The strange thing is, each one would say something different. Some would be from documentaries I had done, others would be from news stories or YouTube. It was a bizarre experience, and after about the tenth time it happened that day, the producer from HBO asked me, "Jeb, does this happen often?"

I looked at him and said, "Not really. Once in a while, someone will ask if I'm 'that jumper guy' or think I look familiar, like someone they went to school with, but this is the first time people are saying my name."

He smiled, laughed, and said, "I had no idea you were so famous." I could tell he thought he was doing a story about a person and a sport no one had ever heard of, and he was surprised that I would be getting recognized in South Africa, of all places. I kind of had to agree with his sentiment though: it was strange.

Joby and I woke up early the next morning, ate a little breakfast, got in the car, and headed to meet the HBO team at the cable car station before it opened. We wanted to have an early start to get in as many jumps as possible before the winds picked up. As we pulled into the parking lot, everyone was already there waiting for us. Iiro, Frank, Christian, Jeff, and Tia, along with the HBO crew. We got on the first cable car to the top and set up as quickly as possible. It was early but already getting blisteringly hot. Putting on a black wingsuit made from nylon is not ideal in higher-temp conditions. The weather report was for the temperature to get over 100 degrees that day, and I believed it. All the cameras got set up and began rolling. Joby jumped first and had a perfect flight. Jeff was standing behind me and let me know he was rolling cameras. I gave him a ten-second call, did my countdown, and *bang*—I was off. We landed safely, Jeff got outstanding footage, and we packed up and did it again.

The next day, we did exactly the same thing, and by the fourth jump, the HBO crew said they had gotten everything they needed to tell an amazing story. They thanked us and then said they were heading out the next day. I told them I would be doing one more day of jumping at Table Mountain tomorrow before moving on to different flights around the country. They asked if it would be okay for their local cameraman to film a few more exits from different angles while we were jumping. I said, "Of course he can. No problem at all." That evening, we all said our goodbyes, and the HBO crew told me they would be in touch about getting the footage I'd been filming with my own cameras the last few days.

I woke up the following morning and just felt off. It took us a little longer to get out of the house that morning and we were a bit behind schedule. This day was supposed to be one of the hottest days on record, and with heat comes wind. I wanted to get to the mountain as fast as possible because the later it got, the more likely the winds would get too strong to jump. Unfortunately, we hit heavy traffic. It turned out to be the first day kids were heading back to school, so every family was on the road that morning. I realized this traffic was going to make us at least thirty to forty-five minutes late, and for some reason this agitated me in a way that it shouldn't have. By the time we got to the cable car, I was feeling unusually anxious.

The day before, I had asked our cameraman, Nic "Moose" Good, to hike up to a ledge located about halfway down the mountain that we had been flying over. I wanted him to set up target balloons six feet above the rocks at the edge of the ledge. I wanted to start practicing for my next project. I was planning on doing the first touch-and-go with a wingsuit in the French Alps six weeks later. I wanted to set the suit down in powder and then take off again. I also wanted to fly down a line of trees covered in snow, hitting the edge of their branches with the tips of my wings all the way down the proximity line. I hoped this would cause the snow to blast off the sides of the trees and get trapped in the vertices coming off the wingsuit to create a beautiful effect. I felt that practicing with balloon targets was a great way to train the type of precision necessary to pull off that project. Nic had agreed to set the balloon and film as I flew into the targets.

Moose was waiting in the parking lot, along with all my friends who had been coming to watch the jumps each day. I handed Moose a walkie talkie and he headed to the trailhead to begin the hike with a few friends to lend a hand. We all got on the cable car and started our way up the mountain. We were quite a bit behind schedule at this point and I felt we would be lucky to get one jump in before the winds inevitably picked up. As we got to the exit point, it was already way too hot. I called down to see if Moose had gotten into position.

"We're close," he replied. "I already put up the balloons, but we need about ten minutes to get the cameras ready." This was the cue for Joby, Jeff, and me to start gearing up. The place was so hot that my helmet burned my hands when I picked it up. It had been sitting in the sun and it was like touching a hot plate. I was so drenched with sweat that I felt like I had just stepped out of a shower, and putting on the wingsuit didn't help the situation one bit. Zero-porosity nylon, as the name implies, doesn't allow any air through at all, so it's kind of like putting yourself in a black plastic bag, in direct sunlight, when it's over one 115 degrees Fahrenheit. It wasn't a pleasant experience, and all I wanted to do was get off the mountain as quickly as possible. Luckily for me, the quickest way out was down.

Moose called up on the walkie and said he was ready. Joby stood on the edge, gave a ten-second call, and stepped off the mountain. He did a perfect exit with a flight directly over the balloons—just gorgeous—topping them by about five feet, and the shockwave from his suit made them dance wildly on their strings. At this point, Jeff and I were so hot it was becoming a problem and I called down to Moose telling him we had to go.

Moose called back and said, "Jeb, I don't think you should go for the balloons. The winds have picked up and they're blowing all over the place."

I called back down to Moose and said, "It's okay. I can see the balloons from here, and if they're moving too much, I'll just fly over the top."

"Alright," he replied. "Just...be careful, Jeb."

I gave him a thirty-second call to give me time to put the walkie talkie away. I waved at Frank and Iiro and checked in with Jeff to see if he was ready. He nodded. I gave ten seconds and started getting ready to jump. I looked down and thought I could see the balloons off in the distance, but they were tiny and I couldn't see any movement. I figured I would get a better view of them as I got closer, so I jumped off the mountain. The heat was getting so bad I could barely breathe in my helmet; I was desperate for the air to start moving. As my speed picked up, I started diving towards the ledge off in the distance. The balloons came into view and I could clearly make out two of them: one silver and one black.

I focused on the black balloon and got total object fixation.

My vision became like a tunnel.

The black balloon became all there was, all there ever would be.

Everything else disappeared from my vision. I was going to hit that balloon at all costs. As I watched it approach, I could tell I was going to hit my target perfectly—when out of nowhere, *BANG!*

Impact.

I was suddenly tumbling, extreme pain slamming through my body like a shockwave. I instantly knew I had gone in. I had just impacted flat, solid granite at terminal velocity. I could already tell my legs were destroyed. I knew—I didn't think, *I knew for a fact*—I was dead. There was a zero percent chance of survival. I had watched Dwain make this exact same mistake and he was severed in half. I'd be dead in a heartbeat. The only surprise was that I wasn't dead already. How could I still be having thoughts?

Time distorted, making seconds feel like minutes. My mind instantly split into two different frames of perception. One was a survival instinct built directly into my DNA; the other was more of a philosophical conversation with myself. The survival side was trying to work out everything necessary to survive. The black balloon had been blown by the wind to a lower ledge, shortening the string from six feet to only a few inches off the ground. This lower ledge created an optical illusion that made the first ledge invisible to my eye, and I couldn't tell the balloon was lying atop flat rock. In order to hit the balloon, I had to hit the first ledge with my legs just above my thighs. After impacting solid granite at over 120 mph with my legs, I bounced and began tumbling over the lip of the lower ledge.

Regaining control of a tumbling wingsuit can sometimes take hundreds of feet, but somehow the years of acrobatic training kicked in and I corrected the tumbling with only a few flips and twists. My left foot had impacted a boulder as I came in to get the black balloon and it had torn apart my wingsuit on the left side. This created asymmetry in the suit that led to it trying to pull me back into the mountain. The survival part of my mind automatically adjusted for the new aerodynamic shape and shifted all my weight to the right to keep me flying as straight as circumstances would allow. My survival instinct could see that I had a series of ledges I needed to clear before I could deploy a canopy safely. You have to remember: this was all happening with two destroyed legs in searing pain.

As the survival part of my mind was working through all this, the other part of my mind was undergoing an existential conversation. I knew I had just impacted at terminal velocity. This was a 100 percent fatal accident. I had witnessed several friends die in similar situations. There was no chance for survival. I felt I only had two choices: Option One—I could deploy a parachute, land somewhere at the bottom of the mountain, and bleed to death in a slow, agonizing way as I waited for a helicopter rescue that would certainly be too late to save me; or Option Two—I could decide not to pull and fly headfirst into the ground at maximum velocity, ensuring an instant and hopefully painless death.

To put this into perspective for you, imagine someone was pointing a gun at you and told you they were going to kill you. You had two choices. They could shoot you in the head, ending it quickly, or they could shoot you in the gut and watch you die slowly. Either way, you're going to die.

This was not an easy decision to make.

In that moment, the part of my mind that had been doing all the important calculations in the background started screaming at me. It shouted, "This is the time to decide! You open now or you die—NOW!" I decided the only thing that mattered was time. If I could get ten more seconds out of this life, I wanted it...even if those moments were nothing but suffering. You see, time (and therefore life) equals infinite possibilities. Death equals the end of all possibilities.

My decision was made.

I deployed my parachute and it opened with heavy line twists. I had a 1.5-second canopy ride before impacting the side of the mountain at high speed right next to a hiking trail. I was able to get my legs out in front of me to take the brunt of the impact, protecting my spine, but they had already suffered so much damage that this only shattered them further.

I quickly regretted my decision to pull. Pain was all I could feel; not regular, everyday pain, but mind-crushing agony. There was no room for anything else. I lay there with my eyes closed, just trying to take my next breath. That was all I could do. With each breath, a new shudder of suffering pulsed through my body. Distantly, I felt the sun beating down on me and realized it felt like I was being cooked alive. My mind was shrieking in torment, but I remained silent. I couldn't even build the strength to cry; I was completely broken, cracked to my core.

Voices drifted through the air around me. A woman and a man approached me from the nearby trail. I couldn't see them because I couldn't open my eyes, but I knew they were there. I could feel their presence. They were two hikers who had happened to see the accident and came to help. At first, I couldn't answer their questions, but after a little while, I was able to tell them my name.

"Jeb," said the woman, "are your legs broken?"

I said, "Yes, one hundred percent sure they are smashed to bits." They gave me water and tried to cover me with my canopy to keep the sun off me. The woman kept telling me not to fall asleep, but I couldn't answer them anymore: the effort was too much. I could hear panic in their voices when I eventually stopped responding, but nothing seemed to matter.

It's hard for me to judge time. I'm unsure of who got to me first. I remained conscious but my mind was clouded, disconnected. My eyes were sealed shut because it was too painful to open them. The only images I have from the accident come from videos that were taken at the time. Most of my memories are of sounds, voices, and pain. I can remember hearing Moose, his voice strained as he tried to move me. When Jeff got to me, he began cutting the wingsuit off my body to reveal the damage to my legs, and I heard his sharp intake of breath as the suit came free. I remember telling him to stop what he was doing and get a camera to film. He thought I was insane, but I knew this needed to be documented. It was really the only coherent thought I had at the time.

I found out later it took between sixty and eighty minutes from the time of impact before the paramedics got to me. Even though Table Mountain is in the middle of Cape Town, my location was difficult to access. They needed to do a long-line rescue from the bottom of a helicopter to pull me off the side of the mountain, and those can be tricky.

I heard the helicopter hovering above me, then came the voices of paramedics talking with Iiro, Jeff, and Moose. I began feeling them try to move me and I started screaming. Someone said they had to give me something for the pain, but I refused. I didn't want painkillers; I wanted to have the experience without being clouded by drugs. I found out years later, when I finally saw a documentary about the accident, that Iiro and Jeff had pulled the paramedics aside and told them to just give me the drugs anyway. I was upset when I saw this. I'm anti-drugs and I deserved the experience I was having. They took that pure experience away from me, without my consent, and I'm still pissed about that to this day. I can no longer be sure how much of what I experienced was real or drug-induced. They gave me the drugs for themselves, not for me. They didn't like hearing me scream. I say, put a stick in my mouth and move me anyway. If you don't like my screaming, put earplugs in, you bunch of pussies.

I had been baking in the sun for over an hour and was extremely dehydrated. All I wanted was water to drink, but the paramedics said that was no longer possible. They explained I was going to need to go directly into surgery when I got to the hospital, and I couldn't have liquid in my stomach. So, they quickly put in an IV to get liquids in me and, as I found out later, to pump drugs into me without my knowledge.

The paramedics put me on a backboard and then into an orange sled. They placed the sled in a fabric sling that hooked to a cable system attached to the helicopter. I can remember the feeling of being hoisted off the ground and floating under the chopper as it took me to an ambulance waiting in a nearby parking lot.

While in the ambulance, my mind became even more clouded. I was drifting from being conscious to somewhere deep in my mind. I was aware of what was going on around me but almost like it was happening off in the distance. There were periods of time that I could hear what people were saying, but I just didn't want to answer them. I think they took this as me being unconscious, so they began saying things I don't think I was intended to hear. As the ambulance pulled away, I heard one of the paramedics working to keep me stable say, "This looks like a double amputation."

Hearing those words did something strange to me. I had thought up to this point that I was absolutely going to die. I felt like I was just going through the motions and, at any moment, everything was going to turn off like a switch and I'd be gone. When I heard them say "double amputation" I thought, *Does that mean I may not die?* It hadn't dawned on me that was even a possibility. Most people would have heard this and been horrified, but to me, it meant there may actually be hope of living. I thought, *Man, if I get to live with two amputated legs, think of all the reading I can catch up on.* I was so excited at the prospect of living that I could barely contain myself. Of course, no one else could see this because I was in an almost-comatose state physically, but mentally I was exploding. An overwhelming sense of joy flowed through me. I had just made the worst mistake a person could possibly make—a fatal mistake that had already killed many of my friends—and somehow, miraculously, I was going to get another chance at life.

As we pulled into the emergency area of the Christian Barnard Hospital, they quickly admitted me and started doing extensive tests and x-rays to see what the damage was. I don't remember this part very well because I think I may have been out during this process, but I do remember lying in a dark room all by myself with a door ajar. I could hear doctors and nurses talking in the next room. I heard a male voice say, "I can't believe his legs aren't shattered."

A man then turned on the lights as he walked in the room. He introduced himself as my doctor and started explaining the damage I had sustained.

"You must be the single luckiest human being on the face of this planet," he began. "To survive an accident like that is remarkable just by itself. But let's talk about your damage: you have a minor fracture in your left fibula and left ankle. Those won't need anything more than bed rest to heal. You have a fracture in your right foot that will need surgery. We have to place two screws to secure a small bone. You have a gaping hole in your right shin that will need surgery to remove shredded muscle, and skin grafting to close the wound. We are pretty sure you have a blown ACL in your left knee but won't know for sure till after we put you under for surgery and can get a better look at it. The biggest issue you're facing, and the reason you'll be in the ICU for the next couple of days, is because of the serious soft-tissue damage to your thighs. Your quadriceps have been badly damaged. They were crushed as you impacted the rock, and the muscle separated from the bone. Your kidneys are now trying to process the significant tissue damage. That, combined with the dehydration, is causing your kidneys to shut down. This is the most life-threatening issue you're facing at the moment."

This was when it dawned on me for the first time: I really wasn't going to die!

"Will I walk again?" I asked, honestly curious if he'd claim anything positive.

He smiled and said, "Jeb, aside from the hole in your shin and the kidney issues you're experiencing, we would have been able to send you home today. Not only are you going to walk again, but you can expect a full recovery."

As his words registered, all I could say was, "You can't be serious."

He smiled and said, "Yes, I am. You are going to have a long road back, but you will recover."

He then explained the ACL was probably going to take the longest, but out of all the bad things I could have done to my knee, the ACL was the best. The surgeries to repair an ACL were tried and true. Athletes get them every day. That's the one thing you could completely sever in your knee and come back just as strong as you were before.

It's impossible for me to express how this made me feel. I had gone from knowing I was going to die, to thinking I was going to have a double amputation, to hearing I would have a full recovery. The emotions were overwhelming, and it may have been the happiest moment of my entire life. I felt joy radiate and tingle through my body. I smiled so big the doctor looked at me like I was insane.

At that moment, a woman walked in and introduced herself as the head of media relations for the hospital. She apologized for bothering me at such a sensitive time but explained she needed me to make a statement to the press.

"What are you talking about?" I asked. "A statement to the press? How does anyone even know I'm here?"

She said, "This was on the news before you even got picked up by the life flight. People filmed it with their cell phones and it's already online. The instant you got admitted, I started receiving hundreds of inquiries from press from all over the world asking about your condition. Dozens of local media started showing up and have been trying to gain access to you by pretending to be your mother, sister, best friends, and so on. I've never seen anything like it."

"I'm not really up to making statements at the moment."

She then explained, "Jeb, I know you are in pain, but please give me something to tell them. They won't stop until they get something."

I responded with, "Okay, tell them this is the greatest day of my life."

She looked at me sideways in disbelief and said, "What are you talking about? How could this possibly be the best day of your life?"

"I just had a fatal accident. I survived something you can't survive and somehow, miraculously, I'm going to recover from it. I have been given a second chance at living my life, and if that isn't a great day, then I don't know what a great day is."

She nodded in understanding and walked out of the room to deliver the message.

The doctor introduced me to a plastic surgeon named Mark van der Velde. I asked why I needed a plastic surgeon. Mark explained that the gaping hole in my right shin was going to need skin grafting and the damage was greater than he'd dealt with in the past. The closest thing he had seen was when a man had gotten his leg trapped in the header of a combine harvester. It was going to be challenging to remove the dead muscle from the living tissue because it was all shredded together. It kind of looked like guts were hanging out of my shin. The hardest part would be performing the surgery without destroying my ability to use the foot properly, and a plastic surgeon was the best type of doctor for this kind of work. Not only did he want to make it functional but also make it look like a leg again.

Mark explained I would be going into surgery in the next fifteen minutes, and when I woke up, I would be in the ICU. I would probably be in there for a couple of days while they watched my kidney functions. They injected my IV with something and asked me to count backwards from ten. I remember getting to about eight before I woke up in a different bed with an uncomfortable catheter attached to me. As my eyes opened, a nurse walked over and injected something into my IV and I asked her what it was. She told me she was giving me morphine for the pain. I looked at her and said, "I don't want anything for the pain. Do not inject me with morphine again."

She looked at me and said, "Doctor's orders," and walked away.

For the next two days, I was in a constant battle to stop the nurse from giving me morphine. I kept saying no and she kept giving it anyway. This infuriated me. By day three, I had finally built up enough physical strength that when she approached me with the needle, I said, "If you come within an arm's length of me with that needle, I will punch you in the face."

She looked at me in shock and said, "Now, that isn't very nice."

I responded with, "I am not a nice person. I have every right to say no to using drugs and you do not have a right to force me to use them against my will."

"Well," she said, "it's up to the doctor, not you, so I'll just go get him."

"Go get the doctor and I'll tell him exactly what I just told you. I am done being injected with that shit."

Sure enough, the doctor walked up a few moments later and asked what the problem was. I told him I had been saying no to morphine for two days and they had no right to force me to use drugs for pain.

"No," he tried to explain, "the dose is recomm—"

"Horse shit," I said. "I don't want it and you are not to give it to me anymore. I have a right to go through this with a clear mind."

You could tell he got exasperated, but he said, "Fine, no more morphine. But you still need to take the anti-inflammatory drugs. We have to bring the swelling down in your legs."

I had to agree with him there: my legs didn't look human. They were so swollen you couldn't even see a knee. They kind of looked like elephant legs.

So, I said, "Okay. I will take drugs that actually help cure a problem. I won't take anything that just covers up symptoms."

"Fair enough," the doctor said, and that was the end of me being forced to use drugs for pain.

I will say this: I have never had drugs pushed on me harder than in the hospital. Not in school, not hanging out with people, not even at the occasional party. Every single morning and every single evening, a nurse would hand me a little cup with painkillers in it and tell me to take them and I would have to deny them. I kept telling her to stop offering me painkillers and she just said, "I have to offer them to you every morning and every evening. It's my job."

I can see why the opioid epidemic has gotten so out of hand. If I weren't a crazy person who wanted to experience my own pain, I would have gotten hooked for sure. It would have been impossible to avoid after six weeks of pills twice a day. Everyone just wants to be comfortable, but they often fail to recognize that comfort is their enemy. The nurses want you to be sedated because it makes their job easier and they don't have to put up with you making noise or being difficult.

After some recovery time, my kidneys finally stabilized and I was moved to a private room. As they wheeled me in, I looked out the window and saw Table Mountain. The hospital staff thought it would be funny to give me a view of the mountain that almost ate me. I have to be honest: it did make me smile.

Shortly after they moved me to my new room, Mark the plastic surgeon came in to check on everything. He took the bandages off the skin graft and instantly his face scrunched up in a way that said something was wrong. I looked down and even I could tell it didn't look right. About 1/3 of the area was discolored and looked like it was rotting.

Mark immediately left the room for a few minutes, and when he returned, he said, "We need to get you back into surgery right away. I tried to leave as much muscle as possible to keep mobility of the foot, but it was hard to tell which tissues were alive or dead. There must have been some dead tissue that prevented the skin graft from adhering. I'll have to remove the part of the skin graft that didn't take and check out what's going on." A few nurses walked in and injected something in my IV without a word. Within seconds, I was unconscious.

I woke up in the same room I had passed out in. The only reason I knew anything had happened was because something new was attached to my shin that was making a strange sound. I looked down at it and had no idea what I was looking at. Mark walked in and said, "Good, you're awake. We had to remove more dead tissue and that exposed the bone. We can't skin graft directly to bone, so we had to move some of the flesh from around the bone to the top. We have placed a vacuum dressing on the wound that will slowly, over time, cover the bone with tissue we can then graft to."

"How long are we talking here?" I asked.

"It's a slow process," he explained, "and will probably take a week or two. We will need to leave the wound open and change the dressing daily."

The thing about the damage to my legs was that I couldn't roll over; I always had to be on my back in bed. I couldn't roll onto my side or get to my belly. I was unable to stand up or go to the bathroom. It was uncomfortable to be immobilized like that. As I have said before, if hell existed it would involve bedpans and salsa dancing. Those are my two most hated things. I was now going to have to deal with the bed pan for weeks and it brought real tears to my eyes. There is nothing more humiliating than having to ring a little bell to have other people help you take a poo. It's truly horrible.

For the first couple of weeks, Iiro and friends would come visit every day and bring me lunch from an amazing Thai restaurant just around the corner, which I loved. The hospital food was barely edible on a good day, so these visits with food were greatly appreciated. But after a couple of weeks, Iiro had to go home, along with all the rest of my friends, and I stopped getting visitors. This shifted my mood quite a bit.

It's a strange thing to be alone all day, every day, for weeks on end with no idea how much longer you'll be stuck in this small box. It gives you a lot of time to think and puts your mind in a strange, awkward place. One night I was lying in bed when something scary dawned on me. Up until this point, I had never really believed surviving BASE jumping was a possibility. I knew what I was doing was dangerous and would eventually lead to my death, one way or another. When I got into the sport, I had given myself five years to live—at best—and my retirement plan was death before thirty.

There I was, lying in a bed at thirty-six, and it occurred to me that I had somehow lived past thirty. The five-year mark had come and gone without me even noticing. I had more than tripled my allotted time of survival in the sport and my retirement plan had failed. I had this twisted way of thinking at the time that I didn't need to worry about saving money, and I felt if I died with money in the bank I would have failed at life. My goal was to die with nothing, having spent everything I had towards turning this dream into reality.

But this accident put a horrifying thought in my mind that had never crossed it before: *What will I do if I don't die?* I had just impacted solid granite at over 120 mph and survived. What if I kept surviving and lived to be forty, or fifty? God forbid, what if I lived to be sixty?

As odd as it sounds, this was the first time I'd thought about any of this. I had always accepted that I'd die young, but now, lying there in a hospital bed all alone for weeks on end, I realized maybe I stood a chance at surviving. The concept shook me to my core. I knew the way I was living my life wasn't conducive to long-term survival. I didn't own a house. I hadn't saved even one penny for the future. My entire existence was about burning all my resources as I got them. I finally understood I had the mind of a child. I was being unrealistic about my life and everything in it. I needed to prepare for the eventuality of surviving to old age because there is nothing scarier than getting to sixty and being destitute. At this point, I had zero regrets in life, but I knew if I lived to be sixty and had thrown away all my wealth when I was young, I would seriously regret that. Also, how much longer could I earn a living doing the things I was doing? This work had a limited shelf life, but maybe I could squeeze another five or ten years out of it? Maybe?

This started me thinking about how my mind was in paradox: I had strange, opposing forces fighting in my head. I was happy with my life and had been for over a decade. I wanted to live but I understood what I did was dangerous and was going to kill me. The thing that gave my life purpose was the very thing that was going to end it. I would try to justify this by thinking I was going to die anyway, even if I stopped. But that's where this accident changed things. It made me understand that time is what mattered. Yes, I was going to die anyway, but how amazing would it be to live two or three more decades? My grandfather lived into his nineties and that had been unthinkable for me before. I had needed to do dangerous things when I was young to help me overcome some dark impulses, but all that no longer seemed necessary. My darkness was gone.

Another thought entered my mind: *Maybe I was taking this all too literally, and deep down it was something more abstract.* Samurai warriors accepted they were going to die before every battle in order to shed their fear of it. Once death became inevitable and they accepted their fate, it freed them to focus their thoughts on the task at hand. This gave them the best chance to accomplish their goal. Maybe accepting my own mortality helped me do the things I did. It sounds suicidal, but really, it's more of a mental exercise that helps a person cope with doing extreme things. I wasn't sure, but I could feel myself growing and my mind seemed to be changing its root programming.

After weeks of the vacuum dressing sucking flesh over bone, it was finally time to do another skin graft. They put me under again and took even more dead muscle out, but this time the skin graft took. They were able to pull just enough flesh over the bone to get it to stick. There was a small problem, though: the donor site on my thigh where they had taken the first skin graft had gotten a small infection in it. The doctor was worried about using antibiotics at this stage of my recovery, so he decided to scrape the infection out while I was under. This would prove to be a mistake and would become a huge issue down the road, but it seemed like the best option at the time.

When I woke from surgery, I was in the most extreme pain I had ever felt (and that's saying something). It was strange because I hadn't thought it was possible to feel more pain than I had already been through, but this sensation was on a whole different level—it was like being branded. Imagine the moment that red-hot metal touches your skin and the flesh sizzles, but somehow the nerves don't die, and that searing feeling just continues nonstop for days. When they took the skin graft, they used a metal planer that looks kind of like a deli meat slicer, and they just flayed off my skin one pass at a time. They took the top two layers of skin, called the epidermis and dermis, leaving the lower layers with all the nerves exposed.

The next few weeks were painful, but I was recovering. At the four-week mark, I was finally getting up from bed and doing small walks down the hall with the use of crutches. They would make me wear these giant plastic boots to immobilize my ankles because the fractures were not weightbearing yet. I had lost a lot of weight and was down to 164 lbs. I am six feet, two and a half inches tall and usually weigh around 190 lbs. My legs looked like sticks and I hadn't had anything more than a sponge bath in a month. I didn't look or smell very good, if you get what I'm saying.

The doctor came in my room to check on me and I asked him how much longer I would have to stay in the hospital. He looked at the skin graft on my shin and said it was doing well and I should be able to travel in a week. He then looked at my thigh where the donor site for the first graft was taken and said it wasn't looking good.

He said, "When you get home, you'll need to find a wound care specialist and have them monitor that donor sight closely. I'm not sure the skin will actually grow back. I may have scraped it too deeply trying to remove all the infection."

"Wait," I said, "what do you mean?"

"You may need to get another skin graft to cover the donor site," he replied. I laughed because I thought he was joking. He didn't smile and said, "I am not joking; this donor site isn't looking good, and if it gets infected again, it could kill you. Wounds should not be open this long."

A week later, I was on a plane back to California. I was weak and traveling alone, but I needed to get home. I couldn't sit in that hospital room all alone any longer. I was starting to lose my mind.

CHAPTER TWENTY-SEVEN

RECOVERY FROM HELL

My mother and little sister Scarlett picked me up from the Palm Springs Airport. Scarlett had bought the house my grandparents lived in for almost sixty years, and that's where I stayed during my recovery. My home in Venice, CA, wasn't going to work because it had stairs, and it would be a while before I'd be able to use those. I was in a wheelchair at this point, and it was looking like I'd be in it for a while. Still, I was alive, and that's all that mattered to me.

I found a rehab center close to where Scarlett lived and started the following week, wanting to get back on my feet as soon as possible. It's funny; when you have such a strong passion for something like BASE jumping, all you can think about is recovering so you can get back to doing it. BASE once again became my whole purpose in getting better. For better or worse, it remained my motivation for everything. I'd get small glimpses of life without needing it, but then it would come rushing back to completely consume all my thoughts.

Taking showers was difficult, if not impossible. I couldn't get my thigh wet, so I had to buy these odd plastic covers to try and keep it dry. But when I went to rehab, the recovery therapy made me sweat, and it got damp. After a week went by, I started noticing an odd smell. I went to a doctor in the area and he had a look at it. He gave me a referral to a wound specialist in Palm Desert, but I couldn't go until it was cleared by my insurance, which took over a week. By the time I got to the specialist, the smell had grown worse and my leg was starting to swell.

I was out of the wheelchair by this time and walked into the wound care clinic on crutches. I signed in and they handed me a bunch of paperwork to fill out. I gave them my insurance card and it took another forty-five minutes to be called in by a nurse after handing the receptionist what felt like a written exam. The nurse sat me in a room and the doctor came in shortly after. He asked me what had happened, and I explained in the briefest way possible the last seven weeks of my life. I explained the donor site had not healed in that time, and over the last week it had begun to smell quite bad.

"You say it smells?" he asked with a look of concern. He leaned down and smelled my leg and his nose scrunched up with disgust. He put on a set of rubber gloves and pulled up the corner of the bandage to take a look. As he saw the wound, he instantly put it back down and asked me to wait there. He opened the door and left in great haste. When he returned, he had two other people with him and they were now wearing masks and wore scrubs covering their bodies. No skin was exposed.

The specialist removed the bandage and all of them made a sound that told me this was bad. He took swabs of the wound and put them in little clear tubs. He handed the tubes to one of the people by his side and they left the room in great haste. The doctor looked at me and said, "Jeb, this is bad. I'm not sure what this is and won't know till the cultures come back, but it looks like MRSA. If that's what this is, your life is in danger. If this infection gets into your bloodstream, it can kill you. We're going to start you on intravenous antibiotics today. You will come in seven days a week for at least one hour a day till we wipe this infection out. We're going to start you on one of the only antibiotics that has shown success against MRSA: it's called Tygacil. Lots of people have strong negative reactions to this antibiotic but it may be your best chance and beating this infection."

I asked, "Do I need to start today? Could I start tomorrow?"

He looked at me and said, "Jeb, I don't know what this infection is, but if it's MRSA you could lose your leg. This looks like a serious infection, so you must treat it seriously."

They escorted me to a room with about twenty chairs all lined up in a semicircle. Each chair had a person sitting in it with an IV sticking out of their arm leading to a bag filled with drugs. Most of them were cancer patients getting their chemotherapy. Others were fighting infections like me and hooked up to heavy antibiotics. They sat me in the only free chair and a nurse quickly put an IV in my arm and hung a bag on a hook above my head. I looked at the bag and it said "Tigecycline" on the side. It took about an hour for the bag to empty into my body, but it didn't take long for me to start feeling nauseous.

As I hobbled to my car, I felt like I was going to throw up. My balance didn't feel right. I started getting violently ill. When I got to my sister's house, I was barely able to get from my car to her front door. The feeling of nausea was the most extreme version of this sensation I had ever felt. The light hurt my eyes and all I wanted to do was go into a dark room and sleep.

The next day, I drove myself back to the wound care center and they hooked me up to another bag of that evil stuff. I told the nurse how horrible it was making me feel and she explained how that was a normal side effect of Tygacil; over 90 percent of people who use it get extremely nauseous. She prescribed me an anti-nausea medication and said it would help. I picked it up on the drive home, hoping it would help me with this horrible feeling. The nausea was so intense I didn't know what to do. I couldn't believe this was a normal reaction.

This time when I got home, I couldn't walk to my sister's door—I crawled there. I slid across the concrete like a lizard on my belly, groaning with every movement. When my sister saw me on the ground, she went and got my wheelchair and helped me to the guest room. That night everything deteriorated horribly. All my muscles contracted and went into spasms. The pain again ratcheted to a new level. I went blind; I could no longer see. I had to go to the bathroom but I wasn't sure how I was going to get there. I became desperate. The combination of pain, nausea, and blindness made me feel for the first time like I wished I had died at Table Mountain. I truly wanted to give up. If I had a gun, I would have killed myself—that's how horrible it was. This wasn't life; this was something so awful that all I wanted was to die.

After I somehow made it through the night, the next day my sister had to drive me to my wound care appointment. As she pushed me in, the nurse instantly contacted the doctor. They took me into a room, where I explained how bad the side effects were. Lucky for me, the cultures had finally come back, and it wasn't MRSA. So, they would be able to take me off the Tygacil, but the doctor said it was still an antibiotic-resistant bacterium. He told me to think of it as MRSA's evil sister: not as bad, but still not good. They were going to try a different antibiotic that my body would hopefully be able to handle better.

After an hour on the new IV, they started me on hyperbaric chamber sessions in hopes that it would help my wounds heal faster, having had some success using the chamber with ulcerated skin wounds that weren't responding to other treatments. The chambers were in the building right next door, so it was a short trip to reach them. They had two chambers side by side that looked like large glass tubes with huge metal doors on either end. Each one had knobs and dials all over the place. I had heard of these chambers in my early scuba diving days and knew they were used to help people with decompression sickness but had never known them to be used in this fashion. They gave me a cloth gown and told me to go to a dressing room and change, explaining it was too dangerous for me to wear my own clothes in the chamber. I wasn't allowed to take any electronics or even books in the chamber with me. They were going to pump pure oxygen and take me to 1.5 atmospheres of pressure. They said if anything were to make a spark while I was in there, the whole thing would explode. Even a static electric charge from my clothing could ignite a powerful burst of energy.

This was all supposed to be beneficial for my body's healing process. I would come here after my IV infusion five days a week and do forty-five-minute sessions in the tank. They said it would enrich my red blood cells with oxygen to promote healing. It seemed strange to me, but I did feel a lot better after my first session. I noticed when I got out of the chamber that I could see my blood vessels at the surface of my skin like little red blossoms. They looked strange and I asked the attendee about it as I came out of the dressing room.

"All normal," she told me.

At this point, the wound on my thigh had been open for over seven weeks. If we couldn't get the wound to heal, then getting rid of the infection wouldn't matter. As long as that wound stayed open, I would keep getting infections until one finally killed me. On my next visit to the infusion center, I asked how long it was going to take for my wound to heal. They said, "It shouldn't take more than two weeks."

I had to stop doing rehab on my legs because the sweat was not good for the wound; I had to keep the area dry. This upset me because I knew how important rehab was. My legs had serious damage, and without rehabbing them properly, I wouldn't be able to return to my normal life. This wound on my leg was a huge issue and it was holding back my progress in a damaging way.

Two weeks went by and the wound on my leg still wasn't any better. They had changed my antibiotics three times and had to install a PICC line in my upper chest near my neck. The regular IV was starting to collapse all the veins in my arms and they needed a more long-term solution. With the new delivery method, they also started me on another new antibiotic, and this one needed blood tests twice a week because it tended to cause kidney damage.

As I was sitting in my chair for the hour it took to get the bag of poison in me, I noticed an older woman sitting in the chair next to me. She was completely bald, so I figured she was fighting cancer. I saw them plug into a line going to her chest and the bag of liquid read, "Tygacil." I said, "Oh my, I am so sorry. That stuff is horrible."

She looked at me and said, "Yes, this is the worst thing I have ever had put in my body. I have been on chemotherapy for months now, and it's nothing compared to this stuff. I hate it."

Another two weeks went by and, as the doctor inspected my wound, he said the infection was finally getting better, but the skin wasn't showing any signs of growing back. I asked him what we should do. He said there was something new called an "Apligraf" where they harvest stem cells from baby foreskins and grow them into billions of similar cells in labs. Once the infection was finally knocked completely out, they could put an Apligraf over the open area and the stem cells would become skin cells, promoting growth of my own cells. I asked how soon he could do the procedure, and he gave me a smirk and said, "Probably two weeks."

"You always say two weeks," I pointed out. "Why is that?"

He smiled and said, "One of these times, I'll be right."

It took four more weeks before the infection was finally well enough to do the Apligraf. It had been almost three months of intravenous antibiotics one hour a day for seven days a week. I had been through eight different kinds of the most powerful antibiotics known to man, and I had spent forty-five-minutes a day for five days a week in a hyperbaric chamber. I was so ready for some actual progress as they put the Apligraf on.

"How long till we know if it worked?" I asked.

The doctor gave me a knowing look and replied with a smile, "About two weeks."

I told him, "You say 'two weeks' because it's an amount of time the patient won't get too upset about, don't you?"

He looked at me and said, "Yes. We're never sure how long these things will take, and two weeks makes the patient feel like it's not too far away. Sometimes we're right, though, and it turns out to be two weeks."

Two weeks later, the Apligraf had not taken. There was a little new skin growth, but not enough to be considered a success.

I asked what we should do.

The doctor said, "We should do another Apligraf. This one didn't take, but I believe it's the correct direction to go."

Each Apligraf cost $6,000 and was not covered by insurance. I had to pay out of pocket, but I didn't know what else to do. I said, "Okay," and the next week they did a second Apligraf.

Luckily for me, this one took. Finally, the doctor's prediction of two weeks came true, and the wound began to heal. It had been open since January 12, 2012, and it was now May 22—more than four months to finally start closing the wound on my thigh. It would still take another month before I could take a normal shower or go swimming, but we had finally gotten the skin to start growing back and everything was going to be okay.

After all that, I was able to begin rehab on my legs again. I went back to physical therapy and started training three hours a day for seven days a week. I still didn't have an ACL in my left leg, and the doctors told me I needed to do something called "prehab" before I went into surgery. It was important for the leg to be as strong as possible before the surgery, since that would make rehab after surgery go much faster and provide better results.

I knew I needed to work as soon as I could manage; I couldn't take an entire year off. I still had to earn a living, and at this point, I had sponsors that made up a large part of my income. If I didn't do something that year, I was most likely going to lose them. So, I decided to get as strong as possible before the summer ended and get in as many paying projects as I could before going into surgery for my ACL that coming fall. That would give me the winter to go through rehab and hopefully be close to 100 percent for the next summer. I got two of the best knee braces on the market, hoping they would hold my knees together long enough to get to the surgery that winter.

My first trip back to work was to film a commercial for Red Bull China in Beijing. I was still too injured to jump but they wanted to film interviews for an ad campaign to promote a new wingsuit competition called the World Wingsuit League. My cave flight had become something of a sensation in China, and Red Bull wanted to do more. Iiro and Frank had asked if I would come help them promote this new venture, and even though I was still bleeding from my thigh, I agreed. Going to China with an open wound was scary because infections were still a huge problem for me, and China wasn't exactly the most hygienic place on Earth. Every single day I had to remove the dressings and clean the wound. Blood would pour down my leg and the wound looked like something out of a horror film. I needed to cover it with this special silicone mesh and put all kinds of medical-grade cleaners on it. If it were to get infected again, I could end up back where I started and I didn't want that. The trip was nerve wracking.

After the wound finally stopped bleeding, I was able to do a series of jumping projects. One was a documentary about my recovery for a new 3D network owned by the Discovery called 3Net. They titled it *Wingsuit Warriors: Jeb Corliss vs. The World* and my buddy Joby was the one who sold the project. We headed back to Africa to try and get permission to jump off Table Mountain again so I could face my demons (or some bullshit like that). The park service laughed at us and told us they would never give permission for me to jump there. But when the cameras were off, they said I could go ahead and jump it, they just couldn't give me written approval. Unfortunately, we needed written approval for legal reasons, so we ended up just finding another jump outside the national park to finish the documentary. I did two jumps that went well, but the landings were tricky with my legs. I couldn't stay on my feet for either landing, and I could tell my legs were too weak to take a bad landing.

From there I headed to Europe, where I had promised my buddy Luigi to film a traveling documentary show before I had been injured. I wasn't sure if I was ready for a project like that, but I had made a promise and I do my best to keep my word. Luigi was shooting ten episodes doing different jumps across Switzerland, Italy, and France. By episode three, I had almost broken myself three different times and I knew I wasn't going to be able to continue jumping till after I got my ACL surgery. My body was too weak and couldn't handle all the hard landings. I was tapped out.

In the middle of this project, I got a message from Iiro about the World Wingsuit League saying they needed me to compete in the event. He explained that I had become a bit of a celebrity, and if I didn't compete, Red Bull China wouldn't sponsor the event. I responded with how injured I was and that there was no way I was in any shape to compete in a race with other pilots. Landing on asphalt just wasn't something my legs could handle. Plus, flying in airplanes was bad for my recovery. My legs blew up like balloons after every flight. I wasn't sure why they were swelling so badly, but it made me feel uncomfortable. I said, "I may be able to come if you guys fly me business class so I can lie down during the flight," but even that would be a challenge. I just didn't know how I'd be able to do it at this stage of my recovery.

I won't go into details here, but let's just say Iiro said things to me he shouldn't have. His words left lasting scars on our friendship, and I came close to never speaking to him again. He had seen my social media posts and didn't realize I had been painting a rosier picture of my situation for my sponsors. So, he felt I was acting like a little bitch. I explained how bad things really were, and when he understood how serious it was, he apologized and we were able to diffuse the situation. I agreed to come and jump in the competition as much as I could. I explained it may only be one or two jumps, and there was no way I was going to be competitive. I wasn't in any position to be jumping, but Frank and Iiro needed me to get the project funded, so I had to suck it up and take one for the team.

I went to China and competed in the first ever WWL grand prix, and sure enough, I almost got injured on every jump. I had them put a thick rubber mat on the road to land on, but even with that, my body couldn't handle landing on asphalt. My left knee was on the edge of exploding every time I set down, but at least the event got funded and a new competitive sport was born.

When I got home from China, I made an appointment with a top ACL specialist in Los Angeles and got the surgery as fast as I could. ACL reconstructions are not complicated surgeries, but they have long recovery times. It takes a minimum of six months before you should return to sports, and that's if you do everything perfectly during your rehab. But in most cases, it takes a year before you should return to high-impact activities.

There are many ways to fix a torn ACL. You can use tendon from a cadaver, which most doctors don't recommend if you're a professional athlete. They are four times more likely to fail when going back to sport. Most high-end sports surgeons recommend you use tendon from another part of your own body. The two most common places to harvest this tendon is either from your hamstring in your thigh or the patellar tendon in your knee. My doctor explained the hamstring would be the strongest over time, whereas the patellar would heal faster. With the patellar, they take chips of bone from both sides of the tendon, meaning there's bone-to-bone healing. The hamstring is pulled through holes drilled through your knee. You have to wait for the drilled holes in your bone to slowly close up and pinch the hamstring in place. This takes longer, but because of the hamstring's elasticity, it holds up better under stress once it's completely healed.

I decided to use my own hamstring and went in for surgery on October 29, 2012. The procedure only took a few hours and I was sent home the same day. I spent a week on bed rest, only getting up to go to the bathroom. They gave me a strange machine that would bend my knee automatically for hours each day. It started at a thirty-degree angle, and each day I was to add ten degrees to the machine until my next appointment with the doctor a week later. I also had to put the heel of my foot across an open space on a coffee table and let the leg hang, using gravity to pull it towards the ground for fifteen minutes three times a day. Apparently, the ACL graft tends to shrink and lock your knee if you don't stretch it in this manner. It was a long process, but easy to handle after nearly dying.

Once I saw the doctor again, he explained how the surgery was a success and I would now need to do at least six months of rehab before it would be safe to start jumping again. He suggested I give it a full year but understood that I needed to work. So, for the next six months, I went to rehab three times a week and worked out in the gym every other day on my own. I was averaging three hours of working out every single day, seven days a week.

At around the three-month mark during my rehab, I got a message from Frank in Beijing. He explained how Red Bull wanted to do another project with me this coming year and asked if I would be willing to come look at possible locations for a new live stunt in China. I told Frank I wasn't feeling well and was just trying to get back in shape.

"They'll pay you just to come take a look," he went on. "If you don't think any of the locations are interesting, they'll still pay you, no strings attached."

"I don't think so, Frank," I replied. "I really need to focus on my rehab right now."

"Come on, Jeb. It won't take more than a week of your time, I promise."

"Alright, bro," I relented. "One week."

CHAPTER TWENTY-EIGHT

THE FLYING DAGGER

A few weeks later, I found myself in the back of a bus surrounded by Red Bull China executives. We were heading to a small town called Jiangshan, located in the Zhejiang province. They wanted to show me a mountain with another gigantic crack running through it called Mount Jianglang. We had already looked at two other possible locations that weren't going to work and I didn't have high hopes for this one either. I had come to realize that people who don't BASE jump or fly wingsuits usually have no idea what we require to do the things we do. I felt like this was going to be a total waste of time, but at least I'd get paid.

As I looked out the window, I saw something off in the distance that looked strange. It was hard for me to understand what I was seeing, but it kind of looked like three colossal fingers sticking out of the ground. As we got closer, they kept getting bigger and bigger. I pointed and asked Frank, "Is that what we're here to look at?"

"I think so," he replied.

"They look so weird. What are they?"

Frank just shrugged and shook his head.

We parked the bus and hiked to the foot of the mountain, which took about forty-five minutes and was hard on my recovering legs, but my braces helped. As I stood at the bottom of the cliff, I looked up at something that didn't seem natural. The fingers looked manmade with almost perfectly straight lines. The cliff had two cracks that went from the ground to the top. One of the cracks was large and wide, while the other was long and narrow. We decided to check out the narrow crack first.

The local village had built a walkway directly at the bottom of the crack through the mountain. It was a well-constructed path, and as we walked along, it felt like we were being engulfed by rock. It was narrow—only about fifteen feet wide. I could stand in the middle with my arms out and only have about four and a half feet from my fingertips to the walls on each side. The distance from entering the path to exiting was about three football fields. So, the mixture of how narrow the path was, how high the cliffs were, and how long the path was, gave me a sense of claustrophobia. I asked Frank, "Exactly how high are these cliffs?"

He said, "About eight hundred and ninety feet tall."

"Well how wide is it at the top?"

Frank asked our guide, who explained it was sixty feet wide at the top and fifteen feet wide where we were standing. So, if I flew into this from an aircraft, it would get narrower the deeper I flew. That was frightening.

So, I did some quick math, rounding the numbers off to make it easier: 900 feet tall, 900 feet long, and probably about thirty feet wide at mid-depth. If I flew a 2:1 ratio glide as I entered at the top of the crack and kept that glide till I exited the other side, I would be at about 450 feet of altitude when I exited. These rough numbers seemed workable.

As we exited the pathway on the back side of the mountain, Joan—the same lovely Red Bull executive we had worked with before from Heaven's Gate—asked what I thought.

"It looks interesting," I told her.

She asked, "Jeb, do you think you could fly through the narrow crack and still have enough altitude on the other side to open a parachute?"

I responded by saying, "It will depend on the landing area on the other side, but from the rough numbers I've been able to work out so far, I believe it could be possible."

From there, we walked back through the mountain to the front side to check out the larger crack and look for possible landing areas. There was a long walkway carved into the rock leading up to the wider crack. This walkway was about five feet wide and had stairs of stone. It also had a concrete handrail that went its entire distance. On the other side of the handrail was a cliff about seventy feet high that gave a great vantage point of the narrower crack we were thinking of using for the stunt. From there, I could tell this would be the only possible place to land. Everything else was dense jungle and steep cliffs. As I stood there calculating, I knew this landing zone would cut about a hundred feet from my altitude, so the 450 feet would be closer to 350 feet. I would also have to fly some distance to make it to the walkway. If I came up short, I would smack into the concrete barriers and fall down the seventy-foot cliff, leading to serious injury or death.

Standing there just feeling the air, I visualized what it would be like coming out of the crack. If I chose to do this stunt, there would be a huge fin to my left as I exited the crack that I would have to clear before deployment. This meant I would lose another fifty feet or so, pushing my deployment below 300 feet. This was getting a bit extreme, considering that there weren't any other possible landing areas and line twists would mean a jungle landing for sure. I looked at the trees and they looked green and soft. At this point I had over ten tree landings all over the world and felt comfortable with them, so I felt, worst case, I pull low and end up landing in a tree. That's not so bad, right?

There was zero wind that day and I felt really good about the prospects of doing a live stunt here. It was going to be beautiful, exciting, and challenging for me. I asked Frank, "If I say yes to this, can we guarantee I'll get a chopper at least a week early that I can use for training? I would want to do four jumps a day for five days. I'll need to jump many times, working my way deeper and deeper into the crack to see where the safe entry and exit points would be. The landing area isn't directly under where I exit the cave, and I'll need to make sure I'm capable of deploying high enough to make it. I can't have a repeat of Heaven's Gate."

Frank said he wasn't sure, but he would explain to everyone that the helicopter practice would be a prerequisite for me doing the stunt. I asked him to get me all the exact numbers: length, height, and width at all the different altitudes. If all the real numbers matched my rough estimates, then I would be willing to do the live show. Joan and the rest of the Red Bull executives smiled and nodded. We were going to have another big show on our hands. Frank suggested we call the show "The Flying Dagger," and I looked at him with a grin. "That's a great name, bro," I told him. "I love it."

I began my preparations the instant I got home. I ordered two new Apache wingsuits from Tony with Red Bull China branding. I purchased plane tickets for Switzerland, which had become my training ground for all big projects because of its ease of access to large cliffs. Walenstadt's cable car service went straight to the top of a 5,000-foot jump and was like a low-budget helicopter, allowing me to get in at least three jumps a day without getting worn out from grueling hikes. A group of wingsuit pilots had discovered new lines from the classic Sputnik exit point that would work perfectly for training terrain flying through narrow spaces. I felt this would be the best way to warm up before heading to China.

I ended up spending four weeks training in Switzerland and did over forty dedicated proximity flights through the trench line and barn lines located in the Walenstadt area. During this period, my good friend Jhonathan Florez showed up to help me with my training and captured many of the jumps on video. The jumping made me current, but I still didn't feel like it was enough to truly prepare me for what was coming. I knew I needed more; I just wasn't sure how to get it without doing things that would get me hurt.

After being home from the Swiss training for a few weeks, I got a call from Iiro saying he had figured out a way for me to train in a safe way for this new stunt in China. He explained how he had been talking with a company from Hungary called AirGlass that specialized in a new technology called "augmented reality." He said they could three-dimensionally render the cliff from the Flying Dagger with all its terrain features, then project it on a special headset I could wear while skydiving. I would look through glass so I would still be totally aware of everything in the real world, but by projecting the image of the cliff in a special way, they could trick my mind into believing the cliff was actually there. This would give me the feeling I was proximity flying without having to worry about the whole impacting-solid-rock-and-dying thing. He asked me if I would be willing to fly to Hungary in order to test out the unit. Iiro was convinced that if it worked, it could be a powerful training tool. I agreed with him, so we set up dates and flights for me to come to Hungary to test out the unit and see if it would help.

I showed up in Budapest a few weeks later to meet with the AirGlass team. Both Iiro and Frank were there to greet me at the airport. We headed straight to a nearby drop zone to begin the experimentation. The lead designer took out an odd-looking helmet with a strange piece of glass over the right eye. It kind of looked like something you might see a fighter pilot wear. They put the helmet on my head to check it for size and make sure the glass aligned with my eye properly. They turned the unit on and had me do a series of calibration exercises.

Once we worked through all the basics, they ran the Flying Dagger program. As I looked forward, I saw numbers counting down. It looked like they were floating in space about ten feet in front of me. As the countdown reached zero, the mountain and crack from China appeared. Everything was brightly colored, making it look a bit like a cartoon, but it made it easy to gauge depth. It was remarkable how realistic it was in size and scale. As I turned my head, the mountain stayed where it was, and I could look to either side without it moving. I was able to walk around the mountain and see it from all sides. I would have had to walk a few miles to walk around the whole thing, but I got the idea of how it worked right away.

They asked me if I would like to try it in the air. I told them, "Yes, let me grab my gear and let's do this." I geared up and jumped on a plane with the head designer, and once we reached 12,000 feet, he turned the unit on. As we got in the proper position to jump, he switched on the Flying Dagger program and the countdown began. This time it started at thirty, giving me time to get into position. I left the aircraft as the countdown reached ten. I was now in freefall, flying my wingsuit as it hit zero and the mountain appeared below me. At the bottom right, I had a readout that told me my altitude. In the bottom middle of the display was my glide angle. Bottom left was my speed. There was an arrow at the top that pointed me towards the entrance to the crack. It was remarkable. As I approached, the mountain grew bigger and gave the sense that I was approaching an actual terrain flight. As I entered the crack, I felt like I was really flying between cliffs; the sensation was amazing. As I flew out the other end, the terrain disappeared, and off in the distance, the mountain reappeared again. On my second approach, I was lined up perfectly to go through the center of the crack, when all of a sudden, the entire mountain moved by hundreds of feet and I impacted the side of the cliff, but as I hit, I flew right through the image and reminded myself was inside a 3D framework. The terrain again disappeared and redrew itself off in the distance. I tried to line myself up with it but noticed it was now moving, almost like it was trying to run away from me. As I flew after the mountain, it just kept moving away from me in all kinds of odd directions. My altimeter told me it was time to pull my parachute, so I did.

I landed right next to the team, and they started shooting questions at me. I told them I was able to get in three runs on the first jump. I explained the first run was perfect, but the second two had serious glitches. After explaining everything I had experienced, they took the unit into a room and worked on it. I was able to get four jumps with three runs each that day. I would say the unit worked about 20 percent of the time. I could tell the technology was still in its infancy and had a long way to go, but when it worked, it was truly phenomenal.

I went home feeling good about the upcoming project in China. As long as I was able to get the five days with at least four jumps a day leading into the live show, I felt we had a high chance for success.

On September 20, 2013, I was once again on a plane heading towards China. My mother was sitting in the seat next to me looking anxious. I tried to explain this stunt was not as complex as my last and should be relatively easy to accomplish. The odd thing was, I believed this statement to be true at the time.

Looking back on this moment right now, seven years later, I realize I tend to underestimate how difficult things are going to be, which might explain how I get myself to do them. I'm pretty sure I trick myself into thinking everything is straightforward and well within my control, only to find out in the execution that things are way more difficult and life-threatening. About 90 percent of the time, I'm way outside my depth and have no idea what the hell I'm doing. In the moments leading up to the action, I become gripped with fear and instantly regret agreeing to do them. I go through a profound debate with myself on the validity of my actions and why I'm doing these things in the first place. I argue and try to talk myself out of doing whatever it is, then remind myself that I've agreed to do it and I am a man of my word, even if giving that word means I have to die doing it. I then swear that if I survive, this will be the last time I ever do anything like this again. After I successfully do whatever that something is, I almost instantly forget the whole interaction and start planning my next thing. It's a vicious cycle, but for some reason, it seems to work for me.

We landed in Beijing to what can only be described as paparazzi. I had personally never seen so many reporters and camera people waiting for someone to get off an aircraft before. Both my mother and I were surprised at how many people were there to greet us and how many questions were being shot at us. Red Bull had been doing a full-court press promoting this event for the last few months and had whipped up a bit of a frenzy.

I looked over my left shoulder and saw a large flatscreen monitor playing the commercial I had filmed with Red Bull earlier in the year, and I noticed it was playing on a loop. During the drive to our hotel, I saw posters and billboards with my face all over them. Everywhere we went, people would get in endless lines to ask me for autographs and to get pictures taken with me. It was a surreal experience.

When we arrived at the Flying Dagger location, there were satellite trucks everywhere. News crews from around the world were setting up shop to cover the events as they unfolded. Everyone from NBC, ABC, BBC, and Reuters all had embedded news crews. It was strange being under constant surveillance. Every time I left my room, I was met almost immediately by more cameras and more questions.

"Mister Corliss, how many jumps will you do today?"

"Mister Corliss, are you nervous about jumping today?"

"Mister Corliss, do you anticipate any injuries today?"

Unlike with Heaven's Gate, the helicopter was on site the day I arrived. We had not only one, but *two* helicopters. Nothing would be left to chance this time. Iiro, Frank, and I were all feeling great about the stunt the first day, but that evening, all of that would change. A report came in that a typhoon was on its way to hit Hong Kong, and even though we were far away from the area, it was going to send bad weather our way beginning the next day. The ten-day forecast shifted to strong winds and rain every single day, and we were only six days out from going live.

This was not good.

Sure enough, the weather was bad the next day with both wind and clouds. My team had shown up the day earlier and we all decided it was best not to waste any time. We would head to the mountain to walk the primary landing area and check for any alternate places to land. I knew that the only alternate place to land was to select the softest, nicest-looking tree to set down in, because that's all there was. My team included Jeff Nebelkopf, Jhonathan Florez, James Boole, Barry Holubeck, and Roberta Mancino. Jeff would be the primary cameraman for my flights, while Jhonathan, James, and Roberta would be part of the live show by doing a lead-up exhibition jump. Barry would be my packer and my ground crew at the landing location.

I walked the team to the staircase that I had selected as our primary landing zone and showed it to everyone. People were looking at it with wide eyes, and as I was explaining how this was where we would be landing, Barry said something that surprised me. He said, "Jeb, I haven't agreed to land here yet. Don't just assume this is acceptable for the rest of us."

For some reason, it hadn't even dawned on me that other BASE jumpers may not think this was a reasonable place to land. I had been landing in such shitty areas for so long that it hadn't even crossed my mind that this spot was terrible. But after Barry expressed his concern, I asked the other pilots what they thought, and they all said no; they were not comfortable landing in that area. The only one who said he would land there with me was Jeff.

"I'll land anywhere you do," he stated with a nod.

Barry and the rest of the team who had deemed the area unacceptable said we needed to look for somewhere else for them to land. I agreed but explained I needed to find a second, even more horrible landing area for myself in case I had to pull too low to make it the staircase. I wanted to check the exit of the crack and find the best trees to land in directly below it. I still wasn't sure what my altitude would be as I exited the mountain, and I felt there was an 80 percent chance I would have to land in the trees and wouldn't even see that staircase anyway.

As we got to the area I would land in if I had an ultra-low pull, I saw I was in big trouble: the trees were not what I was expecting. From a distance, they looked soft and green, but on closer inspection, they only had green on the outside. Inside, they had sharp jagged branches that could skewer you. It didn't take me long to understand that landing in these trees wasn't an option. The chances of a branch puncturing my body was way too high and the time it would take a rescue team to get to me would take too long. I would bleed out before I ever saw a hospital. There was no alternative for me: I'd have to make it to my primary landing zone. This was when it really hit me that this stunt would be far more dangerous than I had previously thought.

We spent the rest of the day finding another location for everyone else to land. They wouldn't be flying through the crack in the mountain, so they could fly high and get to a road further down the mountain. They felt comfortable with this option, so the scouting portion was complete. We all had our landing zones figured out, and I was terrified.

Barry and I got together with Frank and explained how he would need to have plywood placed on all the stairs in my landing area to make them smooth. I couldn't have any right angles because that could break my ankles. Frank said it was no problem and he would make sure it was done the next day.

I woke up the next morning and looked out the window. Sure enough, it was raining and the winds were even stronger than the day before. The whole team got together for breakfast and the mood was somber. The deteriorating weather made everyone concerned about the safety of my landing zone. Frank explained he had already sent people up the mountain to put wood over the steps in an attempt to smooth them out as much as possible, but how smooth can you really make a concrete staircase anyway? After we were done eating, we all headed back up the mountain to see how the work had progressed. I expected to see crooked, wet boards with nails sticking out everywhere, but when we got there, I saw that they had done an amazing job. All the stairs and gaps had been covered up and I was suddenly feeling pretty good about landing there. Barry still didn't think it was acceptable, but he didn't have to land there, so he was fine with it. There was a large concrete bench in the middle of the landing zone, and he asked me what I wanted to do about it. I told him it wasn't a problem because I could land either before or after it. He looked at me like he wanted to say something but then just shrugged his shoulders and said, "Okay."

As we were walking back down the mountain, Frank explained that I had a full day of doing interviews with various news outlets on site. He said we needed to use the time the weather was bad to get as many interviews done as possible so that, when the weather cleared, I could focus on training. I agreed, so for the next two days, all I did were interviews for eight hours a day. It was mind-numbing, but I figured it was better to do it before I started jumping.

By day four, I realized I was screwed. Time was running out, and I had gotten zero training on location. The weather had completely ruined our lead up to the event. I knew I hadn't gotten the training I needed to pull this stunt off safely. On the day before the live stunt, the weather finally cleared enough for me to get in two practice jumps. On the first jump, I flew over the mountain with Jeff so he could film me and to get a look at it from the air. Because we flew so high, we were able to land on the road farther down the mountain where the others had decided to land.

But on my second jump, I flew it by myself and tried to get closer. I needed to see if I could fit in the crack, and how deep I could get and still have the altitude to make it to my landing zone carved into the side of the cliff. I did the flight but didn't get close enough to gather any usable data. I opened high and went for the staircase that would be my LZ on stunt day.

As I came over the handrail, I hit turbulence that took me directly into that concrete bench I had dismissed as a non-issue. Luckily for me, Barry had the foresight to place some extra plywood that had been laying around against it, so when I impacted, I hit the plywood and karate-chopped it in half. That took the brunt of the force out of the impact, so I didn't get hurt, but it made such a loud crash that everyone around thought I had been destroyed. The landing had put me in an awkward position where my legs were up in the air over my head. In this position, it was hard for me to move; I was stuck, so everyone rushed over to help. They picked me up and called for the medic, but I explained I was okay. I then gave Barry a hug and thanked him for saving my ass. Without that plywood, I would have broken both my legs for sure, and the whole stunt would have been over.

The two practice jumps were not helpful at all. The only thing they showed me was how completely screwed I was. The situation brought back painful memories from Heaven's Gate. I still had no idea where I would need to leave the helicopter in order to get the correct glide angle to enter the mountain at the proper altitude. I didn't know where I should begin the line at the entrance of the crack or how high I would be when I exited. I also had no idea if I would even be able to make it to my landing area. All I did know was that if I didn't make the staircase, I was going to get annihilated.

This was all a moot point because the weather report for the next day was abysmal; it was supposed to be the worst day so far.

I told Frank, "If we know tomorrow's going to be bad, why don't we push the event to the reserve days?" I had been promised that we would have two reserve days as a buffer, so if weather screwed us on the 28th, we could just do it on the 29th or the 30th.

"The project has ballooned way beyond our expectations," Frank replied. "We are so far beyond any kind of reasonable budget that we no longer have back-up days. It has to either happen tomorrow or not at all."

"That's a tremendous amount of pressure," I said. "I'm not happy about this at all."

Frank said, "Jeb, you don't have to jump. Red Bull has already said it's not a problem if conditions aren't good. They're getting a huge amount of press regardless. There's no pressure on you if things go wrong. If you don't feel good about the stunt, don't do it. No one will hold it against you."

It's funny how when people say this kind of thing, it doesn't really make you feel any better. It's nice of them, but for me, when I say I'm going to do something, I do it. It's hard for me to step back once I've made the commitment, but this was out of my control—if the weather was going to make it impossible, then there was nothing I could do about it.

As expected, the next day we woke up to strong winds and cloudy skies. This was the first day we couldn't even see the mountain as it was completely encased in fog. Our cutoff time was at 4:00 p.m. At that time, the military was closing down the airspace, and our helicopters would not be permitted to take off. The weather report was bad for the rest of the day. The somewhat ironic thing was that the weather report actually looked good for the next day.

I again tried to convince Frank that we needed to push to the following day, but he explained we had over 50,000 people who had shown up from the surrounding villages, and the local government had brought in over 2,500 extra police officers to help control the large crowd. We had over eighty rescue workers on staff to help in case I had an accident. We couldn't even count how many members of the press were on hand. The slot of time for the TV networks had been set aside, and whatever we got from 1:00 p.m. to 3:00 p.m. was what we were going to get.

I said, "Wait, I thought we had till four p.m."

"Yes, we do," Frank said, "but the TV will only be airing what we do till three p.m. live. Anything we do after that will play on the news later as a recap."

It was time to get to work.

We put everyone in position. Barry was in the landing area with a walkie talkie to give us live updates on wind conditions. Every thirty minutes, we would ask him how strong the winds were, and every time he would respond with horrible news: they were too strong and extremely turbulent. We had the demonstration team at the helicopter staging area with me in case we got a break in the weather, but we were not hopeful.

At around 2 p.m., Iiro came over and said, "Jeb, we can get the chopper high enough to do a jump from around fifteen hundred feet. It's not high enough to do the stunt, but you can do a demonstration jump over the crowd so they can at least see something."

I told him, "Iiro, let the demo team do the jump. I would hate to do a simple jump like this and twist an ankle on landing and then have the weather clear up. I should wait to do the actual stunt." Iiro and Frank sent the demo team up to jump, and sure enough, the winds wreaked havoc on them. Jhonathan got caught in turbulence and was slammed into the helicopter landing pad. We were all surprised when he walked away without any injuries, but his jump showed us that the conditions were not conducive for what we were trying to accomplish.

At 3:10, the fog had risen high enough to see the top of the mountain. I called to Barry and asked how the winds were doing, and he said, "Jeb, they are bad. Very turbulent and way too strong".

"Okay," I said, "but how fast are they blowing?"

"About fifteen mph, but with the turbulence, they are dangerous." The wind was channeling between the two cliffs, and they spiraled as they came out and down the staircase, creating powerful vertices that would grab a canopy and drill it directly into the ground. But I felt I had to give it a try. I told Barry to keep me posted on the wind. If it didn't get any stronger than fifteen mph, I might give it a go. On my way over to the pilot, I grabbed Frank to help interpret for me. When we got there, I told the pilot I wanted to go up and see if we could get lucky with a hole in the cloud cover. He looked at Frank and told him it was impossible. The cloud layer was too low, and we couldn't get anywhere near the 3,000 feet I needed. I said I was aware of this, but we had to try. Frank explained to the pilot that, even if it was pointless, we had to show we were doing everything in our power to try and pull this off.

Right then, James walked over to me and said he had an idea of how I could know the proper glide angle to get to the mountain at the correct altitude. He said, "Jeb, I'll go up in the chopper with you and mark the top of the mountain at the beginning of the crack with GPS. We can then fly to altitude and do a pattern that takes us a few miles from the mountain. As we fly back towards your line, I can let you know the instant we have a two-to-one glide ratio. That will take all the guesswork out of where you need to leave the helicopter."

I told James, "Get your GPS, and let's see if we get lucky." I then called Barry to check on the wind again.

"Wind's the same," he replied.

"Okay," I instructed, "use the aerial walkie, and if the winds get any worse, tell the pilot to stop and we'll call off the jump."

"Alright, Jeb," Barry said, "but I don't feel like the conditions are safe to jump. It's risky."

"I hear you, Barry," I said. "I'm willing to take that risk with this situation, but it's definitely at the max. Anything more and it's time to abort."

I geared up, and by the time I got to the chopper, James was already there waiting for me. We got on and headed towards the mountain. The helicopter pilot flew close to the mountain, right where I would want to enter the line so James could take his measurements with the GPS. When James finished his task, we began to climb to altitude. Within a few moments, we were in a whiteout. The pilot pointed to his altimeter, and I saw that it only read 1,500 feet. He shrugged his shoulders with an "I told you so" expression. That was it; we had tried, but there was no way we could do the jump. We flew around for a few minutes, but it was clear the project was over. I signaled the pilot to head back to base.

The press descended upon us as we landed, and with a heavy heart, I had to explain that we couldn't complete the project. It was 3:30, and this thing just wasn't going to happen. The weather hadn't cooperated with us and made conditions impossible. I went to the tent I had been using to stage from and started taking off my gear. As I was doing this, Frank walked in and asked what I was doing.

"Project's done, Frank," I explained. "No need to keep wearing this stuff."

He told me, "Jeb, I know it's over, but we still have thirty minutes before the cut-off time. Just stay geared up till then. You never know what can happen." I looked at him like he was insane. There was a zero percent chance this was going to happen, and even if, by some miracle, the weather cleared, I hadn't gotten the proper training anyway. It was probably better the weather had moved in, because I wasn't ready for this jump.

At around 3:45 p.m., James' wife Kristina walked in and said, "Jeb, you need to come outside and see this."

I looked at her and said, "I am not in the mood. I don't really feel like seeing anything right now."

She again said, "No, Jeb, you really need to come take a look at this."

I opened the flap to the tent and walked outside to a clear sky above. The clouds were gone. I instantly grabbed a walkie from someone standing close by and called to Barry in the landing area, "What are the winds like, Barry?"

He responded, "Winds are zero. Not a breath up here."

I couldn't believe it. My mind had already shut down, and I had mentally given up.

I noticed a large group of reporters staring at me. My mother was next to me, along with Frank, Iiro, and the Red Bull executives. I stood there contemplating life. What should I do? I looked at Frank and said, "Okay, let's do this." My mom burst out crying. I looked her right in the eye and said, "Mom, don't do this right now. This is hard enough without you adding this kind of pressure on me. This is what I came here for—I have to do this." I moved as fast as I could to the tent to get all my gear back on. This was now a race against time.

I put everything on as quickly as I could and rushed out of the tent, where James was waiting for me. We ran towards the helicopter, but on the way, I passed a reporter from ABC who had been following the event from day one, and she stopped me in my tracks.

She pointed to the cameraman and said, "Turn the camera off." She then looked at me and said, "Jeb, you know you don't have to do this right?"

I looked at her and said, "Yes, I do have to do this. It's what I do." She shook her head, then signaled the cameraman to start filming and followed James and me to the helicopter, firing questions at high speed. James and I boarded the chopper, and the skids left the ground at exactly 3:59 p.m., one minute before the cut off time. As the chopper climbed to altitude, everything became quiet. I felt myself retreat to a familiar place deep inside my mind. I started feeling distant. I told myself, *Barry is going to call up on the walkie and call this off any second. The winds are going to pick up and put a stop to this any moment now. Just wait and see.*

But the helicopter kept climbing. James yelled in my ear over the sound of rotor blades ripping through the air, "We're going to do a dry run to make sure we get all the signals right. I will tap you on the shoulder when you need to climb out of the helicopter. I will then tap you on the shoulder again when you need to let go." I nodded with understanding.

The helicopter did a wide arc in the sky, setting us up for the dry run. At about 1.5 miles from the crack, he tapped me on my shoulder he said, "This is where you get out."

As I looked down, it seemed kind of far away, but I nodded okay. A short time later, James tapped my shoulder again and said, "This is where you jump."

I looked at him with horror and I said, "This is way too far away. I'll never make it."

He looked at me and explained, "This is a two-to-one, like you asked for."

I had no choice but to trust him. I didn't get the practice jumps and this was the only way to be sure of the proper glide. It seemed too far, but for both practice jumps, I had gotten out way too close, so my judgment was obviously off. The chopper started circling back around for the real run when it dawned on me: *I am doing this. Barry isn't going to call this off. I am jumping from this chopper and will be flying through that crack. I'm most likely going to pull low as I end the flight. I probably won't be able to make my landing area and I'll get physically destroyed yet again.* I had just recovered from Table Mountain and, in a few moments, I was most likely going right back to the hospital. Fear flooded my chest. My heart felt like it was going to explode. True terror took over, and I knew I was going to die.

I started pleading with myself, *Please don't do this. You didn't get the proper training. They will understand; everyone will understand. You don't have to do this.*

That was it—I decided, *NO, I will not do this. This is insane. I didn't get the proper training. Not happening.* As I made this decision, my mind tore apart. Tears started welling up in my eyes, and I began to cry.

I understood that if I didn't do this, I was never going to jump again. I would be finished. This would be the end of everything I had been training for and working towards since I was sixteen years old. But then something even deeper came to the surface, a new thought: *I would be lost.* The thing that had given me direction and pulled me through my life would be gone. My passion would be over. My purpose would disappear. My life was crumbling, but from the outside, James or anyone else watching would never have known. My helmet and goggles covered up all emotion.

At that moment, something inside me spoke up, *If you don't do this, you may not die today, but you are still going to die. Maybe tomorrow or maybe in thirty years. Death will find you. If you don't do this, you will look back at this moment as the day you let fear control the direction of your life. I know you are scared, but don't let that decide this for you. If you must die someday anyway, let it be on your terms. Let it be living your dreams. Let it be keeping your word and doing what you said you would do. How upsetting would it be to die in a car crash a week from now? You don't have as much control as you think you do. Today is as good a day to die as any other.*

As those words faded, I felt James tap my shoulder. The fear had melted away like a snowball on a summer's day. I felt total calm come over me. My eyes had dried, and a feeling of warmth had filled my chest. I accepted my fate—I was ready to die. Somehow that helped me shed my fear and find my center. James tapped me a second time, and I let go of the helicopter. As I looked down, I saw I was too far from the crack and there was no way I could make it.

That same calm voice said, *Well, it was a good life.*

After a few seconds, I saw my forward movement and realized, *Wait, I think I'm good. I can get to the opening. I can do this.*

Then I realized, *Wait, I'm totally perfect. I could actually fly over the crack if I want to. I don't even have to fly in it.* But this thought left my mind as fast as it entered. *I didn't come here to fly over it. I'm going to enter it at the beginning and see where I come out on the other end.* I entered the crack where it began at the top of the mountain, and within a tenth of a second, I was deep inside the mountain. I hadn't noticed when looking at it from the ground, but the crack was crooked, like two books leaning slightly to the left on a bookshelf. This meant I had to side-slip to the right as I was flying straight to keep from impacting the cliff on my left side. I had never had to fly like this before, but somehow it was just happening automatically. As I sank deeper, the walls got closer and I could feel turbulence bouncing off the sides and hitting me. Everything got so narrow and so close that I felt like I was about to impact. I hadn't been that close to solid rock at those speeds since I impacted Table Mountain.

I tensed up and *bang*—I was out the other side. I had generated an enormous amount of speed flying through the crack, and I knew I was going too fast to deploy safely, but if I put on the brakes to burn off speed, I would fly too far away from the landing area; I had to pitch. My parachute opened instantly, and the impact was severe. My feet swung out in from of me and all the cameras I was wearing were ripped from my body by the sudden lurch of momentum. I watched as they tumbled away into the jungle far below. I reached up to grab my toggles to turn towards the stairway carved into the side of the cliff and knew it was going to be close. I just started yelling in my own head, *Please make it, please make it!* I aimed for the beginning of the walkway and could see I was going to make it—barely. I had to lift my legs to scrape over the concrete guard rail as I hit the landing area hard. I bounced off the ground and slid into the railing, bruising my ribs on my right side... but I was down, and I was safe.

Iiro ran at me screaming, "You made it, you made it! Are you okay? Did you get hurt?"

I yelled back, "I'm okay! I can't believe we did this!" Just twenty minutes earlier, I was 100 percent sure we had failed, but somehow, we had pulled it off.

The feeling of relief in that moment is impossible to explain. I was sure this was going to end with me going to the hospital or dying, but miraculously, I was okay. I had used up every ounce of energy I had, and a true sense of exhaustion overwhelmed me. Just then, the same reporter who had told me I didn't have to do this earlier walked up and started firing more questions at me. She had about fifty other reporters standing behind her, and I tried to answer their questions the best I could.

It's all kind of a blur from there on. Hours of ceremonies and interviews that seemed to go on forever. By the time I got to my room later that night, I was both mentally and physically depleted. It would take me over six months to recover from the Flying Dagger. It had taken a massive toll on me mentally. Just writing about it now brings back the exhaustion. It's remarkable what an impact it had on me. It sent cracks to my very foundation. I started questioning my purpose more and more. I started feeling like maybe I didn't really need to do these things anymore. Maybe I had gotten everything I needed out of this, and it was time to move on to something new, maybe something with more meaning.

CHAPTER TWENTY-NINE

POINT BREAK

Shortly after my recovery from the Flying Dagger, a dream job presented itself. I got a phone call from a director named Ericson Core. He asked to meet me at a restaurant on Abbot Kinney, near where I was living at the time in Marina del Rey. When I showed up, he was waiting outside for me wearing a bandana. I could see he had a unique style that I liked. He had a kind face and was sincere in a way few humans are. He was calm and collected. Seemed almost wise. I think he is what people would describe as an "old soul," even though I don't believe in the concept of a soul. He just seemed like he had been around for a long time despite the fact that he wasn't much older than me.

We sat down and I asked him what he would like to talk about. Ericson explained how he was working on a script for Warner Brothers, and they wanted to do a reimagining of the film *Point Break*. I smiled. I remembered seeing the original film when I was in my teens, and the skydiving sequences were legendary. It had inspired an entire generation of jumpers and was the precursor to the modern-day extreme sports movement. To get to work on a project like this would be a dream come true and a culmination of everything I had been working towards my entire life. I asked, "What can I help you with?"

Ericson went on to explain that they wanted to have a wingsuit proximity flying sequence with the four main characters flying in formation. It had to be in nature without buildings or manmade structures. The movie wasn't going to be about robbing banks this time; it was going to be about extreme athletes trying to reach the ultimate level in eight different extreme sports disciplines. Each thing done would have to be the apex of what could be achieved in the modern real world. Ericson explained it all had to be practical stunts done for real with no CGI. He wanted me to work as a technical adviser, helping him create the greatest wingsuit flying sequence ever captured on film. He would also want me to be the stunt double for the wingsuit sequence, doubling the Bodhi character.

For Ericson, it was of upmost importance that the stunts be done by the actual athletes at the top of each discipline. He wanted the film to have credibility amongst the athletes within each category. To me, it sounded like an ambitious and exciting project, and I instantly said yes. I told him he would need to contact Jon Devore, the head of the Red Bull Air Force, and probably the best aerial coordinator to have ever lived. I also put him in touch with my friend, Tim Rigby, who had become a phenomenal stunt coordinator. Ericson gave me the script and asked me to think about what would be an interesting proximity line that would fit the script. He wanted it to be spectacular, with many different possible camera locations to film the action, but also needed the safety level to be within reason for a 100-million-dollar Hollywood movie. Spectacular, but not lethal. I understood what he was asking and started thinking about possible locations around the world.

Our next meeting was a week later, and I brought footage from *Grinding the Crack*. I explained it would be the perfect location to get cameras in a position where the pilots could do multiple flybys within ten feet in a relatively safe way. The jump had become more of an intermediate proximity flight but was still an eye-popping visual experience, giving us exactly what we needed for the scene. We could get all four characters in the film to fly past the cameras as the pilots went subterranean with wingsuit cameramen filming from behind, and because of its relatively easy approach, it could be done repeatedly without killing people.

Ericson liked it, but he asked if there was anything in Italy where we could get the same result. They were getting amazing tax credits to film in Italy, and if we could film the sequence there, it could help them save money on the budget. I explained there were many jumps in Italy, some truly remarkable ones, actually, but the logistics would be much more challenging, and they wouldn't be as safe. The risk to the pilots would go up exponentially to get even close to what we could capture at the Crack in Switzerland. He explained Switzerland was probably the most expensive place we could possibly film but understood the level of danger involved in what he was asking for. He said he would work it out and get the money in the budget somehow.

Ericson hired Jon to do aerial coordinating and brought me on as technical adviser, but unfortunately for us, Tim was busy working on *Superman v Batman* at the time. Tim told me it was one of the most difficult choices he had to make in his stunt career. He felt he owed a lot to Zack Snyder, so even though *Point Break* was a dream job, he had to turn it down, but he told me I could pick his brain anytime I needed.

Jon and I started putting together the list of jumpers who would double the actors for the formation. After working with the World Wingsuit League for so many years, I had a strong understanding of who the professional pilots were. Not just people who could do the complicated flights safely, but who could also deal with working on such a big-budget production. Jon and I both agreed we would do a V formation with me at the lead. It's the classic pattern you see birds flying when you look up at the sky, and it's just visually cool to see humans do it.

The other pilots would be Julian Boulle and Noah Bahnson as the pilots on my left and right sides. Julian was one of the best pilots in the world and had already filmed many wingsuit sequences as a Hollywood cameraman, so I felt he could also work as a backup cameraman if necessary. Noah was also an accomplished aerial cameraman and had beaten Julian at the WWL race in China, so they were equal in their abilities. For our primary wingsuit cameramen, we would use Jeff Nebelkopf as camera number one and James Boole as camera number two. Both were dedicated wingsuit cameramen for a living and had numerous large productions under their belts, but Jeff had a little more experience wearing large movie cameras on his head, so that's why he got the main camera slot. Now we just needed to decide who was going to double the Johnny Utah character, and Jon asked me if he could do it. This worried me because he was going to be the aerial coordinator, and I wasn't sure if it was a good idea to have him in both roles. Usually, the coordinator is in charge of making calls that relate to the safety of the stunt performers, and I felt overseeing and performing the stunts could cloud his judgment. I told him I would need to talk to Tim about that one and get back to him.

I called Tim to tell him the situation and asked what he thought about having Jon be both the coordinator and the stunt double for Johnny Utah during the flying sequences. Tim didn't think it would be an issue. He said that most of the coordinating would happen before principal photography started, and he didn't think it would cloud Jon's judgment. He actually thought it might add clarity if Jon was going to be putting his own life on the line with the other pilots. I 100 percent trusted Tim's opinion, so I called Jon and told him that Tim gave him the thumbs up to double Johnny Utah. Jon was ecstatic.

We now had all the pilots in place, and I started working with Ericson on storyboarding the sequence. Ericson wanted to build a powerful story around the action that made sense and integrated into the bigger picture. I was impressed by how authentic Ericson wanted everything to be. He wanted to use as little CGI as possible, which was music to my ears because I hated how fake everything had begun to look in Hollywood. But I made it clear how dangerous everything that we were planning was, and he reiterated that safety was a top priority, which was why he had hired Jon and me.

Meanwhile, Jon ordered the equipment that would be used by the on-camera wingsuit pilots and got the ball rolling. A few months later, the *Point Break* wingsuits showed up and Jon asked me if I would like to go to the drop zone for a few practice jumps to make sure they fit properly. I said absolutely because I always had to make some small adjustments to new suits anyways.

I showed up at the DZ and we did three flights to test out both suits. Two suits had been built for each pilot to make back-to-back jumps easier on filming days. I was excited because the suits fit perfectly, and it was one of the first times I had received not only one, but two perfect suits that didn't need to be sent back for adjusting. Jon said he had to head home to get some work done. I was packing up my gear to head home myself when a young jumper by the name of Johnny Strange came up and asked if I would do a flight with him before I left. I liked Johnny; he was young and energetic. I had taken him on his first shark diving trip in Fiji a few months earlier and we had become buddies. I decided, I'm already here, so why not do one more jump? A little extra practice never hurt.

So, I geared up and followed Johnny to Shark Air, one of Perris' six Twin Otter planes, and took a ride to altitude. We did a jump together that was calm and relaxed. We broke off at about 4,000 feet and I opened my parachute. The conditions were perfect that day with light winds and sunny skies. As I was setting up for landing, I saw a group of tandems lining up to land on the grass. Perris had passed a new rule a year earlier that if tandems were landing on the grass, you had to land in the dirt. I found this annoying because I was in the *Point Break* wingsuit and I didn't want to damage it by sliding in the dirt, but I also didn't want to get yelled at by the person monitoring the landing area. As I got close to the ground, I flared like I had thousands of times before, but for some reason as I set down, I had a little more speed than usual. Had I been on the grass, I would have just gone down on my butt and slid it out, but because I was on hard dirt and the ground could rip the new suit, I tried to run it out. Again, this is something I have done thousands of times. As I took the first two steps, I felt something in my knee give out and I heard a loud popping sound. My leg went out from underneath me, and I ended up tumbling in the dirt.

As I lay there, I knew right away what had happened: I had just blown my ACL in my left knee again. I had spent the last year and a half going through rehab to rebuild that leg, and I had just blown it apart. As I stood up and put weight on it, I could feel the instability. This reconfirmed what I already knew, and I had a breakdown unlike anything I had experienced before. I knew exactly what it meant. An ACL reconstruction meant losing *Point Break*. There was no way I could do the stunts for the movie now. I had an IMAX movie right after *Point Break* and I had just lost that opportunity, too. I was looking at another painful surgery with at least a one-year recovery. I had just been through this, so it wasn't like I could delude myself into thinking everything was just going to be okay. I knew it wasn't going to be.

I became angry. I was tired of being hurt and in pain all the time. I felt jumping just kept taking everything from me. Most of my friends were dead, and my body was destroyed. As Johnny came over to see how I was doing, I told him, "That's it! I'm done with this fucking shit. I'm never jumping again. Everyone I care about is dead. I get hurt all the time. Fuck this sport."

I looked at Johnny and told him he should stop jumping, too. "This sport is death and it just hurts and kills everyone. It's not worth it. You need to stop doing this or you will die." He looked at me in shock and I could tell he didn't know what to say. In the past, he had told me I was one of his inspirations for jumping, which I didn't feel comfortable with. A darkness started growing in me, and by the time I got to the packing area, a feeling I hadn't felt since I was in my teens started taking hold. A rage that I thought had been extinguished started rising up. I was so upset I didn't know what to do with myself. A few people came to talk to me, but all I could say was how over this sport I was and how I was never going to do it again. I didn't know what I was going to do, I just knew I wasn't going to do this anymore. It was the first time since I saw BASE jumping at sixteen that I decided 100 percent, without a doubt, I didn't want to BASE jump anymore.

I got in my car and drove myself home. I called the doctor who had done my first ACL reconstruction and told him I had blown it again and needed to come in for an MRI. He scheduled me an appointment for the next day, and I just sat in the dark, realizing my life as I knew it was over. I was supposed to be going on a scouting mission with Ericson in Switzerland to help set up camera positions the next week, but I wasn't sure if I would even be able to do that now. I waited to call Ericson till after I got the results of the MRI. Sure enough, my ACL was gone, and I'd have to do another reconstruction. The doctor explained I wouldn't be able to do it the same way I had before—using my own hamstring from the same leg to rebuild my ACL—and this time they would have to do something different. When they drill the holes through your femur and tibia the second time, they have to drill them larger. Because of the larger holes, the hamstring wouldn't be as effective, and the doctor suggested we use my patellar tendon because they could harvest bone from each end. This would allow for bone-to-bone healing, which would work better with the larger holes for recovery. He went on to explain they had a new, somewhat radical surgery that could speed healing by as much as 50 percent if they took the patellar tendon graft from the opposite knee. He said he wouldn't suggest it to the average person, but because he knew what a risk-taker I was, I might be interested. I wasn't really in the mood to make decisions at that moment, so I told him I would think about it.

I called Ericson and told him we needed to talk. He lived close by, so he jumped on his bike and road over to my house. I explained my situation and I could see true sympathy in his eyes.

"I'm so sorry, Jeb," he said. "I really am. What do you want to do now?"

"I don't know, man," I replied, "I'm never going to jump again, but *Point Break* is a dream job, and I'd love to still work on it in some way."

"That's no problem. I still need you as a technical adviser, and we can just have you do cameos instead of jumps for the film. It'll work out."

It was an incredible act of kindness from a truly wonderful human being. I'm not sure I adequately expressed at the time how much it meant to me, but it was amazing. Ericson asked if I would still be able to do the scout the coming week, and I said, "Yes, but I'll have to wear a leg brace and walk with sticks. I may move slowly, but I can do the scout."

"Great," he said. "Then I will see you next week."

I called my manager Matt and told him I was done jumping.

He said, "That's fine, Jeb. We'll find something else for you to do."

Matt could tell I was emotional and told me to just relax, that there were all kinds of things I could do. I was more than just a jumper. We would work this out together. I'm not sure he understood how important those words were to me at the time, but they made me feel much better. I then called Gregg, my man at my main sponsor, GoPro, and a good friend. I told him the same thing I told Matt, and Gregg also said not to worry. He told me just to heal up and we would talk when I felt better.

"I'm always behind you, Jeb," he told me. "And GoPro will support you through this." I hung up the phone feeling a bit better, but over the next few days, a darkness descended upon me.

Deep depression seeped back in. At first, I thought I was feeling this way because I was hurt again, but it slowly started dawning on me that it was something else. I had made the decision to stop jumping without thinking it through all the way. BASE jumping had been the thing that brought me out of a dark place when I was young. It gave my life direction and purpose. By making the choice to stop, I had cut myself off from that purpose. I had lost my meaning. Why would I get a surgery? Why would I need to go through rehab? What point was there in getting better? My mind started going into a spiral. A massive void began to open up inside of me. I realized it had always been there, but I had filled it with human flight and everything that came along with that endeavor. Now that I had removed the filler, the black hole churning inside me just consumed everything...until there was nothing left. I started realizing that giving up wasn't going to be that easy. It wasn't like giving up drinking soda or some part-time habit. It was more like trying to give up breathing oxygen or drinking water. Whether I liked it or not, BASE had been keeping me alive. It was the fuel I consumed to exist.

My mind was more broken than I had thought. For some reason, I was under the impression I was all better. I felt I had destroyed many of the demons that had attacked me as a child. But it was quickly dawning on me that wasn't the case at all. If anything, I was possibly more damaged now than I was in my teens.

This understanding sent shivers down my spine. I wasn't upset because I had gotten hurt again; I was upset because I was walking away from the thing that anchored me to life. What a strange paradox. An activity so dangerous that it was almost certainly going to kill me was the very thing keeping me alive. I couldn't give it up; I would have to keep jumping. It was my driving force to keep going, to better myself, to do the surgery, go through rehab, fight the pain, and live to see another day. Without BASE, why would I do any of those things? Why would I need to?

As this all became clear, the dark feelings started to subside. It was as though the black fog that was choking me just lifted away. I called the doctor and told him I wanted to do the experimental surgery, and I wanted to schedule it for the instant I got home from my scouting mission in Switzerland. I needed to get better, and I needed to get better fast. I had things to do.

To paraphrase Abraham Cowley: Life is a sexually transmitted disease that always ends in death; there is currently no known cure. Understanding that death was coming for me and I had no way of stopping it meant I had better get as much shit done as I could with this little bit of time I had to exist. Another quote, this time from my friend Robin Hide, an old-school BASE jumper from the early eighties, goes, "Everyone thinks the reaper is off on some distant horizon. He's not; he's riding your back."

As I was getting ready to head out for the Swiss scout, I got a terrible phone call that kicked me right in the chest. Like I wasn't already dealing with enough confusion?

The person on the other end of the line said, "Jeb, Jeff just died. He was skydiving over Sebastian and did a low pull. His main had a malfunction, and there wasn't enough time to open his reserve. He's gone."

I wasn't sure how to process this information. What shocked me most was that it happened during a routine skydive—I would have expected it to happen while BASE jumping. Jeff had been there when I hit Table Mountain. He was the one who cut my wingsuit off my body. He had been with me on countless film projects. He was my friend. With everything I had been going through mentally over the past few weeks, this news hit me particularly hard. It's interesting how pain has a threshold. You feel it to a certain point and then your body just goes numb. I think that goes for emotional pain as well. Jeff's death was too much for me to handle at the time, so my mind just compartmentalized the emotions and put them away. All the pain was locked up in a little box and placed on a shelf to open at a later date. Problem is, when you put things like that in a box, they tend to fester and rot, and when you finally do open up that box to see what's inside, everything has become much worse.

I called Ericson to give him the bad news: we had just lost our main cameraman for the wingsuit sequence. Ericson, having the big heart that he does, took it a lot harder than I expected. His response impressed me. He said he would make sure there was a dedication to Jeff in the film, even though his accident had nothing to do with the project and Ericson hadn't even met Jeff yet. I told him I was looking for a replacement, but it wouldn't be easy. Jeff really was a one-of-a-kind cameraman and human being.

I called Jon with the situation. We already had to find a replacement for me, and now we had to find a cameraman replacement, which was honestly much more difficult. I told him I wanted Jhonathan Florez. He was a new up-and-coming pilot and had filmed me earlier in the year for another project. I was impressed with his work. I felt he was going to need some training, but I was convinced he would be able to do the job. Jon wasn't so sure. He felt Jhonathan had the skill, but just didn't know if his temperament would be good for the job. He felt he was just a little too green for a movie set. Jon wanted to use one of his close friends from the Red Bull Air Force named Andy Farrington. I didn't know Andy at the time, but Jon explained he was the "ninja of ninjas" and could easily film with a RED camera on his head. I said, "Okay, if you think so, but Ericson was clear he only wanted us to hire people who had flown the crack before and are familiar with the location."

Jon said he would go to the crack with Andy before we started shooting so Andy would know the location before showing up for the job.

I called Jhonathan and told him to start training with weight on his head. There may be an opportunity for him to become a cameraman on *Point Break*, but he would have to be able to fly with a RED camera on his head.

"How much do they weigh?" he asked.

"About twelve pounds," I told him.

He gave a little whistle and said, "Okay, that's heavier than I thought. I'll go online to find out the exact dimensions and get training ASAP."

I knew I could count on him.

While I was on the scout, I got a call from Jon saying Andy was busy during the filming dates for *Point Break,* so he couldn't come. I told him I had already talked with Jhonathan, and he was already training with weight on his head. I knew we'd need him as a backup in case someone else got hurt between now and filming, even if Andy could have made it. This sport seems to hurt people a lot, so you always need people in reserve for a big project like this.

After returning home from the scout, I went straight to the clinic to get my ACL rebuilt for the second time. Before surgery, the doctor handed me a prescription for pain medication, and I told him it wouldn't be necessary. He got an odd look on his face and said, "Jeb, you are going to need these." I told him I hadn't used pain meds during my last ACL reconstruction, and it wasn't going to be a problem this time, either.

He looked at me with concern and said, "Taking a graft from the hamstring is different than taking one from the patellar tendon. The patellar tendon graft removes bone from both sides of the inner knee, and it's a painful procedure. Your pain levels will be far worse than last time."

I said, "I don't take painkillers—I take pain."

He shrugged and said, "Just get the pain medication so you have it on hand. You don't have to use it, but you'll want to have it in case the pain becomes unbearable." I took the prescription paper and put it in my pocket with no plans of getting the prescription filled.

When I woke up from the ACL reconstruction surgery, they handed me a list of instructions and a friend drove me home. When I got there, I had to somehow make it to my bedroom on the third floor of my house to rest. Because they took the graft from my right knee to put in my left knee, crutches weren't going to work. They had done a nerve block while I was under anesthesia, so neither of my legs worked. I have always found it annoying how they do things to you without your permission when it comes to actual surgery, but when you're unconscious, there's not a whole lot you can do to protest.

I ended up scooting out of the car backwards and sliding on my butt, using my arms for movement and just dragging my legs along. I slid through my house to my stairs and slowly, one stair at a time, climbed up to my room. It took quite a while, and by the time I got to my room I was exhausted. I had a chair in front of my bed that I pulled myself into and then used that to make the next move into my bed. Full respect to people who deal with this maneuvering on a daily basis, because it absolutely sucked for me.

The instant I got in bed, I fell sleep and didn't wake up for six hours. The nerve block had worn off and a wave of pain woke me from my slumber. It felt like my right knee was on fire. The pain was so extreme that it made my body shiver like I was freezing cold. I have only experienced that level of pain a few times in my life, but my past experiences with pain taught me that, like all things, this agony would eventually pass. Might take a few hours, might take a few days, but for me, it was a perfect opportunity to test my mind. I think going through these kinds of experiences makes you stronger.

I couldn't sleep the first night. Once the pain kicked in, my mind just refused to calm down. I tried focusing on my breathing, but all thought was focused on the burning sensation in my right knee. Funny thing is, I didn't even notice any pain at all in my left knee, which was the knee that needed surgery. Only the donor knee hurt, and it hurt like hell. The next day, I got out of bed, stood up, grabbed a set of crutches next to my bed, and made the long journey to the bathroom. The odd thing was, walking to the bathroom actually made my knee feel better. So, after the bathroom, I decided to take a little walk down the hall. I then decided to walk downstairs to see my mom, who was there to help me during my recovery.

Mom saw me coming down the stairs and said, "Jeb, aren't you supposed to stay in bed for a week, till after your first check-up?"

I said, "Yes, but it's making my right knee feel better to walk on it. I want to go for a little walk around the neighborhood to see if that helps."

She didn't think it was a good idea, but she got her jacket, and we went for a walk around the neighborhood. We ended up doing a one-mile walk, and when I got home, I iced both my knees. The next day, we did a two-mile walk. By day five, we did four miles and my legs were feeling great. My left knee—the one I had gotten the ACL reconstruction on—would swell and feel hot, but the walking made the pain in my right knee feel way better. By the time I went to the doctor for my one-week checkup, I felt amazing. I drove myself, but Mom came with me to hear what the doctor had to say.

I walked into the clinic without using crutches. I signed in and a nurse put my mother and I in the waiting room. A few moments later, the doctor walked in and asked how I was doing. I told him I felt great.

"How was the pain?" he asked.

"That was, hands down, the most painful surgery I've had, aside from my skin graft."

"Do you need more pain medication?"

"Haven't used it," I said. "I've just been icing and walking to help with the pain."

He then started looking at my legs and a puzzled look spread across his face. He grabbed a tape measure and measured my left thigh and then my right thigh. He picked up a chart and looked at it. He stuck his head out the door and asked for another doctor to come to the room. When the other guy came in, my doctor measured both my legs again and showed him the numbers, then showed him the chart. He said, "Jeb, you have almost no muscle atrophy in your left leg. I've done over a thousand ACL reconstructions, and I've never seen a patient with so little muscle atrophy after surgery."

My mom spoke up and said, "Well, Jeb did go for a four-mile walk yesterday."

The doctor looked horrified and said, "Is this true?"

I explained the walking really helped with the pain, and he said that didn't matter. He told me I needed to stop walking right away. The graft could be damaged by fluids running through the holes between my femur and tibia. I needed bed rest for the graft to take hold properly. He told me I could start with a physiotherapist tomorrow, but I would have to follow an ACL protocol for activity to ensure the surgery wouldn't have to be done again. I was kind of bummed because the walks really helped with the pain.

Physical therapy went super fast this time around and the experimental surgery actually paid off. I recovered twice as quickly as the first time, and my physical therapist was blown away at my progress. Every day, she kept calling me a "rapid healer" and said that she'd never seen someone recover so quickly. But I treated my recovery like it was my job. I would do two hours of physical therapy with her and then go home and work out for another two hours. I did that every single day for months.

I had a life to get back to.

After three months of rehab, I found myself on a plane headed towards Switzerland, where I would work on the production of *Point Break* for six weeks. It was an incredible experience, but I don't feel like telling that story here. For me, one of the most interesting things that happened while working on the movie happened *after* production was complete, and that's the story I'll tell.

My manager, Matt, was contacted by Warner Brothers—the company that was distributing *Point Break*—and asked if I could help them promote the film at an event in Las Vegas. They wanted to use the athletes who worked on the film to explain the technical aspects of the complicated stunt sequences to the media so that people would understand it was all done for real. I was unfortunately busy at the time, and I had to respectfully decline. They didn't like that and told my manager that my contract required me to comply. Matt explained to them that I wasn't an actor, nor had I been paid the amount the actors were paid. He had carved all promotion of the film out of the contract, and they would have to work a separate deal if they wanted me to promote the film. Whoever Matt was talking to got super pissed off and started getting aggressive. All Matt said was, "You don't work for free, and my client doesn't work for free, either. Thank you for the offer, but we must decline at this time." Matt called me and told me the conversation, and I agreed with him completely. I was busy and that kind of press wasn't something I was interested in anyway. A few hours later, the head of Alcon—the production company that made *Point Break*—called Matt and apologized for the abrupt conversation with Warner Brothers. He explained how much they needed me to come to this event in Vegas and they would happily pay me to come do press for them.

Matt called back but I had to explain, "Matt, it's my mom's birthday. I can't just bail on her to go to Vegas." He told me what they were offering, and it was more than I had been paid for the entire six months I had worked on the film.

I called my mom and explained the situation and she said, "Jeb, this is your work. You have to do your job. It's no problem for me; we can celebrate my birthday next week when you get back."

So, I found myself in the Vegas airport a week later. As I was at baggage claim, I bumped into Laird Hamilton, and as it turned out, we shared a ride to the hotel. I introduced myself and could tell he had zero idea who the hell I was, even though we had bumped into each other twice before. In his defense, though, we had never formerly met. He asked what I did on the film, and I told him I was the technical adviser for the wingsuit flying sequence. I could see in his face that he was not a fan of BASE jumping. He asked me if I knew Johnny Strange, and I said, "Yes, Johnny and I jumped together a bit and I consider him a friend."

"Then you probably know this already," Laird said, "but Johnny recently died in a wingsuit flying accident in Switzerland."

I nodded. As terrible as it sounds, this kind of news just wasn't a surprise anymore.

"Johnny's family and I were friends," Laird continued. "I tried to convince him to stop BASE jumping so many times, but he wouldn't listen. That sport is for idiots; you're all rushing to your deaths for nothing."

"You're not wrong," I said with a faint smile. "I had a similar conversation with Johnny where I tried to convince him to stop jumping."

Laird looked at me in disbelief and said, "Why would you—a BASE jumper—try to convince Johnny to stop doing what you do?"

"I try to talk everyone out of BASE jumping. I think the activity is far too dangerous to justify doing it. I tell them, if they can find happiness in their lives doing anything else, then they should do literally anything else. But for some people, they need to do these kinds of activities to feel fulfilled and be happy. Some people feel the same way about big wave surfing as you do about BASE jumping. They ask, why risk your life riding giant waves? You understand why you do what you do and that should help you understand why Johnny was willing to risk everything to do what he did." The conversation continued with a little more understanding from that point.

We got to the hotel and our time was up. It was an interesting interaction, and at times, I felt like I was looking into a mirror. Certain things Laird said, and the way he said them, reminded me of myself. It was kind of surreal to see another me, honestly. But I guess when people become obsessed with taking risks—and dedicate their lives to them—they develop similar mental wiring.

The next day, I met up with Ericson and we spent the entire day doing a press junket where they sent in a new reporter every fifteen minutes for eight hours straight. Each one asked the same questions, which generated an almost maddening sensation for me as the hours dragged on. Your brain just starts to numb out, and I gained a whole new level of respect for actors and actresses who do this shit all the time. It was an unpleasant experience, to say the least. We then went to a massive theater filled with people who represented all the different movie theaters around the country. All the movies that were coming out that year had presentations of why their films should be picked up and shown in these various theaters. I had never seen anything quite like it and had no idea this was how things were done. They showed different clips from each film and the stars would get up and talk about the movies. When it came time for *Point Break,* they showed the entire wingsuit flying sequence. After it finished, Ericson and the entire wingsuit unit got up on stage and explained how everything they had just witnessed on that screen was all 100 percent real with no CGI. After that, it all became a blur. Just one press event after the other.

Finally, after a few days of nonstop presswork, I was back at the Vegas airport heading home. Pretty much every executive from both Alcon and Warner Brothers were sitting at the gate, waiting for the same plane back to LA. I was sitting there, waiting quietly for the plane to arrive, when a woman from Warner Brothers sat down next to me. She was the head of distribution and a lovely lady. I could tell she had been drinking, probably to celebrate, and was a little bit tipsy. She started the conversation by asking if I was religious or believed in an afterlife. I said, "No, not really. Why, are you?"

"I consider myself spiritual, but not religious," she explained. "But I can't understand how someone could do the kinds of things you do without believing in an afterlife."

I thought about what she said for a moment and then asked, "What do you mean about being spiritual? Could you define what you mean by that?"

For some reason, she began by describing her soul and how it was her essence. It was who she really was, and she somehow tried to separate it from her physical form.

"Are you describing the part of you that makes choices in life, whether good or bad?" I asked. "The part of you that's either moral or immoral? Are you talking about the part of you that will be judged by some godlike entity after death, to either be sent to heaven or cast into hell? Are you talking about the way you process information that makes you react to any given stimulus?"

She said, "Yes, that would be a good description of my concept of the soul."

I then said, "To me, that sounds like the same definition as the mind, and it seems to me the mind is the function of the more complex regions of the human brain."

It has always seemed to me that people describe the mind when talking about the soul, but they seem to feel the need to come up with a different word that will allow them to somehow exist past physical death. This, to me, seems like an attempt to separate themselves from the natural world, and doing so helps them feel superior to it. This sense of superiority leads to people feeling like they have a right to subjugate nature, allowing them to justify bending it to their will, but breaking and twisting it in the process.

I told her, "I can logically prove the concept of the soul doesn't exist, and what you're really talking about is the mind."

She lifted an eyebrow and asked, "How?"

I said, "If the soul were truly separate from the brain, then I couldn't change it by damaging your brain. If the soul were not physically connected to the function of your brain, then damaging your brain should have no impact on your ability to make moral decisions. But we both know that if I took a hammer to your head and damaged the way your brain functioned, I would damage the way you respond to information, and I could fundamentally change the way you behave with a whack or two. People suffering from brain damage have gone from functioning, arguably moral human beings, to damaged people who make arguably immoral decisions. That wouldn't be possible if the soul were truly detached from the function of the human brain."

I could see she was becoming uncomfortable with the conversation, and when people want to end a conversation of this nature, they usually just say, "Well, no one really knows what happens when you die," and that's usually the end of it. The subject changes and everyone moves on to something else. When she said this to me,

I decided I wasn't going to allow the conversation to end; I wanted to try something different.

Seeing how I had experienced death myself a few times and was there for many other people's deaths, I felt I had some firsthand knowledge on the subject. I looked at her and said, "I can see this is making you uncomfortable, but I would like to try something. Would you be willing to do a thought experiment with me?"

She looked at me in an awkward way and said, "Sure, why not."

I then said, "Now, this is going to be difficult, but try not to instantly reject what I'm about say. Imagine for a moment that what I'm about to tell you is true. I want to be clear: I'm not saying this is true or even that it's what I believe, but we are going to imagine for a moment that it is real."

"I'll try," she said reluctantly, "but I can't make any promises without know what you're about to say."

"It doesn't matter," I said, "because we're just pretending."

She nodded, so I continued with, "I think you know exactly what happens when you die. Actually, I think all human beings have known exactly what happens when they die since the dawn of man. We have a definition for death in almost every language. In the English language, its definition is in the dictionary, and that definition is not ambiguous. Words have definitions that we all agree upon so we can have conversations about complex ideas. If you want to talk about life after death, you need to stop using the word 'death' and come up with some other word, because life after death negates the word 'death.'

"You know what happens when a fish dies. You know what happens when a chicken dies. You know what happens when a cow dies, and you know exactly what happens when you die. We have billions of examples of what happens when things die every single day. Over one hundred billion human beings have died since the dawn of mankind. We have more evidence to support what death is than almost anything else. It may be the only thing we truly do know. Almost everything else is up for debate, but the fact of death is not. But for some reason, people don't like what they know. People throughout history have disliked what they know about death so much that they have made up thousands of elaborate religions to try and delude themselves into thinking death is something different than what they already know it is. I'm going to tell you something you already know. It will not be a shock when you hear it. You will think, *Yup, that sounds about right.*

"Here it goes: when you die, you melt right back into the universe from where you came, and you are released from consciousness. It's that simple. Now, science has told us energy can neither be created nor destroyed, it just changes form. So, when you die, you get buried in the ground and consumed by microbes, worms, and plants. Your energy becomes part of them for a short while. When birds or other animals eat the worms and plants, that energy changes form yet again. But your consciousness is a function of your brain, and when the brain shuts down, so does your mind. Your energy and your mind are not the same thing. Your mind is a product of a complex network of neurons making connections that create patterns that equal memories. When science talks about energy changing forms, it's not talking about your thoughts."

She looked at me and I could tell this conversation had gotten far too heavy for an evening sitting at the airport and waiting for a flight. I looked around and noticed everyone looking at us in disbelief. No one has these kinds of conversations in business settings. How does the saying go? "If you want to make friends, don't talk about politics or religion."

She said, "Jeb, you have given me a lot to think about, and I'm going home to do some research. This is a lot to process. I want to have this conversation again when I haven't been drinking so I can think more clearly."

I said, "Anytime. This is one of my favorite subjects to talk about."

We both smiled and the conversation ended as the announcement came over the loudspeaker that it was time to board our plane.

CHAPTER THIRTY

THE END IS NEAR

In late 2018, my good friend Iiro Seppänen asked me to come back to South Africa to help him film a four-part documentary series about his life for the European Discovery Channel. Iiro was engaged to a lovely woman named Julia and they had moved to South Africa to settle down. Julia was pregnant with Iiro's first little girl who would eventually be named Freya, after the Viking goddess. Julia also had a son from a previous marriage named Caesar, who Iiro had been raising as his own for over a year.

Iiro said I was welcome to stay at their place in Constantia near Table Mountain if I liked. I asked if it would be okay to bring my soon-to-be fiancé, Aly Demayo (the woman of my dreams who I had built a powerful relationship with over the last few years), with me, and he said yes; his family would be delighted to have her come. We had all done a diving trip the year before to Raja Ampat, Indonesia, so Julia and Iiro already knew Aly quite well. I felt it would be an awesome opportunity to have a little vacation and thought maybe I would go back and fly a wingsuit from Table Mountain again just for fun.

It had been almost three years since I blew my ACL the second time and had struggled with my decision to keep jumping. In that time, I had come back to flying and pushed myself even further than before. I continued doing live shows and honing my skills to a fine point of precision. The last project I had done was putting a GoPro on my helmet through a bullseye the size of an apple suspended over the Great Wall of China. So, I had once again become confident about BASE jumping and its place in my life, or at least I thought I had.

For some reason, I wasn't sure I wanted to jump this mountain again after my horrific accident there, but I was in the process of writing a book about my life and felt it might make for a good ending point. I didn't think jumping it again should be a big deal. It was a relatively safe flight and I had no plans of doing any proximity flying at the location. I wasn't aware of any lasting negative mental effects from the accident and felt it should be a relatively relaxing jump with low stress.

So, I contacted my friend James Boole to ask if he knew any locals in Cape Town I could jump with. All the locals I used to know had either moved away or stopped jumping by this point—or had died. He told me there was a local by the name of Jean-Jacques Wallis who had become a super ninja wingsuit pilot and probably had over 200 jumps from Table Mountain. James gave me his contact info, and I dropped Jean an email that I was thinking about coming back to South Africa to do another flight from Table Mountain. Jean got back to me instantly and said it wouldn't be a problem at all. He said he had the perfect place for me to jump with the perfect flight line. He explained the exit was much safer than where people used to jump, and I would be able to land outside the park, making the jump quasi-legal. I told him the dates I was going to be in Africa and that I would be filming a documentary with my friend Iiro, so I wasn't sure what day I would have free to do the jump. Jean told me to just let him know when I was free and we would work it out. He also said he would let me know in advance what days looked good for weather. I thanked him and said I would be in touch.

A few months later, on January 16, 2019, almost exactly seven years from what should have been my fatal impact at Table Mountain, I was in South Africa heading through customs with Aly by my side. As we walked out, Iiro was there waiting for us. He had a big smile on his face, and Aly and I took turns giving him a huge hug. He helped carry our bags to his car and we started driving through heavy traffic on our way to his new home nestled in the shadow of the mountain. After about forty-five minutes, we pulled into a gate connected to a tall wall surrounding a rustic-looking home. Three large dogs greeted us as we got out of the car, and Iiro escorted us to a guest house across from their main house. As we were putting our bags away, Julia came across with a warm smile and a seven-month-old baby developing in her belly. She welcomed us to their home and asked if we were hungry. Aly and I were a bit jet-lagged after a forty-hour trip from LA, so we said we just needed to rest a bit and maybe take a small nap.

That evening, we all went to dinner and Iiro explained a little more about the documentary he was filming. He explained what the production was going to look like over the next five days: mostly interviews in different locations around town. He asked me if I would be doing a wingsuit flight from Table Mountain, and if so, would it be okay for him to film it for the documentary series. I said I was still thinking about doing the jump, but it would depend on good weather. I started feeling pangs of fear, which I thought was odd. Just being asked about the jump made me feel uncomfortable.

Iiro could see this and instantly said, "Don't worry, my friend. You don't need to do it if you don't want to."

I responded with, "I'll see how I feel if the weather happens to be perfect."

As if he were somehow telepathically listening to our conversation, my phone vibrated with a message from Jean saying the weather was going to be ideal on the 18th. I showed the message to Iiro, and we decided right then and there that we would go for it that day early in the morning. I responded to Jean by saying it was a go and we would see him bright and early on the 18th. The ball was in motion, but a strange nagging feeling pulled at the back of my mind. I wasn't sure what it was, but it was unsettling and different from anything I had felt before.

We woke up early the next day and talked about our lives and caught up over breakfast. The production team showed up shortly after we were finished, and we spent the rest of the day traveling around Cape Town, filming interviews, and reminiscing about old traveling stories. When we got back to the house, it was time for me to start getting my gear ready for the next morning's jump. My BASE rig was already in a stash bag, so I just added my helmet with body armor. As I went through the motions, that uneasy sensation was ever-present. I couldn't put my finger on it, but I tried to ignore it by pushing it far away. My biggest personal disasters had happened in South Africa, and out of six trips to the dark continent, I ended up visiting the hospital five times. Sometimes it was me getting injured, sometimes it was my friends, but it was always something heavy. I'm not a superstitious person, but I had a bad feeling about doing this jump.

There was also another issue: the park service knew exactly who I was, meaning there was a chance I could be spotted and stopped at the cable car. When I had my accident, the press went a little crazy, and the park service did not like it one bit. There was confusion over the permits HBO had gotten for the project, and the park service was thinking about pressing charges against me at the time, so it was safe to say I wouldn't be a welcome sight.

Jumping Table Mountain was a bit of a legal gray area, and I didn't want to cause any problems for the local jumpers. Unfortunately, I had become a little famous over the years and the press tended to report on things I did. Me jumping Table Mountain again could possibly get more coverage than anyone would want at that point. So, beyond my fear of personal injury, I was also concerned I would mess up an amazing jumping location for the local pilots. My work is a balancing act between getting press to make money and not just fucking up everyone and everything. I had not tried doing an illegal jump since my troubles at the Empire, and I wasn't interested in breaking any laws. Jean had explained as long as we landed outside the park, it was totally legal, but he also said don't get caught, which didn't give a feeling of confidence.

Aly, Iiro, and I met Jean at the cable car early the next morning. Jean was with his girlfriend, and he was smiling. This was my first time meeting him in person and I liked him right away. He was glowing with positive energy. I handed my gear to Aly to carry on the cable car in case the park service saw me. Last thing I wanted was for them to see me with a stash bag heading up the mountain. But as I looked around, I noticed stash bags everywhere. At least fifteen people in line had stash bags.

I looked at Jean and asked, "How many BASE jumpers are here today?"

He said, "There will probably be about twenty of them jumping all day long."

"Is it normal to have this many jumpers here?"

He said, "This is a bit more than usual. I think the word got out that you were here, and I think people wanted to see you jump. But yes, people jump here every day the weather is good. I did about two hundred jumps on the mountain last year alone."

I said, "Shit, I had no idea it was being jumped this much. The park service doesn't care?"

"They leave us alone most of the time, and like I said, if we land outside the park, it's technically legal. We're actually trying to get permission to hold a wingsuit competition here next year." That all made me feel a little better in knowing that I wasn't going to harm the location with my presence.

When we got off the cable car on top of the mountain, Aly handed me my bag and we all started walking to the new exit point. Jean led the way and we saw a line of people carrying stash bags filled with BASE gear on their way to the same place we were going.

As we passed the exit I used to jump from, I pointed it out to Jean and he said, "Yes, that's it, but people don't jump from there much anymore. The ledge is bigger, and the area where you gear up is more exposed. The new exit has more cover, so people don't see you as easily."

The paved trail led to an outlook and Jean said, "We are here." He then stepped off the path and started leading us down a series of boulders where there was an outcropping of rock that acted like a roof over our heads. He pointed out the exit and it looked clean. I walked up to it and looked over the edge and saw it was beautiful. The wall was vertical, and you could tell the ledge was much farther away.

I went back under the rock roof and started taking my gear out of the stash bag. As I removed my rig, I noticed I had a problem. I had forgotten to put my wingsuit in the bag with my BASE gear. I looked at Aly and she could see something was wrong. I told her I had forgotten my wingsuit, and Iiro looked over and said, "Are you serious?"

"I'm afraid so," I replied, and Jean just started laughing. I couldn't believe it. In all my years jumping wingsuits, I had never forgotten my suit before. I felt as though my subconscious was doing everything in its power to keep me from jumping this mountain. I apologized to everyone for wasting their time.

Iiro said it wasn't a problem, and Jean said, "Don't worry, I was going to jump today even if you weren't here."

I asked Jean when the next good weather day was going to be, and he said not for another five days. I said, "Let's stay in touch; let me know when the weather is good and when you have time again." Jean nodded and said he would let me know. He then put his gear on and jumped off the mountain.

For the next five days, we traveled around filming for Iiro's documentary and sightseeing. Aly and I went on a day trip by ourselves to see the world-famous Penguin Beach. Many years ago, a group of penguins from Antarctica got lost at sea and found themselves in South Africa. Since they were lost and had no idea where they were, they just moved in and made it their home. Now it's a protected state beach where people from all over the world come to swim with penguins.

While we were on our day trip, Jean sent me a message telling me the next day would be another perfect weather day, but only till midafternoon. So, we would need to be there early and jump as quickly as possible. I responded with, "We'll see you in the morning, bright and early." I then sent Iiro a message, letting him know the jump was a go for tomorrow and that we were on our way back to his house now.

That evening, I put my wingsuit on my rig and made absolutely sure everything I needed to jump was in my stash bag. I was unusually nervous. That night, I had trouble sleeping, which was odd for me since I never had trouble sleeping. I was truly afraid. My rational mind couldn't understand why. This jump was one of the safest jumps I could do right now. I told myself, *I have the experience, the conditions will be good, and if they aren't, I won't jump.* There was no reason to be so afraid. I had been jumping things way more technical and dangerous just a few months earlier. But for some reason I couldn't understand, I just didn't want to do this jump. In the dead of night, I fell into a fitful sleep, exhausted and afraid.

The next morning was kind of a haze. I woke up and went through the motions of getting ready. Aly helped me check to make sure I had everything this time, and then we went into the house to eat some breakfast with Iiro and Julia. After eating, we got in the car and headed for the mountain. Once we got to the cable car, we could see a line of jumpers wearing stash bags again—just as many as the last time we tried to jump. Jean sent me a message that he was already on top of the mountain, so we got in line and headed on up. We got to the exit point quickly and I geared up right away. The winds were already starting to pick up, but they were still safe to jump.

One of Jean's friends jumped as I was getting ready and Jean pointed out, "His jump was perfect. The conditions are ideal."

I walked over to the exit and stood on the edge, looking down. The sun was bright and the sky was clear. Iiro stood behind and to my left, filming. Aly sat on a rock behind and above, watching intently. Jean showed me the flight line and where we needed to land. It was nearly time.

It got quiet. I could feel myself detach. I didn't want to do this. I no longer saw the point. I didn't have anything to prove to myself or anyone else. The fear was welling up and about to overspill. But as I was about to step back from the edge, I saw something out of the corner of my eye—it was a small black bird that flew right in front of me, maybe five feet away. It was gliding on thermals above the exit point without moving its wings at all. It just floated there, frozen in time. For an instant, I forgot what I was doing and wished I could glide on the air like that little bird. A memory surfaced of listening to my aunt tell me it wasn't physically possible to do what birds did, and the response I gave her at that young age.

Maybe you can't, but I'm going to fly.

I snapped back into reality and realized I was standing there on the edge of the cliff in a wingsuit, and all I had to do to glide on the air was to lean forward. My whole life came into focus. Here I was, filled with terror to my core of the thing that had given my life purpose. The thing that had saved me from myself over and over again. The thing that had dragged me, kicking and screaming, through time. My life was a paradox. I was in a constant struggle with my own fears. That was the through line of my life.

I hadn't gotten to where I was in life because I was the best at what I did. I had met many people along the way better than me. But most of them had either given up or died. I found success in life because somehow, against all odds, I survived. I refused to give up, no matter how much I wanted to. This was my gift: not stopping no matter how scared I became or how hard I got hit. No matter how many times my body was shattered, I kept getting back up and somehow pushed through that paralyzing fear. It dawned on me that the entire point of all of this had been to persevere—not just in jumping, but also in life.

Life is just a bunch of experiences you have till you die. That's it. It's simple. I'm just trying to make those experiences as amazing as I possibly can.

With my own words echoing back at me, I leaned forward and joined that little black bird in his domain.

FINAL THOUGHTS

I told an important story in Chapter 2 about almost dying from amoebic dysentery when I was five years old. I felt the need to tell this story for multiple reasons. It was a near-death experience that had an impact on the way I saw my life and it helped form the person I have become. It was one of many experiences that showed me death can take you at any moment, even if you aren't doing anything dangerous. Every time something truly horrible relating to BASE jumping happened in my life that made me question if I should continue, that early brush with death is what kept me going. Even if I stopped BASE jumping, shark diving, riding motorcycles—basically doing anything dangerous—it wouldn't stop death. Dying is 100 percent guaranteed, but it's also a natural part of life. If you're going to die anyway, why not spend your time trying to turn your dreams into realities?

I think suffering from depression helped me see things a bit differently. I went for so many years wishing that I wouldn't wake up in the morning. So many years suffering from my own existence and not knowing or understanding why. So many years of being truly unhappy and feeling like I was in a deep, dark hole. I think hitting rock-bottom and feeling like death was my only escape had a profound impact on the way I choose to make decisions now. This experience helped me understand how important it is to live a life that's honest and true to yourself, and it made me unapologetic for taking the risks I needed to in order to be happy. Chasing dreams was the key to me finding direction, which led to finding my passion, which led to me finding my purpose, which led to me finding happiness. Once you experience the journey from true depression to true happiness, nothing will shake your focus.

When people tell you you're being selfish for risking your life, you will know deep down that you can't love or help others till you figure out how to love and help yourself. Once you have found passion and purpose, you are freed from the crippling darkness, and you will then be capable of helping others come into the light. But as long as you are in darkness, the only thing you can show others is darkness.

When I started writing this book, I thought I would be writing about my adventures in BASE jumping. But it turned into something much more for me: it became a journey into my own mind and the discovery that I suffered from serious mental issues. I had lived a life of doing things without thinking about them. By sitting down and writing my memories from birth till now, I started understanding there was something wrong with me. As I was writing, I kept asking myself, "Why did I do that? What was the point of this?" The only answer I could come up with was mental illness.

I struggled with serious suicidal tendencies from about seven to nineteen years old, and I was filled with an inexplicable, overwhelming rage. Looking back, I'm still not sure why I was so upset. My father was kind of a dick and school was tough, but none of it was any worse than what I saw my friends dealing with at the time. Many people deal with mental issues, especially during puberty; I know I'm not unique in this. Where I feel I may be a bit different is in how I chose to deal with my issues. I feel that many people turn to drugs and alcohol in an attempt to self-medicate, trying to drown out the chaos in their minds. I didn't take that path.

I feel lucky I found something powerful like BASE jumping at an early age to help me channel all that negative energy. It forced me to constantly confront gut-wrenching terror that somehow helped me work through many of my emotional problems.

Writing this book made me take a closer look at the people in my life, and I began to realize that mental illness had always been all around me. From my father to my friends, everyone seemed to suffer from something. Even my little sister wasn't unscathed.

Scarlett was diagnosed with bipolar disorder with psychotic tendencies when she was twenty-four. She would have to be committed to multiple institutions throughout the next fifteen years of her life. Each year, she would have multiple psychotic breaks and they were terrifying to witness. She was never violent towards others, but in her more severe breakdowns, she became catatonic.

I asked Scarlett if she remembered anything from these moments, and she said, "Yes, I remember everything."

Last year, she hung herself, and I finally understood why so many people wish so desperately for there to be an afterlife. I had never wished for it harder than at the moment I found out she was gone. I wanted nothing more than to be able to see her again so I could tell her all the things I wished I'd said while she was still alive. Her death was devastating. I thought I understood what death was because I had seen so much of it, but nothing could prepare me for my little sister taking her own life.

I had been so selfish throughout my life in dealing with my own demons that I never took the time to have a proper relationship with her. My memories of her are so limited, and that's my one true regret. She was a special human being who was kind to everyone and gave everything she had.

Mental illness is something that every human being deals with in one way or another. Either you experience it yourself or you watch people you care about go through it. The human mind is complex and fragile. Consciousness can be overwhelming. I feel we're all struggling to survive, but so many of us don't make it. Maybe seeing someone else make it through the darkness and into the light might give the rest of us hope.

I was able to make it, and this means you can, too. Please, if you are feeling hopeless, just know that time equals endless possibilities. Death is the end of time and the end of those possibilities. Hold on for as long as you can. Death is coming on its own—you don't need to rush it. Look at all the things I would have missed had I taken my life at sixteen. Imagine what you can do with the time laid out in front of you, what special things you can accomplish with even one more day, one more hour, or one more minute.

Don't waste it.

Jeb Corliss with his sisters, Sonia and Scarlett

In loving memory of my little sister, Scarlett

ACKNOWLEDGEMENTS

I never had any intention of writing a book about my life. I was content making documentaries and doing interviews while allowing others to tell my story. But about five years ago, my grandfather, a man I loved and respected very much, died. He was a writer, and from my earliest memories of him, he was always in his study working on his autobiography. He had been in three major campaigns during WWII and wanted the world to see it through his eyes. On his deathbed, as my younger sister was holding his hand, he said, "When I get home, I am going to start working on my book." He had been talking about his book and supposedly writing it for the last sixty years. He died two hours later, at ninety-six, without ever completing his life's work.

When my younger sister told me what had happened, I was saddened. We looked everywhere and couldn't find even one page of his book. At that moment, I realized there was only one book I cared to read, and it had never been written. To read about his life with his words would have been magical. It would have been a form of immortality, making his thoughts resonate through time.

I decided right then I needed to write my own experiences down before it was too late, even if the future generations of my family were the only ones to read it.

It took me over three years, but I finally finished my autobiography. Over 180,000 words describing a life that, if I hadn't lived, I wouldn't believe was possible. When I started the journey of writing this book, I thought it was going to be about my adventures in extreme sports while traveling the world, but it turned out to be something far deeper. It became a story about my battle with mental illness and how I used extreme experiences to cope.

I would like to thank my mother for giving me life and for teaching me how to live it. I would like to thank my little sister Scarlett for showing me how much love exists within my heart, even though I didn't understand it while she was alive. I would like to thank my manager Matt Meyerson for pushing me to keep working on this book even when I wanted to give up. I want to thank Cody Wootton for understanding me and helping me edit this monstrous manuscript into something I could be proud of. I want to thank the love of my life Aly DeMayo for being my best friend and supporting me through anything and everything. I want to thank my father for showing me the kind of person I would never want to be.

Last, but not least, I would like to thank my grandfather. I finished this book for you.

ABOUT THE PUBLISHER

Di Angelo Publications was founded in 2008 by Sequoia Schmidt—at the age of seventeen. The modernized publishing firm's creative headquarters is in Houston, Texas, with its distribution center located in Twin Falls, Idaho. The subsidiary rights department is based in Los Angeles, and Di Angelo Publications has recently grown to include branches in England, Australia, and Sequoia's home country of New Zealand. In 2020, Di Angelo Publications made a conscious decision to move all printing and production for domestic distribution of its books to the United States. The firm is comprised of eight imprints, and the featured imprint, Catharsis, was inspired by Schmidt's love of extreme sports, travel, and adventure stories.

Printed in the USA
CPSIA information can be obtained
at www.ICGtesting.com
LVHW051155120923
757966LV00015B/42/J